THE HEART
OF TRAUMA

Dr. Suzanne Simard (2016) of the University of British Columbia and her colleagues have illuminated the underground pathways that connect groves of trees. Threads of fungus interact with tree roots and direct carbon, water, and nutrients to plants most in need of support, often the younger ones. This fosters a purposeful sharing of resources that helps the entire ecosystem of trees and plants flourish, fostering the beautiful canopy of branches and leaves.

In much the same way, we humans join our inner worlds with one another through many pathways that are largely below conscious awareness. When we are truly present with one another, the silent resources of attention, responsiveness, and love flow in a way that nourishes healing. As we come face to face with one another, we may find shelter like this canopy of trees while the mysterious underground of deep connection works its magic and we may be supported in becoming therapeutic presences in our daily walk in the world.

Suzanne Simard, June 2016, on TED
https://www.ted.com/talks/suzanne_simard_how_trees_talk_to_each_other?language=en

A Norton Professional Book

THE HEART
OF TRAUMA

*Healing the Embodied Brain
in the Context of Relationships*

Bonnie Badenoch

W. W. NORTON & COMPANY
Independent Publishers Since 1923
New York   London

Note to Readers: Standards of clinical practice and protocol change over time, and no technique or recommendation is guaranteed to be safe or effective in all circumstances. This volume is intended as a general information resource for professionals practicing in the field of psychotherapy and mental health; it is not a substitute for appropriate training, peer review, and/or clinical supervision. Neither the publisher nor the author(s) can guarantee the complete accuracy, efficacy, or appropriateness of any particular recommendation in every respect.

Copyright © 2018 by Bonnie Badenoch

All rights reserved
Printed in the United States of America
First Edition

For information about permission to reproduce selections from this book, write to Permissions, W. W. Norton & Company, Inc., 500 Fifth Avenue, New York, NY 10110

For information about special discounts for bulk purchases, please contact W. W. Norton Special Sales at specialsales@wwnorton.com or 800-233-4830

Cover art by Bagamiayaabikwe

Manufacturing by Lake Book Manufacturing, Inc.
Book design by Rebecca Caine
Production manager: Christine Critelli

Library of Congress Cataloging-in-Publication Data

Names: Badenoch, Bonnie, author.
Title: The heart of trauma : healing the embodied brain in the context of
  relationships / Bonnie Badenoch ; foreword by Stephen W. Porges.
Description: First edition. | New York : W.W. Norton & Company, [2018] |
  Series: A Norton professional book | Includes bibliographical references
  and index.
Identifiers: LCCN 2017015270 | ISBN 9780393710489 (hardcover)
Subjects: LCSH: Psychic trauma—Treatment.
Classification: LCC RC552.T7 B33 2018 | DDC 616.85/21—dc23 LC record
available at https://lccn.loc.gov/2017015270

W. W. Norton & Company, Inc., 500 Fifth Avenue, New York, N.Y. 10110
                    www.wwnorton.com
W. W. Norton & Company Ltd., 15 Carlisle Street, London W1D 3BS

5 6 7 8 9 0

For
Coease Scott

The main thing, as Chiviliu had said, was to not only shy away from judging the forms seeds and people took in order to survive strange conditions created by people who'd lost their seeds, but as a spiritual human of a truly indigenous core to simply keep growing the "seeds" in every sense, so they could have a place to direct their ever-ready magical manifestation. The Holy in the Seeds had to direct.

We as people had to provide spiritual ground and physical fertile space and earth for the seeds to do what they already very well knew how to do.

> The seeds had always been there.
> The seeds had always been home.
> It was up to us to be at home
> *keeping the seeds alive.*

—MARTIN PRECHTEL
The Unlikely Peace at Cuchumaquic:
The Parallel Lives of People as Plants:
Keeping the Seeds Alive

Contents

PART ONE: Setting the Table

Section II: How We Attend

PART TWO: Nourishing Accompaniment

Foreword

by Stephen W. Porges

Safety is Treatment

In *The Heart of Trauma,* Bonnie Badenoch artfully provides a narrative to explain the neurobiological mechanisms through which trauma disrupts the capacity to feel safe and underscores that "safety is the treatment." As elaborated in *The Heart of Trauma,* successful therapy accesses the third adaptive system and leverages this system within the therapeutic setting to contain defense and enable co-regulation. *The Heart of Trauma* succinctly informs the therapist that the objective of trauma therapy is to enable the client to experience feelings of safety.

This beautifully written book describes the scaffolding of disparate neural systems with interactive pathways detecting, interpreting, choreographing, and archiving our experiences. The reader is engaged in a vivid narrative linking our neurobiology to mental processes and overt behaviors. As we read, we are informed that the capacity to feel safe in the arms of another, which is the sine qua non of our survival, is selectively damaged by trauma. We learn that effective therapy incorporates an understanding of the mechanisms through which an individual can feel safe as well as understands, witnesses, and respects the vulnerability of these mechanisms to trauma.

By emphasizing contemporary neuroscience, the volume sketches a narrative of how the nervous system is involved in supporting prosocial interactions and enabling defense. When neural pathways down-regulate defensive strategies, social distance is reduced and opportunities to connect and co-regulate are optimized. When contextual cues convey risk to the nervous system, defensive strategies are "disinhibited" and activated to reflexively protect the individual by increasing the physical and psychological distance from a potential predator. Although optimizing survival, chronic recruitment of defense strategies limits opportunities for prosocial interactions and functionally marginalizes the individual from social contact.

Evolution of the nervous system enabled humans to access and regulate two defense strategies: one is associated with the increased energy necessary for mobilization and fight/flight behaviors, and the other is associated with a conservation of energy and manifests in a massive reduction of behavior, enabling the mammalian ancestors of humans to appear to be inanimate. For humans, this system, when recruited, may result in a behavioral shutdown and a mental state of dissociation. Moreover, evolution provided humans and other mammals with a third adaptive system that down-regulates the sensitivity to trigger defense by detecting and responding to cues of safety.

The third system functions as a safety system and provides the neural basis for co-regulation and feelings of trust. It is through the lens of this hierarchical model, proposed in Polyvagal Theory (Porges, 2011), that *The Heart of Trauma* explains the neural mechanisms through which trauma disrupts the capacity to feel safe. This knowledge provides insights into re-engaging the "safety" system to effectively and efficiently contain defense reactions. Insights into the mechanisms that disrupt feeling safe inform therapists to develop trauma treatments designed to awaken the circuits that enable feelings of safety.

Underlying global survival-related behavioral strategies, the nervous system is involved in choreographing a complex scenario by shifting neurophysiological states that serve as "neural" platforms for more expansive emergent behaviors. In one case, the "neural" platform efficiently signals and receives cues of safety, and in the others the 'neural' platform efficiently signals and receives cues of danger or life threat.

In response to cues of safety, the nervous system promotes a *state* of safety with emergent properties including an increased proximity, openness and welcoming to others, a bias towards exploration, a sense of presence, and a neural "desire" or drive to co-regulate with another.

As opportunities for prosocial behavior expand, the individual experiences a great opportunity for the efficient co-regulation that optimizes mental and physical health. Since optimized health is a product of the interactions among humans, experiencing a state of safety promotes social and societal health. Thus, a state of feeling safe functionally transforms the individual from a solitary to a social being.

In contrast to emergent properties of feeling safe, the emergent properties of defensive states functionally transform the individual from a social being into a solitary individual. Defensive strategies encapsulate the individual and limit options for neurophysiological regulation from co-regulation to a more inefficient and limited mode of self-regulation with mental and physical health consequences. In humans, defense strategies provide survival resources when survival is challenged, but these strategies evolved for short-term fixes and not for chronic use. Responses to trauma frequently shift the neural platform to optimize defense. As a by-product of this shift in neural state, behavioral and psychological strategies shift towards aggression or withdrawal, while opportunities for social interactions and feelings of trust and love become vulnerabilities and are adaptively minimized.

Although this shift in neural state optimizes survival through defensive strategies, survival needs of co-regulation and connectedness are compromised. As defense is optimized, it reflexively dominates personal experience and limits the neural resources that foster social interactions and co-regulation. Because humans evolved to connect and to co-regulate, the consequences of being functionally stuck in a neural platform that is optimized for defense compromises all aspects of human health and well-being.

Although defensive reactions are necessary for survival, optimally these strategies should be recruited for acute transitory challenges and not for chronic states of vigilance. Although chronic states of vigilance prepare the individual to efficiently defend, the neural demands to maintain this state result in an adaptive retuning of the autonomic nervous system. This retuning optimizes defense by reducing the latency to defend, but also manifests in the autonomic nervous system promoting an array of mental disorders (e.g., anxiety, depression, PTSD, etc.) and physical disorders (hypertension, irritable bowel syndrome, fibromyalgia, dysautonomia, migraine, etc.). Thus, clinicians "collaborating" with survivors of trauma observe the behavioral and emotional defensive reactivity of their clients even in the supportive context of a therapy session. Clinicians are also aware of the physical and health symptoms that frequently appear to be comorbid with survivors of trauma. As we learn from *The Heart of Trauma*, these comorbidities are manifestations of the chronic recruitment of the autonomic nervous system to support defense strategies.

In the long term, the human need to be social supplants other survival needs beyond the most primitive needs of oxygen, food, water, and physical safety. Social isolation is powerful disruptor of human behavior and physiological health. In the clinical domain of traumatology, isolation, whether physical or psychological, is conceptualized as neglect. In addition, other forms of social marginalization, such as bullying, are interpreted by our nervous system similarly to isolation. Isolation triggers feelings of despair that are captured metaphorically by a nervous system signaling its viscera to initially become aggressive (i.e., fight/flight behaviors) and then subsequently to shut down and appear to be dormant. These responses and this sequence are encoded in our genes.

Typical individuals normally express defensive reactions and spontaneously repair the ruptures in social contact that follow defensive reactions. It is this ability to rapidly and seamlessly repair ruptures that is compromised in the social world of survivors of trauma. Functionally, the survivor's nervous system resists being coaxed and cajoled into a state of safety; it is a nervous system that obstinately refuses to dismiss its responsibility to protect and defend. These neurobiological features, which are frequently expressed following trauma, are independent of volitions, desires, and even explicit cognitive narratives. Survivors of trauma may have thoughts and mental images of welcoming others in a warm embrace, but their bodies are hypervigilant and resist engagement to protect and defend.

In sculpting the theme embedded in *The Heart of Trauma,* Bonnie Badenoch brilliantly centers on the clinical question of how therapists guide survivors of trauma to recover their capacity to connect with humanity when their bodies are in a chronic state of defense. By understanding the mechanisms underlying the trauma survivor's journey into hopelessness and despair, Bonnie Badenoch empowers the clinician with the knowledge that "safety is treatment" to develop strategies to transform their clients from being encapsulated in their isolation to reconnecting with others as social trusting beings.

Porges, S.W. (2011). The polyvagal theory: Neurophysiological foundations of emotions, attachment, communication, and self-regulation. New York: W.W. Norton & Company.

Acknowledgments

I believe that all books are co-authored by many tangible and ghostly presences. I am so fortunate to have such dedicated companions on this path of deepening from vision into words. While there are many, these eight stand very close to me. My daughter Kate is both a companion and an inspiration in her dedication and integrity. Her humor keeps me from getting too serious and her insistence on meeting her suffering eye to eye widens my capacity to sit with what arises within me and within others as well. Her husband, Matt, stands beside both of us, a quiet presence dedicated to kindness and providing support.

I am so privileged to be in daily conversation with my beloved friend Melanya Helene. Because there is a depth of trust between us, we listen tenderly to one another without expectation or judgment. This might be the central gift we humans can offer each other, and I am sustained by this companionship.

My dear friend Kate Cook and I walk side by side. She is a laughing, crying, open, vulnerable testimony to the power of being truly alive to all of it. She opens my eyes to realms beyond the seen and pushes my feet deep into the earth for sustenance.

Another trusted beloved, Coease Scott, has supported, tenderly held, and reflected back to me whatever may be happening within my own inner being so that I can see it with greater clarity. We have explored our wounds and joys together, and in the light of this co-suffering and co-celebrating, capacities have unfolded within me that shape my way of being with the wounds of others and touch every word in this book.

Rich Armington and Heloise Gold, deep friends (and married to each other), have strengthened my resolve in presenting this sometimes challenging vision of where we are in this culture. They have had my back every step of the way. Rich has read every word and, in a very practical way, offered suggestions that have improved this book in countless ways. I am so grateful for this kindness and accompaniment, and no words can capture the value of his contribution.

Companioning me as partner and fellow spiritual explorer, Jo Hadlock-King has touched this book in so many ways. Her love of language and all things poetic as well as her dedication to fostering healing are always in the background to make this book more beautiful in its details and more communicative of the felt sense that is so dear to both of us. Having her at my side eases each day's work.

Others are invisibly at my elbow, beginning with Iain McGilchrist, whose work on the hemispheres has shaped my way of seeing and being in the world in astonishing ways. As I have come to know him a bit more personally, his way of being continues to illuminate the importance of how we perceive this precious world and one another. Steve Porges nourishes me by always pointing toward relational safety, not only in his work on the autonomic nervous system but in his responsiveness to my never-ending questions, the quality of his voice, and his smiling, mobile face.

Deborah Malmud, my always-honest editor at Norton, has provided the kind of challenge and support that strengthens and deepens the final result. Her staff have given help of all kinds at every step. Being part of this community makes the work of authorship so much lighter.

Providing the foundation for this kind of exploration are the three fathers of interpersonal neurobiology (IPNB)—Allan Schore, Dan Siegel, and Lou Cozolino. My years of marinating in their work and sometimes in their presence have left their flavor on every page. And in the deep background is Carl Rogers' reverence for unconditional positive regard.

The inspiration for this writing has arisen from almost thirty years of meeting with the courageous people who come seeking healing, and more recently from students of interpersonal neurobiology who make their way to our experiential trainings and for consultations at Nurturing the Heart with the Brain in Mind. Their vulnerability, perseverance, humor, energy, and emerging capacity for being present with themselves and others touch my heart. Two friends and IPNB devotees, poet Neil Meili and artist Bagamiayaabikwe, have so graciously captured the essence of relational neuroscience and offered their vision in words, color, and form to give deeper life when prose can carry us only so far.

Providing the sense of the sacredness of our work are Leonard Cohen, Jalāl al-din Rūmī, Father Richard Rohr, James Finley, Martin Prechtel, my aged beagle Riley, and my ever-emerging garden all of whom offer the nourishing undertones that hold my soul and the spirit of this project. Accompaniment is everything, and I am truly blessed by all these companions and many more.

Preface

In 2012, I began facilitating my first year-long interpersonal neurobiology (IPNB) immersion training at the invitation of Deborah Dana in Portland, Maine. I had no idea it would be possible for this group of twenty-four to deepen into this work as they did—walking a delicate line between personal work and training, offering the deepest respect for one another while cultivating a safe space for didactic and experiential exploration. I believe the depth of transformation during that year surprised and touched all of us.

By the end of our time, two themes emerged that have lingered with me—the powerful influence of the cultural context enveloping us as we do our work, and the importance of presence for holding what wants to unfold in the space between patient and therapist. If you had asked any of us at the beginning if we felt we were present with our clients, all of us would have said yes. Yet by the end of our time, I believe everyone would have agreed that a different "felt sense"* (Gendlin, 1982, p. 11) of what presence can be had emerged—an openness experienced throughout the body; listening from increasing stillness; fewer thoughts and less planning; a deepening trust that such holding can allow our patients' wisdom to reveal itself. We could not have captured this state in words at the beginning because it had to be felt to be known. It slowly came into being in the context of holding one another, grounding in wisdom about the embodied and relational brain, attending to pace, and cherishing the unfolding quiet.

Another surprise for me was how the conversation about the state

---

* "Felt sense" is a term offered by Gene Gendlin (1982) to name the experience in our bodily awareness of the unfolding life process, what he called implicit bodily knowing, as a form of knowledge prior to and more intricate and full than concepts.

of our culture persistently entwined itself with this experience of presence. On the first day, we spent time deepening our understanding of the seminal work of Iain McGilchrist (2009) concerning the wisdom and beauty of our divided brains. Since research in the last decade had made it clear that both hemispheres fire for everything we think, feel, say, or do (for an example of this, see Van Essen et al., 2013, regarding diffusion MRIs), interest in the topic of hemispheric differences waned. However, McGilchrist's understanding illuminates not *what* each hemisphere does, but *how* each perceives—and then creates—the world. His abundant and meticulous exploration of the research supports the perspective that we are currently immersed in a culture operating primarily according to the viewpoint of the left. This hemisphere sees through the lens of a relationally disconnected manufacturing mentality that we can recognize in the accelerating pace of life, the emphasis on behavior and task over relationship, the tendency to value algorithms over individual process, the polarized and judgmental either/or way of seeing the world, and many other characteristics. This affects the systems within which we work, the way we see one another and define mental health, and even our capacity to be truly present with each other.

My own ongoing interest in the workings of implicit (embodied) memory began to add another stream to this conversation as I wondered how this left shift might be leaving its mark on us. We are continually making implicit memories because they do not require conscious attention to be encoded (Siegel, 2015b). They stay with us as surges of feeling, behavioral impulses, bodily sensations, and perceptions that, when reawakened, color everything because implicit memories have the felt sense of happening now no matter how long ago they may have been encoded. Then I stumbled across an astonishing piece of information. We encode 11 million bits of sensory information per second perceptually (implicitly) while encoding six to fifty bits consciously (explicitly) (Riener, 2011). This suggests that many more of these embodied experiences are taking up residence within us than explicit memories, almost entirely below the level of conscious awareness yet influencing everything we think, feel, say, and do. We are literally marinating in our left-shifted milieu all the time, mostly without our conscious awareness. No wonder we struggle with even having a felt sense of what presence might mean in the midst of such strong unseen encouragement to focus on the *task* of therapy.

In the seven year-long trainings since the first one, the same pattern of concerns unfolded and took center stage in our awareness. These ways of understanding the interplay of culture and presence made sense of so many challenges we were facing in our clinical work, from our interactions with insurance companies to the primary focus on evidence-based treatments, guided more by protocols than responsiveness to what is alive in the moment. We not only gained clarity at the level of concepts but found ourselves attending to our way of being together in the training as we supported one another in slowly, slowly making room for our inherent relational capacities to reclaim us. *We discovered that our inner work with ourselves, particularly as it was being supported by this group, was absolutely foundational to our ability to be with our patients.* Our patients, all of them dealing with trauma in their own ways, began to experience a different level of safety in the room as our quiet receptivity increased. Many of them seemed able to settle into greater depths of healing. We also noticed that we were less tired at the end of our clinical days and felt ourselves to be carrying the suffering we were sharing with our patients a little differently than ever before.

Out of these deep relational encounters, both in the trainings and the unfolding therapeutic story, this book began to shape itself, even though it still seems challenging to hold these lived moments in words. In these pages, the hope is to cultivate a felt sense of both the culture and this way of being present, coupled with a strong, scientifically grounded case for doing the work of opening to hemispheric balance and relational deepening. This intention seems to call for right-centric metaphorical language to embody the felt sense even while seeking to convey solid understanding of what neuroscience tells us about healing from trauma in the context of relationships—a challenging combination at times, as we will see.

It is no small thing to offer to enter this consideration of suffering. To truly deepen into the nature of trauma means that our own wounds will be touched. In the hope that you will feel accompanied as you move into this tender territory, I want to offer several possible ways to read. This book itself may be a kind of companion for you if you prefer to read by yourself. I certainly want to be with you on each page and have written with that in mind. If you would like a bit more interpersonal support, you might want to share the practices that are sprinkled throughout with a partner who is also reading the book. Patty Wipfler (2016), parent advocate extraordinaire, has assisted mothers and fathers in forming Listening Partnerships for decades now, and I have borrowed this suggestion about the value of companionship from her. The deepening that may happen when we are heard is one of the central themes of this book, so practicing together can support embodying the principles. A third and possibly radical suggestion is to invite a companion for the whole experience. *The Brain-Savvy Therapist's Workbook* (Badenoch, 2011) suggested studying with a listening partner as a way to deepen into embodiment of IPNB. We regularly receive emails from people who have been together in this way, expressing their amazement at the depth of learning and healing that unfolds in that space between. For this experience, you might choose a reading partner to share passages or even the whole book aloud. In the midst of this busy world, that's quite a shift from the way we usually approach words on the page. I trust you will find the way that is most supportive for you.

There are way stations for reflection sprinkled throughout these pages, invitations to pause to sink more deeply into the felt sense of what we are speaking about. Their purpose is twofold: to slow the pace a bit so that the words don't pull us too far into the left hemisphere, where meaning has a tendency to get lost; and, if we choose to share with another, to offer some oases where the deepening may be supported by our reflections of each other. These pauses also invite us to practice the very nonjudgmental presence that we hope to offer our patients and others. In addition to the way stations offered here, you will likely find other moments when you are alerted by a rise of attention in your body that a pause is called for. It would be strongly supportive of deeply internalizing this perspective to honor that when it happens.

Finally, while this is a clinical book in many ways, it is most of all about how we might each become a therapeutic presence in the world. What we are coming to understand through relational neuroscience about the astonishing ways we are interwoven suggests that how we walk about in our daily lives will touch everyone, often below the level of consciousness awareness, like the intertwined roots on the cover of this book. Having had the gift of support in cultivating these perspectives for the last fourteen years, I have become convinced that gradually embodying this wisdom—a lifelong process—is to quietly participate in the health of the world. From the viewpoint of becoming a therapeutic presence, I am mainly using the word "people" for those with whom we interact in whatever capacity they come to us, including as patients. There are some places where "patient" also appears, as I hear this word conjuring not someone who is ill but a person who bears suffering with grace. This brings me to another word that finds a place here—"sacred." As we move into close contact with one another, something sometimes happens that can't be defined. The space between seems to hold a deepening sense of meaning, expanding vistas of compassion, co-suffering of great intensity at times, and then, often quite suddenly, "where the two worlds meet . . . the door is round and open" (Rūmī, 1270/2004, p. 36). What happens next is as individual as a fingerprint: an expanded sense of oneness with others, a movement toward action on behalf of those in need, the feeling of being held by the Divine, an experience of stillness spreading throughout the body. There is always a sense of something larger, deeper than words unfolding, touching both people in this sacred space between. The gift of being present for such openings, of participating simply by being present, illuminates our work in a way that we may simply call blessed.

As this book is unfolding, I am fortunate to be able to read each chapter with a "trusted beloved" (Rohr, 2014) or two or three, and what emerges from these shared explorations amounts to co-authorship, as there is an astonishing and often unexpected deepening of meaning in these conversations. I wish you many such experiences as you make your way through these pages accompanied.

THE HEART
OF TRAUMA

Introduction

Being Present in the Context of Culture

We are about to enter the tender territory of human suffering. With grief and hope of healing as our companions, we will begin by exploring the roots of trauma in culture and families, including the pain and fear inherent in our daily lives. Deepening our understanding of these sources of suffering and accompanied by an understanding of our embodied and relational brains, we may find ways to cultivate conditions for deep recovery. As we will discover, the capacity for healing is inherent in us, unfolding in the presence of the long-awaited support.

One of the challenges that a culture dominated by left-hemisphere concerns offers us is a tendency to remove whatever comes to its attention from the context that holds and informs it (Dartington TV, 2011; McGilchrist, 2009). From that viewpoint, the surrounding culture may seem largely irrelevant to the therapeutic process. However, if we remind ourselves that we are taking in 11 million bits of sensory information per second (Riener, 2011), we may begin to appreciate how profoundly we are implicitly embedded in culture as it shapes us below the level of conscious awareness.

How might we understand this implicit and explicit cultural context within which both our traumas and our movement toward healing unfold? How might it be influencing our own lives and what we are bringing as we enter the therapeutic relationship? These may seem like large and abstract questions, but in reality, culture is one tangible and highly influential foundation of our daily practice. To begin, we are all in a stew of too much information together—patient and therapist—shaping the nature of our encounter with each other. We live in a very different world than we did even thirty years ago. According to a study by Martin Hilbert and Priscilla Lopez (2011), we are taking in the equivalent of 174 newspapers' worth of information each day, about five times as much as in 1986, overwhelming our brain's processing capacity (Levitin, 2014). As with most social science research, this statistic holds a metaphorical more than a factual truth for us as individuals, since each of us is probably taking in more or less than the 174 newspapers' worth. Nevertheless, the felt sense of being flooded likely strikes a chord of recognition in most of us. Simply driving down the street, I am aware of the different feeling in my body if the median is filled with signs encouraging me to vote for particular people rather than populated by daffodils.

Whether we feel comfortable considering this deluge to be its own kind of potential trauma or not, it is certainly changing the way we are able to attend to each other. I feel the pull of my email and the insistent call of an incoming text as much as anyone else, while a close colleague who is a dedicated trauma therapist sadly told me that she repeatedly finds herself so distracted by the amount and content of email she imagines piling up while she sits with her dear patients that she realizes her presence in that moment is being compromised. We so often hear parents telling us of their longing to connect with their video game– and social media–absorbed teens that it has become a cliché. Now research is telling us that children and teens are sad, exhausted, and angry as their parents repeatedly turn away to be with their tablets and phones (Steiner-Adair & Barker, 2014). This loss of leisurely, sustained, face-to-face connection is making true presence a rare experience for many of us and neurally engraining fast pace and split attention as the norm. With our best intentions, these patterns may follow our patients and us into the counseling room in subtle and obvious ways.

In addition to the sheer volume of information, much of this inundation involves ongoing exposure to suffering. We are connected moment by moment to far-flung events as they unfold. While there are many beautiful aspects within our society, our exposure to potentially traumatic events is ubiquitous and continuous. Today, as I am completing this chapter, a passenger plane flying over the Ukraine, carrying no one related to the conflict, was shot down by a missile; more children were caught in the crossfire in the ongoing conflict in the Middle East; locally, a young girl who was waiting in the car while her mother ran into the bank lost this irreplaceable person in the midst of a shootout related to a bank robbery—and so much more. This is not a particularly unusual day. Images and sounds of war, natural disasters, and human-made devastation explicitly surround us and implicitly leave their imprint in our muscles, our belly and heart brains, our nervous systems, and the brains in our skulls. We are all touched as time and space collapse with the speed and sophistication of communication.

Like so many changes, this current onslaught has crept up on us incrementally, until most of us are now exposed to potentially traumatic experiences many times each day. Some would say that witnessing trauma can be more harmful than enduring the experience itself because of the acute helplessness we feel. Because we absorb so much more implicit information than explicit, much of the time our bodies may be the only witness to this outpouring of suffering. In response, many of our systems, largely below conscious awareness, have adaptively found ways to not feel so much. While we could call this desensitization, it is likely the product of us protectively shifting away from our right hemisphere neural circuitry that is attuned to the present moment and to relationships as well as sensitive to suffering, toward the left that can stay more distant and analytical (McGilchrist, 2009). This hemispheric movement does not happen by conscious choice but as an adaptive change guided by a sense of increasing danger (Porges, 2011). It is possible that even this shift in our functioning might be considered traumatic as, in the service of emotional survival, we are drawn away from our capacity for offering and receiving compassion and connection.

My growing sense of the depth of our challenge to remain present within this culture is one wellspring for this book. The other is that at the opposite end of the spectrum comes the equally compelling wisdom that we are not designed to live in a sea of disruption and cut off from each other. Instead, we are built to seek out, enter, and sustain warm relationships which allows us to support the emergence of a humane world. Neurobiological research continues to reveal so many signs of our fundamentally relational nature and the crucial importance of safety for our ability to stay connected, with all the cultural and interpersonal possibilities that brings. At the most basic and pervasive level, we shape one another's embodied brains from prebirth to death (Cozolino, 2014; Siegel, 2015b). Our nervous systems continually ask this question: "Are you with me?" The answer is yes when we are present and available to one another, without judgments or agenda in that moment—true safety, true presence, true listening (Porges, 2011). Social baseline theory (Beckes & Coan, 2011) tells us that when we have a felt sense of being accompanied, everything becomes easier and less painful, freeing our resources for relating and creating. Our primary emotional-motivational systems in the midbrain are arranged so that remaining in connection is the first priority (Panksepp & Biven, 2012). Even a small piece of research—like the one showing that the neural circuits devoted to face recognition continue to grow and become more dense throughout childhood and early adulthood, while those devoted to recognizing places don't—appears to affirm the primacy of connection (Gomez et al., 2017). Given all this, it might not be too much to say that relationship is everything—by our very design.

In regard to understanding the challenge we currently have in connecting with one another, one of the primary streams we will be following in these pages comes from the seminal work of Iain McGilchrist (2009) concerning our divided brains. He talks about our two hemispheres not in terms of *what* each does (because both hemispheres fire for everything), but of *how* each experiences—and then creates—the world based on the different way each side of our brain attends and perceives. Right and left literally offer different perspectives concerning what matters and, as a result, shape the way we interact with each other, the kinds of institutions we create, and what values we believe are important. It may be worth pausing to sense the magnitude of this distinction, since it is influencing the way we live and practice.

In a very brief summary drawn from McGilchrist's (2009) work, our right hemisphere orients us toward the space between, the relational space, as it is unfolding moment to moment. As such, everything it sees is held in context and finds its meaning there. The flow of novel experience comes to us here as rich streams of a continuously changing felt sense in the body. This perspective is aware of the uncertainty of the next moment and the next and keenly attuned to both the suffering and the potential meaningfulness of life. There can be a broad acceptance of paradox, a both/and way of meeting what comes, and deep respect for the fullness of implicit experience. It is also here that we make and sustain living connections with one another and here that the guiding vision for a humane society might arise. The individual, the unique, the unrepeatable, the irreplaceable, the unpredictable, the interpersonal all live here.

Pause for Reflection

With this first pause, we are shifting the pace just a bit so we can perhaps listen more deeply to the meaning of the words for us. In the interest of that deepening, it may be helpful for us to slowly read each of the sentences in the paragraph above aloud and then sense what arises in our bodies, feelings, and thoughts concerning this way of being in the world. How is it for each of us to hear about the uncertain and tentative nature of right-hemisphere experience? What novel experiences have come to us recently, and what streams of sensation do we notice in our bodies as we remember them now? What does it mean to us that we are more available to suffering from this perspective? How do we open to a both/and perspective in the face of hearing something with which we intellectually and perhaps viscerally disagree? Is it possible to also have a felt sense of how this perspective opens us to the nourishing joys of deep relatedness?

The left hemisphere's ways of attending and working are very different from those of the right. It is the realm of greater fixity, of creating systems that can potentially bring the right's vision into manifestation. To do this, it mostly *re*-presents information flowing in from the right's experience of the present moment, taking what it needs out of its context, and rendering it static so that the wholeness can be taken apart and made into various elements that can be manipulated like pieces on a chessboard to create these systems, be they modes of thought and relating or institutions. When new experience does come to the left, it is dismembered and parts are sorted according to the familiar categories already encoded. It values the explicit and distrusts the richer but never fully knowable implicit. It is the hemisphere of grasping and using, of autonomy, individuality, and self-reliance, of goal-driven movement, tasks, and behavior. The left concerns itself with algorithms, protocols, and interventions that can be broadly applied without regard to context or individuality. Rather than being aware of suffering, the left perspective tends to be unrealistically optimistic, although this optimism is also colored by paranoia—an uncomfortable combination at best. Additionally, there is a tendency toward an either/or perspective, toward judgment, and the possibility of rigidity and blindness to the present moment and to living relationships, especially if the left becomes less connected to the right. In that state, our world narrows into concern mainly for getting our own needs continually met to ensure ongoing happiness.

Pause for Reflection

As we read through these sentences, we might notice if particular aspects of this perspective resonate with our current experience. Do we have a sense of what it feels like to step out of the stream of experience into the organization of systems? What happens in our bodies when we take that sometimes necessary step? When we hear the words "grasping" and "using," what is our embodied response? What about goal-directed movement—how does that come into our lives? How does the concern for tasks, behaviors, and self-reliance touch us? Is the need to identify and use protocols and interventions part of our professional experience? Do we have moments when we are so task-oriented that relationships feel intrusive? What happens in our bodies as we reflect on optimism colored by paranoia? We don't need to do anything with or about our responses here as we just begin to dip our toes into the felt sense of the perspectives of our bihemispheric world. As our sensitivity to these two ways of seeing increases, we may find that we are more easily able to sense these shifts between hemispheres in our clients as well.

These two different ways of attending are supported by the multiple connections between the cortical columns in the right hemisphere and the relatively isolated columns in the left (Hawkins & Blakeslee, 2004; McGilchrist, 2009). Most simply, we can say that the right hemisphere contains significantly more white matter because the cortical columns of neurons are richly interconnected. These pathways are then myelinated, both increasing synaptic strength and speeding movement throughout these well-wired networks. In this way, experience coming in or being recalled is held in the larger neuronal context and may be felt more as spreading waves in the body than as isolated particles of information (to borrow a metaphor from quantum physics). On the left, these columns are much more like silos with far fewer interconnections. This serves well to order information in a way that allows us to take bits and pieces and rearrange them into new fixed patterns to achieve the goal we have identified. Additionally, new information coming in from the senses has a tendency to be perceived as bits of information rather than a flowing stream, with these bits getting sorted according to the categories already encoded in these silos. Standing in the forest and making a statement like "You've seen one redwood, you've seen them all" reflects this classification and deadening of experience.

At this juncture, it would be easy to align with right-mode processing as the "good" way of perceiving and left-mode processing as the culprit in what is ailing our culture. However, that is not accurate. Difficulties arise when the *relationship* between the hemispheres is altered in ways that prevent them from having an ongoing conversation that supports collaborative expression of their unique gifts.

It seems we human beings are designed to function most humanely when right-mode processing takes the lead and provides the vision—or, as McGilchrist (2009) would say, is the *Master* (no gender intended) and the left mode becomes the vital *emissary* who can provide understanding and build systems to bring the vision of the right into stable form. In the moment-to-moment unfolding in the counseling room, this wisdom can provide a solid enough foundation that we can open into truly following our people. Both hemispheres are essential, and the relationship between them is all-important. By all indications, we in the developed nations are not living in that world now (McGilchrist, 2009). Instead, a pronounced shift toward left dominance has occurred, most dramatically since the Industrial Revolution. The great tragedy of this shift is that it leaves us unable to even notice that we are in trouble because we are cut off from our body's distress signals, an adaptive strategy if the right hemisphere has become uninhabitable.

For herein lies the danger. If our right hemispheres harbor significant trauma in the form of unhealed fear and pain or we feel overwhelmed by the sheer volume of incoming information, we may adaptively shift toward left dominance in an effort to protect ourselves from a crippling onslaught of unmanageable inner and outer experience. Certain streams of research indicate that this may be the case for about 75 percent of us in the United States. One recent study revealed that about 75 percent of college students are significantly less empathic than college students were thirty years ago, and that the decline in empathic capacity has accelerated in the last ten years (Konrath, O'Brien, & Hsing, 2011). We know that the circuitry for empathy is inherent but needs sustained connection with others to mature. As we move away from our right-centric relational capacities, the nourishment for that developmental process is less available. Not surprisingly, there has been a concomitant rise in narcissism among the same population as the left shift has increasingly cut us off from this relational circuitry and felt sense of connection (Twenge & Campbell, 2009; Twenge & Foster, 2010; Twenge, Konrath, Foster, Campbell, & Bushman, 2008). Without that sense of being with others, we are thrown back toward focusing mostly on satisfying our own wants and needs. A third strand of research, this one by Barbara Fredrickson and her colleagues (Fredrickson et al., 2013), looked at epigenetic differences between people who believed they were leading meaningful lives, whether they were happy or not (25 percent), and those who declared they were happy but had little sense of meaning (75 percent). The latter were mainly interested in getting their wants satisfied (a more left-centric value), while the former were dedicated to giving to others and leading lives of connection (more right-centric values). The further results of this study revealed that suffering with meaning is even physically healthier than happiness without meaning. Meaninglessness, rooted in a sense of isolation, brings on epigenetic changes in the direction of inflammation, which we now know to be the headwaters of many chronic illnesses. The epigenetics of meaning offer our bodies more health-supporting anti-inflammatory possibilities.

One indicator of our hemispheric location comes via the language that flows naturally from us. Let me share a story. At a two-day workshop on the interpersonal neurobiology of trauma, in the midst of a touching discussion about the felt sense of moments of silence that sometimes fill the space between patient and therapist, a clinician who had been doing beautiful depth work with trauma survivors for decades asked, "Can you say more about how you would use silence in therapy?" After a pause in which I wasn't quite sure how to answer, I heard myself quietly say, "What if silence just arose when it wanted and left after it had done its work?" For me, the rich conversation that followed was worth the trip to the East Coast, for the difference between *using* interventions and *following* the process unfolding in the space between our patients and us lies at the heart of the matter.

As we talked, it became apparent to us that as much as we might subscribe to the value of flowing with our patients in this way, the push of the culture at large and the therapeutic culture in particular leaves us vulnerable to quickly—almost helplessly—switching into *thinking about* next steps, *figuring out* what's going on, *deciding* how to use interventions, educating, and making treatment plans and goals, even in the midst of our heart's pull toward just *being present* and waiting to see what wants to unfold. Not only do we feel the pressure, but our patients also often come in expecting us to provide solutions, tools, and quick symptom and behavior relief because they have been led to believe that is the desired pattern of healing in this left-centric world. By the end of the conversation at the conference, we came to a compassionate understanding that the implicit pull of our left-laden culture often undermines our capacity to trust in and follow our patients' inherent wisdom about next steps.

One central focus of these writings is that when we can put down roots in the right-mode felt sense of relationship, we arrive at the possible activation of our innate healing capacities, which arise in the relational space between patient and practitioner. Franklyn Sills (2010), one of the pioneering teachers in the biodynamic craniosacral tradition, speaks of the "inherent treatment plan," grounded in deep listening to the wise, adaptive system of the patient. This pathway has the opportunity to unfold as we cultivate our capacity to stay in contact with what is emerging within our patients from moment to moment. With sufficient safety and care in the space between, unhealed implicit memories can be guided toward the surface by the inherent wisdom that knows how to move our patients' system toward greater coherence. Then, from this settled place of interconnection, our next words and actions with our patients may naturally arise as our left-hemisphere capacities respond to what is flowing rather than us taking the lead and consciously crafting next steps.

A felt sense of safety is the bedrock of healing trauma, and consideration of how that arises in the therapeutic relationship is the second stream we will be following. During the last twenty years or so, Stephen Porges (1995, 2007, 2009a, 2009b, 2011, 2013) has been offering a continually deeper and more embodied awareness of how our tripartite nervous systems carry us along in this world, always responding adaptively in the moment. My sense is that this work has transformed him so much that now, when he speaks, we don't just hear his ideas but actually experience what he means by safety and social engagement. In the chapters that follow, we will explore the details of this beautiful, adaptive system, but here it may be enough to quote Porges (2013) and say, "We wear our hearts on our faces and in our voices" (audio recording) as our nervous systems influence our body's moment-to-moment expression, automatically offering a sense of safety or danger to one another. We are keenly and continuously attuned to these messages flowing in the space between, mostly below the level of conscious awareness. These interpersonal communications intertwine with our unique perceptual vantage point, shaped by our life's experiences, yielding our body's sense of how safe we are in this moment. Porges's word for this unfolding process is "neuroception," our bodies receiving, understanding, and adapting in their own unique ways to the flow of information from other bodies, particularly through face and voice quality.

Let me share a personal experience of this. In the hours after hearing about the passenger plane being shot down over the Ukraine because of a conflict having nothing to do with those on the plane, I felt increasingly upset and began to experience an urgent need to be with someone about it. The first two people I approached immediately began to wonder why this happened, speculating about who had done it and how it had occurred. Even before becoming conscious of my discomfort, I suspect I was neuroceptively touched by the intellectual quality of their voices, the tension around their eyes, and the lack of eye contact. My body responded to their disconnected curiosities with rising tension and a kind of heartsick longing for being joined in the immediacy of the experience. No doubt touched and sympathetically aroused by this horrendous and apparently meaningless act, my friends' systems had adaptively (and unconsciously) switched into left-mode processing and, as a result, out of the possibility of connection. Their nervous systems had protected them from the full-body blow of being present to what had happened. With no intention on their part, I was alone in my suffering, the experience that may be central to potential trauma becoming embedded trauma. One of Porges's most important contributions, from my perspective, is that these apparent abandonments don't spring from ill intent or bad character but are instead our nervous systems responding to conditions in the most adaptive way available to them in the moment. As we begin to feel our way into this, compassion for our human condition may begin to soften the protective judgments our left hemispheres so often make when others can't be with us.

As evening approached, I realized that the anguish was settling deep into my belly, my muscles were holding tight, and a kind of hopelessness about the prospects for our species was darkening my mind. Then came another opportunity to speak of my upset. This time, there was only silence after I spoke, and I could see in this person's face and eyes a mirror of my own sense of devastation. Everything changed: Belly and muscles let go, tears welled up, and (though I didn't have words for it at the time) a sense of "this is how we'll survive" came alive in me. As I was truly accompanied, the feeling of being traumatized gave way to standing together clear-eyed in the presence of a terrible truth—and hope arrived. This is one of the central paradoxes. When our systems protectively turn our minds and hearts away from the truth of the moment, there is an element of isolation from ourselves and others that may increase our sense of despair. However, when we come into contact with suffering in the presence of another, even when the depth of pain is very great, the very experience of relatedness—the nurturance we humans most need—prepares a space in which meaning and hope may emerge.

Pause for Reflection

Again making room for a change in pace, let's reflect together on times we have felt met or abandoned in the midst of intense emotion. What happens in our bodies when we are joined by another in our sorrow or joy? What is it like in our bodies to be with someone who has protectively shifted away from connection to our experience? How might we notice, with kindness, when our nervous systems have taken us adaptively away from the experience of this moment? How might we find our way back? It is certainly too much to be continually in contact with the world's suffering, so we may come to appreciate how our nervous systems titrate this exposure for us, and also how accompaniment ameliorates suffering in a surprisingly profound way.

The ability to offer the safe sanctuary of presence is central to treating trauma. It is the beginning and ongoing foundation. As we settle into Porges's work, we may discover that safety actually has a clear definition, although not one that is easy to put into practice. At this juncture, we may find the crossroads where our cultural challenge enters the counseling room. Given the implicit pull of the left, will we be able to stay truly present with one another so that the possibility of deep healing comes alive in the space between? Our work throughout this book is to cultivate this possibility through grounded understanding of the way our embodied and relational brains become wounded and heal, through having our own internal shifts so that we are more able to nonjudgmentally hold what arises in the space between us and our people, and through increasing our capacity for listening from stillness. What happens in our counseling rooms rests on the foundation of our ever-evolving inner orientation.

A third stream runs through these pages as well. Trauma is an *embodied* experience, touching all the neural pathways in our bodies: our muscles, the brains in our bellies and hearts, our autonomic nervous systems, our brainstems, our primary emotional-motivational systems, our limbic regions and neocortices, and reaching down to even finer systems at the level of our cells and genes. As we will see, many of these pathways are gathered into the neural nets of embodied implicit memory, the kind of remembering that is always experienced as happening right now, no matter how distant the original event. When our relational lives have been nourished with warmth and responsiveness, these implicit memories support the ongoing experience of resilience and meaning; when we have instead taken in coldness or chaos, we are haunted by the ongoing presence or potential arising of those experiences in our bodies as well. Most of us have had some of both.

In addition to being an embodied experience, trauma is also a *relational* experience in that the embedding of trauma may arise not primarily from the nature of events, but from who is with us before, during, and after the overwhelming happening (or non-happening in the case of neglect) (Morley & Kohrt, 2013).

My good friend and colleague Connie Lawrence shared this with me about her work:

> You know, I sit with survivors of sexual assault all day, many different versions, colors, degrees, and what people talk about is the relational dynamics: who didn't believe them, who betrayed them, who was cruel, or who started blaming. I also ask clients if the relational dynamics were somehow worse than the original assault. The answer is always a firm YES. (personal communication, July 27, 2014)

We all ache to be heard and held in the reality of our experience, without judgment or any impulse toward fixing.

Perhaps this leads to the natural conclusion that healing trauma might be an embodied and relational experience between patient and therapist as well, with our people's wise inner world leading the way while we hold a safe, warm, stable, responsive space. The research on memory reconsolidation (for a thorough summary, see Ecker, 2015; Ecker, Ticic, & Hulley, 2012) points to *responsiveness to what is alive in the moment* as the central capacity in cultivating a space that supports shifting the felt sense and behavioral patterns of implicit memories. It is this embodied reawakening of embedded traumas in the form of bodily sensations, surges of emotion, behavioral impulses, and perceptual shifts that flow into our daily lives as these unhealed memories (when touched by inner or outer events) well up, coloring every aspect of our world.

Memory reconsolidation research has shown that for the felt sense and implicit pattern to change, we need to not only be in touch with the embedded trauma, but simultaneously in the presence of what has been called a disconfirming experience[*]—most often, what was needed at the time of the potential trauma but was not available (Clem & Huganir, 2010; Debiec, Díaz-Mataix, Bush, Doyère, & LeDoux, 2010; Díaz-Mataix, Debiec, LeDoux, & Doyère, 2011; Jarome et al., 2012). If we felt alone, we needed a sense of accompaniment. If we were frightened, we needed protection. If we were shamed, we needed acceptance. If we were hurt, we needed comfort. It is as though the part of us who experienced the original rupture of safety has been waiting ever since for the repair to arrive. For this reason, we might call these experiences "restorative" or "reparative," leaning toward words that carry more of a healing flavor than might be possible with the word "disconfirmation."

Lack of support in the midst of wounding seems central to the movement from potential trauma to embedded trauma, and the provision of support that is responsive to the particular nature of the wounds is

---

[*] Ecker (2015) also calls these "mismatch experiences" or "prediction errors" (p. 7). The element of contrast and juxtaposition with what is expected is central, and it seems that this can be facilitated at many levels: directly through the body (Ticic & Kushner, 2015), via right-brain-to-right-brain interpersonal encounter (Badenoch, 2008, 2011; Schore, 2012), or with the support of words. So responsive is our whole system to the offer of repair that it is as though we were designed for healing.

equally central to healing. While these reparative experiences can arise internally between two parts of ourselves, they often occur quite naturally in the relationship between patient and therapist. Since our central neurobiological systems are oriented toward making and maintaining connection, providing repair in the space between is to collaborate beautifully with our embodied brain's natural healing processes.

This awareness of the need for restorative experiences carries us back to the territory of our implicit immersion in the current cultural milieu. In the larger sense, this book is seeking to provide a potentially reparative experience in order to possibly ameliorate the pervasive implicit pressure of this left-shifted society. While it is one thing to offer a critique of where we are (the left mode's slant on things), it is quite another to be present to the challenge in a way that offers the felt-sense experience of a more right-centric way of being that also includes the valuable contributions of the left mode as maker of structure and holder of stability. In some small way, this book seeks to begin an exploration of that possibility. Because the right-centric perspective is primarily relational, this may be a good place to remind ourselves that pausing to spend significant time with the reflections and perhaps share them with someone else may help us remain whole-brained. Going for a walk, especially in nature, getting our hands in dirt, or petting any furry creature will foster this as well. In general, anything we can do to remain in a more right-centric mode with our left hemisphere also paying attention will let us experience the words written here with more availability to their meaning and embodiment than to acquisition of knowledge alone.

It is likely that many of us came into this field precisely because we felt drawn to the richness of deepening relationships. However, when we plan interventions in advance, or direct our patients to parent themselves, or hold an implicit or explicit belief that *self*-regulation and autonomy are signs of health, we can again feel the influence of the dominant culture's left-centric perspective shaping so much of what we offer our patients. Our efforts on their behalf are fueled by our good-hearted wish to quickly alleviate their suffering even while we are being drawn into the relationally alienating methods of the left hemisphere's view. How do we begin to trust and ride upon the unsure, tentative groundswells of remaining present with what is here in each moment? The paradox— which brings a big smile—is that getting grounded in clear left-mode knowledge about our embodied and relational brains may provide a secure enough foundation that we can risk being that present. We will spend a good deal of time in these pages developing this clarity.

These three strands of a single braided stream*—hemispheric integration, safety, and the central importance of implicit memory repair within relationship—actually arise from a single river of what it is to be a human being—fragile, tender, easily frightened, body and mind inseparable, resilient, adaptive, and forever interdependent. Many other tributaries will join these three as we seek to open ourselves to the possibility of ever-deepening presence with one another. Since this is the core of who we are and what we long for, surely the journey is possible.

Our own pathway toward deepening relational presence will begin with an exploration of the possibility of a broadened definition of trauma based on what we have learned from the relational neurosciences, and interpersonal neurobiology in particular. As we move into the body of the book, in the first part, we will explore several ways that we can feed our left-hemisphere wisdom with viewpoints drawn from the right-hemisphere perspective. It seems to me that our ongoing connection with the people in our lives, whether they are patients, family, friends, or strangers, begins with one indispensable and ongoing process: *our own inner preparation*. What seems most true is that how we see people has the potential to support true presence based on fewer judgments, more warm curiosity, and trust in the inner wisdom of their system in that moment, all of which lead to gradually expanding compassion and capacity for responsiveness. Such changes begin with viewing ourselves that way, so this part of the book will interweave science and personal exploration. So important do I believe this to be that it will occupy about two-thirds of these pages.

We will begin by spending a leisurely time with a series of chapters about our embodied brains in development, trauma, and healing. We will be deepening into an understanding and particularly a felt sense of the numerous neural streams that converge to offer us the experi-

---

* Braided stream: "A stream consisting of multiple small, shallow channels that divide and recombine numerous times forming a pattern resembling the strands of a braid" (retrieved from http://www.thefreedictionary.com/braided+stream). This metaphor seems to particularly convey the sense of the intermixing of these principles as we move forward. Braided streams continually exchange water with each other, rearrange the underlying and surrounding sediment, and vary their patterns of flow as they move along together yet separately.

ence of both our memories and the newness of this moment. We are truly a buzzing hive of neural activity throughout our bodies, engaging constantly in intricate conversations on behalf of our well-being. As we are able to develop and refine awareness of our own pathways, we will be more able to cultivate a space in which the people in our lives can entertain similar explorations.

In the chapters following the ones about these embodied streams, we will consider how clarifying certain of our perspectives might open us to being more present with ourselves and others. How might viewing us humans as adaptive rather than disordered change our way of relating? When we bring this perspective to ourselves, what happens? If we could also simultaneously sense the inherent wisdom of our systems and the power of implicit memory in guiding our moment-to-moment inner and interpersonal experience, how might that broader perspective support our capacity to be present? Deepening into the work of memory recon-solidation (Ecker et al., 2012), we may begin to discover that implicit memory itself is filled with inherent wisdom. Coming to the heart of the matter, we will explore how we are built more for ongoing interde-pendence and co-organization/co-regulation than autonomy and self-regulation. We will finish this preparatory section by exploring how the language that comes to us naturally concerning the therapeutic process can both illuminate which hemisphere is in the lead and then reinforce that perspective. Shifting to a more right-centric viewpoint can make room for different words that help us see and hold our patients with deepening care and respect.

The final part of the book flows naturally from these shifts in inner perspective. We will move this inner work into the counseling room by spending time in "the space between"—the healing relational space between us and our people that researcher Uri Hasson and his col-leagues (Hasson, Ghazanfar, Galantucci, Garrod, & Keysers, 2012) sug-gest is where two brains may become one in true communication. Lou Cozolino (2014) says this about that precious space:

> The *social synapse* is the space between us—a space filled with seen and unseen messages and the medium through which we are com-bined into larger organisms. . . . Because our experience as individ-ual selves is lived at the border of this synapse and because so much communication occurs below conscious awareness, this linkage is mostly invisible to us. (2014, p. xv)

Making this space a bit more visible and tangible perhaps, we will begin by exploring the process of leading, following, and responding to our people that can help us stay rooted in relationship. As we deepen with these courageous ones, we co-attach, joining our windows of tolerance, and move into waves of restorative experiences. All of this can open a space in which implicit healing can naturally unfold. As an example of how this process may support recovery from trauma, we will spend a good deal of time with practices that help us cultivate compassion within the inner community. While these are the healing pathways most familiar to me and may differ from your own, they may provide valuable guideposts for healing within any paradigm. Then we will spend some time with the often-avoided question—what about when therapy fails? The final chapter will offer the story of a most unexpected therapeutic relationship, one that taught me deeply that I may not have any idea what healing will look like for my people, and often not even for myself. As judgments and expectations loosen, for me, these spaces brush up against the sacred. With this story, we will finish by opening to the possibility of letting go of layer after layer of expectation until we are resting in deep trust of the pathway that is already there within our people. In that open, responsive, supportive space, there is room for everything that wants to emerge.

1

Reconsidering the Nature of Trauma

Leaving her mom at the door, four-year-old Mandy walks confidently into her preschool classroom and is immediately met by the screams of another child as his mother walks out the door. Her brow furrows, her stomach tenses, and her shoulders hunch forward a bit. Understandably, no one notices, and she jets out the door onto the playground. Joyously jumping into the swing, she pumps hard and heads for the sky. Her brainstem likes the rhythm and her nervous system begins to calm a bit. Slowing down, she glances over at the jungle gym and sees two boys who are her friends wrestling over who gets to go first. They are pretty high up on the apparatus and aren't playing so much as fighting. No one gives in, and the shoving turns to shouting and then hitting. By the time the teacher is able to separate them and bring them back to earth, Mandy is wide-eyed and shaking inside. Again, no one notices, so she is left to manage her fear by herself.

As she walks back into her classroom, another friend offers to share her toy, and they wander off together as Mandy's conscious mind forgets about the boys tussling while her body continues to hold the tension. At snack time, still enthusiastically talking with her friend, Mandy accidentally knocks over her cup of juice, and she feels her overwhelmed teacher's frown and impatience flow into her small body as the teacher brusquely cleans it up while talking to another child who doesn't want her apple. Mandy's little chest caves in a bit; her eyes go down as she drops from joyous to quiet, enveloped in a small whirlpool of shame. Things are apparently peaceful for a while, until circle time arrives. She sees the boys who were fighting get close to each other again, both their faces frowning, and her heart speeds up. She looks around to see if the teacher is watching them, but she is helping another child put her things in her cubby. Nothing happens between the boys, but Mandy continues to watch them closely, just in case.

All of this happens during the first two hours of her day. She has explicitly seen and encoded all of these experiences, although they quickly go out of her conscious awareness as soon as a new encounter arrives. Meanwhile, she has also received many more implicit sensory streams, below conscious awareness but registered in her body—children laughing, crying, yelling; parents taking their leave and the felt sense of their departure appearing on the faces of the children; a teacher smiling, frowning, sighing; struggles for control of the toys; the fast pace of the classroom—and so much more. Multiply these two hours times three and we begin to get a sense of her six-hour day. When Mandy gets home and discovers that her anticipated play date has a cold, she dissolves into a tangle of grief and rage.

Without in any way diminishing or dishonoring the devastating traumas so many of us have experienced, is it possible to say that Mandy has had many small potentially traumatic experiences during her day? If we simply say she was distressed (past tense), we may lose the sense of the shards of these experiences that linger in her muscles, belly and heart brains, nervous system, and limbic system and, with repetition, gradually shape her implicit anticipation about the way the world works. It is possible that her powerful response to her unavailable friend arose from an overwhelmed nervous and emotional system that didn't have the interpersonal support it needed to regulate, digest, and integrate the frightening and shaming experiences that accumulated during her day. Perhaps an equally important question is *when* her experience might become a trauma—when her whole body registered fear or shame, or when there was no one available to help her with it?

These may not be questions we usually ask about the experience of everyday life. However, what we are learning from relational neuroscience, and particularly interpersonal neurobiology (IPNB), may help us understand trauma (from the Greek *trōma*, meaning "wound" or "pierce") through a broader lens. IPNB offers particular help here because it is the scientifically grounded, interdisciplinary study of how we influence each other's neural landscape from moment to moment (Siegel, 2015b). It focuses particularly on our essentially social nature, placing the individual brain in the context of relationships (Cozolino,

2014; Siegel, 2015b), something that is essential for understanding the development and healing of trauma. IPNB also sees mental health as arising from increasingly optimal integration between our embodied and relational brain's many systems—taking into account not only our internal resources but also the supports available moment to moment from the interpersonal environment (Cozolino, 2014; Siegel, 2015b). The breadth of its vision invites us to spend years allowing this perspective to slowly become embodied within us so that we gradually begin to see and experience one another through a different lens. This potentially amounts to a profound change in how we attend to each other and, therefore, what we are able to support in one another's development. In a very real way, each moment of our lives is potentially therapeutic as we seek to deepen our presence with each other. While what we will explore here certainly applies in the treatment room—whatever our mode of practice—the hope is that we will begin to notice that this deepening wisdom follows us everywhere.

To understand how we might begin to see certain aspects of daily life as potentially traumatic for all of us, it will be helpful to gain a sense of how our embodied brains are shaped by our experiences and how they then color our continuously unfolding perceptions. First of all, neuroscience tells us that our brains are *complex systems*, and this means they have an inherent capacity for self-organization (among other qualities) (Cicchetti & Rogosch, 1997; Siegel, 2015b). However, what we may next notice is that what is inherent in our neurobiology *doesn't come into manifestation except in relationship* (Cozolino, 2014). The potential remains but is not activated until our developing brain interacts with the brain of another. We know from the experience of the Romanian orphanages that babies left mostly alone suffer the most devastating wounds at every level, from disorganization of all their systems to major deficits in cognition and relational capacity. On their own, their brains don't move toward optimal organization of their neural circuitry. The arrival of another with an already-organized brain is the necessary food for self-organization to be nourished to whatever extent it can within the relationship. Most prominently in the initial stages of life but also throughout life, *co-organization* may be a more accurate term for what is needed to enliven the inherent capacity of our brains to develop the most optimal neural connections they can in the moment.

A second discovery is that each of us comes into this life with the neurons in our limbic and cortical regions mostly an ocean of not-yet-connected cells open to the arrival of others to shape it into patterns of connection. Even the brain in our belly, the enteric nervous system, begins to take on particular ways of being with nourishment as we ingest and digest food interwoven with the quality of relationship with the giver of food (Harshaw, 2008). If the person offering nurturance is attuned to our signals of hunger and satiety, we begin to connect the sensations in our bodies with the arrival of food and the satisfaction of hunger. We gradually encode a felt sense of when to start and stop eating. If the person is not so attuned, our eating patterns become disconnected from our bodies' needs, shaping our way of pursuing nourishment of all sorts. Without the presence of another, we simply have a sensation, but no sense of what it is or what comes next. From this one example, we can perhaps begin to gain a sense of the depth of our interdependence.

Whichever neural system we're speaking about, the quality of our earliest relationships leads to the differentiation of neural nets out of the largely not-yet-connected sea of cells and the development of what are called *constraints*. This means that within these primary relationships, our embodied systems gradually encode neural pathways that will limit our perception of what is possible for this unique individual we are becoming. As we will see, these limits can be in the direction of supporting or hindering our capacity for ongoing neural integration—and are usually a mix of both.

For example, if our mothering person/people* are often able to be present with us with warm curiosity and delight in who we are, to respond to our needs as they arise, to notice when their efforts at connecting haven't landed, and to continue to offer support until the connection is made, then our systems become constrained to expect this kind of nourishing relational experience in the future. It can seem odd to see this kind of pattern of relating as creating limitation because we usually believe that to be negative, but here it means that of all the possible ways of anticipating relationships, this is the one our brains have been shaped to expect. When we have these kinds of nurturing relationships at the beginning of life, the enlivened self-organization

---

* I prefer "mothering person/people" to the more impersonal "caregiver" because I believe the former invokes more of the felt sense of what we need at this earliest stage of our lives. Anyone—mother, father, grandparent, nanny—who is offering primary support for an infant is that baby's mothering person.

in our mothering person (which is a result of her own early and ongoing co-organizing experiences) becomes our own. The depth of this unfolding inheritance is just beginning to be known. The organization of our neural pathways, our capacity to take in and absorb many kinds of nourishment, the strength and balance of our neurotransmitters, the internalization of our mothering people, and the epigenetic stream flowing down through the generations join our temperament to form a rich commingling of constraints that are parallel in parent and baby.

For all of us, no matter how securely we are parented, at some moments our mothering people aren't able to repair the inevitable ruptures. All parents have implicit blind spots that leave them unable to see us children for who we are and also impair their ability to read the experience that is written in our faces when they have hurt or scared us. Left in this fear or pain, our young embodied brains do not have the neural circuitry to sweep these experiences into the ongoing flow of our developing brains, so the felt sense of this interchange is tucked away in limbic-centric circuits in our right hemispheres and held in our muscles, belly and heart brains, nervous systems, and brainstems as well. Our early history, in embodied implicit form, continually whispers the subjective truth that plays an important role in shaping how we perceive our lives, particularly our relationships, to this day. Over time, the felt sense of these implicit memories may change to some degree, but it is the nature of implicit memories to go quickly and deeply into long-term storage and for these neural nets to require certain kinds of experiences to open and take in new information (Ecker, Ticic, & Hulley, 2012). As we will see in succeeding chapters, change at this depth is not as simple as having supportive relationships now.

As this memory is held out of integration, it is also held out of the stream of time. The part of us who experienced the pain or fear stops developing and continues in this disrupted state until the necessary conditions—usually a trustworthy, sustained interpersonal connection—arrive to provide the sanctuary for change. Until that time, the embodied memory can be touched and awakened by internal or external events so that we are physically and emotionally colored with the felt sense of the experience again as though no time has passed. We might say that any part of us that can be touched in this way is carrying a traumatized state. This possibly leads us to a fairly concrete definition of trauma:

Any experience of fear and/or pain that doesn't have the support it needs to be digested and integrated into the flow of our developing brains.

Pause for Reflection

Let's pause to see how our embodied system is responding to this definition of trauma. It would be easy and natural, given our long experience in school, to read through it with our left hemispheres hearing the words while we are disconnected from what it means to us in a personal way. If we reflect on our last twenty-four hours, have there been moments containing some shade of pain or fear that still feels present when we call them to mind and body? It will be helpful to ask this question gently and without pushing for an answer, but just waiting to see what arises when we open to being curious. Taking this gentler stance helps us be drawn in the direction of availability to hear what is unfolding within us.

This definition encourages us to look into the neural and interpersonal aspects of experience for an understanding of how we become traumatized rather than toward the nature of the experience itself or a list of symptoms. We might consider the embedding of trauma to be a *rupture* in the inherent process of neural integration of our ongoing experience, with healing arising through the initiation of an experience of *repair* so that the journey toward integration can follow its natural course.

If we are willing to consider this very broad and inclusive definition of trauma, we will find it can hold so much, from the accumulation of many small unseen and uncomforted daily wounds that begins for many of us in childhood, to the experience of natural disasters, wars, poverty, and cultural distress, to the overt and covert extremes of suffering that happen mostly as a result of the intergenerational transmission of pain. This perspective is in no way intended to diminish the experience of those of us who have suffered the most egregious harm, but instead to diminish the distance between those who are seen as wounded and those who are not. In truth, we are all suffering together in some way. As clinicians, a felt sense of this can often support deepening trust in the space between as our patients begin to rest in our acknowledgment of this common ground.

Now we can return to the question of *when* an experience becomes a trauma. Is it the event itself that lodges the indigestible experience in our embodied brains, or our aloneness with it? This is not a question we may be accustomed to asking, and it may be worthwhile to pause a moment to sense how our bodies respond to it being asked. We may begin to sense an answer by considering that all of us have an ever-emerging, ever-changing threshold for integrating painful and fearful experiences. At any moment, on one side of this doorsill, our embodied brains have enough already-established integration and support from internalized others to meet these events and digest them without additional support. Our ability to do this is often developed within our earliest relationships, or if these didn't support us in building this foundation for integration, later empathic relationships may have offered enough repair for this capacity to be strengthened. On the other side of this threshold, we don't have the internal resources in the face of the current challenge, and without interpersonal accompaniment and support, the experience will go from *potential trauma* to *embedded trauma.*

This suggests it is possible that the origin of trauma has more to do with our interpersonal environment than with the event itself. One of the most touching research areas in recent years explores the experience of child soldiers in Nepal (Kohrt et al., 2010; Morley & Kohrt, 2013). These researchers were asking a specific question about the reintegration of these young ones (who were five- to fourteen-years-old when they joined the rebels) on their return from the devastation of participating in war. Is there a relationship between how these young ones were welcomed back and the development of posttraumatic stress disorder (PTSD) as well as other ongoing symptoms of trauma? The answer from person to person is complex because of the number of societal variables influencing the outcome, but the trend overall suggests that how the young one is held during this period of reintegration by peers, family, and community makes all the difference between whether the child's ongoing life unfolds with few emotional challenges related to these events or with the full-blown experience of PTSD. *In general, those who are rejected continue to suffer in the most painful ongoing ways; those who are accepted and nourished on their return thrive to the extent that there are very few signs of what they have experienced.*

In our own country, the soldiers returning from Vietnam were often greeted with rejection and disgust, some even spat upon, with devastating consequences that they (and we) are still experiencing. Right now, the vision of what is needed for healing our torn warriors, their families, and perhaps society itself is being embodied in the Coming Home Project, developed by Zen teacher and psychologist Joseph Bobrow (2015) and his colleagues. In a recent article, Michael Bader (2016) talks about the vision that guides this program.

> Bobrow and the philosophy behind the *Coming Home Project* emphasize the pathogenic effects of isolation and dissociation and, consequently, of the healing power of community, safety, and unconditional acceptance. Returning vets suffer from both isolation and dissociation—and so do their families, caregivers, service providers, and veteran service organizations. . . . The disconnectedness so rampant in contemporary culture is especially poisonous for veterans who come home wounded, struggling to control frightening feelings and memories, and filled with shame and guilt. . . . In the Coming Home Project retreats, attendees can tell their stories, create rituals that foster mourning, learn techniques to regulate frightening feelings, and, in general, find and create a safe space in which they and their families can begin to heal. (para. 3)

Johann Hari, in his book *Chasing the Scream* (2015), talks about this same principle in regard to the war on drugs. He says that the opposite of addiction isn't abstinence but connection, and makes this eloquent plea: "For a century, we've been singing war songs about addicts; we should have been singing love songs to them all along" (quoted in Bader, 2016, para. 3). Something is afoot in society right now, attempting to reshape the conversation and practice of recovery from every kind of trauma, and we in our counseling rooms may be able to respond to this emergence as we sense that the essence of trauma isn't events, but aloneness within them. Who we perceive as being with us *before*, *during, and after* an event is central to our ability to integrate the trauma throughout our embodied and relational brains.

"Perceive" is an important word here. We may have many people around us, but if we are too activated to have a felt sense of accompaniment or if the people near us are not truly present and available to us because of how their own inner world is taxed in that moment, our systems respond as though we are still alone. In Nepal, there is a greater sense of tribe and community than in the developed world, so these young ones may have an easier time finding a felt sense of being drawn into the embrace of their fellows than teenagers here would in similar circumstances. However, all humans share a common genetic inheritance that yearns for warm attachment, including nervous systems that are always looking for connection, so even in a culture like ours, we do have inherent biological processes as allies that may predispose us to open with the arrival of trustworthy others when we need to digest potentially traumatic events, as the Coming Home Project makes clear.

This brings us to a central question. If it is true that the experience of being alone with pain and fear is fundamental to the development of trauma, how available is the necessary support of accompaniment in our culture? The left-centric nature of our society offers so many challenges in this regard. As this movement into the left hemisphere increases, it cuts us off from the right-rooted relational circuitry that allows us to read distress in the face of another (McGilchrist, 2009). Because of how the primary emotional circuitry in our midbrain has developed, the face of grief or fear is meant to call out to and activate the care response in those around us (Panksepp & Biven, 2012). However, as we take refuge in our left hemisphere's more mechanical reprocessing of the familiar (McGilchrist, 2009), the continuous, microsecond-by-microsecond flow of our emotional state in the faces and voices of those around us (Porges, 2011) goes unseen and is not met with the needed reflection and response.

It is challenging to imagine who is most hurt by this left-centric way of being—the one who knows she needs help in this moment but can't find it, or the one who is so shut off from her own relational resources that her embodied self has the neuroception that she is *perpetually* alone. It seems possible that this dominance of the left itself is a source of ongoing trauma as many of us live with increasing disconnection. This may be particularly tragic because the movement left is often intended to adaptively protect us from the pain and fear held in the right. At the same time, it supports the ongoing accumulation of implicit distress in the right that comes from being alone with the additional challenge of not having any awareness of the need for support.

Pause for Reflection

This hurtful circle can bring on a sense of despair even as we read about it, so it may be important for us to pause a moment to sense what is happening in our bodies as we settle into this awareness. Sitting quietly, possibly with a friend or reading partner, let's open ourselves to what is happening in our muscles, belly, chest, and throat—with as little judgment as possible. Respectfully listening to our body's response can offer a space in which a small change may arise on its own. It may arrive first as a little different felt sense in our bodies that signals the movement from despair to hope. After that, words might come into view. In the case of despair about our culture's propensity for detachment, we are literally stepping out of this particular circle of despair as soon as we connect with another. If you have chosen to have a reading companion, that can be good place to begin sharing support.

Our left-centric way of being offers other challenges as well. Because the left is busy disassembling and reassembling pieces of living experience in order to control and manipulate, it can have the felt sense of a manufacturing plant whose values are "how much it can do, how fast it can do it, and with what degree of precision" (McGilchrist, 2009, p. 430). This drives us to move at an ever-accelerating pace that leaves very little time for the slow, leisurely face-to-face encounters that allow us to truly see, hear, and support each other, particularly in moments of fear and pain. We might say that we are moving at the speed of trauma. At the same time, the left focuses us on task over relationship, correct behavior over moment-to-moment lived experience, judgment over curiosity. All of these lead toward blindness to the opportunity for connection that is alive in every moment.

One of the ways that the left's tendency to take things apart manifests is in our conviction about the ultimate importance of autonomy. A left-shifted mind, divorced from the relational circuitry that is rooted in the right, literally and tragically experiences "I" as more real than "we," and so pushes away from the beauty and necessity of ongoing interdependence starting at the earliest ages. We find one extreme example of this in the well-intentioned advice from Richard Ferber (2006), sleep training advocate. He suggests that in order to fall asleep on their own and sleep through the night, very young babies have to learn to soothe themselves. Even when offered in incremental steps, this is a neurobiological impossibility given how we humans slowly co-develop the neural connections and internalized family that support our capacity for calmness during stressful times (Badenoch, 2011; Schore, 2012). Instead, these little ones who are left to cry have the potential to eventually collapse into exhausted and quiet hopelessness. The title of Ferber's (2006) book is *Solve Your Child's Sleep Problems*, and the *goal* is to create *strategies* for *control* and *predictability* so that parents can be more *personally comfortable*. The vocabulary of both the title and the focus of the book emanates from and further reinforces the left's nonrelational, task-and-behavior-based perspective. The traumatic and tragic outcomes of this loss of relational vision in regard to our littlest ones range from attenuated neural connections to increased anxiety and potential physical maladies later in life (see Narvaez, 2011, and Narvaez, Panksepp, Schore, & Gleason, 2012, for an in-depth exploration). I have no doubt that Richard Ferber feels certain he is providing important solutions for the left-perceived problem of sleep irregularity and overdependence on parents. None of this springs from malice or intent to injure but instead may arise from losses in relational vision that have already occurred without the person having access to the neural circuitry that would allow him to be aware of what has happened (McGilchrist, 2009). If we allow ourselves to gaze at the culture that surrounds and implicitly infuses us, the situation for many of us at work and even at home isn't much different than that of the infant who is left to cry, except that we learned long ago the uselessness of our tears and so flee to our left hemispheres so we don't notice we are drowning in the sea of isolation and abandonment.

Lest we forget, at the other end of the spectrum lies our embodied brain's persistent call for attachment (Siegel, 2015b), our emotional/ motivational system's dedicated focus on connection (Panksepp & Biven, 2012), and our nervous system's ongoing search for faces and bodies that offer true presence (Porges, 2011). These capacities may go underground, but they are never lost. Breathing deeply into that— together—may again nourish sprigs of hope making their way through the concrete of the current cultural conditions.

This is our challenge as we move forward in our consideration of healing trauma—to hold the inherent wisdom and healing capacity of our systems side by side with steady awareness of the cultural surround touching all of us. For those of us who have experienced profound neglect or abuse, the original events and our recovery are situated in the ongoing traumas of daily experience. For those of us who were spared these more overt experiences, we need support to digest the distress of our everyday embeddedness in this culture. And for those of us who have consciously chosen to sit in the midst of the devastation others have endured, we need ongoing support, care, and tenderness around us as we bear witness for others and seek to stay settled in our relational center while the currents of left-shifted society swirl about us.

Returning to Mandy's preschool experience may help us gain a stronger felt sense of these ideas and also settle us internally, since we left her in substantial distress. The moment she realizes her play date is canceled is the crossroads where the experiences of her day may become embedded as traumas or receive what they need to be digested. For many parents (with the covert and overt support of our culture), Mandy's apparently out-of-proportion response might appear to be bad behavior, leading to a parental face darkened by judgment, a voice made harsh by this perception of violated norms, and a demand for Mandy to either quiet down or go to her room. If she does either of those, not only will the earlier experiences go back underground, but they will now also be joined by a further sense of fear, pain, and shame when the parents she loves aren't able to see or attend to her legitimate need for care. A little pool of trauma takes up residence within her embodied brain, and she may be a little less able to anticipate help in the future. In the presence of a fearful, hurtful, or shaming experience and an impulse to reach out, her tightening belly and muscles may warn her to stop before she is abandoned again. If this kind of unintentional and well-meaning parental blindness is a daily occurrence, we can't know exactly how, but Mandy's response to the inevitable daily traumas will gradually shift from a clean and direct request for support into some other less obvious pathway—physical pain, persistent whininess, defiance, silent suffering until she is lost in anxiety or depression, or a left shift into insensitivity to her pain and fear with all that brings. To stay attached within this family system, always our first human priority, she will be shaped according to its needs.

Mandy's mother has a different way of seeing that leads to a crucially different response. She believes that her daughter's behavior is meaningful and exactly in proportion to her upset, even though Mom can't know in the moment what all lies underneath these big tears, and indeed may never know. At a core level, she trusts Mandy's system to be telling an important truth about her inner world as it is right now. Mom's face is concerned, open, and curious, her voice soft, and her body available for what Mandy needs. With this invitation, Mandy crawls into her waiting arms and continues to cry for a while. She has some words about the play date, and then about the two boys, but mostly just releases all that has accumulated in her body through the day. As she pours out her upset in tears and gestures, Mom simply receives it as it is. After a long, slow while, Mandy's muscles and belly let go into relaxation and she is ready for whatever comes next. Safe, unhurried, and accompanied, the two of them have supported a beautiful and natural digestion process.

When a child has consistent experiences like this, the neural circuitry of calmness gradually grows, establishing a longer neural pathway that sometimes allows for reflection under stress. These neural connections also carry neurotransmitters that support the diminishment of fear. We internalize the ones who understand and comfort us, building an inner community of ongoing supporters so we may more often have the felt sense of accompaniment when we are apparently alone. This doesn't make us immune to the distressing events that cross our paths, but it does cultivate a sense of hope and the embodied belief that when we are deeply challenged, others will come help us. We are more likely to have an impulse to ask for support even in the midst of a culture that encourages going it alone and also be inclined to offer that help to others. In this way, we may well become contagious examples of the possibility of a society based on lovely, persistent interdependence.

In our counseling rooms and daily lives, how might we cultivate conditions for recovery for those whose wounds, individual and cultural, have not been embraced? This capacity seems to rest on the foundation of particular ways of seeing, speaking, and being with. It is as though we are setting a table and preparing a meal, which through the power of our resonance with another becomes the world we will inhabit together. The next chapters will explore ways we might support our inner world in becoming a safe haven for those courageous people who come for accompaniment in their movement toward health and wholeness, and a quiet beacon of interdependence in all our daily encounters.

PART ONE

Setting the Table

Introduction to Part One

The Zulu greeting *Sawubona* means "I see you," and the response *Ngikhona* means "I am here"* (deJager, 2006). In some indigenous cultures, the intention is to pause and look with deep eyes to recognize and reflect the humanity of the other person, because *to be unseen is to fall out of existence in some important way*. In these communities, this isn't metaphorical, but a living experience. Implicit in this greeting is the sense that *who you see me to be calls forth that aspect of me*. The tinted lens of my particular perception invites you to manifest those qualities. It is so important for us to stay connected with others that, often without conscious awareness, we will shape our malleable selves around the person seeing us a particular way. A Zulu folk saying says it this way: *Umuntu ngumuntu nagabantu*, meaning *"A person is a person because of other people"* (deJager, 2006).

The discoveries of relational neuroscience continue to uncover ways that this is literally true. How we see one another transforms both the seer and the one seen, and is built on the multiple layers of often unseen entanglement we experience as we constantly affect one another's neural firing patterns (Cozolino, 2014; McGilchrist, 2009; Siegel, 2015b). For decades, we have known that our parents' attachment patterns guide the development of similar ways of attaching in us at least 87 percent of the time (Main, 1996). Even before we see our families for the first time, our nervous systems begin to take shape around our mother's, beginning at about three months after conception, and by the time we

---

* Orland Bishop, youth worker and community leader in Watts, California, speaks movingly about *Sawubona* at https://www.globalonenessproject.org/library/interviews/sawubona. He speaks about how truly seeing one another grants freedom, not from oppression, but freedom to be with.

are born, our neurochemicals (and likely their receptors as well) have also aligned with hers (Field, Diego, & Hernandez-Reif, 2006). Within days to weeks after birth, our mirror neurons and resonance circuits are activated by our mother's imitation of us (Oostenbroek et al., 2016), another example of how our inherent capacities come into manifestation through interpersonal encounters. In this way, we begin sharing the gestures of our family and culture (Iacoboni, 2009) as well as internalizing the people with whom we have emotionally meaningful connections. In a real sense, we carry within us those emotions, bodily sensations, and intentions that were active in them as they related to us (Iacoboni, 2009; Badenoch, 2008, 2011). In this way, we remain in ongoing conversation with them and how they beheld us. The child who is consistently seen as a disappointment feels the echoes of this perception in the underground corridors of her mind, and these stirrings may well shape her behavior to reflect how she was known even decades later. Moving deeper into our heritage, we are finding that epigenetic patterns, shaped by the experiences of our ancestors, underlie some of our tendencies to feel, perceive, and behave in certain ways (Nova, 2007).

When we are in each other's presence, we continue to profoundly influence one another from moment to moment. Here are two examples we likely experience every day. The three branches of our autonomic nervous systems are connected with the nerves that govern the striated muscles in our faces and the quality of our voices so that we telegraph our current sense of safe/not safe to each other in microseconds, shaping one another's nervous systems (and the behaviors that arise from these shifts) below the level of conscious awareness (Porges, 2009b). The three strands are hierarchical to honor our preference and need for remaining in connection with one another. As long as we have a *neuroception** of safety, our ventral vagal parasympathetic pathway (the circuitry of social engagement) remains active, and the physical signs of activity in my ventral circuitry call out to your system, potentially helping your sympathetic arousal settle (Porges, 2009b). Without doing anything, simply by feeling safe ourselves, we provide this support for one another.

One of the most compelling pieces of research about our parallel lives comes from Uri Hasson and colleagues (Stephens, Silbert, & Hasson,

---

* Porges coined this word to indicate how our systems sense safety and danger below the level of conscious awareness.

2010; Hasson, Ghazanfar, Galantucci, Garrod, & Keysers, 2012). They recorded stories in which people were emotionally invested and then had others listen to them. Even without benefit of being in the presence of the storyteller or seeing his or her face and gestures, people who became engaged with the story (as measured by their degree of comprehension) began to demonstrate parallel shifts in many of their brain's firing patterns. The neural activation of those who became the most engaged sometimes even began to *anticipate* the patterns of the storyteller. Based on these discoveries, Hasson says, "Coupling is not a result of understanding. It is the neural basis on which we understand one another. We're suggesting that communication is a single act performed by two brains" (Hasson, 2010, p. 1). He describes this as a visceral process in which we influence one another at multiple levels by linking our embodied brains. In the intimacy of our counseling rooms, the shared narrative of our ever-unfolding relationship gradually takes form within both brains, a process of mutual and ongoing co-organization.

If we take some time to reflect on these discoveries, barriers that appear to separate us from one another may begin to feel like an illusion. What a remarkable opportunity it is then for us to sit in the room with our fellow humans who are seeking healing from their suffering, known and unknown. The way we behold our people cannot help but echo within them and begin to reshape their inner worlds.

This next group of chapters is about setting our internal table in a particular way so we can offer embodied relational attending within which people can be received with profound respect for their wisdom, for the individuality of their experience and their adaptation to it, and for the utterly unique ways in which they can be supported in healing. *All that is offered here is intended to nourish our left hemisphere's store of knowledge with viewpoints drawn from the right hemisphere's way of attending to relationship, while offering opportunities for us to experience these principles within our own bodies.* Ideas drawn from relational neuroscience appeal to the left's need to know because they are grounded in a form of discovery that the left respects. Our left hemispheres need a story that makes sense and brings clarity, and concepts drawn from the right's perspective can provide that while simultaneously encouraging a more collaborative relationship between right and left. It is as though we are offering our left hemisphere's need to know a right-hemisphere lens of understanding. Fortified with this knowledge, the left may be better prepared to be the emissary our right hemisphere needs, allowing our people's flowing experience in the moment to find stability and understanding through what the left has come to know. At the same time, if we pause to experience what we are learning in the chapters ahead, we will also carry *embodied* knowledge of the principles into our time with our patients and others in our lives. More than anything else, these chapters intend to support the interweaving of right and left to foster the essential perceptual shifts that allow us to receptively open to our people while resting in the wisdom of our left hemispheres. From this perspective, perhaps nothing is more clinically relevant than the ways we nourish the relationship between left and right.

Here is a recent example. As one of my people felt safe enough to open into a deep implicit experience, I found myself quietly both supporting her felt sense and narrating her movement from activation into comfort and settling, back into activation and again into settling. We experienced about three waves of this together, both being in the moment (right-centric foundation) and mapping her movement toward resolution (left-centric support). At our next meeting, she shared that she had experienced this kind of implicit arising and settling before, but it had never given her much relief. It seems that giving voice to the spontaneous emergence of the left's stabilizing wisdom in response to her inner need for something more had settled her in a unique and more pervasive way. In addition to the experience itself, the narrative had focused her on the value of such arisings and the possibility of healing. She said she felt more spacious, more known, and more resolved in some way that was difficult to express in words. After a few weeks, she let me know that this feeling was continuing and seemed to be supporting her ability to go deeper in our work together. This is the kind of right-left-right movement that underlies a process of ongoing integration of experience (McGilchrist, 2009). *The more we give our left hemispheres time to digest the learning that arises from the right-centric viewpoint, the more our wise left will able to spontaneously respond to the needs of our people.* Each instance of such a response will be uniquely shaped by what the moment is requesting, so any other example of this process would differ in the way it unfolded. There is no protocol for this beyond preparing our left hemispheres with well-digested learning from the right-centric viewpoint so that it can be responsive to what is arising in the moment—something that may feel quite paradoxical to our left's wish for uniformity, predictability, and stability.

In response to the question of which concepts will best support the left's collaboration with the right, here are a few possibilities. These may be the catalyst for you to make your own discoveries about the kinds of right-centric learning that are most resonant for you. The first section contains a leisurely immersion in some of the neural/experiential processes unfolding within our embodied brains, in development, trauma, and healing, as a body of knowledge that can steady us as we sit with our people. In addition to allaying our anxiety by giving us a sense of what may be happening between us and our patients, a growing sense of the beauty, complexity, and inherent wisdom of our embodied brains can be a powerful antidote to the isolated left hemisphere's tendency to experience the world in mechanistic ways and to apply protocolized solutions for an individual's unique experience. Because we will have taken time to cultivate a sense of these streams in our own bodies, we will be more sensitive to the embodied processes of our people.

In the second part, we will explore how some particular ways we perceive our people can influence how they experience themselves.

- We will begin by considering the felt-sense difference between being seen as having a disorder and being seen as remarkably adaptive then and now.
- Two central themes in this book are the assertions that we possess profound inherent wisdom and that powerful encoding of early and ongoing implicit memories continues to guide us outside conscious awareness. How can we hold both of these in a way that supports healing? Drawing on research concerning memory reconsolidation (Pedreira, Pérez-Cuesta, & Maldonado, 2004) and the theoretical formulations of coherence therapist Bruce Ecker and his colleagues (Ecker, Ticic, & Hulley, 2012), we will explore the scientific foundation underlying our ability to trust that our people's current experience and behaviors are necessitated by the requirements of their implicit memories. Bringing this sense of trust into the room is a strong supporter of our people beginning to believe in their own inherent wisdom, often for the first time.
- Then we'll inquire into the relationship between the viewpoints of co-regulation and self-regulation. We might even ask if there really is any such thing as self-regulation.
- Finally, we will consider how the very language that naturally arises in our minds reveals our hemispheric location while also anchoring our patients and us in that way of attending (McGilchrist, 2009). In

keeping with our belief that healing will best be facilitated by leading with the right, we will explore how changing our language in and of itself may foster our ability to do that.

Over many years of marinating in all these perspectives, I have come to this belief: *It is more important for me to trust my people than it is for them to trust me.* Their trust will grow over the weeks, months, and years as they feel reliably received, but there is little reason for me to expect them to immediately trust a stranger with their precious inner world. However, thanks to these viewpoints arising from relational neuroscience and its theoreticians, it may be increasingly possible for us to trust our people's process enough to truly open into receptivity and listening. When any of us are consistently met this way by anyone in our lives, there is a good probability that our wounds will gradually unveil themselves to be touched by the healing experience and energies of true responsive presence.

Section I

Our Embodied and
Relational Brains in Development,
Trauma, and Healing

2

Introducing Our
Complex and Malleable Brains

Brain scientist woes
they are looking at poetry
reading it as prose

—A. NEIL MEILI (2016)

We are about to enter a most mysterious realm. Our embodied brains are likely so close to infinitely complex, as well as constantly emerging in response to inner and outer experiences, that they can never be known in the settled way science seeks to know. Each is likely so unique in its genetic roots, epigenetic unfolding, sea of shifting chemicals, and developmental shaping that even if we could know one brain, it would not fully illuminate any others. Daunting and limitless as the task is, neuroscience nonetheless offers us glimpses that can provide a foundation of greater understanding that may steady us in our counseling rooms and our lives. In the midst of this unknowable mystery, these discoveries may also nourish the roots of compassion and trust in our system's innate wisdom. Humility is always appropriate in the presence of such complexity and malleability, along with openness to integrating what the constantly emerging technologies offer us, even when the more refined way of seeing asks us to let go of what we already believe we know. Needless to say, what follows is partial, incomplete, and will certainly be modified in some ways long before the publication of these words.

A little bit about the history of exploring the universe of our nervous systems may help us orient to a perspective that honors this paradox of unknowability side by side with recognizing that the general models that do emerge can be helpful. The possibility of doing this kind of research is often catalyzed by the development of some new technology that allows us to peer more precisely into nature's workings from a particular angle. Technology both illuminates and limits what we see. For example, a microscope gives us access to detail at the same time that it can lessen our awareness of the broader interactions that are also present. Perhaps even more importantly, *our way of paying attention* as we do research focuses us on some aspects while rendering us literally blind to others (McGilchrist, 2009). A right-centric way of attending opens us to relationships within the whole and to what is unfolding in each present moment, while a left-centric viewpoint tunes us to fine detail and to generalizing from specific to algorithm. Science generally favors the latter way of attending. We will explore these differences more fully as we proceed. Attuning to these distinctions in ways of attending, we can perhaps find a respectful, inclusive perspective that honors science along with other perspectives that arrive at knowledge in a different way, such as through the rich felt-sense experience of our daily lives (Siegel, 2015b).

We find ourselves at a most interesting crossroads right now in the study of the brain. We have had several decades of various kinds of scans that focus primarily on the brains in our skulls, such as PET (positron emission tomography), which can image blood flow, glucose metabolism, and oxygen through using a radioactive tracer (Johns Hopkins Medicine, 2015), and fMRI (functional magnetic resonance imaging), which follows shifts in blood flow as more oxygen is carried by our red cells to sites experiencing greater neural activation (Rombouts, Barkhof, & Sheltens, 2007). These seek to roughly pinpoint which part of the brain strongly activates for certain kinds of events, not through observing neurons and their connections but through focusing on other brain changes that correlate roughly with activation. The visible result has been pictures with blobs of color indicating areas of increased neural exchange under certain conditions. Now, a newer technology, the diffusion MRI (which creates pictures called connectomes), is able to track the movement of water molecules through nerve fibers so that we can begin to see a small percentage of the actual relational pathways that are constantly active in the brains in our skulls (Collins, 2012; Perkel, 2013; Seung, 2013).

Pause for Reflection

As a beginning exploration and a way to invoke a more visceral experience of these brain pictures, please take a few moments to find images of PET, fMRI, and connectome scans via your search engine and spend some leisurely time noticing what arises in your body as you look at these pictures. You might also listen for the words that naturally come regarding each of them. How do you imagine our vision of the brain is enhanced and limited by each kind of scan?

At the beginning of this recent era of studying the brain via these new technologies, as with many scientific inquiries, there was the tendency to approach what was being studied as an object and then to take that object apart to examine its elements more closely. The most immediate dissection is to cut our skull brain off from the rest of our nervous system, including the belly and heart brains. Our left hemispheres do this kind of division very well, and most science is highly reliant on this single way of paying attention. This knowledge yields approximations to the extent that it provides us with a general picture of certain discrete aspects of structure and function, none of which exactly matches the brain of anyone but the person scanned—and for that person, a snapshot of only that moment (or series of moments). Nonetheless, certain commonalties emerge in a broad way that help us picture correlations between our felt-sense experience and indications in the brain of changes in neural firing (such as increased blood flow). This research can lead to statements like "The amygdala is the fear center" (original version) or "The amygdala is the vigilance center" (more current version).

We begin to experience the brain as a collection of parts, something like a car. This way of viewing also encourages us to explore how we might tweak the various parts in order to improve performance, often leading to speculation about possible drug or other intervention. There is nothing inherently wrong with this approach, but it does limit our relationship with our embodied brains to a single perspective, often treated as though it is the only viewpoint. Herein lies the problem. Such a left-shifted focus and objectification can discourage us from exploring additional approaches to neuroplasticity. What particularly tends to get left in the dust is the contribution that responsive human connections make to catalyzing change in our neural firing patterns because the left has little to no felt sense of relationships.

With all this in mind, how might even this rudimentary knowledge about our embodied brains help us? For us bihemispheric humans, having what we experience as a clear story is important because, without one, we are prone to anxiety as our left hemisphere's need for a sense of clarity, stability, and certainty goes unsatisfied. One of the most striking gains we noticed as the interns at our little counseling agency in California began to bathe in relational neuroscience was a rapid settling of their anxious sense that they weren't quite sure what they were doing or why being one particular way with our patients was more helpful than another. That feeling of floundering in the face of their patients' powerful emotions diminished as the sudden dysregulation of a trauma survivor could now be held by their knowledge of implicit memory awakening and agitating their person's nervous system (Porges, 2011; Siegel, 2015b). Our growing awareness that, thanks to mirror neurons and resonance circuitry, we are able to internalize one another, led to a developing felt sense that we were also with one another when we were with our clients (Badenoch, 2011; Iacoboni, 2009). In terms of being with our own activations in sessions, this understanding of resonance circuitry also helped make sense of why our nervous systems might be agitated when our patients were anxious (Iacoboni, 2009; Siegel, 2015b). As a result, inner criticism decreased and compassion rose. Social baseline theory (Beckes & Coan, 2011; Coan & Sbarra, 2015) tells us that such accompaniment decreases our amygdala activation so that we have more resources for relating with our clients. Our supervision group, also participating in the social baseline experience, became a more supportive community as we beheld and held one another's embodied brains.

It is somewhere between ironic and delightful that because of our culture's overdeveloped reliance on left-hemisphere ways of knowing and our trust in science as the best truth (Weisberg, Keil, Goodstein, Rawson, & Gray, 2008), a little knowledge about the brain seems to settle us so that we become more relationally available for our patients and others in our lives. In this way, the left hemisphere does a beautiful job of fulfilling its emissary role precisely because it needs a story that can give it a sense of certainty.

Returning to the snapshot of a connectome, we may sense that it potentially conveys something a little different to us than pictures of blobs. Inherent in these images is a suggestion of movement. This addition of emergence through time in response to internal and external conditions brings us closer to the way our right hemispheres attend to the world. Brazilian neuroscientist Luiz Pessoa (2013) elegantly describes the consequences of picturing our brains from the perspective of interconnected four-dimensional networks that are rapidly and continuously changing with the flow of time, buzzing hives of activity that are also being shaped by what is coming into our systems through our senses. Because of the constant change in encoding as well as the general complexity of the system, it is unlikely that our brains fire the same set of neurons twice. Our scans are, therefore, likely snapshots of nonrepeatable events.

With the addition of time and conditions, context assumes central importance. Pessoa cites Mesulam's (1990) research showing that networks aren't nonoverlapping sets of measurable connections, but that they continuously change their affiliations with one another depending on the context of that moment. In an interview with Virginia Campbell in 2014, Pessoa put it this way: "So, one region doesn't do much, in my view, but when immersed in cooperating, and interacting, and exchanging signals with many other regions, that's when things really happen. And that's where the human comes from" (p. 6).

In response to this sense of continual emergence and relationship, vocabulary begins to shift toward a more right-hemisphere perspective. As Pessoa seeks to capture the movement, "function" gives way to "process" (Chapter 8, "A Conceptual Scheme," para. 4), and words like "cooperate" flow naturally. The amygdala is seen not as a passive threat detector but as participating in microsecond decisions about what to do next based on understanding what is uniquely valuable and salient to us in our environment (Campbell, 2014). This perspective lends a sense of constant motion, with all the uncertainty that brings.

On the other hand (and the other hand is always important and often neglected in our search for clarity and certainty), there does initially appear to be a constraint in terms of structural connectivity between certain groups of neural networks—the greater the structural connectivity, the more probable that groups will fire together. Except, that is, when certain groups of neurons appear to have no structural connectivity but do have functional connections so that we see them firing together with no apparent structure supporting that neural event (Tyszka, Kennedy, Adolphs, & Paul, 2011). Mystery upon mystery. With each advance in technology, our brains appear less compartmentalized, less composed of independent units that can be measured—either taken as a whole in relation to the outside world or between their parts internally.

Pause for Reflection

What happens in our embodied brains when we are presented with this much uncertainty and paradox? Taking a moment to notice muscles, belly, chest, throat, and head can help us sense if our systems are able to be with this or if the left's need for certainty brings on a sense of wanting to shut the information out or settle on one perspective or the other to relieve the tension. Just noticing and acknowledging is what matters—there isn't a right or wrong way. When I began to be confronted with this kind of information a few years ago, I remember initially feeling irritated (in the bodily sense) when presented with information that didn't allow my left to settle and pushing hard for the next piece of information that would bring clarity (this being one of the core assumptions of most science—that it will all be knowable eventually). Over the years, probably in part due to the foundation of bits and pieces of neuroscience that have calmed my left, my right has gained some strength until sometimes there is a felt sense of delight in the not-knowing—but only sometimes. Return now to sit again with your embodied response to paradox and lack of clarity with as little judgment as possible—just listening and acknowledging.

Pessoa's work has an astonishing breadth to it. For example, in his book *The Cognitive-Emotional Brain* (2013), he considers the two groups of nuclei of the amygdala in finest detail and then expands outward to embrace the ever-shifting relationships between the large-scale structures in our brains. Moving along a continuum from microscope to telescope and back, he encourages us to have the same flexible range of perspectives when we consider our embodied brains—from the settled details that the left prefers to the flowing emergence favored by the right. When we are able to engage more in this both/and experience, we can perhaps begin to sense that the right and left hemispheres are becoming more coherent with one another instead of being at odds. *The right may feel supported as the left takes in knowledge from the right's perspective, and the left may feel nourished and satisfied by the learning arising from the viewpoint of the right.* We come back again to McGilchrist's (2009) belief that our two hemispheres are much like two different people in our brains, seeking to find a harmonious relationship with one another even while having *diametrically opposed, yet potentially complementary,* experiences of the world.

As we begin to sense our brains organically unfolding within the context of the emergent moment, another question arises: "Do brains respond the same way in captivity (inside a scanner) as they do in the wild (daily life)?" Intuitively, we might sense that the answer is no. In accordance with scientific principles, much of the research that has been done with scanners does everything it can to limit variables to see what consistent, verifiable findings about specific situations might emerge. However, in the process, the flowing relational world, with all its unique microsecond-to-microsecond effects on the firing patterns in our embodied brains, is stripped away. We could perhaps say that in a scanner, the person becomes part of the machine with his or her brain operating more according to its rules.

In an attempt to bring the current fMRI technology a little closer to measuring the conditions of daily life, Uri Hasson and his colleagues (Hasson, 2010; Patel, 2011), who are exploring one strand of research that primarily looks at how brains influence one another, are designing studies that can image changes in the brain's blood flow over longer periods of time with more complex relational tasks. Hasson says,

> We're starting from the complexity and messiness of real life and slowly trying to strip away some of the dimensions while making it more simple; most researchers are starting from the other side, going from controlled situations to more complex ones. The hope is that we meet at the middle. *If you start to work with natural stimuli, and you do not simply replicate what other people have done in a controlled setting, it really brings new questions to the table.* (Patel, 2011, para. 5, italics added)

His lab itself does everything it can to not be a lab. The research is conducted under natural conditions, like watching films or sharing stories. Like Pessoa, Hasson is adding the elements of time and relationship, yielding different kinds of images. This innovative approach appears to be a kind of middle ground between snapshots of a moment and movies of our brains as they unfold in the flow of daily life. It is likely the best that current technology offers.

We are in the midst of such a fertile time in neuroscience, one in which we can begin to understand the limits of a more reductionistic and isolationist scientific approach that views our embodied brains as a collection of somewhat discrete parts, while still valuing its contribution as the earliest fascinating steps into formerly uncharted territory. Even as we begin to wonder about the usefulness of images that capture a single moment of a small group of circuits, perhaps, rather than throwing the baby out with the bathwater, we can see this as a developmental process in which this fascinating baby is just beginning to grow into toddlerhood with the prospect of many more stages to emerge. With the help of our right hemispheres, we can perhaps place these earlier scans in the context of their time and value them from that perspective.* They may particularly allow us to make comparisons with images that more closely approximate brains in the wild (which still do not claim to capture what has been called the "impossible complexity" [Patel, 2011, "Foundations of Studying the Mind," para. 4] that is actually unfolding within us). We then have the opportunity to more deeply appreciate the profound influence our brains' neural firings have on each other.

With these considerations in the background, we are now ready to begin the challenging task of talking about our embodied brains as though they have discrete parts, while maintaining a sense of their interconnectedness and flowing mutual influence with each other. Since one of our purposes here is to help our left hemispheres picture how our embodied brains respond to potentially traumatic and healing experiences, we will be exploring a very small subset of all the perspectives from which we could consider our neural circuitry. Even with that, this amount of information might feel overwhelming. Please feel free

---

* Just at the time of this writing, Anders Eklund and his colleagues (Eklund, Nichols, & Knutsson, 2016) have published a study indicating that a bug in the software used to read fMRI scans may have led to up to 70 percent false positives, possibly invalidating up to forty thousand studies in the last fifteen years.

(along with your reading partner, if you have decided to do the reflections together) to take in one chapter, pause for digestion, perhaps read some of the following less technical chapters, and then return to take a few more bites from these chapters. Here is the foundational principle we are seeking to support: *staying with the facts until they become flows of experience.* This takes time, repetition, and inner listening, further supported, co-regulated, and enriched when we choose reflection with another person, to become part of how we attend to ourselves and others. *Our watch words might be "slowly, slowly."*

Pause for Reflection

As we sit with these suggestions, let's see if the phrase "staying with the facts until they become flows of experience" has any echoes for us. Have there been times when we learned something this way? I am remembering my own very amateur encounter with astronomy. It began with reading and then moved on to nights spent with a telescope and a friend. Seeing Jupiter's moons and Saturn's rings felt very different from reading or even seeing pictures. Over time, that beginning of a felt sense became a wider participation in the beautiful, unknowable dance of the galaxies experienced somehow in the body. It is a mysterious process that also seems like a natural one if we give it our time and attention. Our own bodies certainly offer opportunities to learn about them from a distance, as it were, and then to experience what we know through opening ourselves to deep listening along the neural pathways. With as little judgment as possible, maybe we can just open ourselves to that possibility for a bit.

As we move toward the neural streams that inhabit our bodies, we will see a consistent theme. When we have embedded traumas, large or small, overt or covert, our embodied brains' capacity to take in nourishment of all sorts will have been shaped and diminished in unique and powerful ways. One aspect of the healing process is to support the natural opening of our systems toward nourishment once again. The greater our understanding of and relationship with these embodied neural pathways, the more we can engage them as entry points for healing with our people. For example, our belly brains are rich sources of information about our well-being from moment to moment, and will also respond to our attentiveness to their messages. Similarly, an intimate awareness and knowledge of our autonomic nervous system can provide a stabilizing wisdom that can help it calm. With this in mind, we will begin with some of the neural streams that lie largely outside our skull brains yet engage in an ongoing bidirectional conversation with our limbic and cortical circuits.

We already begin to sense that this information for our left-hemisphere way of knowing illuminates the pathways of a nervous system that is as complex as the universe. In the midst of the facts, we may come to appreciate a little more deeply that we are each a bustling nation of highly organized neural activity influencing the intricate neural systems of everyone we meet. We will find that the interpersonal is at the core of organizing what appear to be our individual systems. Much more than mastering the information, we may leave this group of chapters with such a deep sense of wonder and gratitude that we are drawn toward silence as we experience the incomprehensible beauty of the neural streams flowing through these bodies. This may help us develop the capacity to listen to sensation, the language of our bodies, as deeply and naturally as we attend to the more familiar way of knowing—words. When we bring that capacity into our counseling rooms, our patients may well be drawn into listening as well.

3

Skin

Portal to the Brain

You took me
beyond the stars
If you had not held my hand
I would not have had
the courage to go
or the strength to return

—A. NEIL MEILI (2012)

n 1971, when Ashley Montagu's *Touching* was first published, he wrote about "the mind of the skin" (1986, p. 3). The more we learn about this beautiful covering and its neural connections to our inner world, the more prescient that phrase becomes. At the time Montagu wrote, we already understood that in the very earliest process of cell differentiation after conception, three layers of cells form—ectoderm, mesoderm, and endoderm—and that the ectoderm differentiates to become only our nervous system and skin. Montagu, combining science and his more lyrical sense, describes this process.

> The central nervous system, which has as a principal function keep-ing the organism informed about what is going on outside it, develops as the inturned portion of the general surface of the embryonic body. The rest of the surface covering, after the differentiation of the brain, spinal cord, and all the other parts of the central nervous system,

becomes the skin and its derivatives—hair, nails, and teeth. *The nervous system is, then, a buried part of the skin, or alternatively the skin may be regarded as an exposed portion of the nervous system.* It would, therefore, improve our understanding of these matters if we were to think and speak of the skin as the external nervous system, an organ system which from its earliest differentiation remains in intimate association with the internal nervous system. (p. 5, italics added)

The centrality of skin and touch to our way of perceiving the world is attested to by the metaphors that naturally come to us, particularly in regard to how we describe relationships (Linden, 2015). "I am touched by your concern." "I like the feeling of our togetherness." "I don't like it when I find myself using coarse language." "You are a warm person." "That is a burning question." This, the largest organ of the body, continually makes its presence felt even when we aren't consciously aware that it is the source of our metaphors. It envelops us, protects us, provides immune support, and offers ongoing streams of current information about the quality and meaning of contact with the brain above.

Pause for Reflection

Western society has become quite touch-phobic, so our relationship with our skin may be disrupted in some significant ways. In addition, the left-shifted bias of this culture means that we are increasingly out of "touch" with our body's moment-to-moment experience as a whole, although we can still be with our physical being as an object that can be walked around the block or given certain foods or hydrated with moisturizing creams. Now, we are seeking to reconnect with the felt sense of our skin as it brings information about our ever-emerging relationship with the world to our skull brains, and in turn receives guidance about how to respond. As a beginning, you might spend a little time with your two hands exploring one another. If you are with a reading partner or friend, you might then gently touch one another's hands. Is there a preferred kind of touch between your two hands when you do it alone—moving/still, light pressure/firm pressure? Is it different when you do it together? What happens in muscles, belly, and heart as you continue this contact for a while? Is there anything else that arises for you in this experience? Listening and acknowledging with as little judgment as possible is so helpful.

Now that we are being a little more attentive to touch, we might ask how our skin and skull brains communicate. Our epidermis is innervated with a variety of neural receptors that respond to touch and bring the outside world inside, sending streams of information inward along the channels of the central nervous system. These receptors sense pain, pressure, temperature, and vibration and, as we are now discovering, also the emotional quality of contact. Fast-acting myelinated A fibers let us know we are experiencing touch in this moment and what kind of touch it is (warm/cool, light/firm pressure), while slower-acting unmyelinated C fibers tell us about continuity of contact and something about the emotional quality as well (Olausson et al., 2002). Early in this century, it was discovered that some of these C fibers are connected to our skull brains via the insular cortex, one of the pathways that links emotional significance to experience. Researcher Håken Olausson and his colleagues say, "These findings identify CT [C tactile] as a system for limbic touch that may underlie emotional, hormonal and affiliative responses to caress-like, skin-to-skin contact between individuals" (p. 900). Later research found that in addition to the insular cortex, CT fibers are also communicating with a whole network (including the amygdala) that is responsible for social awareness (Gordon et al., 2011). One of the researchers, Kevin Pelphrey, says, "CT fibres activate this whole network of brain regions involved in thinking about other people and trying to understand what their intentions might be" (quoted in Geddes, 2015). These receptors are particularly sensitive to gentle stroking, especially by warm hands, sending a wave of relational goodness along our neural pathways, potentially restoring our nervous systems to a neuroception of safety with all that brings (Olausson et al., 2008). The hairless parts of our bodies—fingers, palms, soles, and lips primarily—are rich in A fibers but do not have CT fibers, while all the parts with the potential for hair do.

Touch is essential for making the transition from the womb to the world—physically, psychologically, and interpersonally. Back in Montagu's day, research with rats had already found that maternal contact in the form of licking the perineal region was essential to initiating digestion and elimination in their newborn offspring, connecting inborn potential to activation. Their small bodies literally did not know how to do these basic functions without this tactile interpersonal support. If mother was unavailable, warm water on a cotton swab could provide an adequate substitute. However, additional research revealed another way interpersonal contact shaped rodent social behavior. Rats who received caring, gentle attention became gentleness itself, exhibiting friendliness, curiosity, and openness to connection with all people. They were also remarkably stress-resistant.* Rats given only perfunctory care were entirely different—irritable, frightened, wary of people, and agitated (Montagu, 1986).

Harry Harlow's monkeys offer a similar picture. Taken from their mothers, the young ones were given a choice between a wooden "mother" covered in soft cloth and a wire "mother" who had food. Both surrogates were warmed with a light. The little monkeys spent as much time as possible clinging to the cloth monkey, going to the wire monkey only for food. Cuddling and snuggling provided essential nourishment. The rest of the story is rarely told. Even though their inherent need for gentle touch drew them to the cloth mother, they did not develop normally either psychologically or socially because there was no living interaction with their mothers or peers† (Slater, 2004). Today, we would say that this clearly indicates that without the combination of warm touch and relational responsiveness, there are integrative connections in the brain that simply don't have what they need to develop and the process of internalizing caring others cannot take place. There's what we can get by with (indifferent touch) and what we actually need to thrive (warm attentive touch).

For us humans, the transition from the swirling amniotic sea to the outer world takes us from the continual caress of warm fluids and the containment of our mother's often-moving body to being untethered in the vast spaces of this earth. Being wrapped up in contact with our mother's skin eases the transition. Messages about the boundaries of

---

* Even in such dire circumstances as having thyroid and parathyroid removed, gentled rats survived 87 percent of the time while those who had not been cared for in this way survived 24 percent of the time. The researchers began to realize that the experiences of regular caring contact had conferred extraordinary resilience.

† There is a lot more to the story of Harry Harlow and his monkeys. For an excellent discussion, see Lauren Slater's article at http://www.boston.com/news/globe/ideas/articles/2004/03/21/monkey_love/. The paradox is that out of so much cruelty arose a much deeper respect for the importance of touch.

our bodies and the safety of our world flow inward toward our limbic system, where our early felt-sense experiences are encoding the perceptual lens that will color our world. The stakes are high when we are most vulnerable, and our skin is continually open to being the conduit for reassurance as it helps shape the neural connections of attachment.

For many of us, the circumstances of our in-womb experience and birth did not allow for this kind of envelopment. To be given minimal or perfunctory touch, or to receive contact that is painful and frightening, is potentially traumatic. It gradually builds up an embodied anticipation that touch brings the felt sense of isolation (along with pain and fear) rather than connection. A number of people have shared with me that even though they have seen pictures of their mother or father holding them, their bodies hold no memory of that experience.

Pause for Reflection

As we are exploring the tender area of receiving touch at the beginning of life, it is likely that something will be awakened within us. It would be helpful to begin by pausing to be open to whatever would like to make itself known as a respectful gesture to the earliest experiences that still live within us in some form. Just notice if your mind is willing to rest into openness, or if it wants to wander away, possibly as a protection from pain. Acknowledging such protection when it arises is another gesture of respect and gratitude. If your mind is ready to rest, just wait to see what will be brought to you—images, feelings, sensations along your skin or in your muscles, belly, or heart, or perhaps something completely unexpected will come. Gently welcoming and holding these experiences and then stopping when it feels right can be a respectful way to touch this vulnerable territory.

The capacity to receive touch is woven into the neural streams embedded in our skin. However, as time passes and implicit memories accumulate, each incoming stream also encounters the thick soup of our past experiences: the inherent wisdom of our system meeting the embodied convictions of implicit memory. In this way, a tender touch entering through the skin can be neuroceived* as threatening, painful, or nonexistent. Thanks to both our inherent capacity to be nourished through contact and ongoing neuroplasticity throughout our system, it is possible that new interpersonal experiences can rewire these pathways so that the messages of comfort carried by the CT receptors can become our lived experience.

Touch is a primary nourishment and a vital resource in healing from trauma. It is concerning that we have virtually eliminated it from the counseling room. Our patients can find touch elsewhere, perhaps with a bodyworker or among friends and family, but it seems odd to remove it from what many trauma survivors experience as their primary attaching relationship. The movement from safety to physical connection is natural. A friend sent me a video from YouTube.com today (Liberators International, 2015). A group of people spread out blankets on the street, sat down, and put out a sign that said, "Where has human connection gone? Share 1 minute eye contact to find out." Strangers came and gazed and then, almost universally, found themselves reaching out to touch one another.

Our concern for the dangers of touching in the context of psychotherapy surely arises from the worthy desire to decrease suffering, from a sense of wanting to protect our patients. However, we seem to have thrown the baby of touch out with the bathwater of ethical violation by the few. Since these breaches occur primarily because of implicit wounds in the therapist, rules don't solve the problem. With the greatest care, respect, and understanding for the experience of our patients, and with particular attention to our own wounds around touch, perhaps it might be possible to restore this primary mode of communication and support to our healing relationships.

I have had my own journey with touch. About thirty years ago, I had the good fortune to fall into the hands of a therapist who could understand and provide support for the depth of trauma that had occurred in my family. As the work deepened and it became more challenging for me to stay connected with him because of the intensity of pain and fear, he offered his hand for me to hold as the memories opened. In the midst of the arising terror, that tangible, stable support provided what was needed in a way that his presence and voice could not—a physical anchor to the

---

* "Neuroceive" is a verb drawn from Stephen Porges's (2011) coined term "neuroception," indicating that the awareness of the safety or danger is happening below the level of consciousness.

present moment. Because I experienced the value of safe body-to-body connection, I have been at ease providing such support for my people. However, I am also clear that if I were to feel anxious about it, my touch would also convey my distress. For this reason, it is essential that we approach our consideration of touch with awareness of our own inner experience and with great care for the meaning of touch for our patients.

Touch joins many other neural streams as implicit memories form within us. The look on the face, the sound of the voice, the condition of the nervous system, and so much more flow from the person touching us, all these streams encoding together in the circuits that gather up our felt-sense experiences into embodied anticipations of what comes next. These then color our neuroception and perception of the next touch that comes our way.

In a more general statement about our relationship with our senses, Montagu (1986) wrote eloquently about his feeling of what he hoped might unfold next:

> We in the Western world are beginning to discover our neglected senses. This growing awareness represents something of an overdue insurgency against the painful deprivation of sensory experience we have suffered in our technologized world. . . . personal frontiers seldom, if at all, permit the passage of a deeply felt communication across them. The human dimension is constricted and constrained. Through what other media, indeed, than our senses can we enter into that healthy tissue of human contacts, the universe of human existence. We seem to be unaware that it is our senses that frame the body of our reality. (1986, p. xiii)

While we can hear Montagu's hope of us reconnecting with and through our senses, and even see some movement toward including the body in our healing process (see Levine, 2010; Levine & van der Kolk, 2015; Ogden & Fisher, 2015; Ogden & Minton, 2006), our culture has simultaneously moved more strongly away from such living contact since he wrote this. The combination of increasing left-hemisphere dominance, with its body blindness, and the ever-accelerating pace of life are among the many forces that keep tugging us toward tasks and distraction and away from the life-giving experience of moment-to-moment relatedness. As we continue to develop our capacity for listening to our bodies, we will turn now to the messages we are continually receiving from our muscles.

4

Muscles

Murmuring Voices of Holding and Letting Go

Let's see if we can picture this. Within the white matter of our spinal cords, we find both ascending and descending neural pathways. The ascending ones carry information from both outside and inside our bodies upward, where it is interwoven with our brainstem, midbrain, limbic circuitry, and ultimately our cortex. As early as the turn of the twentieth century, C. S. Sherrington (1907) gave us names for our experience of these pathways. *Interoception* is awareness (conscious or not) of information from our internal organs; *proprioception* lets us know about our position and movement and is drawn from muscle tension, tendons, and joints (also conscious or not); and *exteroception* brings the external world inside through the senses, much more outside conscious awareness than within it. The experience of being touched follows these spinal cord tracts, while our eyes, ears, noses, and tongues have their own unique pathways closer to the skull brain. The descending tracts carry information from various cortical and brainstem nuclei to support "maintenance of motor activities such as posture, balance, muscle tone, and visceral and somatic reflex activity" (Dafny, 1997, "Spinal Cord Tracts," para. 3). Said very simply, these pathways facilitate the ongoing, emerging, bidirectional conversation between our embodied and skull brains.

For the moment, let's focus on the messages to and from our muscles, picturing the neural circle that carries the exchange. In the presence of an experience that we neuroceive as dangerous, our systems will automatically and adaptively tighten at many levels to prepare for protective action. Numerous pathways (including our enteric and autonomic nervous systems, brainstem, limbic region, and some aspects of the cortex) will participate in sending messages to tighten our muscles. We are designed, also adaptively, to release this tension when the neuroception of safety returns.

However, for many of us—probably most of us—that return to safety is elusive and infrequent for the cultural reasons we have been exploring and because of historical remnants of our own earlier experiences that linger in our muscles. In this case, the ascending arc of the circle, which is always active, sends the message upward from chronically tight muscles that danger is still present. That message, in turn, helps maintain the tension in that particular muscle group and supports an ongoing neuroception of danger, often at such a low level that we have no conscious awareness of it.

All of this is a profoundly personal experience that isn't open for discussion of "real" rather than "imagined" danger because it is subjectively true in that moment. Each of us has a different threshold for neuroceiving danger, one that also varies from moment to moment. As we noted, a good deal of this activation is also likely happening outside our conscious awareness as an automatic adaptive response that is taking into account both what is entering through our senses and what is alive within our complex implicit memory system. Given these circumstances, we might say that our tense muscles are acting as our allies in survival by keeping us alert to danger *as it has been instilled in us over the course of our life so far.* At the same time, the chronic tension is decreasing the nourishment these cells are receiving by restricting the flow of oxygen-carrying blood to the muscles.

Since this circle of tension/fear/tension has a tendency to perpetuate itself, how might we support our body's complementary capacity to begin releasing tension as soon as a felt sense of safety arises? If we follow the primary premise of this book, the arrival of a warm responsive relationship could be helpful in fostering our body's access to its wisdom.

Pause for Reflection

Sitting quietly, with as few expectations as possible, simply ask your muscles if there is a particular group that would like attention right now. Then just listen, noticing if you feel drawn to a particular muscle group. It may be a familiar location of tension or someplace new. Once you feel settled, slowly, slowly bring your hand into gentle contact with these particular muscles, following your sense of just where to place your hand. (If you can't reach the group who called you, gently bring your mind into contact with that spot.) This is potentially a moment of meeting and acknowledgment, of listening and respectful exchange with as little judgment and need for a particular kind of change as possible. Just arrive, settle into relationship, and listen. After a moment or two—or when you feel prompted—slowly lift your hand away and continue listening for a bit. What did you experience before, during, and after your conversation? If you are doing these reflections with a reading partner or friend, you might want to do this with your own muscles while supported by the other's presence; and then, if it feels comfortable to both of you, perhaps you might try it again with your partner making the contact you sense would be most helpful. If you decided to move in the direction of holding one another, do you notice a difference between this and doing it with a witness?

As we develop this practice in ourselves, we can also offer it to our people, particularly when they begin to signal us that they are more in touch with the tension their bodies carry. We might notice a hand finding its way to a muscle group in their shoulders, neck, or along their arms, often without them being aware of it. At that point, we could offer to pause and be with what was calling them. One of the most important aspects of offering practices like this is to also ask them to check in with their inner world to see if this is something their system feels ready to do at this moment. Occasionally, no clear answer will emerge, but more often than we might expect, clarity will arrive. If it doesn't, then we might just try it together and see what comes up. When we are able to let go of our expectations, whatever happens next will be just right.

Denora, a young woman whom I had been seeing for several months began to notice that she was carrying a lot of tension in the upper part of her left arm. She said it felt as though it was a longstanding sensation that she was just noticing. For several weeks, we had been practicing listening to her belly, which had persistently been speaking to her throughout her life. Now we were able to offer this developing capacity to this muscle group. As her right hand gently made contact with her upper arm, she sank into a quiet state of receptivity. Quite soon, tears of unknown origin welled up. We simply sat, holding them in tenderness, without expecting any particular next thing. The tears opened into sobs, and after a few moments, she opened her eyes and softly said, "I'm feeling my mother grab my left arm and drag me toward my room. Then she shuts the door and puts a chair against it so I can't get out. I felt so completely, achingly alone." That ache was palpable in the room as we held this child's anguish.

While this memory may have been touched and awakened at some other point in our work, coming into contact with the strand of implicit experience held for decades in her muscle opened the door for its arrival at this moment. When we approach this practice of receptive listening without expectations, the wisdom in our muscles will guide the next arising.

With this practice, we are getting into relationship with our muscles. What does that mean? We are inviting the neural pathways that support attention to connect with the neural pathways of our muscles (or drawing someone else in to join us in our attending if we have invited a partner). The energy being held by the muscles was often generated in the context of relationship and in response to painful or frightening experience. From this vantage point, providing gentle direct contact that brings acknowledgment of "what is" without needing anything to be different might bring enough receptive presence for the system as a whole to feel safe. As we have seen, the inherent wisdom will know what to do from there to begin the process of release that will restore the system to a more fully nourished and flowing state.

Interestingly, this process of restoration may not feel at all like what our conscious minds imagine. From a left-hemisphere perspective, there is a right way for muscles to be, and they should be moving in that direction. From the more open and listening perspective of the right, anything might happen—and it often does. People have reported a sense of gratitude arising in the contact between muscles and hand. Others have felt either an increase or decrease in tension and pain. The increase often seems to carry the felt sense of the muscles saying, "This is how hard it was." As with Denora, sometimes implicit or explicit memories come, and sometimes there is sadness as the hand departs. Very often, a second group of muscles will come into view, asking for a turn. Some people begin to do this practice every day, morning and evening, since it takes less than two minutes most of the time. They report a sense of ease and growing trust in their body's wisdom.

All of this happens just from listening to our muscles? Bringing the broader perspective back into view, we can again sense how all our neural pathways are talking with each other. As we bring our kind attention to our muscles, we are already engaging parts of our prefrontal cortex and limbic system, including the right insula, whose job it is to keep above and below connected in an emotionally meaningful way. The receptors in our skin attend not only to the quality of the touch, but also to its emotional meaning. Our gentle intention to not fix or change anything communicates with our autonomic nervous system, calming it. This message of safety soothes the fight/flight nuclei in the brainstem and touches the emotional-motivational systems that are sensitive to connection in the midbrain. We can also include the accompanying changes in our neurotransmitters and hormones, from the chemicals of danger to those of safety in connection. *It is likely that every neural system in our body is touched in some way by this simple offer of attentive contact.* We might think of this practice with our muscles as one of many doorways into the wider system that is always waiting for the arrival of what was needed but missing at the time a potentially traumatic event took place. As we consider the other neural systems within the body, our autonomic nervous system next, keeping this ripple effect in view can help us maintain our right-hemisphere balance as we feed our left with helpful information.

5

Autonomic Nervous System
Guardian of Safety

The moment-to-moment sensitivity and responsiveness of our autonomic nervous systems (ANS) to our felt sense of safety and threat is astonishing in its unfailing instinct to protect. Mostly below conscious awareness, these bidirectional neural pathways mediate the activity of our visceral system to support our capacity to be moved in synchrony with our felt sense of current internal and external conditions. These microsecond adjustments that engage the complex interaction of the various autonomic pathways provide a symphony of responsiveness that we can trust to foster our safest possible passage through life, given what is active internally and what is arriving through the senses.

All investigations into our physiology go through stages of development, arising from a curiosity about what processes underlie our felt sense experience. Research moves from a more general sense of how things work to increasing refinement and complexity that moves us back toward unknowable mystery. The older and simpler conceptualization of the ANS spoke about two branches: the sympathetic for accelerating certain bodily functions (while slowing others) and the parasympathetic for slowing down some of those functions (while activating others). With just those words, we can probably sense, in a general way, how these complementary actions unfold in our bodies—the acceleration of excitement or fear, and the slowing of our systems as we head for bed or sink under the weight of humiliation. Moment to moment, each cycle of respiration flows from the sympathetic activation of inhalation to the parasympathetic settling of exhalation, so at a profound somatic level we are always participating in the relationship between these two ways of being moved. It is not surprising that for many decades, we envisioned our ANS as a two-part system.

However, the work of Stephen Porges (1995, 2007, 2009b, 2011) points to a tripartite nervous system that more closely corresponds to our experience of moving in tandem with changing conditions. Social creatures that we are, our ANS seems designed to foster connecting with one another. It is arranged in a hierarchical manner so that the pathways supporting attachment are preferred and remain active as long as we have a *neuroception* of safety.

Returning to our discussion in the Introduction, Porges coined this word to emphasize that we have an embodied way of experiencing emotional safe/not safe that is independent of conscious awareness. The processes of consciousness (involving the neocortex) are so slow compared to those that are responsible for the rapid assessment of threat and safety (arising in the body, brainstem, and subcortical networks) that neuroception is our essential guardian. Receiving information from both current external experience and the ongoing internal flow of implicit and explicit memory, our ANS continually adapts to emergent conditions. For example, I may set out on a walking trip to the corner store, then find myself turning around to head back home without any conscious awareness of what prompted this move. If I attend closely, I might notice that, as I turn, my heart is beating a little faster and there has been a slight shift in my felt sense of the world around me. I feel a little on edge. I may or may not ever know what combination of outer experience and awakened implicit memory has brought on this mild flight response, but I can notice that my nervous system has prompted a rapid and protective shift in my course of movement to match the change in my neuroception.

When our system is sensing safety, the myelinated portion of the parasympathetic pathway, the *ventral vagus*, becomes active. It supports our all-important connection with and co-regulation of one another. This pathway emerges from the brainstem and innervates the organs above the diaphragm primarily, with some projections to the belly. It is also entangled with the nerves that regulate the striated muscles of the face, allowing our expressions to be responsively mobile in relation to what we are experiencing. In ventral vagal*, our vocal cords are automatically tuned in such a way that the nervous systems of those around us recognize our sounds as conveying safety. Similarly, the tension in our a small muscle near our inner ears is increased so we can focus on the human voice and orient to the meaning of the words. Our eyes respond by moving into an alert but relaxed state that allows our system to take in and respond to the internal condition of another. Our heart rate is gentled by application of the vagal brake. Even the mobility of our face sends signals to all who see us that there is safety here and we can settle into relationship with one another. There is no faking a ventral voice or face. We may be able to curve our mouths into a smile even when we are afraid, but our voice, the narrowed focus of our eyes, and the progressive frozenness of our upper face will send the truer message to others' nervous systems.

When our system senses that we are no longer having a neuroception of safety, we adaptively move into intensified *sympathetic arousal*. These pathways strongly innervate the gut and other organs below the diaphragm while also influencing the face, eyes, and heart. While this activating system is always contributing some of its circuits to our aliveness in play and curious exploration, additional neural streams are now activated for protection. Social engagement diminishes so we won't be distracted from the source of threat, and whoever is with us will feel this shift away from connection. The tension in our ear muscle relaxes to take in the whole environment, listening for the sounds of danger— deep rhythmic pounding and shrill sounds—at the cost of focusing less closely on what others are saying. The person we are relating with in the moment will feel this loss of attentiveness. Our eyes focus their narrow beam of attention in the direction from which the threat may be coming, accompanied by an increase in tension around the eyes. The vagal brake is removed so that our heart can pump more blood to

---

* Throughout this book, the words ventral, ventral vagal, or ventral state and dorsal, dorsal vagal, or dorsal state are used in the place of the full descriptions of the vagal processes occurring when the sympathetic nervous system is not recruited in defense. Specifically, being in a ventral state reflects the recruitment of the ventral vagal pathways that promote a physiological state supportive of feeling safe and an ability to socially engage in response to a neuroception of safety, while being in a dorsal state reflects the recruitment of the dorsal vagal pathways that promote a physiological state of withdrawal, collapse, and dissociation in response to a neuroception of life threat.

our extremities in preparation for fighting or fleeing, and our cheeks flush with this increased flow of blood. There may also be a moment of frozen alertness as our system pauses to sense the safest direction to move. These silent signals we send to each other are intended to have the same protective effect as someone yelling "fire." Adding the quality of sound, our vocal cords change so that the prosody of our voice can telegraph this sense of danger to others for their safety.

While most of the shifts are activating, some move in the opposite direction: Digestion, immune responses, and reproduction are viewed as nonessential processes that need to be temporarily turned down or off. We can now begin to imagine what challenges there are to the bodies of those of us who are in a state of sympathetic arousal, mild or intense, most of the time. Given the speed and ongoing demands of our culture, it is more common to be in this state of arousal than we may believe. It may not be surprising that it is estimated that 75 to 90 percent of doctor visits are related to stress (Avey, Matheny, Robbins, & Jacobson, 2003), or that so many of our patients report regular gastric distress, or that autoimmune diseases are dramatically on the rise (American Autoimmune Related Diseases Association, Inc., 2015).

How might we notice when we are moving from a neuroception of safety to danger? In general, when we feel threatened, we initiate some movement toward taking control of ourselves, others, or the environment through impulses to flee or fight. Conversely, impulses to take control inwardly or outwardly can signal that we may be experiencing some sort of threat. Each of our bodies likely responds to this in a different way. For me, just writing those words brought on considerable tension in my belly (my personal canary in the coal mine), some tightening of muscles in my legs and arms, a slight forward movement of my body, and a bit more intensity in my face around the eyes. Adaptively, we generally do not notice these signals because we need to focus our conscious resources on staying safe from this neuroceived threat.

Pause for Reflection

This practice will be particularly powerful if you do it with someone you trust. Can the two of you engage your nonjudgmental curiosity to explore some times when you have felt the impulse to take control of a situation? Can you each begin to sense what happens in your body? Are there different activations for different circumstances? Are there any common denominators? After playing with this for a while together, perhaps you can attune with your partner and sense what happens in your body as you return to a neuroception of safety through co-regulating in the relationship. See if you can gently notice if judgments begin to arise, or if there is a preference for one state over another. It is certainly true that ventral vagal connection is pleasing and healing for our systems, and yet, it is equally true that sympathetic activation is essential for our safety. As we do these practices, we may gradually notice that our capacity for grateful receptivity for all our states is expanding.

When we remain in even a low level of sympathetic activation in the absence of a functioning vagal brake, our digestion, sleep, immune protection, relationships, vision, ability to learn, and even brain integrity may suffer in varying degrees. In regard to this last point, sustained heightened cortisol levels gradually eat away at neural tissue in certain regions of our brains (amygdala, prefrontal cortex, and hippocampus, to name a few). So far, we have only seen stem cells in the hippocampus split and grow into fully functioning and integrated neurons (see Gage & Temple, 2013, for a full discussion of the state of neural stem cell science), fostering regeneration of this brain region. For other regions, the losses appear to be permanent, although the remaining tissue in any area is fertile ground for the rewiring afforded by our abundant capacity for neuroplasticity.

Culturally, we find ourselves at a crisis point in terms of ongoing low-level sympathetic activation. There is a reciprocal relationship between fear and the tendency to shift into left-hemisphere dominance (Porges, 1995). In general, the conditions of our culture are not conducive to ventral settling, and once we have made the adaptive shift into left-hemisphere dominance, our disconnection from others combined with cultural conditions supports remaining in that state. This draws many of us into at least mild ongoing tension and wariness, although we are mostly unaware of this until some major emotional or health crisis overtakes us (McGilchrist, 2009). In this left-dominant state, our attention is drawn to completing tasks and controlling behaviors rather than participating in the relational moment. We lose the orientation toward one another that calms our system (Beckes & Coan, 2011; Coan & Sbarra, 2015) along with the sense of meaning that arises from being connected to something larger than the needs and wants of our individual self (Fredrickson et al., 2013). In short-term conditions of threat, these changes are essential for survival; as a long-term strategy for safety in a threatening world, our system deems them necessary even with the considerable cost they bring.

At certain moments, danger may escalate to the point where we have a neuroception of helplessness. Then, the third ANS branch, the unmyelinated *dorsal vagal parasympathetic* awakens to slow our systems in preparation for the possibility of death and also activate an ancient strategy to conserve metabolic resources in case we don't die. We could say that we feign death to avoid death. These same dorsal pathways in conditions of safety, managed by an active ventral vagal circuit, support our ability to rest deeply, meditate, nurse and soothe our babies, and be together in a state of immobility without fear (Porges, 2011). At the other end of the spectrum, when our threatened system senses that fight and flight are impossible, additional pathways are activated and wisdom guides our movement toward collapse and dissociation as our heart and breath rates slow, signs of aliveness and engagement leave our face and eyes, endorphins are released to diminish the pain of death, and the sacral parasympathetic pathways may release our urinary tract and bowels. At the same time, our system is conserving metabolic resources for a safer time when we can come back into our bodies again (Porges, 2011). When we experience humiliation, we are right at the gateway of dorsal vagal activation.

Pause for Reflection

With the support of your reading partner or even on your own, sense if your system is willing to explore moments of shame or humiliation that you may have experienced. If it feels okay to do this, take turns gently opening to whatever your deeper mind may want to bring you. When the embodied experience arrives, with support, you may be able to notice your bodily sensations (muscles, belly, heart, throat, face, and eyes), flow of emotion, and ways that your body wants to move. You may also sense a shift in your perception of your value and even of the value of life itself. Together, you may be able to offer deep acceptance to this part of you along with whatever circumstances initiated the humiliating event. Notice what happens as this isolating experience of shame is met with accompaniment and acknowledgment. Take as much time as you need to provide this reparative experience for each other.

The movement of withdrawal that shame brings, painful though it is, looks like wisdom when there is an onslaught of criticism, hatred, or disgust. Our systems adaptively move away from the rejection of our being toward a kind of hibernation until the storm passes. In even more severe circumstances, dorsal activation can save our lives as our system abandons fight or flight for submission. As with chronic sympathetic activation, even in the midst of this adaptive response to intolerable conditions, the costs for our bodies and relationships can be quite severe, especially if our circumstances draw us repeatedly toward dissociation.

Our awareness of the intricacies of our ANS can help stabilize our own systems, enhance our awareness of the shifts in activation that our people are experiencing, and also give us words to share with them so they can understand the adaptive nature of the activations of their system. Jake came to our agency shortly after he returned from Iraq where he had served as a medic. While he knew he had seen terrible injuries, he didn't feel it was much different than working in the emergency room at the hospital in the most poverty-stricken part of his town. He couldn't understand why he was having so much trouble concentrating on just about everything, something that was causing him a lot of stress at work and shame at home. His wife had said to him, "You keep going away. We need you here with us. You hardly seem to be able to look at our children."

As we sat together, I soon became aware of frequent shifts in his attentiveness to our conversation. I could feel him focus on us, but soon his awareness would widen to the whole environment, something that registered in my body as him leaving me. Together, we were able to catch these moments and ask his inner world what had drawn his attention. As we listened receptively over several weeks, images of wounded Iraqi children began to come. This still didn't seem different to him than back home, so we simply held the familiar pain of seeking to help these ravaged young ones.

Gradually, a sense of complete meaninglessness began to fill his body with anxiety and then despair. The dorsal heaviness began to fill our time, and he had fleeting thoughts of suicide. He said, "I need words. I need to understand or this will kill me." As if in response, his mind soon began to think about the insanity of this war, of any war. He told me, "I live in a war zone back home, too, but it's my war and I understand it. This war, it's not only wrong morally in my view, but there's something about these unfamiliar children, the ones with no arms or legs, that devastates me differently." He began to be able to weep for them in our times together, sometimes having a sense of gathering up their small bodies in his arms. We both held them.

At times, we also talked about how his ANS had responded to this experience and that his inattentiveness was its adaptive response to these intolerable experiences. He began to believe that his tendency to emotionally withdraw was not his fault. As his shame lifted and he was able to talk with his wife about the origin of his absence, she added her tears for these broken children and the rupture they had been experiencing repaired. Very soon, he was gathering his own little ones in his arms again, too. Jake and I continued our work because the war wounds weren't the only source of his struggles when he came home from Iraq. His experiences there had awakened earlier traumas that had embedded because of the violent neighborhood of his infancy and childhood.

As we are finding with all our neural circuits, our ANS is shaped interpersonally from the earliest stages of life. At about three months after conception, our activations begin to parallel those of our mother. We are already developing a neuroception of how safe this world will be for us (Field, Diego, & Hernandez-Reif, 2006). As our lives continue, the ebb and flow of our ANS has much to do with the quality of our lives. The burn of high anxiety, the narrowing that comes from low-level fear, the cutoff from self and others that arises from dorsal activation—all of these pull us away from the primary nourishment of warm, responsive relationship. In addition, our ANS engages in an ongoing bidirectional conversation with our bellies, hearts, other internal organs, muscles, eyes, ears, and faces. The limbic region, including the vigilance of the amygdala and the neurochemical chain arising in the hypothalamus, join this symphony of protection and play their part in guiding our ANS response to conditions. Eventually, we include the neocortex to translate some small portion of all of this activity into conscious awareness and then some of that into words about how we are experiencing ourselves, others, and the world around us. As Porges (2015) says, "part of Polyvagal Theory is that the underlying physiological state functionally drives the personal narrative. It creates the neural platform upon which higher brain structures are then recruited" (p. 8). So much of our perceptual and then spoken universe is colored by how our ANS is responding in this moment and the next on our behalf.

Our nervous system's window of tolerance—the intensity of feeling we can experience while still maintaining connection with another—is continually expanding and contracting (Badenoch, 2011; Ogden &

Minton, 2006; Siegel, 2015b). When we are physically alone, the continually fluctuating breadth of our window depends on the strength of the regulatory system built in relationship with others as well as the supportive internal presence of those with whom we have close connections (Badenoch, 2011; Schore, 2012). It varies from moment to moment depending on how rested and healthy we are, what might be activated in our own system, and what we are experiencing in relationship with the outer world. It is different, however, when we are with a receptive, responsive other. Then, our *joined* windows of tolerance can allow us to plumb depths and heights of feeling that would dysregulate us if we were on our own (Beckes & Coan, 2011; Hasson, 2010). My emerging fear and pain can be embraced by the wide window of your receptive ventral presence, and in this space, healing potentially unfolds.

We might picture our constantly changing window of tolerance like this:

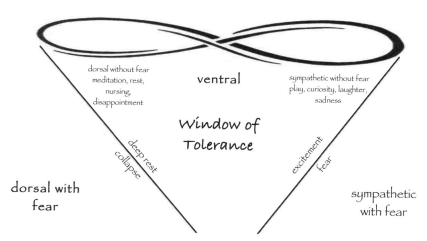

Autonomic Nervous System

Expanding and Contracting Window of Tolerance

ventral

Window of Tolerance

dorsal without fear
meditation, rest,
nursing,
disappointment

sympathetic without fear
play, curiosity, laughter,
sadness

deep rest
collapse

excitement
fear

dorsal with
fear

sympathetic
with fear

FIGURE 5.1 Drawn based on Stephen Porges's Polyvagal Theory. At the top, we have a wide capacity to hold a fairly full spectrum of emotions, and as we move downward, we enter states in which our capacity for maintaining regulation in the presence of intensity is much smaller. From microsecond to microsecond, we are moved along both the horizontal spectrum that embraces dorsal and sympathetic streams under the management of ventral, and vertically from wider to narrower and back. Excitement and fear, and deep rest and collapse, are very close neighbors, arising according to our neuroception in the moment.

Our joined windows of tolerance might look something like this:

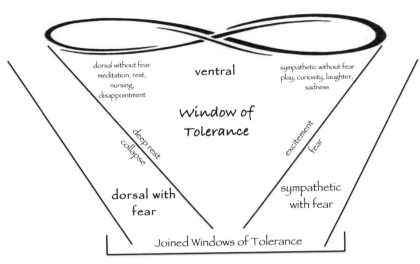

Autonomic Nervous System
Expanding and Contracting Joined Windows of Tolerance

ventral

dorsal without fear
meditation, rest,
nursing,
disappointment

sympathetic without fear
play, curiosity, laughter,
sadness

Window of Tolerance

deep rest
collapse

excitement
fear

dorsal with fear

sympathetic with fear

Joined Windows of Tolerance

FIGURE 5.2 The presence of another (the outer diagonal lines) provides a ventral vagal embrace for the nervous system of the person represented by the inner diagonal lines, a felt sense of containment.

Because of the stability of the outer person's system, the inner person can explore formerly dysregulating experiences of sympathetic arousal and dorsal withdrawal without losing connection. Uri Hasson's (2010) work suggests that in brain coupling, our neural firing patterns become more similar to each other. Since our systems already have a preference for ventral vagal, the inner person can be drawn toward that state of the holding person, so experiences of pain and fear can be witnessed and transformed in the space between as the social engagement systems regulate each other.

Pause for Reflection

It may be helpful to spend some time these two pictures of the emerg-ing flow of your window of tolerance. Inviting your body to bring experiences to you of when you have felt this movement, notice what might come to you. This is good practice for inviting our right-hemisphere felt-sense experience to come to us rather than thinking about such times with the resources of the left. We can notice how our muscles, bellies, hearts, throats, faces, eyes, and ears respond to the widening and narrowing of the window. If our bodies recall times when our window narrowed and we felt alone, the addition of the presence of another, a friend or reading partner, may offer a wonderfully settling and reparative experience.

The embedded traumas we carry continue to influence our autonomic nervous system's sensitivity to both currently emerging experience and the inner arising of implicit and explicit memory. When sympathetic and dorsal pathways become well worn and familiar during the course of our lives, especially if there has been very little activation of ventral, these become our most easily accessed ANS states. Even in such challenging circumstances, we social beings continue to seek and prefer warm, responsive connections. We can rely on our ANS to respond to offers of safety by carrying us toward ventral vagal engagement as soon as the environment turns from hostile to welcoming. Countless times I have seen the wide, tense eyes of fear and the dull eyes of withdrawal gradually soften and enliven as we are able to orient to one another's presence in this moment, drinking in this relational nourishment, sometimes through moments of gazing.

6

Eyes
Diffuse and Focused Seeing

Though if we ask of hows and whys
and what's the magic of those eyes
They do what mirrors can't quite do
they let you see right through to you

—A. NEIL MEILI (2003B)

T here is a tenderness in gazing into one another's soft eyes that offers a unique sense of being known and held.* As we will see, our eyes developed to be able to support this kind of joining as well as to objectify others when we don't feel safe. These changes in our eyes are parallel to the movements of our ANS. Let's begin with the anatomy of our eyes, which returns us to the relationship between our exposed and hidden nervous systems that we explored with touch. The cornea, the outer covering (or skin) of the eye, has six layers. The outermost develops from the portion of the ectoderm that becomes the skin and the innermost from the neuroectoderm that becomes the nervous system (Ort & Howard, 2015). The optic nerve, the neural highway that brings the outside inside, is similarly built from neuroectoderm

---

* Some cultures find gazing intrusive, and it is so important that we honor that felt sense in our relationships. As we are exploring in this chapter, we can remember that there are other pathways that support deep joining as well, including the sound of our voices as we touch one another's auditory system.

cells. More than a biological understanding, this perhaps gives us a felt sense of the fluid intimacy between the tissues that encounter the outer world and the deep nervous system that receives and organizes that world within us.

So much beauty and suffering begin at this particular portal between the world and our felt-sense experience. The morning sun touching the edges of the leaves, the tears of tragedy flowing on the cheeks of those who have lost their loved ones—these reach us in waves of sensation that gather up a multitude of neural networks but begin at the place where light floods cornea. A nearly infinite amount of information is constantly streaming toward our eyes, and the constraints of our system mean that there is a dramatic diminishment between what is available and what arrives at the visual processing centers (Raichle, 2010). Our retinas receive about 10^{10} bits per second, while our optic nerves can handle 6×10^6, and only 10^4 arrive at the integrative portion of the visual cortex. The ratio between what is received by the retina and what is processed by the integrative layer of the occipital cortex is about a million to one. In addition, of the ten thousand bits that survive that journey each second, the maximum that can become conscious is around 100 bits per second (Anderson, Van Essen, & Olshausen, 2005). While these numbers likely exceed our ability to truly comprehend what is lost, it may not be surprising that people have a great deal of difficulty agreeing on what they just saw. In addition, this discussion includes only the visible spectrum. There are both slower and faster wavelengths of light that we cannot perceive at all. Given the intensity of feeling that can overtake us through the portal of our eyes, perhaps there is much wisdom in this modulation of what we are able to take in.

Pause for Reflection

Let's take just a moment to sense ourselves seeing. Can we feel the flow from outside to inside along the neural pathways? If we shift our gaze to a different scene, what else changes in us—muscles, belly, chest, face, thoughts, feelings, impulse to move? Can we feel a difference between looking and gazing? It can be helpful to spend some time with this particular practice, shifting back and forth between looking at and gazing with. When we return to reading this page, is there a change in how seeing feels?

We might begin to wonder how our system selects what is seen, both unconsciously and consciously. Much of this remains a mystery but is likely linked to what is most salient for us in the moment; however, we do know something about certain characteristics of our neural pathways that allow us to have two different experiences when seeing the same scene. The story begins with parallels to Iain McGilchrist's (2009) work. In the simplest terms, *our way of attending* strongly influences what we see and what we feel when we see (Fehmi & Robbins, 2007). Two pathways are built into our optic nerve that facilitate two processes of attention. Both gather information about the outside world traveling along axons from neurons in the cornea and retina through the thalamus and on to the visual cortex. These neurons speak to each other with the same language as other nerve cells—a variety of neurotransmitters. Small parvo cells are neurons specializing in "what" is being seen (color and detail). Their connecting pathways are unmyelinated and, hence, slow moving and longer lasting; they are concentrated in the center of our retina. Larger magno cells specialize in "where," connecting with each other along speedy myelinated pathways that provide a flow of transient information. Located on the periphery of the retina (where they are accompanied by a few parvo cells), they convey information about motion and depth and take in a much larger receptive field than their parvo companions (Livingstone & Hubel, 1988; Yoonessi & Yoonessi, 2011). If we sit with those distinctions for a moment, we may hear echoes of how the left and right hemispheres attend, the former focusing on detail and fine distinctions, the latter concerned with what is emerging in this moment in the broad field of the space between.

Based on evidence from brain waves that are observable through neurofeedback, some researchers, in fact, postulate that the parvo stream is wired to the left hemisphere while the magno stream is linked to the right (Fehmi & Robbins, 2007). This does not appear to be true at the structural level, since both streams reach both hemispheres. However, because of how each stream pays attention, magno cells offer a more right-centric experience and parvo cells a more left-centric. They literally see something different and provide divergent felt-sense experiences.

Fehmi and Robbins (2007) see magno-centric as diffuse attention and parvo-centric as narrow-focus attention. The diffuse way of seeing offers an immersive in-the-moment experience of being present, while narrow focus objectifies what we are looking at, leading to a sense of separation. These messages about our current relationship with the world are sent along the neural highway to join other streams of infor mation and influence our emerging felt-sense experience as the implicit memory associated with the event encodes. How we are attending to what is available via our eyes is no small matter.

Being able to flexibly move back and forth between these two ways of seeing is helpful for navigating the world of tasks and relationships. Thanks to the parvo cells that accompany the magno cells on the periphery, it is also possible to be diffusely attending while also aware of details. This is reminiscent of McGilchrist's (2009) Master and emissary relationship between the hemispheres in which the left/parvo offer their unique capacities in service of the right's/magno's vision (literally). Diffuse attention offers us the opportunity to be present to this emerging moment and receive the flow of light as it is touching us right now, to come into relationship with what is being seen. In this state, muscles release some of their tension, bellies settle a bit, hearts experience connection—even in moments when we are witnessing suffering. In this state, we may for a moment need to attend to a task. Diffuse seeing may move into the background but not go entirely offline while narrow focus comes to the foreground. We can imagine that as children we and our patients had many opportunities to practice each of these ways of attending, depending on the nature of our environment. The more practiced pathways will have a tendency to become our default way of attending, and that has consequences for how we are present in relationship. Are we gazing with or looking at our people?

During the early years of investigating these two ways of seeing, Les Fehmi began to experiment on himself to see how he might generate a state in which alpha waves (abundant in diffuse attention) increased. Try as he might to produce alpha, his neurofeedback machine kept showing no change. After 12 two-hour attempts,

> I was exasperated and gave up and accepted the fact that it was simply impossible for me to create more than baseline alpha on demand. Fortunately, I was still connected when I gave up. The second I deeply accepted my failure, the EEG registered high-amplitude alpha production, five times the amplitude and abundance I had been producing before. (Fehmi & Robbins, 2011, pp. 30–31)

One way we might understand this is that in giving up, recognizing his inability to influence the outcome, Fehmi's system moved out of his effort to control (a sympathetically activating state) in the direction of dorsal vagal activation, but without fear. He was released from the narrow focus on making something happen and fell into the more diffuse state of acceptance. His experience begins to shed some light on how our systems decide, mostly outside conscious awareness, to drop into narrow focus exclusively or move into the more inclusive and nourishing state of diffuse attending, supported by moments of attention to detail.

For most of us most of the time, the process is automatic based on our neuroception. When there is a sense of threat (arising either internally or externally), our focus of attention adaptively narrows so that we are concentrating on the source of the danger without other stimuli pulling us away, activating the central parvo cells (Porges, 2009b). Even low levels of threat that don't rise to conscious awareness call on us to alleviate danger by seeking to control the situation, which requires close focus on the next steps we need to take to survive. Even more subtly, when we shift left at the expense of the right, that in itself initiates a separation from our main source of security, connection with one another. When we sense we have to go it alone, focus narrows. Fehmi and Robbins (2007) extensively explore how our current left-shifted culture of speed, task focus, and overwhelm requires us to stay exclusively in parvo's narrow focus the majority of the time, with harmful consequences for muscles, bellies, nervous systems, and relationships. As with all other neural streams, once this pathway is deeply engrained, it is challenging to leave. Potentially traumatic experience, if it doesn't bring on dissociation, holds us in parvo's tight focus while events unfold. Undigested trauma has a tendency to keep us there as we either protect ourselves by focusing away from reminders of the experience or feel the danger all over again when implicit memory is touched and awakened.

Flexibility can be regained with some astonishing results. In San Bernardino, California, at a prison for juvenile offenders, Stanley Kaseno, a behavioral optometrist, tested the eyes of 1,000 young men and found that 96 percent of them had abnormal vision, likely because chronic tension and persistent narrow focus had pulled their eyes out of shape. Those who didn't have glasses were given them, and all did vision training. There were significant cognitive improvements, but most striking was that the recidivism rate decreased from 50–60 percent to 10 percent with no other intervention (Fehmi & Robbins, 2007). It seems that when their eyes supported the felt sense of connection with other people, acting out against peers and strangers decreased. Our eyes are proving to be another potential healing gateway into the wider universe of our nervous system.

Pause for Reflection

Our nervous systems can detect the difference in the eyes of someone attending to us in a state of receptivity (diffuse attending) versus a state of intention to guide/control (narrow-focus attending). This is another practice that needs a friend for the experience. After you sense you are feeling safe with one another, choose one person to be the seer and one the seen. The seer can simply gaze at his partner with a sense of receptivity, while the person being seen can come and go from this gaze as he feels comfortable. After doing that for a moment or two, it may be possible, when both are in agreement, for the seer to look at his partner as though he were an object to be studied. After a moment, shift back to receptivity for a bit. What do both of you notice in your bodies as you move between these states? When you are the seer, notice especially any differences in the way your eyes and your face near your eyes change. After you finish sharing about this, when you feel ready, change places so that each of you can have a turn being seer and seen. Iain McGilchrist (2009) says that when we are attending to one another, both the one seeing and the one being seen are changed. This has powerful implications for us in the counseling room and in our daily lives.

Offering our diffuse gaze for our people helps create a safe haven in which therapy can unfold. "Offering" is an important word. Our soft eyes can be a sanctuary for our clients to come and go as they feel moved, much in the way babies will gaze for awhile, then look away when they need to rest. If we make ourselves available in this way without expectation, we are cultivating a safe space for their experiment to unfold. Philip Shepherd (2010), student of the bodies' pathways of connection, speaks of gazing in a lyrical way reminiscent of Ashley Montagu on touch:

When you look into the darkness of someone's pupils, though, you encounter her non-objective self—her Being. And let's be clear about this: the pupils are black holes—they are empty and the retina beyond is black; to look at a pupil is not to look at an object anymore than looking into darkness through the mouth of a cave is looking at an object. There is nothing in the dark emptiness of the pupil to actually see or describe or objectify or know, and *yet*: by looking into it, you connect with someone's *life*; you encounter her *Being*. And in that encounter, you precipitate an exchange of energies in which you are both participant. (p. 343)

We may easily remember times when we have engaged in such an exchange and felt known in some profound way.

Our eyes are surely meant to nourish us with their capacity for immersion in one another and the world. This is one reason that newborns crawl up their mothers' bellies toward breasts and eyes to find a safe haven in this vast new environment. We convey so much of our inner state in the quality of our looking and our gaze. If we saw eyes that were terrifying or vacant or anxious when we were very young, we experienced the whole-body upset that wounding eyes can bring. Adaptively, we may become hesitant to share gaze with anyone. Over time, in an environment of safety, permission, and receptivity, we may begin to take little sips of nourishing gaze until these neural streams reclaim their birthright as portals of giving and receiving deep connection.

7

Ears and Vocal Cords
Relational Vibrations

Our ears and vocal cords are receptive and expressive instruments in the whole-body symphony of changes that both follow and influence fluctuations in our ANS. We may notice that at times we are able to listen closely to the meaning of what another is saying, while at other moments we feel distracted by sounds in the environment. Similarly, we may find certain qualities of voice to be soothing while others act as an irritant to our nervous systems. These shifts in how we listen and how we respond to what we hear seem to unfold without our consciously choosing them. They are part of a system of indications of the state of our ANS (which is responding to in-the-moment internal and external conditions) that link us with each other to communicate safety or danger through speaking and listening.

Buried deep beyond the folds of our outer ear (which channel sound waves into our bodies along the ear canal), beyond the flexible eardrum (which is both the barrier and conduit between the outer and inner worlds), and beyond the middle ear (whose tiny muscles and bones move the fluid of the inner ear) lies the complex world of the inner ear. There, the curled up, fluid-filled cochlea contains a membrane that moves in response to the arrival of sound waves, stimulating the hairlike cilia whose job it is to translate vibration into auditory nerve signals that flow via neurotransmitters through the brainstem and thalamus to the higher centers (Murray, n.d.).

The crucial question for us is how these complex processes select which frequencies enter the inner world of our higher brains. Most central for facilitating our felt sense of safety or danger in response to incoming sounds is the condition of a tiny muscle at the gateway to the inner ear and the neural stream of our auditory processing centers. Here, the stapedius muscle contracts or relaxes to either dampen low-frequency sounds in the environment or let them through (Drake, Vogl, & Mitchell, 2014; Porges, 2010). This muscle, less than 1 millimeter in length, influences whether sounds entering our inner ears transmit safety or fear to our higher centers. The current condition of our ANS regulates this muscle because it is innervated by a facial nerve that is part of the vagal system. If we are in sympathetic arousal in response to a neuroception of fear, this muscle relaxes to adaptively allow the low-frequency ambient sounds access to our auditory centers so that we are drawn to orient to the environment as a whole to locate potential danger. If we are in ventral vagal with a neuroception of safety, this muscle tenses so that the low-frequency sounds become background and the human voice emerges into the foreground where we can focus on the meaning of words. In this way, the former adaptively facilitates safety at the expense of relationship, and the latter supports our meaningful communication with one another when we have a felt sense of being safe.

Pause for Reflection

Let's take a moment to sense times when we have felt this shift between orienting to human voice and attending to the larger environment. It may come in response to a sudden sound or an accumulation of experiences that lie well outside conscious awareness. We may notice that there are also changes in muscles, belly, and eyes. Are there judgments that accompany these shifts? Have we experienced the criticism of another when we can't easily attend? As we begin to understand that these shifts happen adaptively and automatically in response to inner and outer events, it may be possible to release some of our own judgments.

As we are in resonance with our people, we may notice moments like this as well. A sudden rise in our person's anxiety may touch our own ANS in a way that we lose our ability to focus on what was just shared. In one way, this is a rupture that can then be repaired by acknowledging our momentary absence and hearing the words again. In another way, we have just experienced what likely happens for our patient quite often and so are having a kind of participatory empathic experience.

When our people have experienced chronic pain and fear without sufficient support to integrate these experiences, they may appear to be easily distracted as their system's anticipation of danger keeps them listening for signals of threat from the larger world. If they have experienced frequent states of helplessness, they may more easily slip into a dissociative state that looks like daydreaming or feels like despair. Jake, our vet in chapter 5, experienced both of these. Instead of indications of attention deficit challenges, these may be adaptive responses to the ongoing inner influence of the neural remnants of trauma.

When we widen our understanding to include both current outer events and what is unfolding internally, it is easier to nonjudgmentally hold that while one person is having the neuroception that the current environment is safe, another may have the felt sense of looming danger. Both are equally real from the viewpoint of each person's inner and outer experience in the moment as shaped by past experiences. *Our current capacity for attending is not a choice so much as a response.* When we hold this view rather than the more critical stance that a person ought to be able to focus his or her attention, we become more likely to be able to support the emergence of a sense of safety in another. A judgmental perspective involves some degree of sympathetic activation that pulls us out of relationship and away from ventral openness to what is emerging in the moment, while the relaxation of judgment into curiosity about what may be touching another's system and making it difficult to pay attention supports our own ventral state.

This is where vocal cords enter the scene. This complex set of muscles in our larynx is innervated by the same vagal nerve as our ears and face. The tension or relaxation in this system, which is responsive to the current state of our ANS, changes the quality of our voices (Lieberman, 2006; Porges, 2011). This allows us to signal danger or safety below the level of conscious awareness to those around us depending on the condition of our own system in the moment. As listeners, while we are consciously attending to the meaning of words, our embodied system is also orienting to the prosody—pitch, loudness, timbre, rhythm, and tempo—for clues about whether it is safe to settle into relationship or necessary to attend to the possibility of danger in the larger environment. As speakers, the prosody of our ventral voice may communicate the reassurance of safety that can help that tiny muscle in another's ear to tense and support connection through attending closely to the meaning of one another's words. From this can arise the sense of feeling felt and known to such a depth that it is possible to vulnerably open our inner world to the care and support of another.

Those of us who have experienced trauma of whatever intensity and duration will likely be especially sensitive to some degree to fluctuations in the prosody of other voices. Small shifts into sympathetic activation on the part of the speaker—the kind that can occur when we are experiencing judgments or have the intention to intervene or fix—may touch and stimulate loud echoes of earlier threatening voices. The accompanying shifts in the ANS of the listener can look out of proportion unless we remember that his or her system is responding from the depth of internalized experience rather than this moment only. At the other end of the spectrum, if we are able to notice this rupture and release our judgments and intentions, our vocal cords will rearrange themselves as we enter a ventral state. The prosody of our voice conveying receptivity and kindness can then become a nourishing elixir bathing the neural streams that are alert for danger in the healing wash of safety.

The well-worn path of ongoing sympathetic or dorsal activation makes it more difficult for anyone to enter a state of safety on his or her own. We have the privilege of offering our ventral voice and ears in the service of joining our window of tolerance with that of another to broaden the range of experience that can be held and healed. On the other hand, any effort we feel we need to make to deliberately simulate a ventral voice or listen more closely is likely arising from a neuroception of danger, leading to sympathetic arousal in us. At that time, our vocal cords and ears tune to our inner state of arousal and communicate that to others. As Fehmi discovered with his eyes, surrendering into a nonjudgmental receptive state will automatically tune our vocal cords and ears so they become instruments communicating safety for our trauma survivors. For those who are uncomfortable with eye contact for any reason, cultural or historical, the sound of our voices and the sense of being deeply heard can provide a path toward co-regulation.

8

Belly Brain

Digesting Food and Relationships

> *My poetry*
> *would like to be*
> *a well worn wooden spoon*
> *in the bowl of your deepest belly*
> *mixing memories—yours and mine together*

—A. NEIL MEILI (2016)

t is a somewhat daunting yet alluring task to enter this gastric universe that influences so many aspects of our well-being. In the last decade or so, we have begun to give this complex belly brain of hundreds of millions of neurons,[*] with its 40 trillion[†] or so bacterial inhabitants, serious consideration. The bookshelf devoted to communicating our new understanding of the enteric nervous system (ENS) and its microbiome (the combined genetic material of our gut bacteria) is becoming wonderfully long. Here, we will be able to focus on only a very small portion, guided by our concern with those aspects that help us acquire a felt sense of

---

[*] Because there are many different kinds of neurons in the enteric nervous system, estimates range between 100 and 600 million depending on which kinds of neurons are being counted. See Gershon (1999) and Furness (2006) for differing estimates.

[†] For a long time, we believed the number was closer to 100 trillion until a recent study by Sender, Fuchs, and Milo (2016) suggested this lower number. In truth, both numbers are likely beyond our comprehension and mainly serve to give us a felt sense of the vastness and complexity of this inner world.

how our belly brains respond to wounding and healing experiences. It may be helpful to begin by getting at least a rudimentary understanding of the intricacies of this highly responsive system and how it communicates bidirectionally with our bodies' other neural streams.

When we can picture something and get a feel for its workings, it seems we develop a kind of intimacy with it, and that is what we hope for here—to cultivate our capacity to listen to the wisdom of our bellies. This is such a good example of how left-hemisphere attention to detail can support our right hemisphere's relationship with what is being studied. As we proceed, it may be possible to sense how our belly brains begin responding to our interest in them. They speak to us through the language of sensation, so while one part of our awareness is on the words, perhaps the other part can be receptive to whatever may emerge into consciousness from our bellies as we read on.

To begin, we find there are many similarities between this second brain and the more familiar brain in our skulls. The neural cells in our ENS are derived at the earliest stages of the embryo from neural crest cells just like the neurons in other parts of our nervous system (Sasselli, Pachnis, & Burns, 2012). Both are accompanied by a large community of glial cells that not only offer debris maintenance and myelin weaving but also actively participate in communication among neurons (Bosemans et al., 2013). These enteric neurons speak with one another via the same language as other neural streams: a wide range of neurotransmitters (Gershon, 1999). In fact, about 90 to 95 percent of serotonin is made in our bellies, along with about 50 percent of dopamine. In all, we believe there are about thirty neurotransmitters present in our ENS (Pasricha, 2011). In very recent research, we have discovered that our gut bugs (collectively called our microbiota) not only aid us in digestion but also make these neurotransmitters on which we depend for our well-being (Lyte & Cryan, 2014). This research suggests that signals from beneficial bacteria are able to find a way through the blood-brain barrier to communicate with the higher centers in our brain (Cryan & O'Mahony, 2011). It appears that our gut bugs are able to touch a "sensory nerve ending in the fingerlike protrusion lining the intestine and carry that electrical impulse up the vagus nerve and into the deep-brain structures thought to be responsible for elemental emotions like anxiety" (Smith, 2015, para. 11). In this way, our microbial colony, belly brain, autonomic nervous system, brainstem, and limbic system carry on a continual conversation, influencing not only digestive health but our perceptions, feelings, and behaviors.

More recently, researchers (Hoban et al., 2016) have found that the microbiome also regulates the production of myelin in the prefrontal cortices of mice through working directly with the genes that instruct glial cells to make the insulating, conducting substance. Since overproduction of myelin is associated with schizophrenia, this may point to a new entry path for treatment by providing support for diversification of our gut bugs. Hoban and colleagues (2016) say this: "In summary, we believe we demonstrate for the first time that the microbiome is *necessary* for appropriate and dynamic regulation of myelin-related genes" (p. 1, italics added). Regulation seems to be a key word here as we picture how our microbial companions are essential for maintaining balance throughout our system. All of this is rather revolutionary news that directs our attention toward the wider networks centrally involved in our emotional life and mental health.

To support digestion, the ENS is distributed along the entire length of the alimentary canal, which we might also call the *nurturant canal,* from esophagus to anus (Sasselli et al., 2012). Its neurons are embedded in the wall of the digestive tract and reach out to the part of our immune system that lies just on the other side of the ENS as well. When we are born, our ENS is not completely developed (Thompson, Wang, & Holmes, 2008) and so does not fully innervate our digestive tract (E. A. Fox & Murphy, 2008). The quality of care we receive, particularly in the context of meeting our need for nourishment in the form of food and emotional support, will guide the emergence of epigenetic* patterns as these new connections to both our digestive tract and immune system are established (Burns, Roberts, Bornstein, & Young, 2009)—another example of *the centrality of relationships in the course of neural development.* These epigenetics will then play their part in our ongoing relationship with nourishment.

It may be helpful to pause here and begin to sense the potential influence of painful or frightening experiences during and after birth on both digestion and immune strength. At the same time, we might

* Epigenesis is the process by which experience switches genes on and off, affecting how cells read the genes. This is an ongoing dynamic process that influences which traits express and guide perception, behavior, development, and so much more.

have a complementary felt sense of the possible amelioration of these experiences if we are surrounded by people who understand our need for ongoing emotionally rich, responsive support during and after such potentially traumatic events.

While the digestive tract itself is similar to our outside skin (and has analogous functions of both protection from harm and reception of nourishment), it is much more delicate so that at certain points nutrients can pass through on the way to entering our cells. The fragility of this barrier both supports nourishment and may make us vulnerable to conditions that can potentially disrupt the lining, ranging from eating processed foods to the prolonged sympathetic activation of stress. If there is such disruption, it can also potentially influence our immune system's response to the inner environment.*

The elegant arrangement of neurons in overlapping networks mirrors and facilitates the rings of muscle that move nourishment along the digestive tract (Costa, Brookes, & Hennig, 2000). Since about 70 percent of our immune system is entangled with this neural stream via synaptic connections, its function is constantly influenced by ever-emerging information in our ENS. The neural stream of the ENS is also connected to the sympathetic (inflammatory) and ventral parasympathetic (anti-inflammatory) branches of the ANS (de Jonge, 2013),† such that our belly brain is exquisitely sensitive to the ongoing fluctuations in the neuroception of safety, danger, and life threat.

Information from the ENS/ANS connection is carried to our skull brain via our central nervous system, bringing news of conditions in our gut to our higher centers, mostly below the level of conscious awareness. At the same time, what we are currently taking into our system via our senses and what is being awakened in our implicit memories also become part of this bidirectional flow of widely shared experience, although the movement of information upward from the gut accounts

---

* While the traditional medical community does not currently recognize diagnoses reflecting lining disruption/immune response, the rise in gastrointestinal and autoimmune challenges parallels the decrease in nutrition and increase in stress. We have much more to learn in this area.

† While it is true that our ENS will continue to support digestion even when its connection with the ANS is severed (Li & Owyang, 2003), we actually live our lives with this flow of communication between ENS, ANS, immune system, and central nervous system intact for more complex and responsive interactions with our internal and external environment.

for about 90 percent of the conversation (Gershon, 1999). The details of these connections may be less important than our emerging sense of how all of these neural streams are woven together into a community of ongoing adaptation and support.

Pause for Reflection

This may be a helpful moment to slow our pace to begin to digest the meaning and importance of these complex pictures. To summarize, our ANS, enteric neural stream, and immune system are in constant bidirectional communication with one another and with our central nervous system and skull brain. This means that changes in our neuroception, most often reflecting the quality of our relationships past and present, directly influence our ability to take in nourishment as well as our body's ability to protect itself. We could go so far as to say that our gut brain is constantly digesting both food and relationships. When we have a felt sense of being alone with fearful and painful experiences, the ability of our intertwined digestive and immune systems to nourish and protect us will be compromised.

To deepen our connection with this system, let's take a moment to sense where we might be drawn to place our hands along this nurturant canal between our throat and lower belly, and just listen receptively for a while. The arrival of this offer of safe connection may facilitate our ability to hear the "voice" of our bellies speaking as sensation. If we continue to visit from time to time, we may become more sensitive to the flow of ever-shifting communication constantly offering its wisdom about how safe we are feeling in this present moment. This developing capacity can then allow us to sensitively receive and hold the belly brains of our patients and others who, through the many pathways of resonance, may feel accompanied in ways that support both digestion and a well-functioning immune system. If we have the opportunity to share our experiences with a reading partner, it can be wonderful practice for this kind of embodied co-regulation.

We find that most of our people, of whatever age, who are carrying embedded traumas experience sensations along their nurturant canal, both in connection with awakening implicit memory and in daily life.

We had such a touching experience with Jerry and Jaylen, four-year-old twin boys, adopted from Eastern Europe, who came to us with difficulty swallowing food and sometimes even water. Understandably, their new parents felt more and more frantic about this. In our playroom, the two young ones often lay on the floor with little energy to engage with each other or anything in this very alluring room.

Before she had time to conceptualize what might be happening, their counselor felt drawn to bring two floppy monkeys from the toy shelf, lie down between the boys, and ask if they could rock the monkeys to sleep with their breathing. She offered to sing a lullaby. As they deepened their breathing just a little, she kept a hand on each of the monkeys so Jerry and Jaylen could feel her presence more tangibly. Both of the boys soon fell asleep. They woke up thirsty after a few minutes, eager and able to drink.

I believe she had instinctively gone toward making connection with their nurturant canal and discovered that her ventral presence with their bellies was able to provide enough of a neuroception of safety for their systems that their throats, at the very top of the canal, could open and receive liquid nourishment. There is such wisdom in our esophagus closing when our belly system is in such a condition that digestion is impossible. Understanding this, she was able to speak with the boys' parents to reassure them that their kiddos' digestive systems were operating as they needed to in this moment, and that working with the embedded traumas from their first three years could gradually relieve their terror so that they could digest well. This good news allowed the parents to settle down so that their agitation wasn't adding to the family upset as much. They were also eager to learn how to do what the counselor had discovered, and so a team on behalf of the boys' belly brains was born.

Working with adults may look a little different, but when our people are experiencing discomfort along this vital canal, encouraging them to gently place a hand on the area of greatest intensity and listen without judgment or intention to change anything can be a healing practice. We may also feel drawn to place our hand in a similar spot on our own belly in support. This warm receptive connection between hand, nurturant canal, and us may soothe their belly's discomfort or open the door to implicit memory, whichever their system deems best in the moment. Even if nothing seems to happen, just the offer of accompaniment begins to relieve the isolation that is at the core of embedded trauma.

The belly sensations that occurred at the time of the original experience become part of the stream of implicit memory. We can likely sense the influence of our own awakening implicit on our ENS as we feel a tightening in our belly or wave of warm relaxation as an old memory of care awakens in our bodies. We are now discovering that our belly brain itself forms molecular memories of previous synaptic experiences (Furness, Clerc, & Kunze, 2000), encoding neural pathways that have some probability of being reactivated by events that remind us of the conditions in which these memories originally formed. The smell of frying bacon or new-mown grass may bring on the belly sensations that accompanied the original event. In this way, our ENS directly participates in the experience of implicit memory.

A deeper source of memory is also present, adding to the ways in which our bodies adaptively look to past experience to anticipate the future. The relatively new science of alimentary epigenetics (Harshaw, 2008) considers how the responsiveness of those who feed us in our earliest days shapes our ability to perceive when we are hungry, thirsty, and satisfied. When we are born, we have certain sensations when these conditions are present, but we don't know what is supposed to happen next. In other words, with the sensation we can now call hunger, we don't anticipate the arrival of food. We simply express our discomfort and await a response. If the person who brings us food comes quickly and willingly, brings what is needed (breast or bottle), and then attends to our signals about when we have had enough, we learn to recognize what is needed when we have that particular sensation as well as how it feels when our bodies are satisfied. This nurturing person mirrors our inner experience and, through that reflection, we gradually learn to listen to our belly's voice as well. With this kind of care, we are much more likely to develop a friendly, respectful relationship with food based on the epigenetic switches that are activated during these lovely exchanges (Harshaw, 2008).

If the person doesn't answer our cries at all or arrives in a state of anxiety or irritation (both feelings being signs of sympathetic arousal), we have no way to connect the sensation we're having with the arrival of food in the first case, and little likelihood of our signals of satisfaction being seen and reflected in the second (Harshaw, 2008). Because the person bringing food is sympathetically activated, her ability to read our body and face diminishes so that she can't easily respond to our needs even when her entire intention is to provide nourishment and comfort. Instead, she can only follow her own perception of what is needed because her social engagement system is turned off. She might also arrive with preconceptions of when and how much we need, making it difficult to attend to the signals sent by our system's innate wisdom. *In general, the greater the disparity between what a baby's belly is requesting and what is being offered, the more this newborn experiences a sense of nonexistence* (Harshaw, 2008). It might be helpful to pause to take that in.

If these ruptures are not repaired, then potential trauma becomes embedded trauma right at the very moment in our development when future expectations about the availability of both food and relational nurturance are being built into our system. To be left alone with the painful and frightening sensations of unnamed hunger and thirst can build a lifelong legacy of rage and despair about who will ever feed us. To have the food arrive but not follow our timing and sense of fullness can leave disorder and confusion in our relationship with essential nurturance. In addition to traces left in implicit memory, these experiences generate epigenetic patterns that will continue to support our deafness to our belly's voice so that we can't tell when we're hungry, thirsty, or satisfied—or when we need emotional support.

Pause for Reflection

Our relationship with food is such tender territory because close by lies the implicit experience of our earliest relationships. Let's take a moment to sense if it is all right to explore this relationship a bit. If we feel that it is, we might begin by dropping a question into our right hemisphere about what our inner world may be ready to share in this moment. When we do this kind of asking, it feels different than when we are actively searching for an answer. Instead of digging through what we already cognitively know, we pause and listen with as little expectation as possible. The response often arrives first in our bodies—sensations in the belly, heart, muscles, the movement of the breath—but may also come as a wave of emotion, a symbolic image, a memory, a shift in perception, or an intuitive knowing. Sometimes there seems to be no response at all. That is likely our system's way of letting us know that this isn't the time for this particular exploration. If a response comes, it may be possible to just sit with it for a bit without needing it to be more clear or specific than it is. Often, there will be a gradual unfolding over the minutes and months ahead. If we have been touched by remembrance of our early experiences of nurturance in a way that feels sympathetically activating or draws us toward dorsal collapse, we might want to pause until we can connect with a companion who can help us return to ventral vagal safety. As we join with another person, our bellies may signal their appreciation by offering a more soothing quality of sensation.

The conditions of our culture also interact with our belly brains in a direct way. Because of our ongoing connection to threat and tragedy around the world (and sometimes in our neighborhoods, workplaces, and families), because of the dominant left shift in our culture (which may be partly an adaptation to the former), and because of whatever unhealed wounds we may be carrying, many of us live in nearly constant sympathetic activation that has become so much the norm that we no longer notice it. Nonetheless, this ongoing stress touches our ENS and microbiota deeply. The ENS is so strongly and responsively connected to our ANS that it was once considered part of that system, so this neural stream that regulates both digestion and immune strength echoes any sympathetic arousal or dorsal withdrawal by moving toward shutdown. Stress, whether from internal arisings or external circumstances, also decreases the diversity of our microbiota, influencing their production of certain neurotransmitters. As we are increasingly aware, our well-being is held in some significant way in the cradle of our belly (see Smith, 2015, for a solid review of the research).

Any healing process that offers considerable nonjudgmental receptive holding of another's world will begin to directly affect the messages from our ANS to our ENS—and from there to our gut bacteria and immune system. All of these neural streams have already learned certain patterns and, through neuroplasticity, can learn differently with this quality of support. This is not a quick process and may not be sufficient on its own to change the gastric tides. Researchers are working every day to discover how to reseed a devastated microbiome. However, this kind of relational care will, at a minimum, decrease the continuing challenge to our belly system. As in the practice above, each of us may be able to remember feeling the quality of our bellies shift whenever we have found ourselves embraced by kind, responsive care. Pausing for a moment to savor this will strengthen these neural connections so that recalling these experiences can become a vibrant and nourishing resource for us.

If we go back to what we have learned from alimentary epigenetics about the entanglement of food with the quality of relationship that arrives with the food, we might wonder about a potential paradigm shift in how we are present with people who have struggles with eating. One primary message from this research is that the epigenetic shifts that occur seem most influenced by whether or not the people offering the nourishment can read the signals of hunger, thirst, and satisfaction from their children, and then reflect them back through both receptivity and action so that these little ones feel an affirmation of the trustworthiness of those signals. *This reflection gives them inner ears to hear their bodies' inherent wisdom.* We might want to pause again for a moment to take in the absolute necessity of having a partner who can see us.

When that reflection is partially or completely missing, a kind of despair about being nourished begins to grow strong implicit and ENS roots. In anorexia, that despair seems to be a felt sense that we should not exist, with accompanying sensations in the belly at the thought of food; in bulimia, what is taken in is experienced as poisonous and needs to be thrown up; and in compulsive eating, we have a felt sense that we must take nourishment into our own hands and rely on the neurotransmitter changes that sugar and fat and quantity bring to provide a sense of being seen and held. Without being able to hear our bodies' voice, we can only follow the engrained implicit and ENS patterns about how we are to relate with food.

Whether our people struggle with over- or undereating or inability to keep nurturance in their bodies, what might happen if we offered what we could call *agenda-less food*? After we have made sure that any health crisis is being supported by a doctor and/or nutritionist, we might inquire about favorite tastes and textures and then bring some of that food into our time with them—without any inner agenda about them eating less of it, not eating it at all, or keeping it down. Our interest would be entirely focused on attending to this person's experience with the food, with acknowledging their current relationship with nourishment, deeply listening and nothing else. Might this receptivity of them, just as they are, facilitate implicit healing and an epigenetic shift that would eventually allow them to reconnect with their bodies' inner voice about its need for nourishment? This can sound quite counterintuitive, because of course we want our people to be able to take in nourishment, but the research suggests we may not be able to get there by continuing to ignore the signals they are currently experiencing because that is what set this struggle in motion in the first place. If we go to the root, attending to what is here right now, accompanied by our felt sense of each person's system having the inherent wisdom to seek nourishment of all sorts, we may be able to provide the support needed for them to regain their connection with this innate capacity.

Pause for Reflection

In my experience, most of us struggle in our relationship with food and water. In a left-shifted society moving at such inhuman speeds, we get disconnected from our bodies and often don't feel the call to hydrate ourselves until our bodies get into an emergency state. Even if we are putting water into our system, when we have a neuroception of danger, our cells may not open to take in this essential nourishment (Lipton, 2008). The same is true for food. If it feels threatening or confusing to us, it is challenging to get into a relationship with it that eases digestion. With great gentleness, let's pause a bit to sense what spontaneously arises when we ask, "What is my relationship with food and water just now?" and then listen with as little judgment as possible. Responses may come in the form of words, images, gestures, or belly sensations. Receiving them gently and not asking them to be any different may be the beginning of connecting with our belly wisdom—the gateway to nourishment for every cell in our bodies.

We have opened a few small doors to this vast universe, sensing some of its intricacies and also some of its connections with other neural pathways. In Eastern cultures, there has been less of a tendency for our sense of self to move upward into our heads. For example, we in the West might say a persistently angry person is "hot-headed," but if we were from the East, we might say something like "his belly rises easily." As we dwell with this accumulating research and seek to feel its meaning in our bodies, we may find that our awareness expands downward to listen with equal respect to the voices of these two brains as they carry on their continual conversation.

9

Heart Brain

One Voice of Connection

B etween the belly and the skull brain lies a third center of neural wisdom, "the 'little brain' on the heart" (Armour, 2008, p.
165). Each of us may immediately relate to the vivid sensations
that radiate throughout our chests, particularly in response to relational
experiences. We may feel the contracting ache that speaks to us of
a personal loss or the suffering of others, and the delight that floods
the whole expanse between our shoulders at the sight of a loved one.
Looking inward, we can begin to picture the intrinsic cardiac neurons
that reside within the heart itself and the rosette-like companions of
the extracardiac neural groups that inhabit the thoracic cavity, together
fostering the capaciousness of these feelings. As they interact with our
autonomic nervous system, insula, limbic circuits, and neocortex, they
hold the truth of our ongoing experience of connection and disconnection with others, sometimes bringing it into conscious awareness but
often not. These sensations, felt and unfelt, arise sometimes from the
awakening of implicit memory and sometimes from our current encounters with one another.

When they do arise in our awareness, it seems unhelpful to label
some of these sensations positive and some negative, but to perhaps
instead view them as telling significant truths about the past and present. *Each sensation has its own story that seeks to be heard.* In the listening, we may often feel moved to respond. Suffering calls for comfort just
as joy wants to be shared, both of them requesting relational joining of
one sort or another. If we come from this more welcoming and inclusive

perspective, we may be able to receive these sensations with compassionate listening for the kind of support each is requesting rather than responding with an urge to suppress some in favor of others.

Pause for Reflection

What is it like to imagine welcoming all these sensations without preference? It is so natural to want to protectively push away those feelings that bring the various shadings of pain and fear. Yet here, at the level of the heart's wisdom, we are invited once again to open to the possibility of equal inclusion and deep listening. We can perhaps begin by welcoming what happens in our chest when we feel the need to move away from a particular feeling. Often, one or two extended arms pushing away is the gesture that comes most naturally. If we follow that, what happens along our arm and into our chest? What happens when we relax that arm and draw the feeling toward us? Perhaps we can gently observe both gestures with as little judgment as possible, even sensing the value offered by each of them. As we become more aware through the day of the protective impulse to push away, perhaps we can begin to experience that as an invitation to offer the complementary movement as well.

The ongoing complex and emergent conversation between the intrinsic cardiac neurons (about forty thousand of them within the heart), the extracardiac thoracic neural rosettes, and the ANS (which carries their messages upward while also bringing messages downward from the limbic and cortical circuits) is exquisitely calibrated to offer the most support for our heart's health in times of quiet and stress as well as make our emotional life available to our awareness. J. Andrew Armour and his colleagues (Armour, 2003, 2008; Armour & Ardell, 1994) have devoted much of their careers to the exploration of what has become known as neurocardiology. Their foundational discovery is that this neural system both retains its autonomy from the central nervous system and is profoundly responsive to it at the same time. They seem to delight in the complexity and the sense of unpredictable emergence this insight offers.

Some of the interconnections between the intrinsic cardiac neurons and the extracardiac rosettes are highly sensitive to the chemical environment and neural firing unfolding within the heart itself without reference to external input. We know this because when a heart transplant is performed, reconnection to the autonomic nervous system happens slowly, if at all (Murphy et al., 2000). Yet the heart continues to support life without this broader conversation. At the same time that this autonomous relationship is taking place, other interconnections within the intrinsic and extracardiac groups are in contact with the overall system, receiving constantly emerging input from the ANS and from regions as close by as our lungs and as far away as our arms and legs (Armour, 2003) as well as from our interactions with one another. When our internal system senses that all is well, the flow of descending information limits transfer of information to the neuron groups that are minding the heart so they can quietly continue their work. There is also no need for much upward flow to alert us to changing conditions. At these times, we have little awareness of our heart's physical or emotional workings.

As we encounter particularly powerful forms of relational goodness, the resulting change in conditions may bring sensations around the heart into our awareness as the upward-flowing stream shifts our felt sense, our perceptions, and even our behavioral impulse. Sometimes this may be reflected by our feeling drawn to place a hand on our upper chest in a gesture of welcome and acknowledgement. This is literally a heartfelt movement. Since our cardiac system is innervated primarily by the ventral vagal parasympathetic branch of the ANS, under these conditions of goodness, our social engagement system has the opportunity to invite others into a sense of connection in these moments of being deeply touched.

Even in potentially traumatic times, this system's wisdom also has elaborate feedback loops to help maintain regulation on a beat-to-beat basis as outer conditions change (Armour, 1976). As our neuroception of danger mounts, our cardiac ganglia devote more of their resources to preparing us to fight or flee. Our ANS removes the vagal brake that quiets the heart in ventral states, allowing for entry into protective sympathetic activation. Often, more information about our heart's functioning becomes available to conscious awareness, perhaps helping alert our system to the need for vigilance. If we enter a neuroception of helplessness and drop into a dorsal state, the cardiac neural system fosters the letting go of consciousness as our heart rate slows, while simultaneously supporting the possibility of healing by conserving metabolic resources for another less threatening time (Porges, 2011). *All of these moment-to-*

moment changes are encoded as part of the implicit memory being formed as each experience unfolds, and will come alive again in this particular rhythm if this memory is touched and awakened in our bodies. Again, we see an elegance and intelligence within the system itself as it promotes our thriving in ventral times and survival during challenge.

These conversations are facilitated by neurotransmitters and support cells that are similar to those in the skull brain and are exchanged via synaptic connections. The heart is also the home of a rich sea of hormones (blood-borne chemicals). This little brain not only is the recipient of the support these chemicals provide, but also makes oxytocin (Cantin & Genest, 1986), the hormone that facilitates trusting relationships of all kinds.* The concentration of this chemical in the heart is about the same as in the skull brain. The presence of oxytocin perhaps further supports our felt sense that this cardiac brain is as central to our ongoing implicit embodied anticipations about relationships as our belly brain is to our core sense of safety.

We can't help but notice that it is impossible to talk about the heart brain without speaking of our ANS as well, particularly the ventral vagal parasympathetic branch. As these joined neural streams move upward carrying information from the heart, the vista opens out toward the brainstem, limbic system, and neocortex, which are shaped by this input. This sense of nested systems in constant communion with each other, working mostly below our awareness to adaptively respond to the emerging moment, may help us settle into ever-growing trust that there is wisdom and inherent health awake at the unseen neural roots of our bodies, awaiting receptive, responsive support to heal the embedded traumas we all carry.

Pause for Reflection

Let's take a little time now to be available to our heart brain's communication in this moment. Gently placing one or two hands on our chests and simply opening to sensation is a good place to begin. As we are making our way up the body, we have been cultivating a will-

---

* Our heart brains also produce epinephrine (fostering concentration), dopamine (supporting focus on what is novel), and natriuretic factor, a hormone that is active in many regulatory regions of the skull brain.

ingness to listen without expectation at each pause along the way. As we focus with patience and receptivity, we may be able to sense how sensation becomes emotion becomes a word as the heart brain's whisperings cascade upward toward the limbic and neocortical worlds. We might also experiment with inviting some past experiences of any kind into awareness and sense how that may change what arises in our chests and also spreads upward.

As our people come to us, they will also have rich sensations arising in their chests from time to time. Our own familiarity with listening will help open the way for them to also get into relationship with their hearts' story. I have found receptivity to the heart to be one of the primary gateways to implicit memory. Just as with the belly, placing a gentle hand on the chest where the greatest intensity arises can offer a sense of accompaniment and comfort for the feelings of disconnection that may have lodged there for decades.

Turning our attention to cultural influences on our heart brain, in 2003, J. Andrew Armour began his article on neurocardiology with these words: "The main reason this burden is increasing is that the ability of many people to cope with daily stressors is being overwhelmed" (p. 1). The burden he was addressing was related to monetary costs and losses of productivity, but also speaks to us of his early recognition that our culture is trauma-inducing in ways that we can measure, as our heart brains, so well adapted to coping with emotional challenge, can no longer fully manage the overwhelming influx of information and the accumulating stress of relational disconnection.

In the presence of potential trauma, whether its origins are subtle or overt, cultural or personal, our heart brains respond to our emerging sense of threat via changes in heart rate variability (HRV). We may imagine that our hearts beat with a steady rhythm, but actually the time between beats varies with emerging conditions (Shaffer, McCraty, & Zerr, 2014). When we have a neuroception of safety, the rhythm is responsive to the moment, so there is greater variation in the time between beats, indicating a flexible, resilient response to this moment's need. However, when a neuroception of danger arrives, HRV decreases, moving in the direction of becoming more rigidly uniform (Cohen et al., 1998). This is likely in response to the restricted focus our system requires to adaptively attend to danger. Over the short term, this may help us because our whole organism remains engaged in protecting us until the danger has passed. However, when these potential traumas are not met with sufficient support and embed in our bodies and subcortical circuitry, the pattern of low HRV is held within the implicit memory and may continue in the body even when the memory is fully out of awareness. This is particularly true for traumas that begin to embed early in life when our system is most malleable and the foundation for ongoing patterns of activation is being built. We know that the majority of information from our embodied brains, including the heart, flows upward to the higher centers, something in the range of 80 percent up from the body to 20 percent down, so when HRV is more uniform, at some deep level our system may continue to feel the presence of danger even when the outer event is over, and this changes our perception of the present moment.

From this research, we might conclude that high HRV indicates health and low HRV suggests embedded trauma. However, another trail of findings offers us a different angle of vision on the heart and invites us to make room for more delightful complexity in our understanding. This research suggests that we are born with differing sensitivities to our relational environment (Boyce & Ellis, 2005; Ellis & Boyce, 2008), and that one of the genetic/epigenetic factors is an inherent tendency toward low or high HRV (Conradt, Measelle, & Ablow, 2013).

These physiological predispositions support different outcomes for children in secure and challenging circumstances. Young ones with constricted HRV display considerable resilience in painful or fearful circumstances, doing as well as they do in warmer conditions. This is the opposite of what the former stream of research indicates. Low-HRV children are often experienced as having a steadiness about them in tough times and easy times. The grandmother of one of these kiddos told me, "He just trucks on through everything without much fanfare." Those with higher HRV seem to be much more affected by the relationships that surround them, blooming gloriously when they are offered secure, supportive connection and withering into anxiety, depression, or physical illness when there is emotional neglect or chaos.

In different ways, both HRV profiles offer certain challenges, with low-HRV children thriving less in good conditions and high-HRV young ones being more hurt in unsupportive ones. At the same time, both also offer protections, with our tender ones thriving to an extraordinary degree with support and our stolid ones doing okay no matter what. Boyce and Ellis (2005) poetically call these young ones dandelion and orchid children, which may give us more of a felt sense for how they grow. Adding to the complexity, I have often seen what seem to be hybrids: dandelion bodies exhibiting strong physical health even in adversity coupled with orchid hearts that are easily frightened and hurt and also struggle to recover, for example.

Pause for Reflection

Perhaps this talk of dandelions and orchids has touched us in some way, so it might be helpful to pause and listen inside. Do we sense we have a preference for one over the other, both for ourselves and for others? Perhaps we can listen gently to our inner response with as little judgment as possible. Do we begin to remember how others may have seen us? Many people in the helping professions seem drawn to the work by their compassionate sensitivity to suffering, and this may have meant that we were viewed as too emotional or tender as children. We may have protected ourselves by shifting left so that there would be less criticism. Or we may be born dandelions who can provide a sense of strength and steadiness amidst the challenge of sitting with so much pain and fear. Or possibly some of both. The value in this exploration is just to receive whatever may be there for us.

These differing understandings of HRV point us again toward attending to individuality, listening deeply to the unique experience of those who come to us. It is helpful to keep all that we've learned in the background, even when it is somewhat contradictory, like ballast for a ship, while suspending expectations and judgments about what it means exactly for this particular person.

In general (while always being cautious about generalizing), higher HRV tends to be correlated with what is called physiological coherence, an orderly yet flowing and responsive-to-the-moment wavelike pattern that has the possibility of integrating with and influencing other bodily systems in the direction of physical and emotional health (McCraty, 2015). When we are in this state, the powerful electromagnetic field that is always flowing with our heart's rhythmic activity may also influence those around us, touching their systems with a sense of our receptive presence (McCraty, 2015). We may, in this moment, recall encounters that felt particularly nourishing in this heartfelt way.

As we know and have likely experienced, embedded traumas often leave our systems in ongoing protection and constriction at so many levels that some kind of support is needed for us to open to healing. The Institute of HeartMath, whose researchers have collaborated with cardiac experts for many years to deeply understand the heart brain's processes, offers one pathway for supporting higher HRV through various techniques, coupled with a device that reflects our heartbeat patterns to us (McCraty, 2015). The intention is to provide exercise for neural pathways that foster increases in HRV through focus on what they call positive emotions in order to move away from negative ones. With ongoing reinforcement, these neural supports are more apt to be available to us in stressful situations. There is no doubt a great deal of value in strengthening these circuits. At the same time, it isn't clear that the implicit memory containing restricted HRV is also changing. This may leave us with two parallel pathways, one containing the implicit pattern and one holding the new heart rate pattern. Under stress, the implicit pattern may make itself adaptively known so that it can heal.

There may be an additional way to foster a more coherent state of heart. Any movement in the direction of increased HRV involves activation of the ventral vagal parasympathetic pathways. Stephen Porges (Porges, Badenoch, & Phillips, 2016) would tell us that there are passive pathways by which we are drawn toward our preferred ventral state. Primary is our receptive nonjudgmental presence with one another, often supported by a quiet environment. As the neuroception of safety deepens, we can be present to whatever is alive in the moment, including the full range of emotions without labeling them positive or negative. This often opens the doorway to implicit memories holding embedded traumas that then become available for disconfirmation and repair (Ecker, Ticic, & Hulley, 2012). In the background, the activation of these ventral pathways will support increased HRV. As the healing implicit memory reconsolidates, it may permanently hold this new heart brain pattern in place of the constriction that was there before. Beckes and Coan (2011), our social baseline colleagues, would also suggest that having the support of another means we need to call on less of our own resources in the effort to regulate. Perhaps these two ways of fostering increased HRV can complement each other, both developing neural strength as a resource and healing embedded traumas for deep and permanent change.

So far in these chapters, we have been exploring pathways that are mainly external to our central nervous system. They provide the vital moment-to-moment unfolding felt sense story that is gathered up and integrated by our higher centers. So much of their input remains outside conscious awareness yet guides our perceptions, emotions, thoughts, behaviors, and relationships. Now we arrive at the brainstem, the gateway to the brain in our skulls.

10

Brainstem

Moving to the Rhythm
of Memory and Experience

Sloshing and chugging sloshing and chugging
as I curled up beside it
in the great pile of laundry
rich with the smells of the people I loved
Half asleep half awake I floated there
all my senses safely cradled and warmed
and part of a rhythm and a sound
like a heartbeat in a womb

—A. NEIL MEILI (1994)

We may often picture the brainstem as a river that gathers in the tributaries of some of the senses along with the neural messages from our muscles, belly, heart, autonomic nervous system, and more, delivering this rich flow of information to our skull brain.* While that is true, our brainstem is far from a passive pathway. At the core of the brainstem is the reticular activating system (RAS) that filters out and streams an infinitesimal fraction of the information that

---

* The conversation is bidirectional, but it is good to remember that the flow is about 80 percent upward and 20 percent downward, giving us a sense of the importance of the embodied streams in the shaping of the skull brain.

arrives there to the midbrain and thalamus, with the latter then distributing the flow to the limbic regions and neocortex (*The Brain From Top to Bottom*, n.d.), all part of a single neural system providing access to this moment's internal and external experience. We can picture how this rich upward stream of information/experience spreads to every corner of our higher centers, influencing feelings, thoughts, perceptions, behavior, and relational patterns. In this way, the brainstem functions both as the gatherer and gatekeeper for what can possibly come to consciousness, apparently selecting tiny streams from the flood for their relevance to us in this emerging moment.

The information/experience that does arrive at the thalamus and is sent to the higher centers is then met by the thalamocortical sweep, moving from the back to the front of our brain in forty-cycle-per-second pulses. It brings together the neural nets that are active at the time of the sweep, binding them so we consciously experience a flow rather than discrete events. From what was already a very small stream arriving from the brainstem, the sweep makes a further selection of what is deemed most salient. It is then delivered to our working memory, where an additional refining process delivers a much smaller slice to consciousness (Llinas, 1990, 2008). It may be helpful to pause for a moment and feel into this ever-narrowing process that flows from the totality of potential experience to the actuality of our awareness. This sweep happens across the neural landscape of both hemispheres, bringing the often-wordless experience of the right as well as the worded narrative of the left into the possibility of being known (Siegel, 2015b).

This unseen, nonconscious selection process may seek to guard us from drowning in the flood of possible experiences available to us. It seems we are currently living at the edge of overwhelm a great deal of the time, so this process may be quite wise and protective of us now. At the same time, it may cause us to wonder how much of what is available in the world we are unable to take into our awareness, and offers another opportunity for humility about how little actually reaches consciousness.

Pause for Reflection

Perhaps we can picture this process of gradually diminishing streams and sense its meaning for us. How is it for us to be aware that there is so much that never reaches our higher centers, much less consciousness? Just the pausing is good for us to allow this flow of information about our brainstems to settle in us a little more deeply.

We now arrive at the core of the core of the RAS and find an ancient ridge present even in reptiles whose neurons secrete the serotonin that is carried upward to our skull brain (Törk, 1990). Two very old systems, the belly brain and brainstem ridge, supply this crucial neurotransmitter that has so much to do with our physical and emotional stability and well-being. That it has been conserved in our neuroanatomy throughout evolution points to its significance (Panksepp, 1998). Nearby, the locus coeruleus is making norepinephrine, priming the neurons throughout the brain for activation in times of danger as it receives messages from the body as well as subcortical and cortical circuits (Benarroch, 2009). Because of this ongoing conversation, when potentially traumatic events arise, norepinephrine begins to increase, interacting with the part of the brainstem that participates in mediating our level of consciousness[*] (Kinomura, Larsson, Gulyás, & Roland, 1996). When our neuroception of danger is moderate, attention and working memory increase, often encoding the memory in a highly detailed way. However, when the threat reaches a certain threshold, possibly approaching terror, conscious awareness decreases as norepinephrine floods the system (Ramos & Arnsten, 2007). At that point, explicit memory encoding may become fragmented and can finally no longer be recorded at all. This shift may correlate with the movement from sympathetic to dorsal activation in the ANS. Many of our people struggle with memories that have no explicit story but only linger in the body's implicit circuitry. Sharing the wisdom of our system in shielding consciousness from the intolerable may help us settle our people into work with implicit-only memories as they gradually gain trust that their bodies have acted in supportive ways at the time of the trauma and now provide one entryway into the process of changing implicit memory.

---

[*] Another of the processes in which our brainstem is implicated is our sleep-relaxed/awake-focused attention cycle.

Pause for Reflection

It may help us to pause here to more deeply picture and feel into this information about our brainstems by slowly and tenderly placing a hand at the back of our neck, up into the hairline where our brainstem lives. Arriving, pausing, listening, and perhaps even feeling gratitude, we might be able to open to the flow that is happening there, to the winnowing of experience to what is most relevant for us, to the ever-responsive flow of neurotransmitters, and to the modulation of conscious awareness on our behalf. Perhaps we can arrive without expectation and just listen.

It won't surprise us to discover that traumas that don't receive the support they need to integrate (sustained abuse, war, neglect) can affect the anatomy of our brainstem. In 2005, a study of the brains of World War II veterans with probable combat-related PTSD showed a significant decrease in the number of neurons in the locus coeruleus, particularly on the right side of the brainstem where the conversation with the right amygdala takes place (Bracha, Garcia-Rill, Mrak, & Skinner, 2005). The location is significant because the circuits of emotional regulation are right-centric. Because these neurons are involved in a delicate and intricate regulatory dance that unfolds throughout the body and brain, this diminishment of resources affects the whole system.

It isn't the potentially traumatic experience that initiates this loss, but rather the continuing effects of embedded trauma that at each moment remind our system that danger is ongoing. At these moments, we are directed again toward the crucial importance of relationships. We are foundationally and eternally attaching beings whose neural circuitry is open to the nourishing, co-regulating influence of others who can offer us a safe, nonjudgmental, receptive space. The neurons in our locus coeruleus may never be replaced, but the effects of this loss can be ameliorated as our capacity for co-organized neuroplasticity allows us to weave supportive circuitry around the injured parts. Settling into that picture of potential healing may allow our bellies and muscles to soften, our heart to quietly expand, and our breathing to deepen a bit as hope and gratitude arrive.

Before we leave our brainstem, we are going to explore one more process, this one centered at the boundary between the spinal cord and the base of the brainstem where we find our central pattern generator (Shubin, 2009). From here, our brainstems send nerve impulses that activate muscles in a particular sequence. As we feel the rhythmic movement of our heartbeat, breath, peristalsis, and cycles of sleeping and waking, we may begin to sense how much our lives are held by the many rhythmic pulses within us. The most ancient beings would have participated in their own version of this process. Given the sophistication of our overall neural system, might this area of the brain also be sensitive to other kinds of internal and external rhythms?

Taking a slight rabbit trail away from the brainstem, the answer to this is suggested by research regarding our cerebellum that points to an overall principle of brain evolution. Until recently, this part of our brain adjacent to the brainstem and containing almost half the skull brain's neurons was thought to be in charge of balance and fine motor control. We believed it helped us ride a bike and write legibly. However, thanks to research with people born without a cerebellum, we now know that this area is devoted to a particular *principle* rather than just specific activities. The cerebellum is involved in refinement of thought and emotion as much as adding grace and balance to physical movement (Schmahmann & Caplan, 2006). As our higher centers became more complex, the cerebellum donated its expertise to our expanding emotional and intellectual possibilities. We see a similar pattern in how pain centers and pathways that were originally devoted to physical pain now also light up for emotional anguish (Eisenberger & Lieberman, 2004) and how our amygdala has taken on increasingly sophisticated emotional processes (Pessoa, 2013).

With this principle in mind, the question about the possibility that our brainstems are sensitive to rhythmic patterns of all sorts is certainly a reasonable one. The work of Bruce Perry and his colleagues (Perry & Hambrick, 2008) has illuminated how much this is true. His concern with the brainstem springs from his awareness of how our brains develop sequentially, bottom up, not only in the womb but also outside as they are formed in relationship. If our brainstem doesn't receive what it needs in these early encounters, the brain circuits that develop later will feel the influence of the disorganization of this developmentally earlier region as reflected in our thought patterns, perceptual biases, feelings, behaviors, and ways of relating (Perry & Hambrick, 2008). What we have understood so far about the wide-reaching innervations that arise from the brainstem certainly supports this view as well.

Pause for Reflection

We can perhaps begin to sense the physical rhythms our bodies have taken in, beginning with being rocked in our mother's womb, listening to her heartbeat. We might pause here to listen for what wants to be shared about this. These early experiences of rhythm that begin patterning our brainstem are already relational, perhaps preparing us for the less tangible flow of back-and-forth between us and our closest people. What might we sense about the difference in the relational rhythms of our mother and father? Over the months and years, our world gradually widens into a circle of connections with a great variety of pulsing patterns. Who comes to us as providing a sense of easy flow? At the same time, we are already participating in the cadence of our culture, side by side with the larger natural rhythms of day and night, the tides, the seasons, the planets, even the galaxies. As we sit with each of these, we may notice how our other interconnected embodied systems respond to the different rhythms we welcome. What happens in our muscles, bellies, hearts, and breathing? If you are reflecting with a partner, does anything change when you share this experience? How might the two of you sense the rhythm of your relationship?

These rhythms become part of the implicit memory forming to hold each experience, and arise again in our bodies when that memory is touched and awakened. We can perhaps call to mind and body times when we have experienced the pulsing in our bodies changing. As I write this, I feel the shift in rhythm that occurred for me in the transition between my frightening home and the safety of school. There is particularly a change in tempo as my system's pace slows, accompanied by an expansion of breath. With every experience, multiple networks in our bodies act in concert as they adaptively respond to emerging conditions, almost entirely without effort or conscious awareness.

If our early days were shaded by fear and pain without the support we needed, the inherent wisdom in our brainstems will not be enough to organize this system. That innate capacity will need the support of others and, as Bruce Perry (2014) notes, can be assisted by other repetitive, rhythmic, embodied practices. Here is what he and Erin Hambrick say:

An example of a repetitive intervention is positive, nurturing inter-actions with trustworthy peers, teachers, and caregivers . . . using patterned, repetitive somatosensory activities such as dance, music, movement, yoga, drumming or therapeutic massage . . . This is true especially for children whose persisting fear state is so overwhelming that they cannot improve via increased positive relationships, or even therapeutic relationships, until their brain stem is regulated by safe, predictable, repetitive sensory input. (Perry & Hambrick, 2008, p. 42)

When we have embedded traumas from long ago, we are all children deep inside, where time has stopped as the trauma is held safely away from our conscious awareness in our subcortical circuits and bodies. Bruce Perry's work is relevant for healing wounds at every age. Perhaps there could be drums and an invitation to share music in the midst of every therapeutic relationship. Perhaps we can find ways to engage in rhythmic movement together, or inhabit rocking chairs side by side. When children come to us, the back-and-forth of playing catch can help these young brainstems settle into the embodied patterns of safety and security. This combination of consistent relational rhythms accompa-nied by regulating activities that we do together can activate our brain-stem's innate capacity.

Our current culture has moved far away from the rhythms of com-munal life. At that time, the group came together throughout the day around the sound of corn being ground, the slap of clothes on rocks as they were washed, the rhythm of butter being churned. Babies were rocked in time with the tribe's life, and children often organized their games in harmony with these daily activities as well. For us, rhythms have largely become individual as our earbuds offer a private world of sound and movement for much of our day and night. Adapting to the overwhelm of daily life, we can perhaps understand the value of this privacy, even as we recognize that it isn't easy to remain connected to something more embracing. If we remember Mandy's story in Chapter 1, we can perhaps feel the disrupted rhythms of her day and sense the wisdom in her system as she headed for the swings. At the end of her day, she returned to the warm embrace of her mother's love and under-standing, to the rhythms of safe, predictable relationship, so the day's potential traumas never embedded at all.

11

Midbrain

The Emotional-Motivational
Roots of Selfhood

*The deep sadness
the red anger place
the "hang on tight we might
end up in the next county" passion*

—A. NEIL MEILI (2003A)

With just a small shift of focus, we now arrive at the top of our brainstem, an area called the midbrain. It lies between and joins the centers that are lower down and behind (brainstem and cerebellum) with those that are above (thalamus, subcortical, and cortical regions), making the midbrain a region of *integration and transmission* (Breedlove, Watson, & Rosenzweig, 2010). *Streams of experience about the ways in which the world (particularly the interpersonal world) touches, sounds, and looks to us gather here alongside the emotional-motivational circuitry at the root of our affective experience and impulse to move in a certain way.* Like the rhythms in our brainstems, the experiences rooted here underlie and shape the felt sense and words that emerge in the higher regions of our brains.

Let's pause here and see if we can feel more deeply into how the ever-changing sensory world is shaping our emerging feelings and behavioral impulses at this moment. For me, the warm air from the heat pump is touching me on this cold day; I hear the soft snoring of my old beagle who is nestled next to me on the couch; and, raising my eyes from my laptop, I see and feel the strong old trees out my back window. My breath deepens and I find myself recalling the beautiful companions who visit this home regularly. I feel surrounded and held, content to sit quietly in this moment. The neural firings in my midbrain have been taken up into my subcortical and cortical circuitry so that I can share the narrative of the unspoken experience rooted in these ancient pathways with you. In the midbrain itself, there is the confluence of some of the senses and the full range of primary emotions and the movements correlated with them, all of which are aspects of implicit memory. As we will see later in this chapter, this region can be accessed directly in the healing of embedded traumas.

Because so many streams gather here, encoding our body's behavioral impulses and emotional experience, the midbrain is likely the area where there is sufficient integration between multiple circuits that the possibility of a sense of self and conscious awareness begins (Damasio, 2000; Panksepp, 1998; Panksepp & Biven, 2012). That is quite a statement, indicating that *who we experience ourselves to be is more rooted in our sensory experience, primary affective nature, and its corresponding movements than in our thoughts.* The long and tantalizing story of how neural firings become subjective feelings of which we are aware is still an unresolved mystery in many ways, but we can certainly leave it as a lingering question for our embodied brains to mull in the days and decades ahead.

In the midst of all this complexity, it may be most helpful for us to focus on aspects of the midbrain that will further ground us in an understanding of their nature and contribution as well as how they respond to traumatic events and the processes of healing. This invites us to enter into the work of Jaak Panksepp and his colleagues—some of whom are laughing rats (Panksepp, 1998; Panksepp & Biven, 2012; Veebiakadeemia, 2013). Beginning with these mammals and others, this team of researchers has discovered that our midbrains contain the root circuitry of our emotional life, what they call primary-process emotions. As a result of their work, we now know that we have inherent emotional systems that are not dependent on higher cortical functions. We may need our cortex to name or reflect on them, but we

)n't need it to experience and be conscious of emotion or to share in
.ivid emotion-based relationships. Animals (Kolb & Tees, 1990; Panksepp, Normansell, Cox, & Siviy, 1994) and human children (Shewmon,
Holmes, & Byrne, 1999) without a cortex can live emotionally rich lives
when they receive responsive loving care, and people in severe cognitive
decline are still often able to richly respond to offers of kind connection
when we let go of our judgments and expectations that their cognitive
capacity defines who they are in favor of simply receiving them as they
are (Pearce, 2009).

Panksepp and Biven (2012) speak of seven distinct midbrain circuits and their associated neurochemicals that mediate our emotional-
motivational life. This region evolved to foster our survival and has
become the foundation for lives anchored in meaning through the richness of emotional aliveness and movement toward social connection.
Because as adults we now experience these emotions after they have
been shaped and differentiated into categories of feeling by higher processes, it may be difficult for us to get the flavor of the midbrain experience. As Panksepp and Biven say, "raw emotions are not everyday
occurrences for mature humans, but most can remember clenching
their fists and turning red in anger, being incredibly scared, and feeling
both deep sadness and joy" (2012, p. 13).

Panksepp (1998) originally chose to capitalize the words for these
pathways to indicate that he is speaking about specific circuits in the
midbrain while using common terms that try to capture their essence.
The first, and what Panksepp calls "the 'granddaddy' of them all" (Panksepp & Biven, 2012, p. 86), is the SEEKING system.[*] It is an "anticipatory eagerness" (p. 96) supporting curiosity and exploration, and
particularly animated by anything new. Before being shaped by our
daily life experiences, it is "a goad without a goal" (p. 96), a feeling of
eye-brightening interest. We could think of it as the "psychobehavioral
push" (p. 86) that animates most of the other primary emotions and
behaviors. It is anticipatory delight rather than the reward we expeirence
when we get what we were seeking. Not surprisingly, its circuitry is in
a midbrain area that is rich in dopamine production.

---

[*] One of the other most ancient circuits for survival is the LUST system, which animates our sexual desire. While it doesn't fully awaken in us until puberty, in terms of
evolutionary time of origin, it is side by side with the SEEKING system.

Pause for Reflection

As we are borrowing words from Panksepp and Biven to try to capture something about the SEEKING system, what begins to awaken in our bodies? Do our muscles, bellies, hearts, eyes, and breath begin to shape themselves around our experience of this emotion? We may be able to both touch the core of it when it is still "a goad without a goal" that engages our energies and sense some of the ways it has been shaped by our experience.

This emotional feeling is paired with the behavioral impulse to move outward in our world to locate resources that are most meaningful for our survival. For us humans, that means a primary focus on seeking connection with other humans, for without these links with one another, we wither, become ill, or die (Beckes & Coan, 2011; Cozolino, 2014; Porges & Phillips, 2016; Siegel, 2015b). Right after birth, if we are placed on our mother's bellies, guided by SEEKING, we crawl upward toward breasts and eyes even with our very immature systems. When we are fortunate, our mothers respond with their CARE systems in full flower. Flooded with oxytocin and the opioids that our bodies make (the neurochemicals of CARE), our mothers are also animated by SEEKING as they joyously anticipate each new movement, sound, or smile that their infants may offer next. As little ones become more mobile and move out of sight, CARE and SEEKING propel mothers to find them. CARE isn't limited to mothers. Our fathers have what Panksepp and Biven call "latent maternal circuits in their brains, waiting for the right environments to amplify their potentials (de Jong et al., 2009)" (p. 284). That opportunity may come as they touch their babies for the first time.

Pause for Reflection

The descriptions of SEEKING and CARE offered here are the foundations for secure attachment. Let's take a moment to check in with our bodies to see how we are receiving these words and images. If we have had less than optimal experiences as little ones or as parents with our own babies, it may be challenging, even painful, to take this in. If we notice a protective tightening, let's see if we might welcome it as a guardian of our heart. If there is pain, perhaps we can surround that with CARE, ideally with the support of another. As we stay in this compassionate place, more feelings or images may come forward or not. Perhaps we can hold a space for either outcome without judgment. For those of us who feel the warmth of recognition in these images of CARE, perhaps we can sense that as a cause for gratitude.

Close by our CARE system, we find its complement, the SEPARA-TION DISTRESS/PANIC/GRIEF system. The development of CARE* is intimately intertwined with the response to its loss. All of us, even in times of warmth and connection, carry the equal possibility of GRIEF at our roots. The PANIC/GRIEF behaviors that are animated by the loss of CARE, including clinging and crying, are intended to bring our person back. At the midbrain level, we aren't talking about the circumstances in which these two become activated but about their presence prior to any experience at all. GRIEF and CARE are fundamental to who we are, and we could imagine that the presence of our GRIEF system supports our urge to bond with each other.

Viewed this way, we can see the adaptive beauty of this pairing. Without our GRIEF system, both the feelings and behaviors, we would not be able to let others know we need them. Without a CARE system, we would have no feeling or motivation to respond. Some would say that the relationship between these two systems is the inborn root of our empathic capacity. Research tells us that when parents hear their babies' distress cries, the GRIEF system lights up in their own brains (Swain, Lorberbaum, Korse, & Strathearn, 2007). What happens next between parent and baby may have a lot to do with how the parents' GRIEF was met when they were small, but the foundation for the possibility of empathy and responsiveness is nonetheless there in the midbrain circuitry of us all. In the process of healing our traumas, the inherent health in the system can return, allowing us to reinhabit our inborn capacity for CARE.

---

* Some would speculate that the CARE system evolved from the LUST system as a nonsexual social feeling and impulse necessary to nurture young birds, mammals, and humans. That they share some common neurochemistry points in that direction.

Pause for Reflection

Reading about the intertwining of GRIEF and CARE may have touched our own experience because all of us have suffered and been comforted in these ways. What response does awareness that suffering is inevitable because it is built into our systems evoke in us? We may have said words about the inescapability of suffering to ourselves and others many times. Does it feel different to have our capacity to suffer confirmed as an ever-present and even helpful part of our biology? If times of loss have reawakened with these reflections, perhaps we can receive and hold them with compassionate care right now or, even better, seek out a friend to hold them with us.

When we experience disconnection at any stage in life, SEEKING lends its energies first to the SEPARATION DISTRESS/PANIC/ GRIEF system. When we are unwillingly parted from a loved one, whether for a time only or through death, we often cry out in distress, and if our person can't or doesn't reconnect, we may feel a sense of panic and desperation. Then, as the separation becomes final, we may descend into what seems like an eternal ache of lonely desolation. SEEKING dims, and we may sink toward depression* if we remain in this isolation.

If our person is not lost to us permanently but is unresponsive now, the pain of separation is nonetheless intense. As we become uncertain of whether our person will ever return, our SEEKING system may begin to devote more of its energies to our FEAR system in response to the pain. Panksepp and Biven tell us that GRIEF and FEAR are different primary emotions that are held by separate circuits, but their activation may overlap at times. We can sense the difference in the behavioral impulses they both animate. GRIEF brings a biologically healthy and helpful social behavior of wanting to cling, while FEAR activates the bodily impulse to fight or flee, specifically not a social but a survival response. Their dominant neurochemical environments are also some-

---

* Panksepp traces the experience of depression to our midbrain circuits. When SEEK-ING quiets because another midbrain system has come online and shifted our neurochemistry, we experience a loss of hope, and the immobility of depression may set in. This may be a helpful way for us to understand our patients' darkening moods.

what different. GRIEF diminishes the CARE chemicals of oxytocin and endogenous opioids, leaving us feeling deeply alone, sad, and yearning, while FEAR increases the threat-response chemicals to prepare our bodies for action.

Pause for Reflection

Let's take a moment to see if we can sense how GRIEF and FEAR inhabit our bodies differently. What happens with our muscles, bellies, hearts, eyes, and breath? Are there times when we have felt both at once? Can we bring in our CARE system (or the support of another's CARE system) and see what happens then?

We might imagine a small child whose parent is unable to focus her attention on him. She ignores his distress cries, perhaps even punishing him by putting him in isolation in his room. With his pain unmet and increased by the very person he needs, he becomes afraid, withdrawing from efforts to cling in order to protect himself. His cries escalate, and the look on his face shifts from GRIEF and yearning to FEAR. His SEEKING system experiences mounting frustration when his efforts at reconnecting go unheeded. At some point, a third system related to disconnection may awaken—RAGE. The energy being held in the SEEKING system intertwines with the strong onset of RAGE to amplify the response.

The primary experience of RAGE arises in times of scarcity, not times of abundance. Its behavioral corollary is striking out to protect ourselves. Panksepp and Biven say this about RAGE: "[It] is not fundamentally designed to punish but rather to bring others in line, rapidly, with one's implicit (evolutionary) desires" (2012, p. 146). In other words, the protective intention is to draw our person back to us again. However, by the time this primary-process emotion encounters our higher centers, it has transformed into all manner of feelings and plans: anger, hatred, revenge, aggression, ongoing irritation, or blaming, to name a very small sample. All of these have a tendency to produce the opposite of the original intention to renew connection.

Pause for Reflection

It may be helpful to see if we can feel the movement from the awakening of GRIEF to FEAR to RAGE in our own systems. Whether we express any or all of these, do we feel the behavioral impulses in our bodies? These potential movements, or what Panksepp and Biven call intentions-in-action, may be the most direct road to the felt sense of these core midbrain circuits that are activated by a sense of disconnection. We might also remember that when we become left-shifted, our awareness and relationship with our physiological responses diminishes to the point that we are unable to attend to them. As a result, our bodies carry the visceral experience of unmet GRIEF, FEAR, and RAGE as embedded traumas. There is a tragic quality to this, because our culture often requires us to divorce ourselves from the foundation of our humanness.

This experience for our young one could have gone a different way with a mother whose own inner world could be touched by his cries, activating her own inborn GRIEF system without plunging her into her own painful implicit memories and moving her to comfort him. His wails would suddenly or gradually subside to be replaced by the warm responsive sounds of being together. Once connection is reestablished, the RAGE system is quieted by the release of endogenous opioids and oxytocin. At that point, another system is free to come online—PLAY. No longer required for focusing on maintaining connection, the SEEKING system's energies can begin to range freely as exploration and add their enthusiasm and love of novelty to the unpredictable world of interpersonal PLAY. It is spontaneous, joyful, and explores the edge where connections can be made and lost. In this way, it becomes a process of social learning in the midst of just playing. Panksepp and Biven tell us that the PLAY system is both "robust and fragile" (p. 354).

Play only occurs when one is safe, secure and feeling good, which makes play an exceptionally sensitive measure for all things bad. PLAY, however, is also a robust system: If young animals are healthy and feeling good, they almost invariably play together when given the chance. (p. 355)

One could say the same thing of young children. In our teen years, that free-ranging exploration combines with our PLAYful tendencies to include the seventh system, LUST, as we SEEK not only to procreate but to honor a deeper connection through the inclusion of romance and sexuality.

> ### Pause for Reflection
>
> *Complementing our exploration of the more distressing emotions, let's spend a little time to see if our bodies recall the joy of PLAY and LUST, accompanied by the spontaneous engagement of SEEKING once relational safety arrives. As always, we might notice a shift in our muscles, belly, heart, eyes, and breath, a little differently perhaps for PLAY and LUST. Just allow yourself to enjoy how these three systems intertwine, giving meaning and delight whenever they arrive.*

These seven systems—SEEKING, PANIC/GRIEF, FEAR, RAGE, CARE, PLAY, and LUST—are our common inheritance. They animate our emotional life, contribute to our behavioral impulses, and tell us again that connection heals and supports growth, while disconnection deepens pain and, without the needed support of others, embeds trauma. The midbrain system as a whole is highly sensitive to our lived experience. When events bring unmet pain and fear, these circuits adaptively respond with repeated activation of the PANIC/GRIEF, FEAR, and RAGE systems, supported by our SEEKING system's energies that have to be directed primarily to our survival in such challenging and lonely times. Since all of these systems are interrelated at the level of neurochemicals, the hormones and neurotransmitters needed to manage traumatic experiences, large and small, seen and unseen, dampen our system's capacity to offer endogenous opioids, oxytocin, and other molecules that support the awakening of the CARE, PLAY, and LUST systems. Our seven systems begin to be shaped by these events when they are repeated, and especially if they are the dominant experiences of our lives.

A small boy came to our playroom after living his first six years in a war zone in Africa. His parents, also suffering from PTSD, loved him, but because their own primary emotional systems were now dominated by PANIC/GRIEF and FEAR, they were unable to provide what he needed to begin to heal. At first, he was unable to stay in the playroom at all, so strong was his FEAR. As he was repeatedly met with CARE, showing itself as deep understanding and receiving him just as he was without judgment or expectation in those brief moments before he pulled his mother out of the room, he began to stay longer. His GRIEF system was still active in the clinging, but his FEAR was diminishing, making room in his system for the neurochemicals of comfort and relationship. Gradually, he began to explore the toys as his SEEKING system no longer needed to devote all its energies to protection.

Initially, if he encountered any obstacles in his PLAY, he would fall to the floor in a heap of despair. In his life, his SEEKING system had met almost nothing but tragic disappointment when it sought to reconnect with his terrified parents or maintain even a modicum of safety. Moving beyond RAGE, which also turned out to be useless, his SEEKING had learned to simply withdraw in the presence of frustration, collapsing in the face of challenge. Rather than encouraging him to try again (something that would add more pressure to his overloaded system), his therapist sat near him on the floor, offering CARE right where he was. Because our primary need in life is to connect with others, he would gradually come back toward her, and they would begin again. Whether we work with little ones or adults, the way our midbrain circuits were shaped by the experiences of our early childhood and beyond will be with us in the room. If we can develop our capacity to see this core circuitry underneath all the ways it manifests through the involvement of our subcortical and cortical ways of feeling, knowing, and behaving, our own midbrain propensities may guide us in our CARing responses.

In recent years, many new healing modalities have emerged as we understand more about how our neurobiology develops, embeds trauma, and heals. Each provides a different entryway into our embodied systems that have adaptively shaped themselves around adversity experienced in emotional isolation. Because our midbrain circuits are strongly implicated in the emotions and behavioral impulses of implicit memory, discovering the pathways that might lead to healing at this level could be valuable. Several years ago, David Grand (2013) was doing EMDR (eye movement desensitization and reprocessing) with one of his people and began to notice that there were moments in tracking when her eyes wobbled. With experimentation, he found that staying with that spot helped his people gain access to the visceral experience of trauma.

Along with so much else, the orientation of the eyes was encoded as part of implicit memory.

Subsequent research (Corrigan & Grand, 2013; Corrigan, Grand, & Raju, 2015) has revealed that because the visual orientation response in trauma is encoded in the midbrain and intertwined with the emotional-motivational systems, identifying and staying with the spot where the eyes locked during the trauma could give access to the emotional and behavioral parts of the traumatic memory. As with all other pathways toward the roots of trauma, awakening one strand of the neural net that has gathered up the memory of the experience has some probability of bringing more of it into the space between therapist and patient where the possibility of disconfirmation and implicit change arises. Because the midbrain holds the circuits at the foundation of our sense of self, as the embedded traumas are released, they may offer a profound change in how we experience our bodily self. Since these midbrain circuits are richly connected to the subcortical and cortical regions, this change in sense of self can then be further supported to gradually influence the way we feel and think about ourselves.

Grand stresses the importance of sustained mindful connection, not only with the visual orientation that provides the strongest visceral sense but also between therapist and patient, providing the necessary support for entering this potentially dysregulating territory. That connection fosters what we would call interpersonal disconfirmation. Blending Ecker's (Ecker, Ticic, & Hulley, 2012) work on implicit memory change with Grand's, we have another opportunity to nourish our left-hemisphere emissary's understanding of the pathways of healing. These knowings then become readily available supplies that our people can call forth in us at the moment of need.

In very brief summary, these upper-brainstem circuits in the midbrain are the place where we see evidence of our evolution from survival in emotional isolation to survival through social connection, from reptilian to mammalian ways of being in the world. The LUST system is perhaps the bridge from asocial to social, as it requires some degree of relatedness to provide its vital support for procreation and eventually fosters the systems that give us the pleasures and meaning of romantic love and nurturant care.

As we now finally arrive at the limbic regions and neocortex, we may be able to sense a little more deeply than ever how these lower streams are constantly speaking to us and shaping how we feel, think, and behave. A concluding word from Jaak Panksepp and Lucy Biven:

> The overall premise of this discourse is that primary-process affective arousals always participate in the diverse experiences of our higher emotional processes, but we can all agree that no one has devised good scientific methods to get at those mental subtleties, which reflect the way our cognitions are modified by our passions. (2012, p. 147)

Once again, we are at the crossroads where science meets mystery.

12

Limbic~Neocortex

Lateralized Resources for Integration

W̲e have spent a long, leisurely time sampling the neural streams that move upward to become a river of neural firings and experiences that are then filtered through our brainstems and thalamus on the way to integration in the limbic and neocortical regions of our lateralized brains. As at every level, there is a seemingly infinite amount that could be said of these higher regions, and some of it is quite paradoxical.* Here, we are going to speak less of what each smaller region does and see if we can get a sense of the relationships between these larger systems. It is customary to speak of the limbic region and neocortex as two distinct areas, but the work of Brazilian neuroscientist Luiz Pessoa (2013) might persuade us to picture their affiliation differently. They both receive input from all the embodied streams, and they both reach downward to influence the neural firing in all those streams, forming a continuous circle of ongoing mutual modification in light of emerging experience and memory. They are also profoundly interwoven with each other.† We traditionally

---

* One small example: In general, the left hemisphere displays an affinity for what are called positive emotions and the right for negative emotions. Yet studies have found that fear activates the left amygdala more than the right (Hardee, Thompson, & Puce, 2008).

† Because of the abundant connections the amygdala makes with many circuits in the neocortex, it emerges as the primary contributor in a network that links together the cortical and subcortical brain regions involved in emotional processing. (Petrovich, Canteras, & Swanson 2001; Purves et al., 2001). Thinking and feeling are inseparable.

think of the limbic region as the center of emotional processing and the neocortex as the realm of cognitions. Pessoa suggests we take a more whole perspective.

> As discussed by B. Scott Kelso and David Engstrøm (2006), it may be time to stop describing concepts in terms of dichotomies . . . and to adopt a vocabulary that views concepts as complementary pairs that mutually define each other *and, critically, do not exclude each other*. Thus Kelso and Engstrøm propose that light should be understood in terms of complementary pairs of "wave~particles" (quanta). In this vein, behavior should be understood in terms of "emotion~cognition." (p. 5, italics added)

Kelso and Engstrøm use the symbol ~ to invite us to the perspective of complementarity. They ask the question, "How are these two concepts/processes in relationship with each other?" Built on the both/and way of attending that is uniquely right-centric, we can begin to experience how the subcortical and cortical worlds belong to each other, how right and left hemispheres support one another, and how emotion and cognition are interwoven in a particular way.

This idea of complementarity can sound quite philosophical, and we might ask what this has to do with helping our people. It is certainly supportive of our clarity to keep in mind the ways that thought and feeling are intertwined and influence each other, because that can guide how we listen and what healing methods we offer. For many people, the attempt to shift the trajectory of their lives by adopting different cognitions without attending to the limbic and embodied precursors of their thoughts has led to disappointment as the underlying implicit memories and their attendant perceptions remained unchanged. Fourteen-year-old Jordan came to us because her parents were concerned that she had so few friends and seemed to be sad most of the time. With a previous counselor, she had talked about feeling like she was fundamentally uninteresting and could find no reason for anyone to befriend her. With every intention of relieving her suffering and building on his experience that she was indeed interesting, he talked with her about changing how she thought about herself and gave her some exercises: affirmations and social coaching. Always seeking to be an obedient child, she practiced diligently and left therapy about two months later because she felt like a failure when her inner experience and her outer life didn't change.

When Jordan arrived at our center, her counselor was grounded in the awareness of how thoughts arise from implicit roots and can then continue to hold those perceptions in place. To begin with cognitions and behaviors as though they are independent of implicit memory might generate a new set of neural nets, but would not address the foundation of worthlessness arising from Jordan's deep implicit stream. Attending from this angle of vision seemed to make room for her to begin to speak of her sadness that her father didn't seem to like her. He wasn't vicious or mean, but rarely looked her direction at all. With her counselor's support, she could feel a core of emptiness along her nurturant canal, and together they could hold the embodied and emotional experience of being ignored along with the thoughts this repeated relational experience engendered. Honoring both the implicit root and the beliefs made room for the possibility of a disconfirming experience.

Our left hemispheres have a strong tendency to separate processes into components and then privilege one over another. Coming from the more right-centric view of our embodied brains, we are more able to work in the complexity and sometimes confusion of multiple systems in interaction with each other. This kind of respectful holding of the whole is the foundation for safety and opens the door to healing. Because of their close relationship, we are including the limbic region and neocortex in a single chapter as a gesture acknowledging how they are interwoven.

Some details may helps our left hemispheres picture this relationship. At the level of structure, subcortical and cortical areas are not always clearly defined. Our hippocampi, makers and part-time retrievers of explicit memory, are an elaboration of the edge of the neocortex, of the temporal lobe in both hemispheres. At this point, the cortex thins from six layers to the three or four layers that make up the hippocampi (Amaral & Lavenex, 2006). The insula or insular cortex, tucked deep inside a fold of the cerebral cortex, is well placed to connect our bodies to the higher regions. Some say it is part of the cortex; others, part of the limbic region (Kolb & Whishaw, 2003). We might say it is part of both. The same is true of our orbitofrontal cortex, because while it is continuous with the prefrontal cortex, it curves deep inside behind our eyes and makes intimate contact with our amygdala to support secure attachment and emotional regulation (among many other functions) (Barbas, 2007). It is challenging to see where one begins and the other leaves off. Our anterior cingulate cortex, just above the corpus callosum, has two sides, one facing the neocortex, one facing the amygdala, so it is a place where cognitive and emotional experience meet, although it is unclear how much interaction the two sides have. What we do know is that it is "involved in a form of *attention* that serves to *regulate* both cognitive and emotional processing" (Bush, Luu, & Posner, 2000, p. 215, italics added). All of this is just to help us picture that even at the level of structure, there is less than clear division between cortical and limbic regions. Instead, physical proximity and sometimes even shared structure, supplemented by the vast network of neurons that reach into each other's territory, speak to a single system.

The clearest divide in our skull brain is between the two hemispheres, because it is crucial for our functioning that these complementary ways of perceiving remain relatively isolated from each other (Devinsky & Laff, 2004). Too much incursion of one into the other may be part of the underlying process of schizophrenia (McGilchrist, 2009). Paradoxically, as our corpus callosum, the major connector between the two hemispheres, matures in childhood and adolescence, inhibition increases. McGilchrist says,

> All in all, my view is that the corpus callosum does act principally as the agent of hemisphere differentiation rather than integration, *though ultimately differentiation may be in the service of integration.* This complex, almost paradoxical, function at the very core of the brain, form[s] a bridge that nonetheless separates the worlds of the hemispheres. (2009, p. 213, italics added)

From Dan Siegel's work (2015b), we are certainly familiar with the principle of differentiation preceding the linking that leads to integration at every level of experience. In terms of the hemispheres, differentiation is a given by the time we are adults. What might integration be like between these two halves? In research, when conditions are set so that each hemisphere independently receives information, certain brain circuits become active. However, when both hemispheres are given access to the same experience, inviting cooperation, different regions come awake. This suggests that integration across the hemispheres isn't simply the sum of what the two do, but a process energizing different possibilities (Banich, 2003; Marzi et al., 1999). We might have an experience of the essence of this kind of integrative process when we meet with a deeply listening friend and find that we have realizations and emotions that would not have come if we were on our own. *Something about our availability to one another, while also maintaining our separateness, cultivates the possibility of something more that is unpredictable and hard to describe.* And so it is with the hemispheres as well. We have begun to consider how the well-educated left hemisphere emissary may help the right-centric Master by providing an underlying stability of understanding that holds the tentative emergent processes of relationship. It is a theme we will follow throughout this book.

Pause for Reflection

As we are picturing the interweaving of subcortical and cortical structures and functions as well as the necessary divide between the hemispheres, let's just take a moment to feel into them as well. What do we sense about the relationship between our feelings and our thoughts? Can we sense how they co-modify each other? In terms of the relationship between the hemispheres, can we feel the difference between left-centric task focus and right-centric relational focus? Are there times when we also experience how they support each other? As we gain more practice with how these states show up in our bodies, this awareness will accompany us into our counseling rooms and, through resonance, help our people develop this way of experiencing themselves as well.

What are some ways that our cortical~subcortical regions uniquely contribute, building on what the rest of our system offers?

- *They encode and retrieve implicit (embodied) and explicit (declarative) memories* (although the other neural streams also have their own kind of memory that contributes particularly to our implicit sense of things). When potentially traumatic experiences occur and then embed, the implicit aspects are wisely sequestered in the amygdala-centric circuitry and the body, awaiting arrival of the support needed to disconfirm and integrate them (Jovasevic et al., 2015). In this way, the fullness of emotional and bodily distress is held away from conscious awareness much of the time, although still available to be touched and awakened later by internal and external events. This keeps implicit memory malleable enough to be accessible for healing. The wisdom and delicate balance of this process is astonishing.

When we turn to explicit memory, research produces some paradoxical results in terms of how potentially traumatic memories are encoded. In general, it appears that at the onset of stress, explicit memory may encode more strongly with amygdala activation (greater emotion) and the concomitant rise in cortisol until both reach levels that block encoding and/or retrieval (Cahill & McGaugh, 1995; Elzinga & Roelofs, 2005). This may leave our people with implicit-only memories of highly stressful events, not only from early childhood but also from later traumatic experiences, which impairs the formation of a coherent autobiographical memory stream. In Chapter 20, we will explore how to support our people when they are challenged by this loss.

- *They integrate the many streams of information flowing upward from the body and inward from the senses*, although the wisdom of how these flows of information enter our lateralized brains comes from the circuits below. For example, activation of the ventral vagal parasympathetic nerve lateralizes right, as does information about the state of our bodies in the moment. The former supports social engagement, a primary concern of the right hemisphere, and the latter serves to give us the felt sense of what is emerging in the moment.

Bruce Perry and Erin Hambrick (2008) along with Jaak Panksepp and Lucy Biven (2012) have developed models for how these systems are nested from lowest to highest. Perry and Hambrick's Neurosequential Model of Therapeutics focuses on the need to regulate/heal the lower systems, beginning with the brainstem, before turning attention to wounds in the systems above. In their experience, the effect of dysregulation in the brainstem is strong enough to disrupt daily life and hamper healing the higher levels. Panksepp and Biven speak about how the primary-process emotions arising from the midbrain are elaborated and refined by the subcortical (secondary) and cortical (tertiary) circuits. RAGE takes on many shades from irritation to righteous indignation. CARE becomes a mother's gentle holding and the way a child empathically responds to a friend's scraped knee. We give these emotions names and make charts of them in case we forget the subtleties of expression. Panksepp and Biven see the upward pathways predominating in early life and the downward pathways strengthening with maturation so that they potentially have a dampening effect on the primary emotions. We might imagine the formation of an oval in which the initial vivid impetus is upward from the body beginning before birth. As experience wires in certain implicit patterns, which gradually become explicit beliefs, the higher cortical and subcortical circuits send what they have learned back into the embodied brain, along with whatever regulation of intensity may have been co-organized. This becomes the lens through which we experience the world and the foundation from which our behaviors arise. Perhaps a little more than ever before, we can appreciate the importance of a wise, listening other entering this system to be a consistent, caring, responsive presence that can disconfirm what has been so deeply engrained.

In general, when traumas embed and are held in amygdala-centric circuits, the capacity for integration is disrupted in the optimal protective ways described above. As support for healing arrives, our system's inherent capacity for integration resumes its developmental course (Siegel, 2015b).

- *Based on how our entire system is shaped by our implicit memories and accompanying beliefs, combined with what is happening right now, they send information downward to adaptively regulate the circuits below.* As an example, our amygdala, hypothalamus, and prefrontal cortex (along with other pathways) combine to contribute to the adaptive shift of our autonomic nervous system, muscles, belly and heart brains, breath, and quality of attention to meet emerging internal and external conditions. When we are carrying embedded traumas, our amygdala will be more sensitive to possible signals of danger (such as neutral faces) and less integrated with our prefrontal cortex. This will influence the nature of the downward flow of neural firings as our amygdala sends its perception of danger into our bodies.

- *Supporting self-consciousness, they give us the capacity to reflect on our experiences and to develop narratives that hold our ever-unfolding story.* Both hemispheres do this, as we have felt-sense and behavioral narratives as much as worded ones. Cortical and subcortical capacities also contribute to the creation of these stories. For those of us without strongly traumatic histories, the flow of autobiographical memory generally begins around five or six years old. Prior to that, explicit memory more often contributes discrete memories that don't yet hold the story of our lives. If we have lived in ongoing pain and fear, the development of explicit memory, the precursor of autobiographical memory, is impaired and a sense of our life having narrative coherence is disrupted. With healing, even in the absence of significant explicit recall, it seems that an intuitive and compassionate sense of the trajectory of our lives can be known. The gradual emergence of this flow is one way we can know that we are moving toward integration of embedded traumas.

What our cortical/subcortical system doesn't uniquely do is let us be conscious and in relationship with each other, although it certainly supports and amplifies those processes. As we were discovering in the last chapter, the source for both of these seems to lie below, before lateralization, in our midbrain. McGilchrist offers this:

> Panksepp sees consciousness as something that begins very deep indeed, in the so-called peri-aqueductal grey matter in the midbrain, and "migrates" through higher regions of the brain, especially the cingulate, temporal and frontal regions of the cortex. So he sees it as something that is not all or nothing, but has a continuous existence, transforming itself as it travels upwards, through the branches, to what he calls, by analogy with the forest canopy, the "cerebral canopy," until in the frontal cortices it becomes high-level cognitive awareness. I like this image of the cerebral "canopy" because it reminds us that consciousness is not a bird, as it often seems to be in the literature—hovering, detached, coming in at the top level and alighting on the brain somewhere in the frontal lobes—but a tree, its roots deep inside us. *It reinforces the nature of consciousness not as an entity, but as a process.* (p. 221, italics added)

Once again, we may be drawn back to the cover of this book where we see not one tree, but a forest in which nurturing interpersonal relationships support the development of the individual trees. For us, too, relationships begin deep down, as all our circuitry points us toward one another beginning before birth. What happens between us shapes the nature and felt sense of the consciousness that arises in us from moment to moment.

> ## Pause for Reflection
>
> *As we are nearing the end of this exploration of our embodied brains, it may be possible that we are developing a felt sense of the roots and canopy and the conversation between them, of the flow of embodied processes upward and emotional~cognitive influences downward. Without too much thought, let's sit with our bodies, spending a little time at our feet to anchor us first. What might we sense about the quality of our muscles, our belly and chest, the flow of our breath, the quality of our face? What emotions and thoughts well up spontaneously? As best we can, let's allow any judgments that come to recede as we are available with open receptivity to what is.*

Now, let's turn our attention from what the cortical/subcortical community does to how it flows in challenging circumstances. The complexity involved in this system would take volumes to fully describe, and we can only address some of the major pathways here with the intention of gaining a felt sense of the adaptive movement of the system. In times of potential traumas involving fear and pain, the insula, which connects bodily sensations to emotional meaning, carries these signals upward (Vilares, Howard, Fernandes, Gottfried, & Kording, 2012; Wager, 2002), where they have special relevance for the small jewel of the limbic region, our right amygdala (Markowitsch, 1998). In rapid fashion, it assesses what this newly arriving information is and what to do about it* (Pessoa, 2013). It is the center of a decision-making process that affects our entire system. The choices, mostly below the level of conscious awareness, at least at the beginning, are made in light of what is implicitly being awakened and what is happening in the moment.

As our amygdala communicates with our hypothalamus, it responds by initiating a flow of chemicals to prepare our bodies to meet this challenge, while our basal ganglia reaches up to the motor regions of the cortex and down into the body to select, connect, and refine the movements that will support our protection (Chakravarthy, Joseph, & Bapi, 2010).

---

* Our amygdala has the same evaluative functions in times of safety as well, attending equally to the sensate messages that we may approach each other and connect. In addition, our amygdala grows calmer in the presence of a trusted other (Beckes & Coan, 2011; Coan & Sbarra, 2015).

If the stress isn't too great, our hippocampi* will also memorialize the event in explicit memory, holding it for a while before passing it on to long-term storage. An implicit memory is also being encoded that contains the multiple streams from the body, including behavioral impulses and fragments of sensory information that support our perception of this experience. Strong emotions increase the strength of neural firing, anchoring the implicit memory in place.

At the same time, we are also internalizing the other person/people involved in the experience via our mirror neurons and resonance circuitry, a collaborative cortical/subcortical process (Iacoboni, 2011). They will become permanent inhabitants within both implicit and explicit memory (to the extent the latter encodes), carrying their bodily sensations, emotional surge, and intention into our implicit system, along with how they look and sound, the quality of their touch, their odor, and possibly their taste. Now part of our neurobiology, they will be available for healing, as we will see in Chapter 21.

At the point where our amygdala receives the upward-flowing message, we find ourselves at a crossroads that defines whether a potential trauma will embed or be resolved. If the emotionally rich information awakens an implicit memory of formerly embedded trauma or is simply overwhelming for our system, the longer pathways between our amygdala and orbitofrontal cortex will quiet to make room for the fastest possible actions of protection in light of our perception of the magnitude of the danger. All of our resources will be devoted to this response, and without support, this trauma will embed and be held in amygdala-centric pathways and the body. If the new experience does not overwhelm us, the encoded experience will be held by the confluence of our amygdala and orbitofrontal region (with the help of a wide network of other activations), where the process will slow down and it will be possible for us to weigh decisions about what to do next, a process called response flexibility (Siegel, 2015b). Here, drawing on internal resources, potential traumas can be given the support they need to integrate rather than embed. At the meeting of our neocortex and limbic system, often fostered by having someone with us, lies the possibility of both healthy development and of healing when embedded traumas have stopped our process along the way.

---

* Some very recent research with mice (O'Neill, Boccara, Stella, Schoenenberger, & Csicsvari, 2017) is suggesting that other brain regions may be equally and independently involved in the encoding and retrieval of explicit memories.

We could say that our amygdala is one center that holds our well-being and distress.* From about the eighth month of gestation onward, our amygdala-centric pathways build up an implicit perceptual lens based on the quality of our interpersonal and cultural experience. In one sense, we can't step outside this lens to see and feel ourselves and our lives differently; in another, with our neocortical capacity to generate a bit of distance from our experience, we can begin to see the patterns and have both an understanding and felt sense of their origin (McGilchrist, 2009). When we turn to the process of healing implicit memories in Chapter 20, we will explore how our receptive, responsive presence can support this process with our people.

The description of the neural pathways in these last chapters contains just an infinitesimal part of the multitude of interconnected circuits that are actively working together at every moment as one new experience after another comes to us, as memory awakens and colors our moments, as opportunities for interpersonal healing arrive. For now, perhaps it is enough to get a sense of how all the streams join each other, not like a relay runner passing the baton, but more like braided streams. They flow together to pick up water from adjoining streams, which changes them in often unpredictable ways. This new emergence is then offered to the next stream to join, to receive and give the richness of its own journey until they are interwoven to produce the experience of a life. In closing, it is perhaps fitting to return to what we quoted from Luiz Pessoa (2013) back in Chapter 2: "So, one region doesn't do much, in my view, but when immersed in cooperating, and interacting, and exchanging signals with many other regions, that's when things really happen. And that's where the human comes from" (p. 6).

---

* We could equally say this about our autonomic nervous system or the quality of our interpersonal relationships.

13

Where We Have Been
and Other Intriguing Explorations

As we have made our way through these beautiful bodies, from the ground up (muscles, belly, heart, autonomic nervous system, brainstem, midbrain, subcortex, and neocortex) and from the outside in (skin, eyes, ears), we have taken in a lot of new information and perhaps now find some new pictures of these flows coming to our mind's eye. Maybe we are becoming more comfortable listening to the language of sensation side by side with the more familiar world of words. While this is a good way to begin getting acquainted, the most profound meeting happens when we then patiently and repeatedly sit with these streams, listening from as much stillness as arrives in that moment. As we attend, our bodies seem to share more information. Perhaps it is our listening that allows this, but it is possible that our bodies also offer more of their truth-telling wisdom when they are heard, that it is a bidirectional process of understanding and care. As we leave these chapters, perhaps we will feel drawn back to the reflections frequently so we can amplify our awareness of these embodied streams.

Recalling the practice we did with our muscles, many people have told me that they have a strong sense of their muscles somehow expressing gratefulness at being met, a felt sense of "thank you." After that, some have the sensation of another muscle group calling for attention. We might say this is imagination, but it seems to be more than that. What does consistently happen is that when we attend without expectation or judgments, our muscles begin to find their own, often-unexpected way of moving toward release, sometimes after waves of increased tension. Both of these movements are part of the process of sharing their story when we invite them into the safety we are offering with our listening. As we have more of these experiences, we may begin to inhabit our bodies just a little differently than ever before, with a deepening respect for the conversation they offer. From a right-centric perspective, we have gotten into relationship with the flows of energy and information that speak the language of sensation. Why would they have less to tell us than the worded conversation in our mind? I believe we are simply more accustomed to listening for language.

While the majority of the information exchange moves up from the body (about 80 percent), we may also feel the returning loop as our emotions and thoughts flow downward to touch our moment-to-moment embodied experience as we did when practicing in the last chapter. In this mutual exchange, they shape one another in the many ways we have explored here. From the interpersonal viewpoint, perhaps we are also becoming more sensitive to how responsive our systems are to those near us, to the point that we can say that we are not completely two but also not entirely one, as we find that our individuality is built by these nourishing contacts as well. What a beautiful waterwheel of merging and emerging. Most of all, we may experience a gradually developing sense of wholeness and cooperative conversation within this system and beyond our skin, accompanied by waves of gratitude for the wisdom dwelling within us.

We have also explored how embedded traumas affect the nurturance each of our systems can receive and give. Skin that remembers painful contact may become afraid to take in the emotional reassurance that comes from kind touch and reluctant to reach out to comfort others. Tight muscles are partially closed to the flow of blood that nurtures their cells and continue to send a message that danger is near. Belly brains struggle to digest both food and relationships in ways that limit health and make us wary of connecting. Hearts constrict and color our choice of partners. Eyes tense and narrow their focus so they can attend to the source of the threat, ears loosen to take in the whole environment at the expense of attending to human sounds, and the quality of our voice changes to warn everyone of threatening conditions.

Our autonomic nervous system's ongoing neuroception of some degree of danger may keep our baseline in sympathetic arousal or dorsal withdrawal, states that preclude social engagement. This closes the door to our primary nurturance—each other. The dysregulated rhythms in our brainstem affect all the systems above and make it challenging to find harmonious relationships. The emotional-motivational pathways in our midbrains shape to the experiences of the trauma. Instead of their resources being available for curious SEEKING, PLAY, CARE, and LUST, they will be more drawn to GRIEF, FEAR, and RAGE. Our cortical~neocortical world receives all this, becoming sensitive and hyper-vigilant as its perceptual lens colors our world with the anticipation of painful and frightening relationships, shaping how and when we reach out to others. Our felt sense and worded narrative about ourselves and the world is also touched by the perceptions these embedded traumas leave in their wake. The depth of pain and fear can encourage us to shift into left-centric experience for protection, a change that takes away the nurturance of relationship almost completely. Each of these shifts is wise and adaptive in light of what we have experienced, even though it has resulted in us becoming isolated with it. Without the arrival of support, we can remain caught in the continually circulating conversation among these neural streams.

At the same time, we also found celebration for the inherent health that remains alive within each of these systems even when they are burdened with extensive embedded trauma. We are so responsive to one another that the arrival of someone who can listen without judgment, agenda, or expectation may awaken the "inherent treatment plan" (Sills, 2010) that can guide the resolution of these long-held traumas. In the space between us and our people, co-suffering and co-regulation can support the emergence of this potential-health-in-waiting. In my experience, scars remain that both strengthen the injured spots and serve as reminders of former wounds. Certain areas of implicit tenderness may always remain, and these may also become resources for deepening wisdom and compassion.

If we ask about the clinical relevance of what we have learned, we might again be reminded that the practice of nonjudgmental, agenda-less attention to our bodies' communications helps prepare us to receive our people with the same openness to "what is" in this moment. In this way, we offer the emotional-relational safety that is the foundation for healing. Over time, this listening builds trust in our bodies' inherent health and movement toward healing, a valuable resource on behalf of our patients. We will likely also deepen our appreciation for the influence our system has on our people and rededicate ourselves to finding the support to both heal our own embedded traumas and to resolve the daily stress we encounter before it lodges in our limbic region and body.

As we attend to our bodies, we come into direct contact with the streams of implicit memory, refining our capacity to hear the truth-telling voices of embedded traumas that have no words to offer while also discovering the memories in need of healing in us. Then we will be better able to support our patients when the only witness to their earlier experiences is an upset stomach or tension around the heart. Our left hemispheres may want procedures and step-by-step directions for how to undo the symptoms of embedded traumas, but the wisdom of the right-centric way of attending that we are cultivating suggests that we let go of linearity in favor of fluidity. Then these well-learned methods can be allowed to flow with what is emerging in the moment rather than according to a predetermined pattern.

With every chapter, we have sought to provide our left-hemisphere emissary with stabilizing pictures of how we function, side by side with honoring the paradoxical nature of some discoveries and the overall mystery of our unknowable brains. When our left has a science-based story to hold what is happening in the emerging moment in therapy, it offers reassurance to the right in terms of both the information and the overall feeling that what is happening makes sense. Both hemispheres settle when things make sense to the left.

Along with all the ways that our own system is being reshaped by our growing awareness of the universe inside, we are also gaining the capacity to share this knowledge with our people, not so much as psychoeducation, but as bits of wisdom drawn forth from this growing storehouse to meet our people where they are. When this offering is embodied in us and arises in response to the need of the moment, there is a greater probability that it will take root in the minds, hearts, and bodies of our patients as well. The processes of their inner worlds become felt sense companions for us along this healing pathway, providing hope and regulation.

Because so many of these discoveries point in similar directions—we are built for relationship at every stage of life, there is more neuroplasticity rather than less with almost every new piece of research, our inner systems are working on our behalf at unimaginable speeds and complexity, interpersonal safety is the ground of healing—an overall pattern of unseen support arising from who we are as human beings begins to be a felt sense reality for us. It changes how we are present in the room with our people, and that changes everything.

Now let's turn for a brief visit to just three areas of exploration that we haven't had space to be with here: epigenetics, the work of the tiny glial cells that outnumber neurons 85 to 15, and the cerebrospinal fluid that guards the well-being of our brains.

Deep Roots of Memory: Epigenetics

Dreams that aren't yours
neurons firing like the war's still on
and mines set off by a word or a touch

So please be gentle with one another
and your mother and your mother's mother

—A. NEIL MEILI (2012)

We have occasionally mentioned epigenetics, a new science just being born that helps us understand and feel into the roots of memory that are deeper and more invisible than any we have known before. While implicit memory often remains the hidden substrate of our perceptions and behaviors, it can come to conscious awareness as we notice patterns and feel the inner links between our past and present. On the other hand, the shifts in gene expression in response to experience, the realm of epigenetics, lie more distant historically, having come down to us in the heart of each cell from parents, grandparents, and possibly beyond. Events and relationships that we have not personally experienced are shaping our perceptions, behaviors, choices, and quality of relationship at each moment. At the same time, each new experience we have is initiating changes in our gene expression now (for a review of the history of these discoveries, see Hurley, 2013). Changes in gene expression, called phenoptypic plasticity, runs parallel to neuroplasticity.

When we first unlocked the genetic code, we thought we might have found the essential and immutable process for who we become, only to discover that the complexity of what it is to be human is more related to the way genes express in response to the environment at a particular time. The malleability of our genes doesn't change our DNA but makes possible an almost infinite array of possible expressions. Turning to our simpler cousins, mice, we can see a clear example of how this works. Brian Dias and Kerry Ressler (2014) paired a cherrylike smell with a small shock to generate fear of this odor in mice before they conceived their offspring. This new experience induced an epigenetic change. For at least two generations, the baby mice were born with fear of this smell even though they had never had an unpleasant experience with it.

In two other studies, we see these same effects in humans. Children of Holocaust survivors who developed PTSD as a result of their experiences have lower cortisol levels day to day than offspring of survivors without PTSD or without this trauma history. These lower levels make them more vulnerable to developing PTSD as a result of any potentially traumatic experiences in their lives.[*] This gene pattern may be passed to the next generation, although more needs to be learned about this in humans (Yehuda et al., 2007). Rachel Yehuda and her colleagues found similar results for women who were pregnant and in proximity to the World Trade Center during the September 11 attacks and developed PTSD (Yehuda et al., 2009).

There is evidence for this even in the more complex case of attachment patterning. One of the seminal studies with mice suggested that high-licking mothers and low-licking mothers generated epigenetic expressions that endured through the next generation. However, if the offspring of low-licking mothers were gently handled early in life, this appeared to promote an epigenetic change in the direction of their becoming more available mothers later on (Meaney, 2001). As with our neural pathways, the malleability of gene expression allows for changes in the direction of both trauma and healing.

Cellular biologist Bruce Lipton (2008) adds an important perspective. It isn't experience that changes our gene expression, but our *perception* of experience. Our perception of the environment becomes a chemical signal in our bodies: Fear becomes cortisol and warm connection becomes oxytocin. As these signals reach our cells, they respond by moving adaptively into a state of protection or growth. We can begin

---

[*] While we associate our response to danger with heightened cortisol levels, the development of PTSD is associated with lower levels (Meewisse, Reitsma, de Vries, Gersons, & Olff, 2007). This may reflect the descent into helplessness and the onset of the dorsal response of withdrawal and collapse.

to sense how embedded trauma decreases our capacity to take in nourishment at all levels, down to our cells, while co-healing of those experiences restores our inherent capacity for growth.

How many of our own daily experiences are being touched by unseen
and unknowable influences from past generations? As clinicians, parents, partners, and fellow human beings, this awareness may deepen
our humility and kindness concerning what we believe we know about
the roots of another person's thoughts, feelings, behavior, and relational
choices. It can become a helpful practice for reducing judgment. As I
work with my people, I find I am less concerned these days with understanding the explicit history of their implicit patterns. These connections and stories often do emerge, and that can be helpful in settling our
people's left-hemisphere need for something concrete. However, if they
don't emerge or if it seems there is something beyond the connection
with what was experienced earlier in life, perhaps we can make room
for multiple influences on memory. Epigenetics is an infant science, and
we have the privilege of growing in compassion and understanding with
its emerging discoveries.

The Other Brain: Glia

This section borrows its title from a book by R. Douglas Fields (2011),
a researcher whose laboratory is devoted to studying these small cells
that companion our neurons. What follows likely has no clinical relevance for us right now beyond fostering awe at the intricacies of this
unseen world within us. However, it is just beginning to revolutionize
our thinking about how our brains work at the most fundamental level,
so this seems like an important story to follow.

A little history first. We have known for a long time that neurons
and glia share space in our brains. In fact, glia outnumber our neurons
85 to 15. However, discoveries by Santiago Ramón y Cajal in the late
1800s focused our attention on neurons, and this view became gospel
in the 1950s when advances in technology let us see neurons and their
synapses. From then on, neural processes were considered primary, and
glia (which means "glue") were relegated to support cells that cleaned up
the debris left by neural activity and wrapped axons with myelin (Fields,
2011). They were basically viewed as janitors with duct tape. This is
in part understandable, because the methods used to study neurons

attended to the way they communicated through electricity. Since glial cells don't connect that way, they appeared to be passive in regard to information processing.

Then, in the early 2000s, something surprising happened in Fields's lab.

> And here in my studies, and other studies (others were making sim-
> ilar observations) I was startled to find that information was leaving
> neurons and going into a part of the brain that involved cells that
> were not neurons, and couldn't communicate with electricity. So,
> we were wondering what this meant. (Campbell, 2010, p. 4)

As Fields and his colleagues looked more closely, they found that the information was going underground below the cortex, home of neurons, to the place where axons were being wrapped by glia. Watching more closely at this level, they found that when the neurons were actively fir-ing, the glia were also awakening and communicating with each other via calcium waves, speaking to each other in the language of chemicals rather than electricity.

Once scientists could see this conversation, their perception of glia began to change, opening the possibility of listening to what these tiny cells are actually doing (Fields & Stevens-Graham, 2002). It seems that they are the regulators, the nourishers, and the protectors of the neural activity that we believed was the main actor in processing information (De Pittà, Volman, Berry, & Ben-Jacob, 2011; Fields, 2010, 2011; Koob, 2009). One indication of their importance is that in a petri dish, neu-rons die if they aren't accompanied by glial companions. Glia don't need neurons to survive.

As far as we know, there are three groups of glia. One—Schwann cells and oligodendrocytes—is primarily responsible for the process of myelination in the skull brain and peripheral nervous system, coordinat-ing the speed of connection between associated networks of neurons. Another—the astrocytes—provides daily nourishment and supports healing when there has been injury, controls blood flow, guards the blood-brain barrier, and connects neurons into broader networks. The third group—the microglia— provides our brain with an immune sys-tem that contributes to repair when there has been injury.

Let's look at the function of the myelin producers for a moment. Far from passively wrapping axons in a more mechanical way, they respond by adding myelin as neural firing increases so that the pathways deemed most important by our perception of environmental conditions receive the greatest support. Without myelin, nerve impulses propagate very slowly, if at all, and with the insulation, transmission speeds up by about 100 times. Then a new question arises. Since what fires together wires together, how does our system coordinate impulses coming from many parts of the brain to fire together at the same time? If one group of neurons is farther away than another, how is speed of transmission modulated to provide this perfectly timed ballet that creates our multifaceted memories? Glia's control of the myelination process has to be at the core of it, regulating which neural firings are sent on and when (De Pittà et al., 2011), although more is to be learned about how this actually happens. One other aspect of myelin is that once an axon is wrapped, further sprouting of the axon stops, so no new connections can form. This is helpful for stabilizing learning and hurtful for injury recovery when new connections are crucial for regaining functioning.

As vital as the myelin producers are, the stars of the glial world are astrocytes. They actually looked like stars when they were first seen through microscopes because of how the cell staining process works. We see now that they are more like fuzzy balls of various sizes. Fields tells us some of what they do:

> So the things astrocytes do are they take up neurotransmitters, they release neurotransmitters, but they also release growth factors—which are substances that stimulate neurons to live and grow, and protect them after stress and injury. . . . Astrocytes respond to disease. So after stroke or brain injury, the first responders are astrocytes and microglia. And we can see them change their structure in their genes, and they begin to spew out different kinds of chemicals that initiate the healing process. (Campbell, 2010, p. 17)

In a very direct way, they also influence information processing and learning. Astrocytes monitor the activity in neurons, and in response to what is found, one astrocyte can wrap around as many as a hundred thousand synapses, controlling how they connect with each other. This puts a higher-level structure on our brains, drawing brain regions together to facilitate the complexities of learning something over a longer period of time. If we think about individual neurons firing, it makes sense that another process would need to link these firings into the vast networks that Pessoa (2013) describes. Until recently, no one thought these web weavers would be glia.

There's more. Astrocytes take up neurotransmitters that are left over from neural firing, making them more or less available to neurons for future firing. They have a role in the pruning of unused neurons also. They provide nutrients to feed the neural cells and control the flow of blood in the brain at the micro level. In fact, this latter contribution is how fMRI imaging works. Astrocytes are responding to neurons' need for oxygen and nutrients as they work, and they do this by controlling the diameter of capillaries. This change in blood flow is what we see in the images. In the big picture, research finds that the greater the number and size of astrocytes, the higher the intelligence. In fact, they appear to be the main reason for the increase in intelligence in humans. They tend to congregate in areas responsible for higher, more integrative thought and have particularly strong communities in areas of our specialty. As we step back a bit to take in the larger picture, it seems that our neural world would not function without the abundant and varied supports the glial underground provides.

Andrew Koob (2009), another researcher who has been captured by these tiny cells, offers an additional speculation about their function, one that is far from proven but is indeed intriguing. In recent times, scientists have found quantum behavior guiding the macroscopic world, as in the process of photosynthesis, which transforms sunlight into chemical energy (Engel, 2007). Because glia communicate via calcium waves, which are molecularly small enough to possibly operate according to quantum rules, Koob wonders if the underlying glial world holds all the wavelike possibilities that collapse into a single manifestation at the level of neural firing. To say it another way, he wonders if the neurons are there to support what the glia are doing.

Sometimes new discoveries are enjoyable just for their own sake, even without them leading to any particular change in how we do things. It must be satisfying for our SEEKING system to explore new territory. For me, reading about glia literally makes my brain feel different in a positive way, more substantial, more supported, more filled with the wisdom of multiple systems working continuously on our behalf.

Sweet Restorative Sleep:
Our Cerebrospinal Fluid's Night Work

Scientists have long wondered why sleeping has been conserved by evolution, because in earlier times sleeping in the wild was such a dangerous activity. We have learned that memories consolidate, events of the day and our lives get processed, and chemicals that repair our bodies are released to do their work. A new discovery about what is happening when we sleep may be the strongest reason we need to let go of conscious processing each day.

Dr. Maikin Nedergaard's research has revealed that when mice (and probably humans, too, although this research is yet to done) go to sleep, their brain cells shrink and make room for more of the pristine cerebrospinal fluid to flow to every corner of the brain (Konnikovajan, 2014). The increase may be up to 60 percent. As it makes its way along these expanded channels that surround blood vessels, it can go much deeper in the brain, gathering up and carrying away the debris that is generated in abundance in the active thinking we do when awake. Beta amyloid, implicated in Alzheimer's disease, is one of the waste products, so a good night's sleep may be actively working to prevent this kind of cognitive decline. In light of the section just above, it may not be surprising that this process is under the control of our glia—and thus called the glymphatic system.

We are ending on this note because we Americans are a dramatically sleep-deprived people who are also living longer. This is an encouragement for each of us to get our deep rest regularly. It is also a beautiful example of the wisdom of our embodied brain's numerous systems of support, waiting to work on our behalf if we give them the time and space to do it. Now we'll move on to some other ways we can prepare ourselves to be present with our people.

Section II

How We Attend

14

Disorder and Adaptation

Now that we are gradually settling into a richer felt sense of the beauty and sensitivity of our embodied brains, particularly their responsiveness to relationships past and present, in the next few chapters we will consider how our way of perceiving our patients has a profound effect on their experience of themselves and the way they move into relationship with us. Our offer of "I see you" is followed by their response: "I am here." This act of reflection is not primarily a cognitive process, not what we think about this person, but instead is rooted in how we experience ourselves and our fellow human beings through the lens of the unique implicit cellar that guides our moment-to-moment perceptions.

Changing places, let's see if we can step into our own experience of being patients for a bit. We may be able to feel how profoundly sensitive we are to the inner world of our helpers at multiple levels. In a microsecond after catching sight of them, we will have a neuroception of how safe the environment is for us in this moment and move into or away from relationship accordingly (Porges, 2011). Usually, this happens invisibly at speeds that prevent it from becoming conscious. Our attachment system, carrying the burdens and gifts of previous experience, responds to the way our therapists offer connection, shaping our approach to them (Cozolino, 2014). At the same time, our resonance circuitry encodes their emotional and bodily state and their intention, along with our sensory experience of them—how they look and sound, at a minimum (Iacoboni, 2009). They are becoming part of our developing inner landscape, a presence that fosters or hinders ongoing neural integration (Badenoch, 2011). In short, how we are attended to shapes the next emerging relational moment and influences the course our connection takes.

Iain McGilchrist (2009) says something quite powerful about how we see one another.

> Attention is not just another "function" alongside other cognitive functions. Its ontological status is of something prior to functions and even to things. The kind of attention we bring to bear on the world changes the nature of the world we attend to, the very nature of the world in which those "functions" would be carried out, and in which those "things" would exist. Attention changes *what kind of* a thing comes into being for us: in that way it changes the world . . . In all these circumstances, you will also have a quite different experience not just of me [the one attending], but of yourself: you would feel changed if I changed the type of my attention. And yet nothing *objectively* has changed. (p. 28)

Here, we are going to consider how seeing our people as having a "disorder" calls forth a different *person* in them than experiencing them as adaptive. Let's begin with sensing how these two perspectives feel in our bodies.

Pause for Reflection

This would be a particularly helpful reflection to do with a friend or reading partner. See if you can experience yourself from the viewpoint of having a disorder or being disordered. "I have an anxiety disorder." "I am dissociative." After settling into this, spend some time sharing what you discovered. What happens in your body? How do you feel and think about yourself? How familiar and comfortable are you with this way of seeing yourself? These are just preliminary explorations and may not lead to clear inner responses right away, so gentleness and acceptance of whatever comes is helpful.

What happens if someone else sees you that way and speaks these words to you: "You have an anxiety disorder." "You are dissociative." After you have both had the opportunity to sample the "I" and "you" perspectives, see what happens if you experience yourselves instead as continually adapting to the internal and external conditions that arrive. Again, what happens in your body, thoughts, feelings, and comfort level with this perspective? There are no right or wrong answers—only the gentle awareness of what uniquely happens for you.

As with just about everything we've explored so far in this book, both the perspective of disorder and of adaptation can have an upside and downside. Being seen as disordered has a tendency to provoke the sense that there is something wrong with us, something that perhaps needs to be fixed. When that observation is offered by another, there can be a kind of objectification of the person that may lead to a felt sense of separation rather than connection. Disorders are a collection of symptoms based on discrete pieces of data boiled down into an overall picture that likely doesn't apply to any individual exactly or continuously. Once we have been settled into a category by the one observing us, curiosity about what else might be here, the sense of the uniqueness of the person, and fluid contact with the emerging moment may all be limited or lost. In general, the perspective of disorder arises from a more left-centric way of attending, so it isn't surprising that there can be both a quality of judgment and felt sense of disconnection. One of my people shared this about her experience with a previous therapist: "When he said I had an adjustment disorder, I felt boxed up and dealt with in some way. He had me figured out, so I felt little inclination to share anything that didn't match his belief about me. I wonder now if I just abandoned myself." My thought at the time was that without any intention to do so, her therapist may actually have abandoned her, in all her uniqueness and complexity.

On the other hand, for both patient and therapist, there can be a sense of greater settledness with a diagnosis in place. Our left hemispheres bring us certain gifts—stability, predictability, clarity, and relative simplicity compared to the teeming unknowability of the ever-emerging right. Our patients sometimes find that a previous sense of "just being crazy" is quieted by a diagnosis that gives their upset a recognizable shape. At the same time, we clinicians may find comfort and relief from anxiety in the process of putting a boundary around our patients' distress, while also creating some cognitive distance between them and us so we do not feel so overwhelmed as we continue to resonate with their inner world.

There is an additional pressure. Currently, the culture of our profession demands that we diagnose in finer and finer ways, especially if we want to be paid by insurance. Each edition of the *Diagnostic and Statistical Manual of Mental Disorders* earnestly seeks to enumerate with greater accuracy the symptoms of particular patterns of mental illness, often identifying subtypes through noticing that people with a given diagnosis aren't all alike. As the categories proliferate and narrow, there is a tacit sense that the pressures of individuality are trying to crack open the boxes, but the needs of the left-centric system can only respond by creating ever-smaller boxes.

It isn't primarily the process of identifying a diagnosis that disturbs the ground of safety and openness with our patients. Often, this is just something that has to be done and may have little influence on how we see our people. However, if at a deep level we experience them as disordered, mentally ill, and diseased, that will often call forth in them a part who likely already believes they are damaged goods. Shame, protectiveness, and helpless/hopeless feelings are often nearby companions of this perception, making connection more challenging. We may also notice that the tendency to insist on diagnosis gets stronger as the symptoms become more challenging for us. When we say, "He has borderline personality disorder," there can be a sense of putting up a shield between his inner disruption and us. In this case, diagnosis can become a weapon that annihilates any chance of connection.

The roots of this view of others often reflect our implicit sense of ourselves. How many times do we think, feel, or do something and hear "What's wrong with me?" or "What's wrong with you?" in our minds? Something fractures inside us as we judge and then often want to push away the part of us who just transgressed some value we or society holds. A left-shifted culture urges us toward perfection, happiness, and a set of values that prioritize tasks, behavior, success, self-reliance, and constant improvement. We might pause here for a moment to feel what happens in our bodies just reading that list. We may sense there is an embedded trauma here expressing itself through this protective unkindness toward ourselves when we ask, "What's wrong with me?" If we are harsh in our judgments, maybe we will be goaded back onto the path of conformity with what society requires. Attaching—being part of—is so core to who we are as human beings that these cruel voices may be trying to adaptively herd us back into line.

Pause for Reflection

What happens for us as we begin to consider that the critical voices that bring on so much pain may be adaptive? Is there a shift in body, mind, and emotion? Do we feel drawn or resistant to this possibility? Does our body feel one way and our mind say something else? Does curiosity about how this might be so begin to awaken? As always, there are no right/wrong, better/worse answers here, only the opportunity to listen and sense what is true for us in this moment. From this place of vulnerability, we may be able to slowly, slowly deepen into understanding the roots of our experience. In these moments, the cruel voices of judgment and rejection may begin to soften into the movement toward gently accepting ourselves in all our complexity and confusion, simplicity and clarity, just as we are in this moment. This is a lifetime's work.

We are going to begin our consideration of adaptation with a broad and perhaps challenging statement. It may be possible that we have always been and always will be adapting to internal and external conditions. If this is true, then regardless of how a perception or behavior influences our outside life, we can't call it maladaptive. From the viewpoint of its effect on the course of our current life, it can certainly be seen and experienced as hurtful or limiting. However, when we broaden our perspective to include the implicit pain and fear being protected, we may be able to gain a sense of its current necessity.

Over the years, a number of my people have protected themselves through self-injury. Coming from a deeply held belief that the intention behind these behaviors is adaptive rather than destructive, I offer to listen for the value of these actions. Over time, each person has eventually been able to come into contact with his or her unique story about how this form of protection has helped. "When I cut myself, I see that I'm alive because I don't feel alive." "When I plunge myself into freezing water, the self-hatred is less and I let myself live another day." Our own protective instinct is no doubt to want these behaviors to stop so the suffering can be less for our people. However, the shortest road to this happening may be through coming into relationship with the part who views this action as absolutely essential *given the current context of the implicitly held trauma that has been touched and awakened, and the perceived level of outer support in this moment.*

Our growing felt sense understanding of the need for these protections opens the path toward warm, nonintrusive curiosity about the pain and fear being so fiercely guarded. It can potentially draw us toward healing these deeper wounds and then, also adaptively, the protections that may have been bringing more pain can gradually become oriented toward current life rather than based on the needs of the inner, implicitly held trauma. When our left hemisphere holds this picture of the primacy of adaptation, we can begin to sense the value of every part of every person even when our left hemisphere doesn't have the explicit details yet. We become less inclined to just push away those protective parts.

Here's a story of that experience. One of my people kept herself consistently withdrawn from others and was aware that she also felt lonely most of the time. Understandably, she became quite frustrated with herself for not "just getting out there." I certainly sensed that she would be a wonderful friend for almost anyone. Coming from trust that her reclusiveness must make adaptive sense in the big picture, we began to see her frustration as a protection that was urging her to be more social and her withdrawal as a guardian of some pain and fear we couldn't see quite yet. So we welcomed both, and that opened the door to curiosity about the underlying embedded trauma. Following the signals her body gave her whenever she contemplated going toward others with any kind of vulnerability, we arrived at early paradoxical experiences of her being both safe (from the violence) and terrified (of the rage between her parents) when she was alone in her room. It became clear to us that until those locked-away experiences of isolated terror were met and held by us, any approach to the outside world raised the threat that she would begin to feel that terror again. Over the many months that these embedded traumas healed, her protections continued to adapt, gradually shifting from isolating her and being angry about her continued aloneness to wisely and cautiously approaching new relationships. The rigidity required by the terror gave way to a flowing and respectful sense that some people might be safe companions.

Our capacity to place ourselves in this broad context of seeing ourselves as adaptive then and adaptive now arises out of a more right-centric way of attending. It brings with it the impulse to get into relationship with whatever is present in the moment, including our apparently harmful protections. We are more prone to listen than to assess, to acknowledge than judge. Porges (2011) would say that these are important elements for emotional safety, which is the bedrock of healing. One of his statements that has been most influential for me is that so many of the actions to which we assign motivation—"You're reading the mail while I talk because you aren't interested in me"— actually reflect the mail-reading person's nervous system response to ever-shifting neuroceptions of safety and danger (Porges, 2013). These responses take into account both the outer environment and whatever is implicitly awakening internally. Perhaps the person who has turned toward the mail heard something specific below the level of conscious awareness that scared him or her, or is feeling overwhelmed by the intimacy of the sharing, or is simply tired. From this viewpoint, these autonomic nervous system (ANS) responses are fully adaptive to keep us safe, not a judgment about the person we are with.

In general, the more painful and frightening the embedded trauma, the more profound the need for protection, and often, the more hurtful to current life that guardian may be. It is such a paradox and may call up in us an ever-stronger need to have the protection stop, especially when it manifests as self-harm and suicidal thoughts or actions by our patients. When the lives of our people are threatened, we must take action to modify the intensity of the protection. We may be able to do that while also acknowledging that the system currently believes fully that these actions are needed at this moment. In my experience, just that acknowledgment often allows the protective part to feel seen and aids in the reduction of intensity because help has arrived for the intolerable pain and fear beneath.

If this perspective seems to be valuable, how do we move in the direction of it becoming the way we experience the world? Not surprisingly, we need to begin with ourselves, and this is no easy process. We can offer to listen for the parts of us that are eager to push away what we may have called "maladaptive" behaviors, like eating to excess when anxious, getting angry with our loved ones, or falling into shame at the slightest criticism. This new understanding asks us to notice our impulse to push away these feelings and behaviors with a gesture of rejection, and instead change that gesture to one of inclusion.

Pause for Reflection

Let's slowly explore the felt sense of these gestures. Calling to mind and body one of our least favorite protections, feel the understandable and adaptive impulse to push it away, make it stop. If we allow that impulse to take its natural behavioral course, it may become something like an arm extended to shove it away from us. We can begin the process of inclusion by fully feeling into that gesture and acknowledging its protective intent—it doesn't want us to feel the discomfort of these protections we don't like. It can be helpful to take some time with this, sensing how this gesture also activates our belly, chest, muscles, nervous system, and eyes, along with other bodily responses. Again, the paradox. We can feel the value of this protection even while acknowledging these activations.

Now we can move to the next layer and focus our attention on the protection we wanted to push away. What happens to that protection when it is rejected? Does it go away quietly, push back, or transform into something else? It may do a fourth thing we haven't even imagined here, but the disliked feeling or behavior will respond to the gesture of rejection in some way. Because this process may be unfamiliar, clarity may not come right away. We are just beginning to develop a pathway toward radical inclusiveness, so being gentle with ourselves is most helpful. If we notice we have judgments about our performance, that awareness can begin another round of exploring the gesture of rejection.

After we have done as much as we can with the action of rejection, let's allow our bodies to show us what a gesture of inclusion might look and feel like. For me, it is the movement of my curved, extended arm toward my body as though I am gathering in something/someone precious to me. What feels just right to you? As we explore this, we can notice how this action activates belly, chest, muscles, nervous system, and eyes—and whatever else may be responding in our bodies.

When we feel settled with that, we can invite this gesture to begin to draw the protection we dislike close to us. Any response we have is valuable, including one of disgust, hatred, shame, or automatic rejection. "Welcome and entertain them all!" as the Sufi poet Rūmī says in "The Guest House" (Rūmī, 1270/2004, p. 109). If there is a substantial reaction, let's also pause to acknowledge the power of this process, and, if you have a friend or reading partner with you, co-regulate with one another by sharing what is happening and being received without judgment. After that, we can begin again with the gesture of inclusion. If we get to the point of actually welcoming this part of us, let's notice if warm curiosity about the meaning and necessity of this protection is a possibility. We are literally building a new neural highway that will gradually be able to carry the experience of adaptation and radical inclusiveness into our daily life.

Given the healing potential of developing this perspective, what is the possible downside? As we may sense from the reflection we just did, getting settled into this way of perceiving asks a lot of us. We are challenging not only a basic human impulse to push away what is painful, but also society's preference for judgment and blame. As we bring this perspective to our patients, they, too, may find it runs against so much of what they have always believed about themselves.

Developing radical inclusiveness is not primarily a cognitive process. Neuroscience gives us support for making a case that our protective feelings and behaviors are adaptive both then and now, so we may be able to accept this premise fairly easily. However, this alone isn't enough to change how we perceive and receive our people and ourselves. The important movement is toward the embodied acceptance of "what is" as being meaningful and valuable even when we don't understand it or like it. When we are confronted with protections that are doing active harm to our patients, there is such a delicate balance between accepting these actions as meaningful and protecting our patients from their protections. As a result, the downside is not so much about this perspective on adaptation itself as the need for us to be gentle with ourselves as we slowly move down the path toward a profound level of vulnerable inclusiveness, recognizing that it is likely a lifetime's work in progress.

How might disorder and adaptation work together, since our right-centric way of attending values both/and rather than either/or? Perhaps we could approach diagnosis not as a series of small, confining boxes but as a set of fuzzy lines that point us toward a general sense of how our people have adapted to the suffering in their lives. We might be able to let go of the word "disorder" to see these categories as a way our left-hemisphere emissary can support some focused attention on particular adjustments their systems have made in an effort to survive isolating experiences of pain and fear. Then, rather than diagnosis becoming a left-centric strategy that fosters separation, it might become a support for clarity and deepening empathy.

We will conclude this chapter with a beautiful example of the healing potential of this paradigm-shifting perspective that we are adaptive rather than disordered, one that is beginning to change the face of addiction treatment. In the late 1970s, Bruce Alexander (1987; Alexander, Beyerstein, Hadaway, & Coambs, 1981) was asking an out-of-the-box question in regard to research on drug addiction. Is the drug itself the source of addictive behavior in caged mice, or might their predilection for the substance have to do with the conditions of the experiment itself? In other words, is addiction a medical problem/disorder or is it an adaptation to conditions? And thus Rat Park was born.

Here is the story. As an experimental psychologist between 1960 and 1980, Alexander observed the behavior of rats in cages, called Skinner boxes because they kept their small subjects from any contact with each other for the sake of controlling the experiment in behavior modification. When they were offered morphine in unlimited quantities, the rats eagerly took it until they died. Most scientists then concluded that this proved that certain drugs are addictive by nature in rats and humans. Alexander's different hypothesis seems to have sprung from his growing empathy for the caged rats, social creatures by nature, who seemed tormented by their isolation. He reasoned that humans placed in solitary go crazy and would be happy to consume mind-numbing drugs as well (Alexander, 2010b).

Based on this dawning curiosity, he and his colleagues built Rat Park, a large area strewn with everything rats enjoy and populated by rats of both sexes (and very soon, their babies). Sweetened water (rats have a sweet tooth) with morphine and plain water were readily available. Some rats sampled the morphine concoction occasionally, but then returned to the plain water while continuing their joyous lives together. Even previously addicted rats were less drawn to the morphine water when they were turned loose in Rat Park, enduring some withdrawal symptoms to be more available for the joy of companionship. It appeared that rats prefer connection to drugs, and can even consume some of these drugs without becoming addicted (Alexander, 2010a). Because some follow-up experiments didn't get the same results (while some did), Alexander and his colleagues had difficulty getting their research published, and once it was published in a small journal, it still wasn't taken seriously.

After sitting with this defeat for a while, Alexander began to wonder about evidence in humans and turned his attention to the results of colonization of native peoples in western Canada (Alexander, 2010a). Robbed of their natural environment, their culture, and often their children, these people experienced feelings of loss, isolation, dislocation, rage, and helplessness—not unlike rats locked in a Skinner box. Prior to such spiritual and social trauma and incarceration (being placed on reservations), the native peoples exhibited no tendency toward addiction. Once these events occurred, addiction (beginning with easily available alcohol) was almost universal. Even more telling, he found that in the absence of addictive substances, the people so devastated by the loss of their way of life exhibited many of the symptoms of addiction anyway: They stopped doing work and no longer cared for their families. In spite of all the obstacles he has encountered, Bruce Alexander has continued to be the voice for the adaptive nature of addiction when the cage of the culture creates a "hyperindividualistic, hypercompetitive, frantic, crisis-ridden society [that] makes most people feel social (*sic*) and culturally isolated" (Alexander, 2010a, para. 34). Johann Hari (2015a, 2015b) has now become one additional voice speaking strongly about addiction as an adaptation to the felt sense of isolation, slowly influencing how we perceive and treat the burgeoning number of addicts responding to the stress and loneliness of this left-shifted society. It is worth repeating Hari's words that were quoted in Chapter 1: "For a century, we've been singing war songs about addicts; we should have been singing love songs to them all along." Bruce Alexander's work on addiction as an adaptive strategy is finding acknowledgment after almost fifty years.[*]

How we attend to the world, each other, and ourselves does matter. As McGilchrist and the indigenous people of Africa remind us, we call forth in others what we see in them—"I see you" and "I am here." Receiving people as continually adaptive because we have done the work to embody the knowing that this is true for us and for all gives them and us a solid foundation of hope and respect on which we can both stand throughout our work.

---

[*] Another pioneer in shifting how we understand and treat addiction is Canadian physician Gabor Maté. He also places addiction in the context of the culture. *In the Realm of Hungry Ghosts* (2010) provides the basis for compassionate understanding of our compulsions, leveling the playing field between those who are perceived to be addicts and the rest of us.

15

Inherent Wisdom
and Implicit Memory

Our next way of preparing ourselves to attend so that we are supporting safety and vulnerability for our people is a little different than the contrast between disorder and adaptation. Rather than considering alternative viewpoints, it involves expanding our perspective to hold two potentially opposing angles of vision in our minds and bodies at once, which is never an easy task, particularly for left-mode processing. Some of us who have been doing this work for a long time may have an advantage here because we have experienced and internalized so many iterations of the movement from pain and fear to healing that we may already have at least an implicit sense of the *inherent health* that lies within each of us as well as the profound power of *implicit memory holding embedded trauma* as it continuously shapes our perceptions, actions, thoughts, and feelings. We may also have experienced that the presence of receptive and responsive relationship is the indispensable ingredient that offers what is needed for health to manifest and cultivates conditions for healing implicit memory. As we are discovering, if we make this awareness explicit and deepen into our own experience of both the availability of inherent health and the power of implicit memory, our left-hemisphere emissary may be able to more easily support keeping both perspectives alive in our minds as well as our bodies. This often allows us to hold onto our trust in the inherent wisdom of our people's system even in the midst of the necessary co-suffering that comes when strong implicit experiences are awakening.

Early on in my own practice, I began to appreciate the power of implicit memory to shape our perceptions when I met with a young man who experienced himself as ugly and unlovable. That isn't what I saw. My perception was that he was good-looking in a swarthy sort of way, with deep eyes that easily shared his suffering. I actually felt drawn to him, not only through compassion for his suffering, but because I sensed the kindness that was evident in the way he talked about everyone but himself. The dichotomy between our two perceptual worlds was upsetting for my body, and I had an impulse to try to correct the way he saw himself.

Fortunately, my supervisor during my first year of practice was a wise and gentle man who helped me sit with my own discomfort long enough to be curious about how this self-rejection had been fostered in my patient's childhood. In essence, my supervisor was supporting me to endure my own discomfort in order to feel my resonance with this young man more clearly. In my immaturity (even though I was forty-eight years old), I moved into his suffering to an extent that I began to feel how broken he was because of the way he had been continuously disliked by his parents. At the time, feeling his brokenness was helpful in that I began to be able to sit quietly with his suffering rather than follow the impulse to insist that his self-perception change. At the same time, I believe I lost sight of the inherent health that lived side by side with his pain, and because of the power of our resonance circuitry, I may have inadvertently helped him lose sight of it as well for a time. We went through some months when we both lived so fully within his early experience that we felt that the weight of his emotional abandonment might have crushed any possibility of him reaching out toward connection again. In those moments, I was unable to inwardly hold the conviction, and through resonance reflect to him, that his capacity for attachment was still alive within him.

Having this felt sense of the power of the implicit has been an invaluable companion throughout practice, but it needed the gradual development of its complementary perspective of inherent health for me to begin to more fully hold people in both their woundedness and inborn resilience. Deepening into the inherent wisdom of our systems has been a slow development that was significantly enhanced when interpersonal neurobiology and relational neuroscience became central to my understanding of what it is to be human (Cozolino, 2014; Schore, 2012; Siegel, 2015b).

One of the gifts offered by seeing from these two perspectives at once is that we are less likely to be drawn into the need to control the process, to intervene, to fix, all of which are adaptive responses to the anxiety that may arise when we are in the tentative, liminal movement of therapy. Without the support of trust in the wisdom of our people's system and the inherent health underneath the symptoms, we may feel quite uncertain about the outcome. The sympathetic arousal that accompanies our anxious need to take control may move us toward left-centric dominance, often manifesting as the urge to craft interventions. When this happens, safety and connection diminish as our social engagement system is no longer available. Similarly, a deepened understanding of the processes of implicit memory may also help us trust the felt sense veracity of the experiences our people are bringing. We will be less likely to see thinking as disordered or emotional and bodily responses as maladaptive or out of proportion. This kind of broad receptivity is the very ground on which healing rests.

Let's begin by talking a bit about these two perspectives. How might we picture inherent health? Beginning with some specific examples, we know that the circuitry of PLAY lingers in our midbrain, no matter how our experience of play may have been stunted, and this playfulness will spring into joyous life as our felt sense of connection grows (Panksepp & Biven, 2012). A man in his mid-fifties taught me about this natural emergence. "I never expected that to happen," he said to me. I had made some sort of silly joke, and we laughed so hard we had tears running down our faces. Now, in a quieter moment, he was reflecting on how unexpected this joyous eruption was for him. The silence grew deeper in that moment as he listened inwardly for the meaning of this experience that somehow felt so important. Very quietly, he said, "You know, when I came here, I believed I would never laugh again, so I believe this means I'm getting better. How can laughing at a stupid joke mean that?" I don't remember what I said in response that day, but now I understand that this burst of joy was the awakening of his PLAY system as we began to get more connected, and he had rightly sensed that it was a sign of healing. Together, we had been moving through the extremely painful territory of early abuse by a drunken father and neglect by a terrified and dissociated mother. Suddenly, the sun came out as the growing connection between us fostered steps toward healing. Once his system came to trust our joining, the playfulness that had been waiting all the time was touched and awakened in the space between us. Once there, it became the spice sprinkled in with the challenging painful work we were doing, a way to remember that he was tapping into the core of inherent health side by side with the suffering.

As another example, we also know that our nervous system retains its preference for social engagement even when it has spent most of its time in sympathetic arousal or dorsal collapse (Porges, 2011). Even people who have experienced dramatic early abuse, who have spent little time in anything but sympathetic and dorsal adaptations to threat, will gradually respond to our offer of ventral presence with a slowly expanding window of tolerance. Three seconds in ventral gradually becomes one minute, then two, then often goes back to one before suddenly expanding to five blessed minutes. The process isn't linear, but the change is unmistakable over time because our inherent capacity for social engagement has just been awaiting the arrival of support from another.

Our belly brain also begins to remember how to digest and support immune health as soon as our autonomic nervous system feels safe enough to spend regular time in ventral (Porges, 2011). Our right orbitofrontal cortex and amygdala always have the capacity to find one another and begin to weave the circuitry of warm attachment and emotional regulation into our system as soon as someone with a well-woven brain arrives to activate these patterns of connection (Siegel, 2015b). At one level, this is neuroplasticity in action, but guiding the development of these neural pathways are deep resources of inherent health that are not destroyed when potential traumas embed, although they may be undeveloped or expressing in ways shaped by those neural processes.

As we have seen, at the beginning of life, so much that is inherent in us flowers in the context of the receptive and reflective presence of another. We retain our responsiveness to this interpersonal yeast throughout our lives. To draw on a different metaphor, this is why therapy is more like gardening than manufacturing. Rather than applying certain algorithms to get certain outcomes, we water the seeds of what is already uniquely present in each person and lovingly watch over what wants to grow. Keeping this felt sense of the near availability of inherent health in view can foster hope as the necessary co-suffering that accompanies healing emerges.

Side by side with this growing confidence in the wisdom of our embodied system, it is helpful to also deepen our awareness of how our encoded implicit memories shape our perceptions in ways that often elude conscious awareness while influencing every thought, feeling, behavior, and relationship. The development of this perceptual lens begins with conception in ways we are just beginning to understand, including discoveries being made by the burgeoning science of epigenetics and the better-known influence of our mother's emotional and physical state (for a review of the research, see Weinstein, 2016). In the early days after birth, we build on these seminal implicit-only encodings in a way that provides significant foundational organization for our ongoing experience (Schore, 2012; Siegel, 2015b). The depth and pervasiveness of this process is challenging to fully appreciate because it creates the invisible glasses that color our world and are simply experienced as "what is." Then, throughout our lives, we accumulate many more implicit than explicit memories (Riener, 2011), building a rich and completely individual library of perceptual guidance that shapes what we see and how we see it. There is no stepping away from this multifaceted lens. These embodied memories hold the full spectrum, from the felt sense of those encoded experiences that support the sense of hope and goodness in us and the world, to those that contain the remnants of frightening and painful experiences. The former integrate more fully throughout our brains, providing easy access to what sustains us, while the latter are tucked away in subcortical and bodily pathways, awaiting healing (Jovasevic et al., 2015). The two themes of inherent health and implicit memory come together as we consider the wisdom embodied in the processes of how potential traumas embed and how they always remain available for healing.

As we begin this exploration, we are going to call on one of the leitmotifs from the last chapter—radical inclusiveness—to support us in experiencing the arrival of painful implicit memories just a little differently than ever before. Instead of our natural impulse to dislike them and want to push them away, we can perhaps gradually cultivate an appreciation for the truth they bring and the way they offer a pathway toward healing. At the same time, we can perhaps also acknowledge that opening to receptivity of the painful and frightening is no easy task, given the suffering that often accompanies these awakenings. Our ability to extend welcome may well rest on trust in the inherent wisdom in the way these embodied memories are encoded, stored, and retrieved. As we will see, they are patiently holding the key to changing our daily felt sense experience of embedded traumas. Let's briefly review what we know about implicit memory as a starting place.

Bearing in mind that every memory has an implicit layer, here are some of the more significant aspects of this kind of memory for us. You may wish to spend some time with each of these qualities, pausing to reflect on how you experience them. There are some questions at the end of each statement as a beginning. Dropping each one into your right hemisphere and pausing to listen will allow your deeper mind to offer what it can in this moment. Reflecting on experiences in this way will help the concepts live differently than simply reading the list.

- These kinds of memories are embodied as behavioral impulses, bodily sensations, surges of emotion, and perceptions, usually encoded with snippets of sensory experience that occurred at the same moment (such as the smell of cookies, the angle of the afternoon light, the scratchy sensation of Grandpa's beard, and more) (Siegel, 2015b). They gather up information from the neural streams arising from our body's experience of events. *Can you get in touch with your behavioral impulse when something unexpected comes your way, when you are surprised?*
- When we have the same kinds of implicit experience over and over, they become what we might call embodied anticipations,* flows of expectation about how life will unfold for us, held mostly out of conscious awareness (Siegel, 2015b). They guide our perceptions, thoughts, actions, and particularly our relationships. *What comes to you about your embodied anticipation as you approach new relationships?*
- As infants, we are able to form behavioral, perceptual, and emotional memories (Bauer, 1996; Fivush & Hudson, 1990), and for the first twelve to eighteen months of life, implicit is the only kind of memory available for encoding.† Then, while the capacity for explicit and

---

* These expectations are often called mental models. However, that sounds too cognitive for the actual experience, which is one of embodying the next step in the dance. For that reason, embodied anticipation seems to better reflect this process.

† That being said, several of my people have reported clear explicit memories all the way back to the womb. Experiences at odds with this nascent science of brain and mind can be our guides toward more expansive curiosity about what it is to be human.

autobiographical memory slowly develops, implicit encoding remains the dominant mode until we are about four or five years of age, the time when many securely attached people report being able to offer a more connected narrative. *Do you have a sense of the age when you began to experience your narrative emerging?*

- Implicit memory encodes without us needing to consciously attend to the experience, while explicit memory requires conscious attention (Squire, Knowlton, & Musen, 1993). Riener (2011) reminds us that we encode 11 million bits of sensory information per second perceptually (implicitly) while encoding six to fifty bits consciously (explicitly). While it is difficult to know exactly what this means for us, it does suggest that we are being shaped implicitly in profound ways, below the level of conscious awareness. It seems quite likely that we are making many more implicit memories than explicit. *What is it like for you to get in touch with the overwhelming flood of implicit compared to explicit experience that is available to us?*

- While implicit memory often remains below conscious awareness, when we practice attending to our patterns of activation, sensation, and behavioral impulses, these memories can come into consciousness. *Can you recall a time when you became aware of an implicit pattern as just that—"I respond this way because that is what I had to do to stay connected to my father."*

- Experiences of warm, responsive, nurturing care live on implicitly in our bodies and provide the foundation for a sense of life's burgeoning possibilities. When we revisit these experiences, the neural nets strengthen with each firing so we have a reservoir of inner resource with us always. *Can you make room for a number of these lovely sensations to move through your body?*

- When we have experiences of fear and pain that don't have enough support to integrate, implicit memory is held mainly in subcortical circuits and the body (Jovasevic et al., 2015), becoming embedded traumas awaiting support for integration in the future. *Does an example of such an embedding process come to you easily? If not, that's okay, too. The awareness will come when we're ready for it.*

- As traumas embed, time stops for the parts of us who experienced these events. *Do you have a felt sense of this? Again, we can open to this without needing to push for it to happen.*

- When implicit memory associated with embedded trauma is touched and awakened in our bodies and perceptions, it is experienced as happening in the present moment, often without our being aware that it has origins in the past (Siegel, 2015b). In this way, we might call implicit memory "the eternally present past" (Badenoch, 2011, p. 8). *Does a time like this come to you easily?*

- The felt-sense quality of implicit memory as well as our understanding of the meaning of the behaviors generated by the implicit can change through the process of memory reconsolidation, often fostered within warm, responsive relationships (Ecker, Ticic, & Hulley, 2012). We will explore this process in detail in Chapter 20. *Are you aware of having a memory's feeling state change through the support of another?*

- Implicit memory never becomes episodic explicit memory because the latter has a time stamp so that we have the sensation that it is over. To avoid confusion, we might say that implicit memory comes into conscious awareness rather than that it becomes explicit. In the process of integrating embedded traumas, however, the implicit memories that encode during healing experiences become interwoven with the explicit aspects of the memory (when these are available). At that point, there is a *knowing* that the events from before are over (explicit) even while we continue to *experience* the sensations and behavioral impulses from the healing experience in the present moment (implicit). For example, in the place of fear, we now feel safe and protected when we explicitly recall the original events; in the place of shame, we feel the warmth of acceptance. We could say that the implicit past is gradually transformed into the implicit present during the healing process, which goes on to become a healed implicit past as time moves on. The experience is something like this: When we recall a healing experience in which fear was transmuted into safety through the presence of another, it will awaken the feeling of protection in our bodies that never recedes into the past, which is really quite a blessing. This change will likely be accompanied by shifts in behavior from actions based on greater fearfulness to ones that reflect more openness to relationship. In this way, as healing experiences accumulate, our reservoir of supportive implicit sensations and perceptions, along with our deepened understanding and the accompanying change in behavior, continues to expand into an increasingly firm foundation for a life of meaning, hope, and relational richness. *Perhaps you have experienced this as you have touched some painful or frightening places and found that the listening presence of a therapist or friend has brought a felt-sense change in that memory. Is it possible to return to the felt sense of that experience now?*

Pause for Reflection

By combining reading and reflecting with each of these statements, our capacity for hemispheric integration is being supported. We are nourishing our left hemisphere with information that may help steady us in the storms of co-suffering while also making it easier to offer this wisdom in the most helpful way with our people. It is this living, embodied knowledge that will guide us to notice when that right empathic moment emerges inviting us to share some small bit of information. This might be a good time to return to the list again, making even more room to deepen into your experience of the concepts. If you are working with a reading partner, sharing these experiences will allow you both to deepen even further.

Our implicit memories encode in a similar but more foundational way at the beginning of life than when we are a little older and our embodied brains have become more differentiated. While our autonomic nervous systems (Field, Diego, & Hernandez-Reif, 2006), amygdala (Qiu et al., 2015), and other systems have already been developing in utero in parallel with our mother's emerging experience, the transition to the vastness of the outside world places us face to face with this precious person and others for the first time. Our system is open, vulnerable, and eager to make connection. At that stage, our neocortex, subcortical regions, and many of the associated embodied streams are mostly a sea of neurons, carrying the richness of our individuality, awaiting the reflection of another to shape that individuality *in ways that let us stay connected with one another.* That does seem to be the outcome and perhaps the underlying purpose of our responsiveness to the gaze and perception of another—to remain in connection no matter what.

These earliest relationships lay down core relational patterns that are The (implicit) Truth about who we are and how relationships unfold for us. Similar experiences with our parents likely played out over and over, deeply engraining the felt sense of what it is to attach. This relational encoding combines with our inborn temperament to establish a

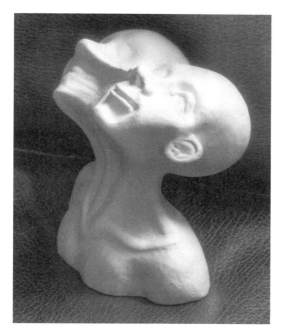

FIGURE 15.1 This beautiful sculpture (made for sand tray) can give us the sense of the movement from formless to form, as nascent possibilities take on solid expression, through reflection—"I see you." "I am here." Sculpture by Bagamiayaabikwe.

baseline of what is perceptually real for us. At the same time, the surrounding culture is also implicitly and continuously shaping both us and our parents. The richness and complexity of these intertwining layers of encoded experience can't be cognitively grasped but perhaps can be intuitively sensed. Because we are in such different states as adults as we read this now, it may be challenging to fully experience the pervasiveness of the perceptual lens that takes shape, even though it is the ground we are standing on right now (perhaps somewhat modified by later experiences).

How profoundly available we are right after birth is suggested by some research done in connection with the so-called "negativity bias" (Baumeister, Finkenauer, & Vohs, 2001; Kanouse & Hanson, 1972), which suggests that we devote more resources to attending to negative information of various sorts than to positive information when both have equal emotional weight. However, some research done with infants during their first seven months revealed that these little ones are apt to have a stronger response to positive emotional expressions than negative ones when mother and baby are focusing on each other, perhaps indicating a "positivity bias" (Farroni, Menon, & Rigato, 2007; G. M. Schwartz, Izard, & Ansul, 1985).* Let's linger with that for a moment.

The timing is not accurate for every infant, and we can imagine that some persist in their positivity longer than seven months, others less.† However, these research findings are an indication that most of us come here expecting to be met with warmth and responsiveness, actively looking for and responding to reflection of that relational goodness in the faces and bodies of those close to us. This search for the most nourishing attachments we can imagine is one of the roots of our system's wisdom that persists throughout our lives, even with the inevitable multiple disappointments we all encounter (Siegel, 2015b). This anticipation of warm connection is alive in our families and counseling rooms, in both parent and child or patient and therapist, no matter what the outer expression of attachment patterns may be in this particular moment. As we take this in more deeply, it can become a support for hope and trust when we are drawn deep into the pain, fear, and despair of those we are accompanying. Then, as we stay in a ventral state more often, that hope becomes a living experience for our people, opening the way for them to explore more secure attachments, first with us, perhaps, and then with others.

This inborn surge toward connection is supported by the neurobiology that draws us to live parallel lives with those nearest us, and this has an apparent upside and downside, as we have discovered with many of our other explorations. Our social circuitry, root of our surviving and thriving, wires in whatever implicit pathways will allow us to stay

* Most interesting is that at times when the focus of attention isn't on the relationship but on a toy, babies' emotional response to the object follows their mother's. If she looks afraid, they look afraid as well (Mumme, Fernald, & Herrera, 1996). It appears that this positivity bias is relationship-specific as part of our robust and optimistic attachment system.

† It may be a question of how many experiences of fear and pain it takes before a baby needs to allocate more resources to protection, so my preference would be to call this a "protectivity bias" rather than a "negativity bias." We also know that when we are comfortably in relationship, our system calms because of the accompaniment (Beckes & Coan, 2011; Coan & Sbarra, 2015), so what we may be seeing here in the greater activation with negativity is the relative change in the system between the calmer ventral and more activated sympathetic pathways.

in connection with those closest to us. If abuse or even neglect is the only path for staying in connection, we are placed in the terrible bind of belonging as an object of harm or hatred. We may become isolated in the attempt to be invisible, or pass the abuse on to others. It may be very challenging to imagine these are forms of attachment, and yet because of the primacy of connection, our neurobiology's wisdom is that we adapt according to the offered belonging even when it results in suffering or disorganization.

If emotional distance is the norm for our family, then attaching looks like remaining relatively autonomous, even though this brings with it a great cost in terms of deepening emotional pain. If emotional chaos is how our family connects, then we may sacrifice our own course of development in an attempt to regulate our parents, or simply join the chaos. In both cases, our developmental course will be disrupted to maintain our sense of belonging. If warmth and responsiveness are at the heart of our families, it is possible to be connected and supported along our natural developmental course at the same time. All of this happens because that is how we are neurobiologically built.

Pause for Reflection

This last paragraph contains some strong statements about attachment in adverse circumstances. It may be helpful to take some time to sense how your nurturant canal from throat to lower belly, along with muscles, eyes, and autonomic nervous system, is responding. Pause to just receive whatever sensations might be present. Are any images spontaneously arising as we touch into these pathways of early attachment? Do you notice any wish to not slow down right now and get in touch with your emerging experience? If that is happening, it makes such good sense, since we are getting into relationship with our most foundational encounters. Please honor any sense you have of timing about welcoming these implicit arisings. You may also be feeling warm and held, likely a sign of the many nourishing experiences between you and your parents early in life. If there is a sense of disturbance, seeking some deep listening with a reading partner or friend may provide just what is needed to begin to heal these earliest embedded traumas.

Where is the wisdom and gift in these various forms of attaching if they potentially lead us into pain and disruption? One part is simply that isolation is more harmful for us than attaching, even in disorganizing ways. Our systems simply can't take shape without others. As much as painful attachments are hard to bear, the primacy of connecting, a biological imperative for our autonomic nervous system (Porges & Phillips, 2016), means we will keep seeking as best we can to stay in contact with what is offered and eventually find more nourishing attachments.

Now let's turn to the process by which potential traumas embed to see what we can discover about the wisdom it holds for us. Just recently, researchers have discovered the neurochemical process by which overwhelming experiences are stored in our subcortical circuitry when we don't have enough resources (internally and externally) to integrate them (Jovasevic et al., 2015). Looking at how amino acids in the hippocampus support the formation of memory in mice, they found that glutamate, an activating neurochemical, is turned on in nontraumatic memory encoding. These events are stored in distributed brain networks, including both subcortical and cortical networks, for easier conscious recall of the full embodied and narrative experience. A separate system, extrasynaptic GABA, activates when there is overwhelming stress, storing fear memories in subcortical circuits while inhibiting cortical memory pathways, so the embodied and sometimes narrative experience of these events is less accessible to conscious awareness (Jovasevic et al., 2015). While the study doesn't overtly distinguish between implicit and explicit memory, we can infer that the subcortical-only implicit memories are separated to some degree from whatever explicit memory there might be. In my experience, there are varying degrees of explicit recall, from none to full narrative, depending on the severity of the potential trauma, the degree of emotional isolation associated with it, and the unique ways each person adapts to pain and fear. When the narrative is present, it is most often severed from the implicit memory as a way to enhance emotional safety. However that is for any embedded trauma, our system's capacity to sense when an experience is too much for us to bear and to shield our awareness to some degree from overwhelming sensations and emotions until such time as sufficient support for integration arrives offers evidence of an inherently wise ally.

That implicit memory remains so malleable is also part of this wisdom, with both an upside and a downside. While these experiences are often sequestered for our protection, they also need to be accessible to make healing possible. This means that they can be touched and awakened through any of our senses, as well as through shifts in our inner world, even in moments when healing support is not available. It is almost as if the memory comes up, looks around for support, and, if it isn't there, gradually deactivates and recedes out of awareness to wait for another day. In the process, the embedded trauma may also be strengthened to some degree because the neural network has fired again in this process of awakening and receding.

Returning to the encoding study (Jovasevic et al., 2015), the researchers note that reactivating the brain state in which the memory was encoded is one key to these memories becoming accessible again, thus affirming earlier research on state-dependent learning (Fisher & Craik, 1977). The richness of a well-endowed playroom can offer our little ones a wide array of potential stimuli to support awakening and exploration of their implicit worlds within the embrace of warm, responsive relationship—the necessary conditions for disconfirmation to emerge. When we make room for these little ones to guide the play, their wisdom coupled with the safety of "just playing" allows embedded traumas to be held as they awaken (Kestly, 2014). Daisy came to us when she was seven and caught in an implicit world created by unintentional neglect that left her alternately enraged and collapsed, with little in between. Her older brother's cancer treatment had so engulfed the family since she was an infant that these tragic circumstances had generated a great deal of anguish and terror with very few resources for reflection or regulation of her experience. The resulting disorganization left her helplessly in the grip of frequently awakened implicit encoding, leading to disturbing behaviors that had kept her isolated from the help she needed.

In Daisy's initial play, her counselor noticed that she stayed far away from the corner that had hospital-related toys, while being frequently drawn to the small mountain of stuffed animals. For weeks, at her request, she and her counselor repeatedly tucked the soft critters around her, getting to know one another in the process. As trust increased, Daisy began to look over at the hospital corner, then back at her counselor for reassurance. "Are we just playing?" she seemed to ask with her eyes. With warmth that had no push in it, her companion let her know they were in this together. As long as they remained connected within this joined window of tolerance, there might be enough safety for Daisy to begin to explore the deep well of pain and fear opened by images related to hospitals and doctors. This playroom contained the two necessary ingredients: images that could touch and awaken her implicit world and the warm, wise, responsive presence of another who could follow her, hold her suffering, and provide disconfirmation. As we also offer sand and miniatures for our adults, the same possibility of activating the innate healing process is in place.

This entire sequence of experiences, from the embedding of traumas, to the arising of implicit sensations, to our deepening sensitivity to and trust of them, to our openness to receiving disconfirmation, speaks again of the depth of embodied wisdom that permeates the encoding, retrieval, and healing of implicit memory. This unfolding process is also guided by the inherent wisdom of our embodied brain's innate movement toward greater integration (Siegel, 2015b), not in a reliable, predictable, left-centric way, but in the messy, tentative, unpredictable manner that is the hallmark of right-centric processes.

As we stay with the emerging moment, we will find that each person's internal pathway is as unique as a fingerprint, stopping/starting/pausing, jumping around in time sequence, communicating when a break is needed, and so much more. If our paradigm of healing can embrace this, we will be more able to remain responsive to the inner wisdom that is unfolding, even when we can see it only in retrospect.

Our left-centric culture has a tendency to want to define and control the way healing unfolds. This is understandable when we consider the potential anxiety that arises when we open a space in which the deep implicit of our patients can awaken, bringing considerable pain and fear into awareness. At those moments, we are co-participants through resonance. We are asking both of us to become vulnerable to the unexpected. At that moment, the door to the potential for deep healing also opens. Understanding the specifics of the retrieval and repair/disconfirmation process that supports change can perhaps steady our left hemispheres so that there is less need to control, more capacity to trust that both our systems already know what to do. Then, our left can become the indispensable supportive emissary of the emerging process. A solid grasp of the principles can help steady and guide us as strong emotions and sensations arise in our people and resonate in us so that we are more able to remain a solid ventral container for that person.

For the specifics of the processes of retrieval and repair, we can turn to the work of Bruce Ecker and his Coherence Psychology Institute colleagues (Ecker, 2015; Ecker, Ticic, & Hulley, 2012) for a thorough summary of the research and some guidance about a helpful perspective on therapeutic change. Until the last decade or so, we believed that once implicit memories moved into long-term storage, they were forever synaptically locked in place (LeDoux, Romanski, & Xagoraris, 1989). Encoded in the presence of powerful emotions, these circuits were experienced as especially strong and durable, generally persisting over the course of our lifetime as the unseen guides of perception, emotion, and behavior (Pine, Mendelsohn, & Dudai, 2014). In terms of our life experience, this meant that at no point would we be free from the possibility of these memories being touched and awakened. If we consider our earliest implicit memories, which are foundational in a different way than those that encode later, this indelible encoding would mean that we would be vulnerable to being engulfed in the panoramic and pervasive sense of our value and of how relationships unfold forever. This way of perceiving and experiencing would linger in the background even if we co-built a second set of neural nets with another person that would hold a different sense of self and relationship.

At the beginning of this century, new research let us know that this challenging picture isn't an inevitable prison for us.* Instead, several researchers found that there is a process by which these implicit synapses become destabilized and open to new information, followed, about five hours later, by reconsolidation of the neural net that now contains this changed implicit memory (Nader, Schafe, & LeDoux, 2000; Przybyslawski & Sara, 1997; Sekiguchi, Yamada, & Suzuki, 1997). While the emotional, behavioral, and belief components of the memory can be completely changed or modified, the explicit component, the narrative memory of our experience, remains unchanged and available to us (Duvarci & Nader, 2004; Pedreira & Maldonado, 2003; Walker, Brakefield, Hobson, & Stickgold, 2003).

The key to this neural opening is the arrival of two embodied experiences at the same time: the awakening of the implicit memory and the offering of what is called a mismatch or disconfirming experience (Ecker, 2015; Ecker et al., 2012). This second part needs to also be an embodied emotional experience, not only a cognitive idea offered by the left hemisphere. It appears that at the moment embodiment meets

---

* We are speaking here of implicit memories holding painful and fearful experiences, and it is helpful to remember that this durability of warm, responsive embodied memories is also the unseen ally of our ongoing sense of ourselves as lovable and of our world as full of hope, goodness, and the possibility of caring accompaniment.

embodiment, the neural net offers itself to receive new information and will reconsolidate about five hours later, bearing this precious healing cargo. It may be possible for both parts of this process to arise within us without the other person providing the disconfirmation directly.

Bruce Ecker (2015) writes about a woman, now fifty and married with children, who was experiencing sexual aversion with her husband, depression, and panic attacks. As they worked together, one particular memory emerged about her being a young woman who had become pregnant with her boyfriend and, while contemplating an abortion, miscarried instead. Because of strong messages from childhood about the kind of woman who would have this experience, she felt she was ruined for life, that she would never be married or have children. With no one available to comfort her at the time of the pregnancy and miscarriage, this painful implicit memory had been embedded in her subcortical circuitry and was now reawakening in Bruce's kind presence. As she deepened into embodied contact with the memory, another part of her neural circuitry that held the felt-sense experience that she had indeed married and had children suddenly became available for integration. With considerable emotional intensity—this time joy—these two aspects of her knowing touched one another. The mismatch between the two implicit memories initiated the possibility of destabilization, allowing the old felt-sense knowing of a ruined life to be replaced by the new knowing of a fulfilled life. Some hours later, this neural net would reconsolidate, carrying this updated implicit memory, allowing her depression to lift once and for all. While she had held these two pieces of experience within herself all along, the anguish of the unaccompanied earlier event had been adaptively buried but was still generating these painful symptoms. As long as the earlier experience was being held subcortically only, there was no way for these neural nets to join. As the older experience came into embodied conscious awareness, it was potentially available for *getting into relationship* with her current lived experience.

We could say that all the ingredients for this disconfirming/reparative experience were already present within this woman, and yet, like so much in us, what is inherent needs relationship to come into being. Without Bruce's depth of understanding, capacity for attending to what is emerging in the moment, warmth, and confidence in her ability to change, this transformative experience may never have happened. We can refer to the power of accompaniment offered by social baseline theory to understand the calming of her amygdala that allowed her to feel safe enough to open to the memory (Beckes & Coan, 2011). Such a neuroception of safety opened the door to the greater likelihood that her awakened implicit could be held within their joined windows of tolerance (Badenoch, 2011; Porges, Badenoch, & Phillips, 2016). We also can be drawn again to Uri Hasson (2010) and brain-coupling for ways in which her brain began to align more with Bruce's, amplifying her integrative capacity. Once connected, curiosity supported by her SEEK-ING system became available to listen for the messages from her deeper mind (Panksepp & Biven, 2012). All of this unfolded because Bruce's accumulated wisdom and cultivation of presence made it possible for him to offer deep listening, with his right-mode attending supported by his abundant left-mode understanding (McGilchrist, 2009).

None of this is to say that we might not also have many spontaneous experiences of disconfirmation and repair from within our own storehouse of accumulated conflicting memories. Perhaps many of these healing moments happen below the level of conscious awareness. However, when we are in the shadow of embedded traumas, the assistance of another is valuable, both as the co-holder of the experience and as one who can be internalized as an ongoing companion, both within that particular memory and throughout our system.

Often, it is another who holds the needed felt-sense experience as well. A young woman I had been seeing for quite some time began to touch in with early memories of what she described as "my mother's turned back." She felt the heart-wrenching ache of needing to see her mother's eyes and smile, particularly when she arrived home from school each day. As she touched this place of embodied need and disappointment, she glanced at me for a moment and then came to rest within our gazing. In that moment of deep quiet, what she described as "warm waves of noticing each other" moved through her body, which, in that instant, was also the body of the aching child she had been. Without any words, the longed-for but unexpected face of the other arrived and she was comforted by being seen. What Ecker and his colleagues (Ecker et al., 2012) call a mismatch experience had silently arrived in the space between us. Most of our embedded traumas arise because of the absence of another to help us integrate the painful or frightening experience. When we couple that with our awareness that our systems are uniquely prepared to receive and co-regulate with others, the co-holding of the disconfirmation and repair lets us powerfully collaborate with our brain's inherent developmental and healing process.

Ecker and his companions (Ecker et al., 2012; Ecker & Hulley, 2000; Toomey & Ecker, 2007) have chosen to call their work Coherence Psychology because of a particular phenomenon that they observed repeatedly and consistently. *They found that our symptoms are adaptively generated by the underlying implicit memory, which is to say that we were adaptive at the time of the wound and continue to be adaptive now to protect this injured part of ourselves and our whole system from the pain and fear carried within this implicit trauma.* In a broader way, this adaptability was the subject of the immediately previous chapter. Describing symptom coherence, here is what they say: "A client's seemingly irrational, out-of-control presenting symptom is actually a sensible, orderly, cogent expression of the person's existing construction of self and world, not a 'disorder' or pathology" (Toomey & Ecker, 2008, p. 210).

Pause for Reflection

How would it be for us to view our most distressing "symptoms" as a wise gift of protection? Let's listen for one part of ourselves that we have a tendency to reject. It might be anything—a critical voice, a part with addictive tendencies, an aspect of ourselves that has a fearful or angry response under certain conditions, a hard-heartedness at times. Simply getting into receptive relationship with this part, particularly in the presence of another if someone is available to us, will begin a conversation that may open us to awareness of the underlying implicit memory that requires this protective part. From there, the possibility of mismatch/disconfirmation/repair comes closer. For now, we are simply offering to become aware of the presence of these protective symptoms.

A strongly held, whole-brain sense of this adaptive coherence and the pathway of disconfirmation/repair opens the possibility of respectful receptivity and trust, which are the conditions for safety for both our patients and ourselves. Our left-hemisphere emissary who holds this knowledge can support our right-centric attending as we move into the deep waters of embedded implicit trauma, widening our window of tolerance so that we are able to hold ourselves and our people even in times of strong activation.

On this foundation, we may even begin to be able to cultivate a sense of gratefulness when we notice the leading edge of an implicit arising. We may begin to sense that the door to healing is opening in that moment. We may begin to experience these awakenings as vital truth tellers that can illuminate our lived experience rather than as torturing or annoying remnants sent as hated reminders. This has the potential to change how we relate to our inner world. In response to this movement toward acceptance, gentle curiosity, and gratitude, the way our embedded traumas share themselves seems to modulate, significantly decreasing the degree of activation when our implicit world is touched.

Of these shifts in perception, the movement toward gratefulness may bring on the most significant neurobiological and neurochemical changes. Gratefulness shapes our brains in some remarkable ways that may account for this greater gentleness (Korb, 2015). Dopamine increases, supporting enjoyment and motivation (Ng & Wong, 2013). Our ventral vagal parasympathetic engages, leading to serotonin increase (Perreau-Linck et al., 2007). Thankfulness activates the hypothalamus, which regulates sleep and stress (Zahn et al., 2009). Activity also increases in the anterior cingulate cortex and medial prefrontal cortex, which enhances bonding and empathy (Fox, Kaplan, Damasio, & Damasio, 2015). However, perhaps the most profound discovery is that once we initiate a cycle of gratitude, it has a tendency to continue so that gratefulness and its benefits become an ongoing state (Kini, Wong, McInnis, Gabana, & Brown, 2015). Overall, sustainable changes in mood, fulfilling social interaction, lowered stress, and resilience in trauma, arise when we feel grateful. Many of my patients find a growing sense of mutual receptivity between their awakening implicit world and their conscious awareness as we welcome these emissaries of healing.

Expanding our practice even more, we may be able to hold the arising of implicit memory and the emergence of inherent health as equally valuable and equally welcome. To truly trust the undulations between these two kinds of experiences and feel the relationship between them, how they support each other, is likely the work of a lifetime. Only gradually might we begin to let go of our longing for the more pleasant times to stay indefinitely. It begins with doing our own work, hopefully with a therapist or friend with a similar perspective on the value of the implicit and the inherent. As we gradually modulate our impulse to control our own recovery process, we will likely find ourselves extending this grace to everyone—patients, family, friends, and possibly the world at large. This may help us become ever more skilled listeners with fewer agendas and judgments. We may begin to notice that the listening itself initiates some movement that points the way toward what our patients' system needs in that moment. We may find ourselves responding in that instant from the deep well of cultivated wisdom born of study and experience. Sometimes when the emergent need is met with disconfirmation, an implicit learning will completely change, and sometimes there is more of a spiral movement as we deepen into a long-held implicit pattern. At some point, the healing implicit and inherent wisdom merge. Rachel Naomi Remen says it this way:

> Until we stop ourselves or, more often, have been stopped, we hope to put certain of life's events "behind us" and get on with our living. After we stop we see that certain of life's issues will be with us for as long as we live. We will pass through them again and again, each time with a new story, each time with a greater understanding, until they become indistinguishable from our blessings and our wisdom. It's the way life teaches us how to live. (1996, p. xxxviii)

Pause for Reflection

Let's take a moment to sit with the suggestion that our wounded implicit world and our inherent health are equally valuable. This is basically asking us to not have a preference for one over the other, to greet the arising of implicit pain and fear and the arrival of harmony within our bodies and minds with equal welcome. How do our bodies respond to this suggestion? Our minds may or may not be willing to sign on to this right now, but even if we can cognitively make a case, our bodies may have a different response. For now, we can just be aware with as little judgment as possible.

Moving beyond the general principle, perhaps we can each go back to a recent time when we had an implicit arising. What did we want to do with it? The impulse to push it away or change it is a most natural human gesture of protection. For now, maybe we can just notice that gesture if that's what we felt, and then, as we did in the last chapter, for a moment play with the gesture of inclusion again. What would it be like to draw this implicit experience close to us?

What would it be like to get into a relationship of care with it? What happens if we change "it" to "him" or her"—instead of criticism, the part of you who protects by judging? Is there a shift in how you feel toward this experience with the change of pronouns?

For now, we are just seeking to nourish our left hemispheres with a deepening awareness of implicit memory and inherent wisdom as our right-centric experience of both becomes the foundation for the development of stabilizing concepts. Later, in the second part of this book, we will circle back to spend time in the counseling room to settle into the particulars of practice. We have one more stop in our consideration of ways of attending. How might we understand the relationship between co-regulation and self-regulation?

16

Built for Co-regulation

In 2014, the *New York Times* published an article titled "Teaching Children to Calm Themselves" (Bornstein, 2014). Bornstein wrote about a Head Start program in Kansas and Missouri that works with traumatized preschoolers to help mend early brain development influenced by adverse circumstances in the first years of life. Like many of us in today's culture, Bornstein's stance is that self-regulation and emotional self-reliance are the goal, and that this is accomplished through teaching children a number of steps to achieve self-control. He writes about one of the children in the program:

> When Luke gets angry, he tries to remember to look at his bracelet. It reminds him of what he can do to calm himself: stop, take a deep breath, count to four, give yourself a hug and, *if necessary*, ask an adult for help. (para. 1, italics added)

However, as an observer reporting the practices of the school, he tells us, "One key is remembering that children who have experienced trauma feel profoundly unsafe. When they are acting out, their primary need is often to feel a sense of connection" (para. 16). As he watches the teachers at work, he notices that welcoming adult eyes, voices, and laps are always available for these children, not as a last resort, but as part of their understanding that this brain-building project thrives through partnership. At every step of the way, these young ones are accompanied. Because Bornstein is legitimately an observer rather than participant, his stance may be a more left-shifted one, leading him to believe that these are strategies designed primarily to lead to self-regulation rather than part of a broader picture of an ongoing commitment to connection and support held by the teachers.

While the distinction may at first seem subtle, the author and the teachers offer differing perceptions of the role of co-regulation. For Bornstein, the support of another is a necessary stepping-stone to self-regulation, which is the desired outcome. For the teachers, this partnership is central to the ongoing process of healing and possibly beyond. As a reader, I got the impression that these teachers would respond to a child asking for support at any time. They seemed to recognize that these children's legitimate need for safe connection would be a constant, and that the overt request for support could be seen as a wise guide to their healing and as essential for ongoing development. These two ways of seeing likely reflect the viewpoints of the two hemispheres. Left-centric seeing stresses self-reliance, while whole-brained seeing with our right in the lead emphasizes relationship, supported by the wise resources of what our left knows. In this case, what the left may hold for us is an awareness of the principles of relational neuroscience that show us how we are built for ongoing co-regulation.

Because we find ourselves in a left-shifted society, it may not be surprising that the former viewpoint rests on the implicit or explicit assumption that co-regulation is merely a stepping-stone to autonomy. This arises, in part, because once we are in a left-centric state, we are without a felt sense of "we" some or all of the time. With our relational circuitry out of reach, the need to become emotionally self-sufficient seems self-evident, perhaps even urgent. Our left-centric viewpoint tells us it isn't safe or possible to rely on others. This underlying experience may be part of what drives the assumption that self-regulation is healthier than an ongoing need for co-regulation. The latter then is merely the necessary means to attaining the former. When we carry this assumption into our counseling rooms, there may be an inherent preference for the signs of a steady trend toward less need for support (rather than the more undulating pathway of more-less-more that emerges in the natural process of deep healing), along with a tendency to encourage our people to comfort and parent themselves without much reliance on us. Out of our care for our people, we may teach skills, but we may be inclined to do it from an inner distance lest our people become dependent on us.

Often, our patients contribute to this sense that they must regulate themselves because they have been criticized for being too needy, too emotional, or too sensitive. The clear message many of us have received is "get ahold of yourself," often offered by well-meaning family and friends who have also been influenced by the cultural implicit, which experiences self-reliance as an aspect of good character.

Pause for Reflection

Does this injunction to somehow self-regulate touch and awaken any experiences you have had? What happens in your body with this phrase? What is your emotional response? I can feel a mix of anger, shame, and sadness coupled with some tension in my chest and lower belly. We may intellectually know that "get ahold of yourself" doesn't reflect a healthy way to live, feel a strong visceral response to the injunction, and, at the same time, feel driven toward behaviors that encourage self-reliance in ourselves and others. Because of the implicit power of the culture in which we marinate, coupled with the way we may have been raised, it isn't surprising that our care for others might also be influenced by this message. With openness to how this enters our work with others, perhaps we can begin to be aware of certain clients who struggle with regulation and of what unfolds within us when we are with them.

As the research on mindfulness strongly reminds us, there is a place for self-guided practices that support integration of the circuitry that helps us regulate (see Flaxman & Flook, 2012, for a brief summary). However, often in the teaching of mindfulness, there may also be an unseen co-regulatory process at work because of a teacher whose ongoing presence multiplies the effectiveness of the practice itself, particularly fostering the student's ability to continue a new practice. For example, in the contemplative traditions, the role of the teacher is central in transmitting the practice through resonance with the student and then supporting the new meditator in settling into the process. How might this co-regulation unfold in our system? Stephen Porges (Porges, Badenoch, & Phillips, 2016) speaks of the neurophysiological processes that link us through activation of the social engagement system (ventral vagal parasympathetic) when we are having a neuroception of safety. In the presence of another who is in social engagement, our own system has the opportunity to respond by moving in that preferred direction as well. He calls these processes that open the way for a rich experience of co-regulation the "passive pathways," because we are neurobiologically designed to respond to one another's offers of connection simply by *being* together without *doing* anything. Social baseline theory (Beckes & Coan, 2011) and brain-coupling (Hasson, Ghazanfar, Galantucci, Garrod, & Keysers, 2012) support this same vision of how the possibility of co-regulation is thoroughly built into our system at many levels. Because this process is simply our inborn response to a receptive and responsive other, it is easy for it to go unnoticed in the moment and for us to completely forget about the longer-term effects when such experiences of co-regulation are internalized.

Here is a story that may help to make this process more concrete. A friend who works with homeless men shared his experience with me. For a long time, he had been encouraging his street dwellers to drink more water so they were less in danger of falling ill from all the challenges dehydration brings. He offered suggestions, resources, and his concern. Over time, he realized none of this was making much difference and, in fact, seemed to be creating shame when his men had to report they still weren't doing as he asked. Most often, they said that they simply didn't remember. Then, one day, he noticed one of his men had a cracked lip and offered him a bottle of water while they talked. They drank together, a kind of communion perhaps, and the man left with the bottle. When he came back the following week, he was clutching the bottle and said with a smile, "I drank at least twice as much water this week and I thought about you every time. You really do want me to feel better, don't you?" He asked his counselor to refill his bottle before he left, sacred water infused with the felt sense of the deepening relationship. They repeated this ritual every time they met, and after a few weeks, he declared that water bottle to be his most prized possession.

How might we understand why this non-intervention made such a difference? When my friend taught water-drinking as a skill, he realized he was in a more left-centric state, passing on information in the hope of a behavior changing and perhaps also communicating anxiety along with his concern. Left dominance and the intention to control means that the ventral pathways of connection are likely offline (Porges, Badenoch, & Phillips, 2016). Because of this, such skills training is no match for longstanding implicit and epigenetic patterns. As you may recall, our awareness of even being thirsty arises from the way our genes expressed according to how our first need for liquid nourishment was met (Harshaw, 2008). We only learn what this sensation we call thirst is asking for if our parents see our need and satisfy it. When they don't, our bodies can't remind us to drink. Well-meaning instructions to do something different are often not enough to initiate change.

The act of my friend and his client drinking together is potentially an entirely different neural event. The gift of water brought not an idea, but instead offered this man a felt-sense experience of a primary need being seen and met by someone who valued him. This allowed the possibility of initiating change at an implicit and possibly even at the epigenetic level. His intellectual knowing that his counselor cared about him became a whole-body experience of mattering that was reflected in his words at their next meeting. It is almost as though he *experienced* this care for the first time, even though he had *known* about it for months. As they drank together, the sharing of this primary nurturance with another initiated the process of internalizing the two together with the water. From then on, there was the possibility that the act of drinking also brought the presence of the person. Even when the man was back out on the streets, he was no longer drinking alone. With the water came the felt sense of accompaniment and care. I suspect this encounter was as warming and integrating for my friend as it was for his street dweller.

Both the experience of being met and the process of internalizing the counselor are right-centric events that have some possibility of beginning the process of disconfirmation we talked about in the last chapter. Our street dweller's familiar state of not noticing his thirst is juxtaposed with being met in his need by his counselor bringing just the right resource. The water bottle itself is encoded in this changing implicit neural net as a reminder of the whole healing experience. The sight and feel of it may open the implicit experience of warmth, care, and liquid nourishment. If we were to say his relationship with water was dysregulated before, now we might sense it is becoming co-regulated in an ongoing way. It may have been helpful that my friend didn't do the water-sharing as a planned intervention, but simply as a responsive gesture of care. He had no intention of using this as a way to change behavior, but simply as a moment of being together. These human acts of sharing arise in right-centric, ventral times when our systems are open to responding to each other in the emerging moment and taking in each other's presence, laying the groundwork for the ongoing relationship. It might be that this process of internalization holds the key to perceiving self-regulation a bit differently.

We can turn to the work of Marco Iacoboni (2009, 2011) and his colleagues to understand this process by which we take others into our embodied system so that we can experience their accompaniment even when they are not with us physically. The discovery of neurons with mirroring properties, first in macaque monkeys (Gallese, Fadiga, Fogassi, & Rizzolatti, 1996) and then in humans (Iacoboni et al., 1999), began to open the door to understanding how we are so deeply and permanently connected. As with so many discoveries, the initial phase suggested these neurons were only the basis for imitation and learning, while ongoing exploration has revealed more complex processes that help us understand our capacity for empathy and our impulse to act in ways that are responsive to another's state (Iacoboni, 2009). Most recently (Iacoboni, 2011), observations of mirror neurons in many parts of the brain (including our amygdala, hippocampus, anterior cingulate, medial temporal, and medial frontal cortex) are suggesting that our neurobiology provides us with a most dynamic and sophisticated system of co-internalization. Iacoboni (2011) says it this way:

> We empathize effortlessly and automatically with each other because evolution has selected neural systems that blend self and other's actions, intentions, and emotions. The more we learn about the neural mechanisms of mirroring, the more we realize that the distinction between self and other may be almost fictitious in many cases. We have created the self-other distinction in our explicit discourse, along with many other constructs that divide us. Our neurobiology, in contrast, puts us "within each other." (Iacoboni, 2011, p. 57)

This is a profound statement, one that may send both a wave of warmth and a shiver of concern through our systems, because we are again in the presence of what we might call the upside and downside of this process of inner communion. Those who have hurt or scared us live on within just as much as those who have nourished and warmed us. As we will see, they become ongoing resources for co-dysregulation as well as co-regulation. However, as we also often discover, we will find that even this downside has a possible upside.

Pause for Reflection

As we begin to move toward our own complex, ever-emerging inner community, it may be helpful to get a sense of our embodied response to the awareness that we are carrying so many others within us. Checking in our muscles, bellies, chests, and breath, we may be able to receptively listen to the sensations that accompany this awareness without much judgment. Do we have both a sense of welcome and caution? It may be that we see certain faces or feel the presence of some of our internalized others. Do we have a preference for certain of them over others? This may be our natural first response, and perhaps we can just receive that without judgment, too, noticing how our bodies respond differently to the various imported others inside us. We may begin to sense those who support regulation and ventral experience as well as those who stimulate sympathetic arousal with fear or the shame and terrified helplessness that tends us toward dorsal. If we have the opportunity to hold all of this within the regulating experience of being with a reading partner or friend, it can be healing in and of itself.

As a way of further grounding our left hemispheres in knowledge that gives us a sturdy foundation, let's explore the process of internalization a little more deeply. The story begins with research that discovered that only one-third of mirror neurons are strictly congruent, meaning that the neurons that fire when we perform a goal-oriented action also fire when we observe the same act. The other two-thirds are broadly congruent and, as their name suggests, relate and respond to the action being witnessed in ways that are complementary.

> The properties of broadly congruent mirror neurons suggest that these cells provide a flexible coding of actions of self and others. This flexibility is an important property for successful social interactions because even though imitation is a pervasive phenomenon in humans, people do not imitate each other all the time but rather often perform coordinated, cooperative, complementary actions. Broadly congruent mirror neurons seem ideal cells to support cooperative behavior among people (Newman-Norlund et al. 2007). (Iacoboni, 2009)

As both of these kinds of neurons fire, the observed action both echoes in us and initiates a response. If we see a sad face, resonance will activate sorrow in us, and then there is some probability we will be moved to extend comfort. Meanwhile, the entire sequence is being encoded within both of us so that the experience of comfort in distressing times remains alive and available. Part of that Hebbian encoding process (what fires together, wires together, and then survives together) (Hebb, 1949; Post et al., 1998) includes the sensory aspects of the experience as well: our dynamically changing expressions, the prosody of our voices, possibly the quality of touch, any smells or tastes or other sensory bits in the environment (the quality of the light, the feeling of our clothing, bodily sensations). As we experience recall, these are often more like virtual reality movies than snapshots, filled with the streaming sensations of affiliation and regulating connection that we now carry within us.

Pause for Reflection

These inner pairs (or larger groupings) carrying experiences of comfort and connection continue to be resources of reassurance and regulation for us even when they are out of awareness. However, when we can bring the memory of them into our bodies to reexperience the felt sense of support, they become stronger with each firing. We may or may not remember the explicit details of these encounters, which is all right because the support they offer comes primarily from the embodied experience. Let's pause to invite a nourishing pair to come into our embodied awareness. This is another opportunity to practice opening without expectation, as we have been, to see what arises spontaneously from our implicit world. If a pair arrives, we may be able to feel the sensations that inhabit our bodies in the presence of these inner ones. How do our muscles, belly, heart, and breath respond? Can we feel our nervous system's response as well? Are there some fresh words that also arise spontaneously? If we were to visit these states regularly, they might develop enough neural strength to begin to come to us in moments of distress without our needing to consciously call them forth.

All our mirror neurons, both strictly congruent and broadly congruent, also participate in a delicate, responsive dance of excitation and inhibition that helps us distinguish between our own experience and the sensations, feelings, movements, and intentions of those we are importing. About one-third of our mirror neurons are excitatory, one-third inhibitory, and one-third what Iacoboni (2008) calls super mirror neurons. The majority of these have the unique property of increasing firing for execution of an action and decreasing firing for observation by changing to inhibitory properties. A minority do the opposite dance. Overall, about 85 percent of our mirror neurons are excitatory and about 15 percent inhibitory, dampening our impulse to perform the actions we are witnessing and facilitating the distinction, below conscious awareness, between self and other. This is so valuable for us, both as clinicians and patients. Our system's potential ability to feel what belongs to us and what belongs to our patients may be central in preventing what we call secondary trauma.

At the same time, if our resonance with another's wounds touches and awakens our own unhealed implicit world, the power of that arising is often stronger than the inhibitory mirror neurons, so we can't differentiate between our experience and theirs. Instead of co-regulation, we find ourselves in a moment of co-dysregulation. As we become more aware of what is occurring within us, our window of tolerance may expand to return us to a more ventral state, and from there, we can offer the repair of drawing our person toward regulation as well. We will visit examples of this in Part II.

As a result of the internalization process, there is also another kind of differentiation available to us. When we are in our own healing process and turn inward to listen to our inner community, we are often able to sense the difference between the felt experience of each member of the pair. The inner worlds of the depressed mother and the abandoned child feel distinctly different in our bodies, opening the door to healing what we might call both our *native parts* (our experience) and *imported parts* (the experience of the internalized other).

This is the point where we can perhaps sense the upside to the downside of internalizing those who have wounded us. Because they remain within us as living parts of our experience, they are also available for healing in ways that the person who hurt us may not be. A parent dies or a brother has no interest in exploring the painful parts of our relationship with him. The part of this person we have internalized is now part of us and so available to be received and acknowledged, to be touched by disconfirming experiences in ways that have the potential to resolve the pain and fear in the relationship. In Part Two, we will explore how this deeply healing process slowly unfolds within the embrace of the therapeutic relationship.

How does the story of self-regulation intersect with our tale of co-regulation? In the embrace of warm, responsive relationships, our orbitofrontal cortex becomes interwoven with our amygdala in the right hemisphere. As this wiring strengthens and stabilizes through repetition and the subsequent myelination of the new circuitry, our window of tolerance* for strong emotions widens. From the outside, we appear to be more able to regulate without the assistance of another. Inwardly, the very process of neural weaving is anchoring the internalization process. Our mirror neurons are near the beginning of an intricate network of circuits that support resonance. What we are about to describe happens in microseconds and largely below the level of conscious awareness. When mirror neurons are coupled with the superior temporal sulcus, we gain both a sense of the intention of the other person and the beginning of moving with him or her internally as a precursor to complementary action (L. Carr, Iacoboni, Dubeau, Mazzlotta, & Lenzi, 2003). At this point, the insula becomes involved, bringing the accumulating information to the limbic region and body, where we begin to resonate with the physical and emotional experience of the other as well as sense the meaning for us of what is unfolding (L. Carr et al., 2003). If our unhealed and sequestered implicit memories are not touched and awakened by this stream of powerful information, the neural journey culminates in the highly integrative orbitofrontal and medial prefrontal cortices, where we experience most fully the presence of the other. All of this is being encoded in a widespread single neural network (what fires together, wires together) that gathers up the rich experience happening in both people. In this way, we gradually accumulate a valuable storehouse of what we might call nourishing pairs (or groups) that continue to participate with us in the ongoing inner dance of co-regulation. Increasing neural integration and co-regulating internalizations blend into the outward picture of what we call self-regulation. In truth, we are never alone.

---

* Just as a reminder, the window of tolerance doesn't have to do with the intensity of the emotion itself, but rather with our ability to stay connected with another (externally or internally) no matter the strength of the emotion.

Pause for Reflection

As we settle, we may first notice how we are receiving a robust meal of neuroscience, nourishment for our left hemispheres that we may need to snack on a few times until we gain a sense of the neural flow. Are pictures beginning to form of how mirror neurons and the associated resonance circuitry move in us? It will be far more helpful to sense the flow of this through our own experience than to try to memorize the pathways. Perhaps we can recall a recent experience in which we felt held without judgment or agenda, sensing the presence of our companion. As we invite this memory, can we gain a sense of the other person's intention, body, and emotion? How do we experience this in our own bodies? At first, it may be challenging to discern what is arising from the other person and what is coming from our own experience, because with these nourishing encounters, the experience for both people is often similar. You may want to play around with other nourishing pairs, perhaps even exploring how you provide that possibility for others in your life now.

When trauma embeds because we don't have the internal and external support we need for it to integrate, implicit memory of these pairs (or groups) is tucked away in subcortical circuits by extrasynaptic GABA to await healing (Jovasevic et al., 2015). One of the prominent features of trauma is the sense of being alone with the experience. Even though there was often another person with us or we had the felt sense of a needed person's unavailability, that person was taken in as a dysregulating presence or absence. There was no sense of safe, warm, responsive connection, but instead a profound sense of aloneness and isolation while enduring the pain and fear. When our people's implicit memories begin to open in their bodies and we arrive with the equally embodied disconfirming experience, one of the first experiences is that the needed other has come. The movement from "I am alone" to "we are together" is, in my experience, most often the beginning of healing. Anything we can do to support this process of internalization will relieve the core of the suffering and make it possible for us to go more deeply into the wounded areas, bringing what was needed at the time. In Part Two, we will explore some of the ways we can foster this profound joining.

By now, we likely have a growing sense of how thoroughly and continuously relational we humans are, so when we meet in the field of deep connection, we are collaborating with our system's neurobiologically implanted process of healing. We can certainly be grateful for the individual practices that can help build the neural integration that supports regulation even while recognizing that our systems are so gratefully receptive and open to all offers of co-regulation. As social baseline theory teaches us, we simply work less hard at everything when we are accompanied (Beckes & Coan, 2011; Coan & Sbarra, 2015).

All of this information about our profoundly relational nature may invite us to practice mindfulness in a particular way that blends development of our ability to compassionately observe with the support of co-regulation, what has sometimes been called interpersonal mindfulness (Kramer, 2007). It is not so much a formal contemplative practice as a way of being together that involves the deep listening we have been cultivating with our practices here so far. It begins with us receiving support for our own capacity to experience our inner world more deeply. When we are held in safety by another's nonjudgmental receptivity, we naturally open to more awareness of sensation, feelings, and the thoughts that arise from and accompany them. The stability of our joined windows of tolerance makes what was intolerable and necessary to ignore available for awareness and disconfirmation. In the process, the circuitry of regulation develops more strength as our community gains another dyad for ongoing co-regulation. On this foundation, we gradually become more able to extend this safe holding to others, ripples of supportive connection that widen the possibilities of cultural healing, too.

As we continue to build this inner realm of support and deepen into a felt-sense awareness of our own inner community pairings and groups, we may find it helpful to consider changing our language concerning the process of regulation. *Rather than advocating teaching self-regulation, we might speak about entering into relational environments that support internalization of nourishing others for ongoing co-regulation.* When these words spring from our inner sense of their truth for us, it changes how we inhabit the space between us and our people. Receptive nonjudgmental presence, responsiveness that meets our people where they are in this emerging moment, and sensitivity to rupture that opens the possibility of repair supports internalization of co-regulatory presence for both people. To practice in this way means gradually letting go of the greater certainty granted by our taking more control of the process and instead moving into the uncertainty that is the hallmark of right-centric awareness. To balance this sense of tentative insecurity, we have spent many pages now preparing our left-hemisphere emissaries to provide a stable foundation of wisdom about the right-centric processes that support ongoing co-regulation in the midst of uncertainty. In the final offering before we turn to application in our counseling rooms, we will explore how the language that naturally draws us offers some guidance about which of our hemispheres is in the lead while also inviting others into that way of perceiving. Small changes in language may foster large changes in depth of connection.

17

The Music of the (Hemi)spheres

The limits of my language mean the limits of my world.

—LUDWIG WITTGENSTEIN (1922)

About seven years ago, a new friend came into my life, a man whose twenty-five years as a practitioner had sensitized him to the importance of the language that arises from our inner experience. When he would hear me speak in ways that were judgmental or indicated my wish to get rid of some part of me, he would gently say, "A more respectful word may want to emerge soon" (C. Scott, personal communication, September 8, 2010). He encouraged me to just listen for it, not try to find it by digging around. Something always came and gradually opened me to a more kind and inclusive way of being with myself and others. I began to notice that my words and perceptions were inextricably linked, so as the words changed, my perceptions were also shifting (and vice versa, I imagine), and this led to more changes in language to better reflect this continually emerging felt-sense experience while encouraging it to deepen further as well—a beautiful circle of transformation. Slowly, slowly, I found myself moving away from a more judgmental, analytical, disembodied, left-shifted viewpoint toward a more open, curious, accepting way of being that emerges when right-hemisphere processes take the lead.

Because of this experience, we are going to dare to respectfully approach the vast subject of language here near the end of this preparatory journey, touching on several aspects, from its origins to its influence on the therapeutic relationship. We may find that the words we are naturally drawn toward when we speak to others or ourselves have a great deal to say about our ability to be present with one another. To explore the importance of language to presence, we need to lay down a bit of a foundation first, beginning with revisiting the seminal work of Stephen Porges (1995) concerning our autonomic nervous system. His Polyvagal Theory suggests that presence becomes possible when there is a felt sense of safety. To briefly review, when we are in the role of practitioner, if our autonomic nervous system is receiving what it needs to have a neuroception of safety (our system's felt sense, below the level of conscious awareness, that we are safe), then our social engagement system (the ventral vagal parasympathetic) will be alive in the room as our patients arrive (Porges, 2011). In this state, we become a potentially safe landing strip for them. When we are able to offer this safe haven, the possibility of the other person moving toward a similar felt sense of safety awakens in the healing space between us through resonance. There is also additional support for this happening since our systems have a preference for being in the ventral vagal state because it supports connection. As we may already be seeing, such joining makes room for the inherent healing capacity in the other to begin to emerge, so the widening and deepening of our ventral window is a primary gift we bring to others. In his early work, Porges (1995) discovered that *this ventral state has a bias toward right-hemisphere processes*, so if our language can help us orient our system toward the right-hemisphere perceptual world, we may be able to offer a more profoundly safe space for the relationship to take root. Porges's realization about this lateralization invites us to again turn our attention to the work of Iain McGilchrist (2009) on the wisdom of our divided brains.

We are going to take a little time to revisit the fundamentals of McGilchrist's work here, to further deepen our felt sense of our two hemispheres. Our right and left hemispheres encounter the world from very different perspectives, almost as though there are two people within us taking different vantage points (McGilchrist, 2009). In the process, these two viewpoints shape our perceptions and then the words (arising from the core metaphors of each hemisphere) that surface within us as we feel, think, and eventually speak from these two stances. McGilchrist (2009) says, "If it is the case that our understanding is the *effect* of the metaphors we choose, it is also true that it is a *cause*: our understanding itself guides the choice of metaphor by which we understand it" (p. 97). These two viewpoints offer us different ways of orienting to the world that lead to strikingly divergent values, ways of relating, and behaviors. As we may feel more deeply now, the essence of the right-hemisphere perspective involves attending to relationship, embodiment, and what is unfolding in the unique moment in the space between. *We could say that from this viewpoint, the central metaphor is living beings in relationship with each other in this moment.* In contrast, the left-hemisphere viewpoint steps out of the relational moment to focus on division, fixity, disembodiment, and the creation of algorithms (standardized step-by-step solutions to problems that do not take individuality and context into account) (McGilchrist, 2009). *The central metaphor here is the machine, with our bodies, our brains, and our very selves viewed as mechanisms to be analyzed and shaped.* We might immediately sense that the perspective of each hemisphere has substantial consequences for how we are able to be present with one another.

Pause for Reflection

Let's pause to go beyond the concepts that are likely becoming more familiar to spend some time noticing the subtle and not-so-subtle shifts that inhabit our muscles, belly, chest, face, and breath as we move between right dominance, left dominance, and the more whole-brained experience of right-centric perceiving supported by the able emissary from the left. It may help to sense and talk about how this is unfolding with a reading partner or friend, as always, with as little judgment as possible. Embodiment of any of these principles is likely a lifetime's work, and it is also true that the small steps we take in that direction often yield substantial increases in connection.

As we speak from a particular perspective, our words not only reveal something about our hemispheric vantage point, but they also go on to reinforce this way of seeing, wrapping us within a distinct perceptual slant. Then, because of our resonance with each other, we are simultaneously issuing an invitation for others to join us in this mode of attending. As we shift toward left dominance, we move internally out of relationship and into isolation, no matter how many people may be present, and we are inviting others into disconnection from themselves and others as well (McGilchrist, 2009). It may feel odd to speak of "join-ing" and "disconnection" as occurring together, yet research on avoid-ant attachment (a left-hemisphere-dominant form of relating) suggests that a mother's inner state of relative disengagement is reflected in her infant's biological response of needing to go it alone through increased attempts at self-regulation even at one year of age (Hill-Soderlund et al., 2008). It is as though there is an unspoken communication that life is about independence, encouraging mother and baby to move apart into more separate universes—together. For both parent and child, the long-term effects of such isolation are profound, even leading to changes in their epigenetic profiles that support increased inflammation, the head-waters of many chronic illnesses (Fredrickson et al., 2013).

How might language separate us or draw us together? If our words center around grasping, creating, using, knowing, efficiency, step-by-step procedures, problem-solving, interventions, tools, and a sense of good-better-best (an ever-upward trend), we are likely attending mostly from a left hemisphere that is operating more or less autonomously, without support from the right's perspective. There is often a sense of judgment and certainty, along with an intent to guide, shape, or con-trol another that arises from and is reflected in this way of speaking. Because the left hemisphere has a tendency toward either/or, good/bad distinctions, there is often the sense of preference or wanting to get rid of something in favor of something else (i.e., getting rid of sadness in favor of happiness or peace).

If, on the other hand, we hear ourselves speaking words that convey attunement to the process unfolding in this moment—a felt sense of receiving, cultivating, believing, supporting, and trusting—we are more apt to be attending from the right with support from the left. This way of experiencing may also be coupled with attention to felt sense, comfort with being rather than pressure to do, and a respect for the undulating rise and fall of healing that unfolds naturally in the space between. When we are in this mode, we have a tendency to speak more tenta-tively and to check in with our relational partner about how he or she is receiving what we are offering. This last part is particularly important as it reflects our growing felt-sense awareness that the system of the person we are helping knows more about what needs to happen next than we do. In addition to the humility and respect this engenders, we may also notice that instead of wanting to get rid of some state, we are more apt to acknowledge its meaningfulness and be present to it just as it is. Listening in this way, the so-called negative state may reveal itself as telling an important truth and become an opening toward healing. We may also be aware of the limitation and incompleteness of words, leading us to honor silence as well.

There is a place for both left-dominant and right-anchored ways of seeing, being, and languaging our experience. If I want to purchase an airline ticket, it is useful that the online reservation system works in a reliably familiar way each time and that my mind can narrowly focus on the details to complete the purchase. Even though I am having an experience in the moment, my attention is appropriately on a step-by-step process to finish this task. I am likely not very aware of my body or the surrounding environment. In fact, if someone were to come in, I might experience that as an interruption rather than an opportunity for connection. If I were to speak with someone about the experience, I would likely use words that reflected the efficiency and dependability of the reservation system. And that would be that.

If my daughter then walked into the room, perhaps everything might shift toward attending to the space between us. My chest might warm as curiosity about her well-being in this moment took center stage. Neither of us would know what would happen next as we moved into the flow of this unique moment of relationship. No words could begin to capture the felt sense of all that was unfolding between us. The multilayered, embodied, ever-shifting complexity of our human interactions literally defies the confines of language. Being able to flow flexibly from one perspective taking the lead to the other, depending on context, reflects our embodied brain's growing integration, and very likely also illuminates that the right is in the role of Master while the left is the essential emissary (McGilchrist, 2009).

As we consider these two ways of attending, we could easily begin to imagine that one way of seeing is better than the other, mainly because of the left's lifelessness when left to its own devices; however, as always, relationship is everything, and the capacities of the left are essential for the expression of the right's vision. If we can find ways to support leading with the perspective of the right hemisphere, the left's capacities can then offer essential assistance from its storehouse of prior learning. One of the struggles with this is that while the right trusts the value of hemispheric collaboration, the left, with its relative blindness to relationship and tendency toward paranoia, is challenged to find value or security in the ever-flowing experience of the right. As a result and with the support of our cultural biases, the left can feel the necessity of maintaining its independent and nonrelational viewpoint (McGilchrist, 2009). Our awareness of this negotiation between the hemispheres can support the gradual integration of their viewpoints.

As we open to listening more deeply, we may begin to sense how language illuminates and influences our hemispheric location. Small shifts in the words that silently emerge within us or that we offer our patients can be one doorway into reestablishing a flowing balance between the right (in its role as Master) and left (in its role as emissary). Even though we have been so influenced by the left hemisphere's ascendency, we also have an inherent capacity to be rooted in the relational right because we are, after all, first, last, and always beings whose embodied brains hunger for connection with others, literally shaping one another's ongoing experience in every moment (Cozolino, 2014; Siegel, 2015b).

Like so much in this culture, our profession has been strongly influenced by the left dominance of this society. We find ourselves surrounded by *protocols*, evidence-based *interventions* that seek to become *algorithms* for remediating narrowly focused behavioral problems. We are urged to find *strategies* to get our patients moving in a particular direction. The concern for *speed* of recovery often engages us more than curiosity about how deep healing might be supported. Forms used in many clinics ask patients to rate their state on a regular basis, hoping to see an *ever-upward trend*, and sometimes *judging* the efficacy of the therapist by that measure without regard for the complexity of the challenges they are holding together in the space between. All of this is well intentioned with the primary *goal* being rapid reduction of suffering. However, it is built on the assumptions of the left hemisphere.

Coming from a perception of our inherent separateness, the left has the felt-sense experience that one person needs *to do* something to or for another, as one would manage a machine's performance. This is not to suggest that we stop caring about the other person when we come from this viewpoint, but that we start relating in a different way. If we begin to attend to our bodies, we may notice that our muscles, bellies, throats, and perhaps other areas respond in distinct ways when we move into this mode of relating. As we step out of responsiveness in the moment into the need to act from our own disconnected sense of what should happen next, we are no longer truly present with the other.

Pause for Reflection

Given the implicit and explicit influence exerted by the state of our culture, it is likely that all of us regularly step into this mode of doing. With as little judgment as we can manage, let's ask our systems how they might let us know when we are taking that step into left-hemisphere dominance. We may find that what helps most is dropping this open curiosity into our receptive right hemispheres and waiting for a response. Sometimes the felt-sense awareness of how our bodies announce this hemispheric change will come quickly, sometimes not until we are engaged in that shift. Often, the respectful gesture of simply pausing to pose this curiosity is enough. Our systems will respond as and when they can. Returning to glance at the question from time to time can help our inner world sense that we believe noticing how this experience feels is important.

Gradually, we may also begin to notice what initiates the movement toward the left. To what is my system adaptively responding? For example, I notice that when the other person has been in despair for a prolonged period, I begin to feel myself crumbling into discouragement internally. One of the ways my system seeks to protect both me and the other person is to activate into helpful doing. Even though it is a pseudo-engagement, the intent is to shelter us both from being engulfed in despair. As we begin to open to this practice of noticing, it is enough to just acknowledge without doing anything to change this response—good preparation for the kind of presence and receptivity we are cultivating. Paradoxically, often just acknowledging seems to open the possibility of this experience unfolding just a little differently than ever before. We may find ourselves drawn to this curiosity about what initiates the hemispheric shift more and more frequently over time as we refine our sense of how our system speaks to us.

Now we will begin to be with some words and phrases that can potentially reveal our hemispheric location and suggest some alternative language that may help anchor us in the right. One challenging part here is that if we are going to truly be in the both/and way of perceiving that is characteristic of the right mode, we will need to open ourselves to the value in the left's perspective as well. How might these two ways of seeing move into a relationship that draws on the strengths of both? These few pairings are just a bare beginning, and the hope is that the ones offered here will begin to sensitize us to listening to our body's response when words are drawn up internally and externally from our own particular storehouse of language. We might then find ourselves opening to how some of those coming from a left-dominant stance might be ready to shift to expressions more supportive of leading with the right hemisphere's perspective.

Since all these pairings are arising from seeing and experiencing the world in distinctly different ways, we will find they aren't the usual kinds of antonyms or necessarily even the same parts of speech. As much as possible, they arise from the felt sense of how we might experience life from within a left- or right-centric perspective. These may not even be the most respectful words possible, but they are a beginning with a growing edge that each of us might explore in our own unique way.

Mechanism/emerging: Any of us who read the abundant research literature, either in its original form or in the condensed versions in the press these days, will find the word "mechanism" used in regard to what is being discovered about the correlation between our experiences and the areas of our brains that light up during these experiments, as in "the mechanism for communication between the gut brain and the skull brain." The world of science is largely charged with taking things apart to look closely at how things work, then reassembling the now-inert pieces so that the feeling is often one of cogs and gears. This can be valuable in a general way, and yet it is equally valuable to recognize that the act of taking apart also removes context (the uncountable other excitations and inhibitions that are happening in our embodied brains at the same time, for example) and individuality (no two brains respond identically and no one brain responds to similar circumstances the same way all the time) in favor of looking for a somewhat artificial stability, certainty, and predictability. In this sense, neuroscience can be seen as offering metaphors that point in a general direction but don't exactly match anyone's individual experience.

It bears repeating that the intention of these scientific activities is often to increase understanding in order to relieve suffering. If we can see the scientific viewpoint as one way of perceiving rather than as offering the only or the superior truth, then we can learn from these discoveries without shifting into a more mechanical viewpoint ourselves. One danger of experiencing our brains as mechanisms is the invitation to step out of relationship with them and tinker with them as though they are machines devoid of their own kind of wisdom. The majority of research-related articles I read move automatically toward suggestions for doing something *to* the brain—finding new medications, applying techniques to train the brain, and other ways of treating the brain like an object that is separate from ourselves. In addition to this objectification, there is per-haps the greater danger that when we are viewing ourselves or another that way, we have already stepped away from being truly present, so the person being so scrutinized will not feel safe or have a felt sense of being heard, seen, or held. This includes our relationship with ourselves.

Let's spend a few moments sinking into the experience of "mech-anism." We may notice that we step back out of flowing relationship toward fixity. We have a tendency to become detached observers rather than participants. There might also be a sense of disassembling a com-plex, flowing process to focus on a small part of it. If we expand our focus to begin to include *emerging*, one of the first changes we may notice is the bodily felt sense of being in the midst of something, of constant motion, lack of clarity (in the left-hemisphere sense), and unpredictability.

Pause for Reflection

Let's pause here for just a moment to open to deeply feeling into these two words as they live in our bodies. The possible experiences offered above are small samples of what we might become aware of as we take time to sit with our experience. We could check in with our bellies, chests, throats, and muscles, as well as be open to the arrival of images, sounds, and possibly textures and colors, as we practice deep listening with "mechanism" and "emerging." Our open curiosity can support the unhurried arrival of the felt sense, which may deepen each time we revisit this pairing.

If we go to the roots of "mechanism," we of course find "machine" in the line of descent. Etymologically, we can trace this all the way back to a Greek verb that means "to be able" or "to have power over" (*Online Etymology Dictionary*, 2014), so it is rooted deeply in the left hemisphere's viewpoint. In philosophy, use of the word "mechanism" is associated with the belief that eventually all things will be explained by science, no mystery remaining.

In contrast, we find the roots of "emerging" in a verb that means to rise up or come forth from the surroundings (*Online Etymology Dictionary*, 2014); context and the relational vantage point were thus built into the word's meaning at the beginning. There is an element of the unexpected and unknown until it arrives, as well as a deep sense of interconnectedness and interdependence, all things moving together and modifying each other. This more accurately holds our felt-sense experience from the right hemisphere's perspective.

How might these two viewpoints work together? Outside my window, there's a sudden loud noise; my head turns rapidly toward the sound, my heart pounds, and I feel tension throughout my system, all automatic, visceral responses emerging in the moment. After ascertaining that there is no imminent danger (my neighbor dropped a pallet of bricks on his driveway), my left hemisphere might volunteer this: "That's my autonomic nervous system and amygdala protecting me," identifying the process that keeps me alert to new experience. My body responds by taking a deeper breath that moves me back toward a more relaxed state, as though the left hemisphere has reassured the right that all is adaptive and well. Interestingly, my left can only offer a couple of small pieces of what all was going on, and yet having that story satisfies the left (which always needs a story) as well as normalizes something for the right. This left-hemisphere response is also without judgment and focused on how the unfolding moment was adaptive, suggesting that its universe of meaning has been impregnated by the right's viewpoint and that it is truly serving as the valuable emissary who gives shape to what the right perceives and experiences. This may be the signature of the right hemisphere's leadership—that over time the left is infused with knowledge and wise principles based on repeatedly perceiving experience through the lens of the right, a kind of true nourishment for optimal relatedness between the two. Then, when the left speaks, it can support and add stability to the interpersonally rooted vision of the right.

Create/cultivate: These two words are more parallel than the two we just considered. These verbs lie at the heart of what we believe our role as practitioner might be. Let's begin this exploration by first sitting with the felt sense of these two words.

Pause for Reflection

As we open to the word "create," attending to our bellies, chests, and muscles may lead to us to also sense a movement or gesture that our bodies begin to spontaneously offer. Images may also arise. Can we just be with all this for a bit, without judgment? Then let's try on "cultivate" in a similar way—what bodily sensations, gestures, and images might we notice? Is being present with these two words tinged with a positive or negative evaluation of either of them?

Carrying with us whatever we experienced in doing the practice above, let's attend to the etymology of "create." We find the origins in "making," "producing," "causing," "bringing into existence" (*Merriam-Webster*, 2014; *Online Etymology Dictionary*, 2014). However, there is also a fourteenth-century meaning that has to do with growing and arising (as in a crescent moon), something that we may sense is a little more akin to cultivation. Over the centuries, under the influence of increasing left dominance, the meaning of words has focused on certain aspects of their origins while attending less to others. It seems that the sense of agency in the word "create" has moved to the forefront, while the complementary experience of receptivity has receded. We might recall Michelangelo speaking about how the marble would reveal to him what was inherently in it:

> *The best artist has that thought alone*
> *Which is contained within the marble shell; the sculptor's hand can*
> *   only break the spell*
> *To free the figures slumbering in the stone*

> —MICHELANGELO, N.D.

It seems he experienced the act of creation as being rooted in receptivity to what was already innately present. He and the stone participated in a silent conversation that was initiated by the marble.

Let's return to the felt sense that arose when we sat with the word "create" a few moments ago. To offer an example, when I open to the sensations that come with this focus, I notice a prominent sense of being responsible for doing something that announces itself through a subtle tightening in my belly, sharper focus of my eyes, and a gesture of moving forward that particularly localizes itself in my hands, arms, and torso. My body aligns itself with the sense of agency in the word. How is that similar or different from what you felt in sitting with "create"? There may be many occasions that call for just this way of being and doing. However, in our human encounters, this movement toward needing to create something has the potential to pull us out of connection in the emerging moment into the distancing stance of planning. It also suggests that something needs to be created because something is lacking.

The felt sense alive in "cultivate" seems to offer a different perspective—a belief that there is something inherent that is awaiting support perhaps, an essentially relational stance. When we cultivate the soil or a friendship, we offer to collaborate with what we sense is already present. Turning to etymology, we find the roots of this metaphor in breaking up the soil in preparation for growth (*Online Etymology Dictionary*, 2014). This then extends to language like "foster," "encourage," "make friends with," "seek closeness with" (*Merriam-Webster*, 2014). There is less sense of personal agency and greater focus on how being actively present with one another can offer nourishment for the next unfolding.

We may feel ourselves move into a role similar to that of a gardener as we cultivate a space in which healing can naturally unfold. In terms of neurobiology, this stance encourages us to lean into the reassuring awareness that our systems already contain seeds awaiting our attention. For some examples, we humans are always seeking the warmest attachments we can imagine (Cozolino, 2014; Siegel, 2015b), our brains are continuously yearning for the arrival of a co-organizing other (Badenoch, 2011; Cozolino, 2014; Schore, 2012), emotional regulation flows naturally from being in the presence of someone we trust (Beckes & Coan, 2011), and even our nervous systems have a preference for the social engagement circuitry that sustains connection (Porges, 2011). With this kind of support from the biology inherent in both practitioner and patient, our bodies may begin to open into a welcoming state as others come toward us, with a sense of a partnership being established rather than one person doing something to or for another. However, this also means letting go of the potential certainty that comes from feeling as though we are in charge. How can we increasingly be with the challenge offered by each moment's ambiguous and tentative arrival? This can possibly be one of our ongoing open curiosities, encouraging us to allow space and time for our own unique responses to emerge, possibly with the support of our reading partner.

To honor the both/and tendency of our right hemispheres, how might we include "create" within "cultivate"? We might begin by reclaiming the felt sense of receptivity that lies within the origins of create. Cultivation seems to presuppose that there is something inherent that can be relied upon as a starting place if we can open to receive it. In gardening, the soil is already here and able to let us know what it needs in order to become the most receptive medium for growth. As we till the soil, we may find that rocks need removing or rich compost might be added, and that will have been shown to us by the soil itself. Entering into relationship from this perspective may turn out to awaken the creative potential that is innate and now being enlivened within this connected space, a kind of co-creativity just waiting to have what it needs to manifest. Then creating isn't something one person does alone but instead unfolds in a dynamic, emerging partnership.

These two pairs—mechanism/emerging and create/cultivate—seem foundational in some way, and we can likely spend weeks, months, and years listening to our bodies as we shift our words and our hemispheric perspective. Gaining familiarity with the felt sense of this movement can become a central support in being more frequently grounded in a right-centric relational stance, a perspective that can help us sustain safety in the space between. Now, we're going to be with two other pairs that are likely familiar from our day-to-day professional environment.

Protocols/supplies: When my daughter was young and we would head out on a road trip, often with a couple of her friends in tow, we didn't have *protocols* for when and how snacks would occur. Instead, we had abundant nourishing *supplies* that we could offer according to the need of the moment. It was our responsibility to attend to the quality of nourishment as well as having awareness of what the children could take in with joy, and from there, we followed their lead for the most part. With the possible exception of "it's almost time for dinner," we flexibly grazed our way along the back roads.

The various definitions of "protocol" (*Merriam-Webster*, 2014) suggest some kind of codification as a reference point for how to undertake similar procedures in the future. There is a distinctly left-hemisphere sense of agreements or conventions to be followed, a code that details correct etiquette and precedence for the future—a sense of freezing processes in place so they can be repeated; in essence, an algorithm. If we turn to "supply," we find more of a sense of making something available to meet the needs of another according to what is happening in this particular moment (*Merriam-Webster*, 2014). Turning to origins, "supply" (which is both a noun and a verb) carries the sense of completing, compensating for, filling up for another—a greater sense of flow, flexibility, and moment-to-moment responsiveness. Protocols exist outside of context, while the offering of supplies is context-dependent and inherently relational.

Pause for Reflection

Let's take a moment to come into contact with the felt sense of each word in our bodies—first "protocol" and then "supply." How do our bellies, chests, and muscles feel? Are there images that emerge? Is there a gesture that our bodies might make in regard to each? What is it like to imagine letting go of protocols? How does having them serve us? If we open ourselves to having abundant supplies that are called forth by ever-changing circumstances, how is that? Just dropping these curiosities into our right hemisphere may make room for the gradual emergence of felt-sense experience.

Protocols we may have learned have the opportunity to become supplies when they encounter the solvent of this moment's need, softening to become flexible and adaptive. If we have first developed sound left-hemisphere knowledge about particular practices for interacting with another (e.g., EMDR, sand tray, body-based therapies, and many more), we may then be able to let go of the need to decide in advance what the other person requires. This process of letting go of being in charge often unfolds over time as we develop greater trust in the wisdom of our patient's system as it awakens within the embrace of the relationship, so that we gradually need less and less to find our own security by taking the lead.

Over the years, at least partly in response to our left-shifted environment, I have found that much that happens in supervision/consultation focuses on what needs to happen next. There can be a sense of the person under consideration becoming a static object to be analyzed, and then advice may be offered about how that person could/should be shaped in a certain (presumably healthier) way. This can sound cold, but is actually often accompanied by a warm sense of deep care for this person's well-being, so there may be a mixture of right- and left-hemisphere perspectives. However, in the moment of encounter, if our attention is on what we're going to do next to accomplish a specific goal (often decrease a symptom) rather than on openness to what the other person is bringing in this moment, we have stepped into our left hemispheres and out of relationship—and our patient will feel that as a kind of subtle abandonment (S. W. Porges, personal communication, October 19, 2014). This interchange will likely happen below the level of conscious awareness and yet lead our person to step back a bit internally, awaiting the arrival of true presence, without agenda or judgment, so that safety can arise in the space between. At that moment, the healing power inherent in this co-organizing/co-regulating relationship arrives. We have been returning to this crucial distinction in these pages, as much as possible with ongoing compassion for the challenge we experience as we open to the right remaining consistently in the lead.

Intervention/following: This final pair is central to our work. Hardly a day goes by that the word "intervention" doesn't enter the conversation. At its root, it invites us to step between, to interrupt what is currently happening, and do something (*Online Etymology Dictionary,* 2014). Interestingly, one of the earlier meanings was also related to intercessory prayer, which carries much more of a relational sense, a yearning for the Divine to step into our human world to help us, but this meaning has been largely lost, not only in the cognitive sense but also in the felt sense (*Online Etymology Dictionary,* 2014).

Pause for Reflection

As we have been, with as little judgment as we can manage in this moment, let's invite our body to share its response to "intervention"— bellies, chest, muscles. What gestures and images come? How does it feel the same or different from "protocol," "create," and "mechanism"? If we imagine not intervening, what felt sense and gestures might arise? Can we be gently curious as we sit with these experiences, perhaps with a reading partner, allowing them the time, space, and support to reveal themselves to us?

The dictionary definition of "intervention" adds the idea of systematic assessment and planning to remedy a problem with the intention of preventing further harm (*Merriam-Webster*, 2014). The struggle here is the original perception that there is a *problem* to which *we* can *apply a specific cure*, a cure that we know in advance will remediate the perceived difficulty. All sense of context, individuality, and the emerging moment has a tendency to be lost. Much of what we are calling evidence-based intervention these days rests on these assumptions and guides us away from being present in the complexity of the unique moment. Intervening from this perspective has the potential to keep us from being able to provide safety in the space between, meaning that both practitioner and patient are less safe and, therefore, less able to connect. This may seem counterintuitive, because taking steps to intervene can feel like it provides us with security as we take charge. However, what we are coming to understand about our autonomic nervous systems (Porges, 2011) suggests that anything we determine to do in advance has already separated us from being in this emerging moment with ourselves as well as the other person. Part of the challenge to remaining in the moment is rooted in the original perception that there is a problem, which immediately draws our attention away from wholeness of the person toward a split-off bit of him or her. If we are practitioners in the field of psychology, we have an entire manual (the *DSM-5*, at this point) (American Psychiatric Association, 2013) that seeks to *define* what is *wrong* with people via *lists* of *symptoms*. For me, just writing that sentence brings on a sense of fracturing, accompanied by a feeling of separation between me and the others being studied.

If we want to explore a different way of being with ourselves and our patients, we might try on the word "following."

Pause for Reflection

Remembering that anything may happen when we do these practices, let's open ourselves to the possibility of surprises. What happens to our muscles as we listen for the felt sense of "following"? How about our bellies and chests? Gestures, images, textures, colors? What is the emotional tone that arises when imagining "following"? Taking time to let our bodies offer a range of responses can help us develop trust in the depth of wisdom our bodies carry.

If we follow this word back to its roots, we find "full-going," which then moves to "serve or go with an attendant" (*Online Etymology Dictionary*, 2014). Among a whole host of definitions offered, we find "watching steadily," "keeping the mind on," and "attending closely" (*Merriam-Webster*, 2014). In this sense, following is about linking with another and keeping that one in the center of flowing awareness, which is exactly what the right hemisphere has the potential to do beautifully. In fact, we may best begin by following our own internal movement as it arises in the presence of the other person.

Let me share a story. In a conversation with my friend Rich Armington about the art show that offers the work of Austin's street dwellers, he said, "Over the years, Art From the Streets has become an intervention on behalf of the homeless" (R. Armington, personal communication, December 9, 2014). I was just writing this part of the chapter, and so we began a discussion about whether it was an intervention or more of a following. So here is the story about the origins of this festival. Many years ago, Rich's wife, Heloise Gold, and her friend Beverly Bajema, felt called to help at a homeless shelter, serving food to hungry humans. They went in with the intention to get to know the people first and then offer an opportunity for creativity. They quickly became uncomfortable being on the other side of the table and so came around into the midst of these people, bringing art supplies, sitting with them, drawing and painting together. Over time, this gesture of respect and kindness became a small art show and now has grown into a large annual community-based gathering, Art From the Streets (artfromthestreets.com). Heloise's original impulse followed her awareness of her relational yearning for greater contact and interaction. Now the show continues to provide opportunities for the familiar barriers to dissolve as artists sit with their art so there is no temptation to separate the beauty from the one through whom it arrived—the relational core of it.

As Art From the Streets has grown into a major event, it has been necessary to create procedures so everything unfolds smoothly, and this is the province of the left hemisphere. Because Heloise has continued to quietly guide the process, these procedures organize around the relational intention, even in the spaciousness of the Austin Convention Center. This community endeavor has faced the crossroads where there was the potential to shift into left-hemisphere, impersonal organization or retain the right-hemisphere perspective with the left in service. Since Heloise has continued to hold the values, the original intention is still honored.

Moment to moment, she and her people continue to follow, responding to whatever is arising, maintaining proximity with the artists—who may be facing mental, emotional, or physical challenges—through gentle and playful co-regulation. As Heloise's hand moves outward to comfort a frightened young woman who is a first-time exhibitor, we witness the intersection of intervention and following, as her gesture is called forth by the expression she sees in this young one's face. What unfolds in that convention center is the fruit of trusting relationships established over years of contact. What began with Heloise attending to her own inner world has flowered into being attentive to the world of the homeless in a way that has broken through stereotypes (creations of the left-hemisphere perspective) and altered a city's perception of these people and themselves—a profound example of relieving trauma through relationship.

While we could say that technically this isn't a clinical example, this event, as well as the whole year of preparation as the artists' creativity emerges in twice-a-week open studio sessions, is clearly therapeutic for the whole community. It will always be my viewpoint that interpersonal neurobiology asks us to place no boundaries on where and how it might illuminate our world. It is possible that every moment has the potential to be therapeutic in some way. As we deepen into an embodied sense of IPNB's way of seeing, a profound right-centric shift may begin to color every aspect of our perception. In our counseling rooms as well as our daily lives, how might we maintain a similar sense of following, allowing each moment to bring forward from the left's storehouse what may be helpful and responsive? This is the ongoing curiosity at the heart of this book. The challenge—which is also at the center—is that what animates the process of following is letting go of certainty, control, planning, clear-cut goals, and so much more that may feel settling even as it separates us from those we want to help. This letting go requires cultivation of trust in the innate processes that support the movement toward healing, something that grows with time and experience, especially when compassion for this depth of challenge to our need for security is present.

In the not-so-distant past, I had an experience that has become a visceral marker for the difference between how the hemispheres offer presence. As Lila stepped into my office, I smiled and said, "I was thinking about you this week." At this moment, I can still see and feel how her eyes lit up with the felt sense that she existed for me at other times than when we were together physically. Then, as we sat down, I went on, "And I thought of something I wanted to share with you." I have no memory of what that was, but the feeling of contraction in my belly as the light went out of her eyes is still strong. In that moment, she experienced me abandoning her because I was relating to the Lila who was in my office last week, not this unique person here today, who hadn't even had a chance to speak for herself yet. In fact, I had frozen her in time within me for a whole week and was now prepared with an intervention that would somehow help. On another day, this may have gone differently, depending on Lila's inner state. However, I have learned through experience that it is always more risky for me to intervene than to first be present to where we are in this moment. In the development of language, before there was the word "intervention," there was the impulse to step in between a person and his experience, without checking in first, a particular relational style that arises from the combination of left dominance and the wish to help. I believe we find ourselves implicitly and explicitly nudged in that direction by our current cultural milieu, and it takes a good deal of attentiveness to notice as it happens. Fortunately, when there are ruptures, there are also opportunities to repair if we are able to sense these breaks in connection.

An infinite number of pairings might present themselves to us once we begin to be continually curious about the influence of the words we speak and hear. After five years of opening to this, my belly and muscles in particular offer me a running commentary on the conversation going on around me and within me. Here are three more pairs we may want to play with, or we could just drop them into our minds and see what they might want to do when we aren't looking, since most of our thinking goes on without conscious awareness.

Pathology/opportunity: I wonder if the right hemisphere believes there is such a thing as pathology or if our symptoms might all be seen as truth-telling and adaptive. Then they might become opportunities—favorable junctures, openings with a good chance for advancement (*Merriam-Webster*, 2014).

Goals/curiosity: I do not remember one time when the goals my patient could articulate on the first visit had much to do with why his or her whole individual self had brought this person into my office. What would happen if we led with warm curiosity about this unique individual in this moment? What if we had no treatment plan beyond that?

Triggering/touching and awakening: We have been exploring the possibility of there being a gift in the awakening of our implicit memories. It might be possible that "triggered" may not be the most helpful word to apply to these arisings. For me, there is a sense of violence in this word, while "touched and awakened" more accurately describes what happens to these sequestered neural nets. This gentler wording helps us cultivate a sense of meeting the experience every time we are so "touched" with an appreciation for what it might be offering. Then, the neural firings and neurochemistry of gratefulness we visited in Chapter 15 come to support us, and we begin to find a new gentleness in these embodied awakenings as they are related to just a bit differently. In this way, we return to the principle that perhaps relationship is everything.

We may find more pairings begin to spontaneously arise and offer themselves for exploration now that we have begun this process.

Whether or not we ever actually speak the words we've explored here, the relational feeling of them likely permeates our work because they are central metaphors for our profession and hold such distinct viewpoints about how we are with one another. Once wrapped up in either of these ways of seeing, our conversational language arises from these comprehensive felt-sense perspectives that are informed by our hemispheric location. From there, we and those around us are drawn either away from or toward true presence with one another. Since presence is the foundation of healing, the stakes are quite high.

If, after this exploration, we feel drawn to align a little more with right-centric words, surprisingly, we may be seeking to return language to its origins in the right hemisphere, to reembody it. Following the work of anthropologists, including Robin Dunbar (2004), McGilchrist (2009) takes us on a journey from great apes grooming one another through music to the gradual appearance of language, with referential left-hemisphere language being a late arrival to the neighborhood. Instead, the emergence of language is an embodied, right-hemisphere-centric story in which these acts of communication are intended for establishing and maintaining cooperative community rather than analytic dissection and competition. McGilchrist (2009) says,

> One theory is that singing, a sort of instinctive musical language of intonation, came into being precisely because, with the advent of humans, social groups became too large for grooming to be practical as a means of bonding. Music, on this account, is a sort of groom-

ing at a distance; no longer necessitating physical touch, but a body language all the same. (p. 106)

The trail of evidence for such origins is complex and beyond the scope of our study here (see McGilchrist, 2009, pp. 94–132, for a more complete account); however, at the core of it is the sense that first music and then language were originally intended to be invitations to inhabit one another's emotional world, to resonate with each other in an embodied way that promoted the possibility of truly encountering each other in the space between. It seems true that about 90 percent of communication is nonverbal even while we are using the linguistic materials of left-hemisphere based words to indicate our intention to build felt-sense bridges to link with our fellow humans. It is intriguing that language "involves the same processes, and even the same brain areas, as certain highly expressive gestures" (McGilchrist, 2009, p. 122), possibly keeping the tendency toward embodiment alive. Additionally, listening to one another activates our mirror neurons and resonance circuitry (Iacoboni, 2009), so that we can be said to literally begin to inhabit one another's embodied emotional universe (subject, of course, to some coloring from our own system).

Recently at a retreat, one of our members was clearly deeply moved, touching into a painful memory. In a diffuse way, we were able to be with her in her suffering. She initially felt hesitant about sharing the content of the memory, but as we sat together, she found the words to offer something about an experience of being abandoned in ways that raised a lot of shame for her. As the words of the narrative entered the room, it was as if our compassion came into sharper focus, surrounding this wounded part of her with such tenderness. Several members of our group said they felt more able to be present with her as the content was added. While the words themselves could never hold the experience, once the living implicit was in the room, they could give it a shape that our whole brains could take in. This kind of partnership, beginning with the right's experience, moving to the left for words and then back to the right for a deeply shared interpersonal experience, is the essence of embodied language.

As we explored our pairs above, we saw that many of the earlier, more relational meanings have been stripped away by the growing blindness of the left hemisphere to a felt sense of "we." As a result, many words have been incarcerated in somewhat impoverishing boxes. Ours is a quest for liberation of language back to its roots in the body. With mixed results, I feel sure, this book is seeking to honor language in this way. Having marinated in the perspectives of the last few chapters, it's time to step into the counseling room. Having set our inner table, we may now offer our people a nourishing meal of safety, receptivity, respect, responsiveness, and repair.

PART TWO

Nourishing Accompaniment

Introduction to Part Two

Now we move into the counseling room with all that we have developed in ourselves through spending time and attention with the previous chapters:

- the practice of nonjudgmental, agendaless presence as the foundation for safety and co-regulation,
- deepened awareness of the neural streams flowing in our bodies,
- the conviction that we are adaptive rather than disordered,
- the hopeful understanding that implicit memory can change,
- the depth of our sensitivity to one another's presence,
- appreciation for the profound resources of inherent wisdom and health that are alive in us, and
- perhaps some supportive shifts in language.

Taken together, these may have deepened our trust in our people's inborn capacity to heal. Studying and practicing these concepts has also been feeding our left-hemisphere emissary so that it can support our increasing capacity for right-centric attending with its clarity about how embedded traumas can heal as they receive the support they need.

We also bring humility, recognizing that ruptures are a daily occurrence in all our relationships and grateful that our systems only need to receive resonance and reflection on the first try at connecting about 33 percent of the time to cultivate security. All the rest is optimally rupture and repair (Beebe & Lachmann, 1994; Schore, 1994; Tronick, 1989, 2003). "Optimally" is such an important word. When we experience a break in connection followed by repeated attempts at repair until the bond is restored, we build the implicit pathways of resilience. We come to know in a visceral way that when things break down interpersonally, someone will return to help us come back into relationship. That wired-in optimism and expectation makes it much more likely that we will form relationships that have this quality. Most of the people who come to us haven't had this experience consistently in their lives, so when they encounter it with us, it is often surprising to the point of tears. As we accept and then rejoice in our humanness, we offer this vital gift of rupture and repair to those around us.

The clinical stories that make up a good deal of this part of the book are drawn from my experiences with the courageous people who have come to our clinic over the years. Most of them have felt so broken that they thought they would never heal, but somehow we have made our way together through the uncertain territory of their inner world toward their own version of what healing can look like for them. I have been struck by the uniqueness and creativity of their systems when they have been given support to unfold along their natural path. Often, the results have been unexpected and certainly not in conformity with any list of outcomes. Sometimes, from a certain viewpoint, we could say that therapy failed, and yet something has happened that has been meaningful and transformative in its own way. We will explore all of this.

Each of us has cultivated certain ways of working with our people. Mine include deep listening to the wisdom of the body as a guide to what is needed right now, sand and miniatures, nondominant hand drawing, and exploration of the gestures, sounds, and images that arise as we touch the deep implicit places within us. We also work directly with emerging implicit memory in ways that make room for disconfirming experiences of many kinds and do this from the perspective of multiple selves, what we call our inner community. Each of you have your own repertoire of cultivated expertise, so what will be offered here is more of a guide for how any process can arise from and rest on the foundation of presence. With that, we move toward the rich stories of recovery that I have been blessed to share with so many courageous people.

18

Leading, Following, Responding

Safety IS the treatment.

—STEPHEN W. PORGES, 2016

Today I am seeing several people in various stages of integrating the embedded traumas that have troubled their quality of life and relationships. Between each meeting, I usually feel drawn to do a brief practice to let go of what was just experienced and settle into the felt sense of opening into receptivity. It begins with rooting my feet into the stability of the earth; then listening to the sensations of my muscles, belly, and heart with no intent to change anything; glancing upward at the spaciousness of the sky as the complement to the solidity beneath my feet; following the flow of my in-breath and out-breath a couple of times, again with no intention to shift anything but just listen and experience; and opening into a bowl of receptivity, which may feel like an expansion and quieting of my heart.* The experience is different every time. Sometimes there is pervasive distraction, sometimes a wish to change the tension in my muscles or the depth of my breath, sometimes judgment about how I'm doing this practice, and sometimes it flows like a sweet river. Most important is being present to *what is* with as little judgment as possible, even when this means being present to judgment itself. *That level of acceptance, much more*

---

* If you want to do this receptivity practice in a longer format to ingrain the pattern, there is a recording on the resources page of our website, nurturingtheheart.org.

than the practice itself, is what can prepare us to receive our person with the same quality of attending.

It is rather paradoxical for our task-focused self when it isn't the quality of the practice, but our honest and humble acceptance of the emerging moment, that prepares us for nonjudgmental, agendaless presence with another. Being kind to ourselves can be helpful as we seek to practice this way of being, because it places us at cross-purposes with our culture, where performance and improvement are so valued and the limits and variability of our humanness are cause for criticism and correction. Many aspects of our training as well as our everyday experience in this society urge us to take control to achieve a particular result, and this can become so implicitly ingrained that it feels wrong to sink toward our innate humanity. Again, just listening with kindness to the competing voices inside is such good preparation for extending this attentiveness and kindness to all aspects of the person about to come in our door.

Pause for Reflection

Taking a few minutes to reread these two paragraphs, let's notice what happens at this cultural crossroads. What is it like to imagine doing a meditative practice without critiquing how well we're doing it? When the evaluation does arise, does it set off a cascade of judging the judgment? Sometimes a little humor might be possible around this particular pattern of hamster-wheel criticism. Then we might see if it is possible to step back and hold the entire sequence with kindness.

Changing perspectives, let's reflect on our experience of whichever patient comes easily to mind. Perhaps we can sense something about how openness/receptivity and/or control/intervention may both be present during different parts of our sessions with him or her. Remembering that the impulse to control is an indication that we are having a neuroception of danger, perhaps we can be compassionate rather than critical of ourselves when we do step in to overtly manage the process. Perhaps we can begin to ask inside about the nature of the threat that brings on the need to assert control and fix. As always, dropping the questions into our right hemisphere and not expecting a particular answer in this moment opens the way for a deeper understanding to emerge bit by bit.

Having done this preparatory practice of receptivity and with what-ever depth of presence is available to me today, I meet David at the threshold. I sense that my eyes are warmly curious to take in his face and gaze this day, this moment. There is often a good deal of warmth between us from long familiarity. We have been working with his sea of embedded traumas from a cruel and violent childhood for about three years. When he arrives, I believe we initially experience safety most days because we have moved through rupture and repair dozens of times, and many of his traumatic experiences have been held in safety, finding what they needed to integrate. An implicit foundation of assumed security has slowly grown beneath our feet so that we believe we will go forward together through whatever stumbles may come.

We also have our reassuring rituals. He has a preference for getting the exchange of funds out of the way, so he tucks his already-written check under the box of tissues. I nod my thank you. He prefers this minimalist acknowledgment that money is involved in our encounter. I believe his child self needs to sense that he is simply welcome here and that the monetary exchange has nothing to do with the quality of holding and care, so his adult organized self quietly manages the finances for both of them. A cup of warm water is waiting for him this day. When I occasionally forget to do this, it has become a source of rupture and repair for us.

As we settle more deeply into our familiar couches, a moment of silence invites me to fill the space, to intervene, make a suggestion, remember something from the last session. Instead, I breathe a bit and wait. On another day, I might offer something else: "What comes with you today?" or "I'm glad to see you." More important than the words or silence is my inner stance of making room for what is stirring within him, becoming alertly still enough inside that his inner world senses safety, the precursor to him opening into vulnerability. Some time ago, I had realized in my own therapy that my system began to prepare for our sessions about twenty-four hours before we got together. When I was met with openness, it might take me some time to drop into what was present, but I usually got there, and I grew to appreciate the agendaless space and time that made it possible.

If David and I are in the moment, neither of us knows what is going to happen next, which is a tentative, uncertain, and potentially sym-pathetically activating state. When patients tell me of the mild anxiety that comes with them to each session, I no longer think of it as a problem, but instead as an indication of their aliveness at the brink of the unknown. For me, the accumulated resources of what my left hemisphere knows about the healing process often provide some stability and a greater likelihood of remaining in ventral in these moments of uncertainty. When my neuroception of safety is present, it supports the other person's ability to bring his or her anxiety under the larger ventral umbrella supplied by our two joined systems.

David and I share a history, and it affects how we come together. From the moment we see each other, a rich interchange is already taking place below the level of conscious awareness as our two systems converse along multiple lines of communication. Since we began with a felt sense of safety this day, several neural streams are initially supporting the renewal of our connection. In our midbrain, the energies of the SEEKING system are animating the CARE system, which can both foster the good feelings between us and support offers of repair should we have a rupture (Panksepp & Biven, 2012). Once in connection, our ventral vagal parasympathetic system is affecting the prosody of our voices, our facial mobility, and the attentiveness of our listening, maintaining social engagement (Porges, 2011). Since ventral lateralizes to the right hemisphere, we more easily stay rooted in the right-centric way of attending that keeps us in connection with this moment and with each other (McGilchrist, 2009). In this intimacy, our brains are coupling in many regions, so there is an experience of emotional engagement and embodied communication as we become a single system in two bodies (Hasson, 2010). Because we are trustworthy partners in this healing process, social baseline theory tells us that our right amygdalae are calming just because we are together (Beckes & Coan, 2011). All of this is happening without *doing* anything, without even saying anything, in microseconds below conscious awareness because of the safe space we have cultivated over time. We can more clearly understand why Porges says, "Safety IS the treatment" (Porges, Badenoch, & Phillips, 2016).

An additional process is also unfolding. Through mirror neurons and resonance circuitry, we are taking in each other's bodily state, feelings, and intention in each emerging moment (Iacoboni, 2009). This gives us an approximate empathic sense of what is happening in the other person, but it is important to be aware that the information is also being filtered through our own implicit lens. This filtering colors our perceptions and pretty much guarantees that there will be ruptures that invite repairs, as our offers of empathy will sometimes not reflect what the other person is experiencing. Resonance also means that whatever may be stirring in David's implicit memory will be felt by my internal world as well, even though it may not rise to the level of conscious awareness. At the same time, his limbic circuitry may be alert for anything I might do that more strongly awakens something implicit in him that is already close by.

After a moment, without my conscious direction, I glance at the clock. David tightens and says, "You did it again." I am immediately able to respond with "I know I did. I'm sorry." Making contact with the clock has always been one of my go-to protectors when something gets stirred inside, almost always outside my conscious awareness. I'm not sure if this shift provides reassurance, a distraction, or is an attempt to regain stability via a small movement to left-centric attending—maybe some of all of this. I am rarely aware of what has made this protection necessary, although I mostly assume there was some hint of danger in the underground resonance between us that required me to shift out of connection for a moment. This time, I am able to notice that the prosody of my apology has a ventral quality and eye contact is easy, telling me that I haven't slipped toward a dorsal state of shame with this rupture, at least not enough to pull me out of connection. This is perhaps the gift of me saying inwardly, "thirty-three percent with rupture and repair" many times each day, declaring human imperfection to be optimal rather than shameful.

Because this is a familiar rupture for David and me, there is usually a tinge of humor in our exchange about it these days. However, I am also aware that his body tightened significantly when I broke the connection. The rupture seems repaired, so it is likely okay to move on. Responding to the physical tension I noticed, I ask him if he is aware of what happened in his body when I looked at the clock. With practice, he has strengthened his capacity to listen inwardly with interest and with far fewer judgments. Today, he might equally find that the moment has passed and the sensation is gone, or that the sensation is still wanting to be heard and comes into his awareness as he offers attention. *If we trust that our inner world knows what is needed next, one outcome isn't preferable to the other.* It is so easy for us to want healing to pursue a more linear path: Something arises and it would be best if we could stay with that. There can be a sense of disappointment in therapist, patient, or both if the sensation doesn't return. This might be perceived as a lack in our patient's ability to maintain contact, a reflection of our inadequacy as a therapist, or simply discomfort that the therapy feels stuck.

Pause for Reflection

Let's take a moment to see if we remember a time when a process that had begun simply stopped, faded away, or became unavailable in some other way. It could be in our own therapy or with our patients. What was our experience of this? We might check in with muscles, belly, heart, and breath as a beginning place. Then we can move to the feelings and thoughts that arose from these sensations. Do we feel at ease with these kinds of experiences, or does it feel as if something is wrong? We may find that other examples come to our awareness as well, bringing similar or different cascades of sensation, feeling, and thought. As best we can, we may offer all of them welcome with warmth and kindness.

This day, the sensation does not return. Because of our long experience with each other, David and I are able to acknowledge the wisdom of his system rather than judge it as a lost opportunity, even though we may never know exactly how or why the tightening sensation was unavailable. Because we have grown to trust the process, this acknowledgment happens along the pathways of our out-of-awareness embodied conversation (detailed above) and is then translated into words. With this coherence between the felt sense and thoughts, we both feel settled.

I continue to be so appreciative of how much these communications that arise in our embodied brains outside our conscious awareness influence what happens next. For David and me, because we have both gotten to the place of ease with not knowing, there is not much of an impulse to push or control the situation and no interpersonal tension because one of us feels we are doing it wrong. Instead, we are free to remain in connection with each other and await the next arising from his inner world. "Let's see what wants to come now," I say, and we become quiet again. After a moment, he says, "I am realizing that I felt drawn to the sand tray even before I got here." Together we move toward preparations for honoring his inner sense of what is needed in this moment.

When we talk about cultivating a nonjudgmental, agendaless space between, we might easily believe this means we are passively present. Quite the contrary. We are dynamically awake in the midst of the inner stillness and receptivity, attending to and following what is emerging in our people. At the moment some direction makes itself known, all our left-centric wisdom (in the service of right-centric relationship) arrives to support the path the person's inner world has offered. With David, my twenty-three years of working with sand and miniatures comes forward to actively support him.

The difference between how we might usually practice and this way of working is that *the focus comes from our patients' receptive listening inside, not from us having a sense of what to do to correct, change, heal, or fix the symptom or concern our people are bringing.* It is as though we become the Sherpa to accompany them on their self-chosen Himalayan journey. Our long acquaintance with the vicissitudes of the trek lets us know what supplies may be necessary and most helpful. We have some idea of the road ahead, but our Trekkers have chosen this path of healing and will guide us about the direction, the pace, how far they want to go, and what this experience means for them at each step along the way. Actually, in its own quiet way, our service began when we offered safety so that there was enough support for our people to listen inside for what is needed.

David had clarity about what his system was asking for and could overtly share it with me. However, often our people will be far less aware of what they are needing, but nonetheless tell us in subtle ways often having to do with the quality of our relating. I am remembering a young woman who was deeply disturbed by responses she was having to lectures in a college course concerning World War II. Her distress about these arisings, in the form of confusion and anxiety, was present in the room as she shared how she could barely sit in class because she felt like throwing up or running away. In response, I felt my own breathing deepen as if to offer a little containment for her upset. She told me she had never had any kind of noticeable reaction in any class before, including history courses that contained a lot of violent conflict, so she was at a loss to explain her intense reaction. What confused her most was that it didn't seem as if it was the Holocaust that was so upsetting, but little things like a description of Hitler's bunker or Goebbels's family life. She never knew which bits of information would set her off. Slowing down a little, looking away, she told me she felt deeply ashamed of not being able to hold it together.

Right at this point, we arrive at a crossroads. Out of my concern for her distress, my mind might get busy with ways to alleviate her symptoms. There are so many valuable techniques for regulation, for exploring and integrating traumatic experience, and so on. Once we know these protocols, they may pull on us in ways that invite us to seize control of the therapy. The other pathway suggests that her system holds the answers and that if I can offer enough safe support, it will likely begin to speak with us. At least cognitively, I can recognize that this person's inner world contains much more information about the root causes of her upset than I do. From this perspective, I am less interested in dealing with symptoms than moving toward making room for the implicit origin to emerge so that the protective symptoms can take care of themselves.

Pause for Reflection

Let's take a little time to sense what happens in our bodies when we go in either of these directions. What do we notice in our bellies when the impulse to take control arises? In our heart region? In our muscles? Does our breathing change? Is there a change in the area around our eyes? What about our posture? We will each have our own set of bodily responses that announce the arrival of the need to take control (which is accompanied by a shift, however subtle, into sympathetic activation and a decrease in connection with our person as she is in this moment).

Now let's take a couple of breaths to release this orientation. When we move into the experience of receptivity as best we can, what do we notice about belly, heart, muscles, breathing, eyes, and posture? It may be helpful to rest there for a bit and then to feel the difference between these two states of body, heart, and mind again to gain more familiarity.

What effect does it have on us if we imagine someone else being in these two embodied conditions while he or she is trying to help us? What is our body's response to offers of control and offers of deep listening? There are no right or wrong or preferable answers here, just the experience of making contact with what actually happens for us.

My multifaceted canary in the coal mine signaling the impulse to take control is my belly tightening, my posture changing slightly to lean forward, and tension increasing in my upper arms. It feels as though I am preparing to thrust myself into the middle of the problem with everything I know. It comes from a good-hearted place of wanting to relieve suffering and also diminishes interpersonal safety as my system enters mild to medium sympathetic arousal.

If we take a step back, we might become curious about how the neuroception of danger arose in the first place, because that is what initiates this chain of events. If we were to explore this, many answers might come: We have been trained to intervene; we don't have any experience that tells us our patients' systems are trustworthy guides to healing; the upset in our patient is severe enough that we fear for her safety; if we can't heal this person, there's something wrong with us; strong emotions are uncomfortable for us and we need to regulate them before they overwhelm us. The list is endless, individual, and likely changes with each new circumstance. It is always a most valuable inquiry, especially if we can begin it with compassionate curiosity, which makes it less likely that we will feel shamed by the answer that presents itself. When we remember that neuroception is an automatic adaptive process, it may take character condemnation out of the equation when we invite awareness of what frightens us.

If our fear feels heard and acknowledged, there is some likelihood that our bodies will be able to find their way back toward receptivity. As we feel our own openness returning, we can be certain that this embodied change is also influencing our patient and the quality of the connection. With this young woman, I found that my quiet attentiveness seemed to make space for her to deepen her exploration without me needing to add much more. She moved over on the couch to sit a little closer as her fear began to rise while she described a particular interchange between Goebbels and his wife. As our eyes met, I felt drawn to ask her if she was feeling something in her body. Most importantly, at a deep level, I had no wish for her to answer in a particular way. It could be that my question was not aligned with where she was and we would encounter our first rupture. It could equally be that she would shift her attention to her body and come into contact with part of the implicit root of her struggle. As long as I was aligned with listening rather than with an intention to receive a particular response or to shift something, we would stay on safe ground.

She noticed that the familiar nausea was rising. As her system spoke to us, we could move into following its lead. My left-centric emissary/ Sherpa knows the general pathway from bodily sensations to implicit memory, so I could begin to tentatively offer some practices for responding to her sick belly.

"How would it be if you put your hand on your belly right where you feel it most intensely?"

Closing her eyes, she tried it, and I found that my hand was moving toward that spot on my belly as well. "It feels warm and a little scary," she said.

"Does it feel like your belly would like your hand to stay there?"

She paused for a second or two to listen. "Yes, for now."

We sat quietly for a moment more, allowing her belly to get used to the contact. I was savoring the warmth of my hand on my belly, my unspoken contribution to the goodness of making this connection. When I had the sense that things had settled a bit, I felt drawn to ask another question, again knowing that it might or might not be helpful. "Do you hear or see or have a sense of anything else besides the nausea?"

"Something keeps flickering in and out of my vision, and it scares me." She opened her eyes, took her hand off her belly, and moved away from experiencing. I didn't know if I had initiated a rupture with my question or if her system was ready to stop the exploration for now. My own hand was lingering on my belly. This was one of those moments of uncertainty and a bit of unease that come in the midst of following an unknown path. I sensed that little rise in my body's tension as it responded by wanting to take charge and felt a deeper breath draw me back into listening.

After a moment, she said, "You know, I feel like we'll find the answer right where we were, but I can't do it all at once. Does that make me a coward?"

I smiled broadly. "My goodness, no! This is your body's wisdom speaking to us, sensing when it is safe to go forward, pulling back a bit when it might be too much. You and I are just getting to know one another, so I really respect the caution and protection in your inner world." Over time, with equal parts of study and practice, we may develop strong convictions about the wisdom of our inner world, our body's ability to show us the way, and the adaptive protection that guides pacing. Then our well-fed left-hemisphere emissary can step forward with clear reassurance at certain moments. This integration of right-centric relatedness and left-centric understanding comes and goes for all of us, but it does seem to gain strength and reliability over time.

With visible relaxation in her body and strong eye contact, she said, "All my life, people have criticized me for being cautious. It means a lot that you like that I'm that way."

"Like it and appreciate its value," I replied. Beyond the words, the depth of our engagement was held in the meeting of our eyes. As we prepared to end our time, it seemed her inner world had made its first solid contact with us, her shame had lifted for now, and we had passed through moments of uncertainty into restored connection. We parted from that first meeting with the sense that we were becoming a team on behalf of whoever inside was so distressed.

In these pages, we keep returning to one foundational principle: providing the possibility of emotional/relational safety for our people, be they patients, children, partners, friends, or strangers. We are able to make this offer when we are experiencing our own neuroception of safety, not continuously, but as the baseline to which we return after our system has adaptively moved into sympathetic arousal or dorsal withdrawal in response to inner and outer conditions. When we neuroceive safety, we humans automatically begin to open into vulnerability, and the next movement of our "inherent treatment plan" (Sills, 2010) has a greater probability of coming forward. When we have a neuroception of threat, we adaptively tighten down at many levels, from physical tension to activation of the protective skills we have developed over a lifetime (Levine, 2010). In that state, our innate healing path will often wisely stay hidden until more favorable conditions arrive.

Reading these sentences, we might be drawn into a more left-centric way of hearing them and experience the promotion of safety as a somewhat mechanical process in which A inevitably leads to B—my being in a ventral state will automatically draw you into one, and if it doesn't, there is something wrong with one of us. Viewing it that way encourages us to turn being in social engagement into a technique, even a manipulation of the other person's nervous system toward what we view as a more desirable state. Ironically, when the left hemisphere is dominant rather than supportive of right-centric attending, we have already moved out of social engagement and thus are in no position to offer safe space to another. When we make an effort to return to it, we have forgotten that neuroception is continually arising automatically and not under the control of our will. The very pressure to activate ventral makes the space between unsafe.

The other way we could hear these words is from a more right-centric viewpoint in which we have a felt sense of times in which the listening, nonjudgmental presence of another person had a significant influence on our autonomic nervous system (ANS). Without access to our own storehouse of such implicit experiences, it is challenging and sometimes impossible to do anything but turn an idea into a protocol, intervention, or technique. When we touch these living memories, we likely sense the fluidity and constant movement of our emergent ANS as well as our tender responsiveness to small shifts internally and interpersonally. We might even experience a surge of gratitude for these relationally rich encounters. The activation of these memories draws us toward the lived experience of ventral and allows us to offer it to our people without strategy or expectation of any particular result. This lack of agenda is the primary essence of safety, giving our people implicit permission to bring forward any aspect of themselves that needs attention.

Pause for Reflection

Let's see if we can take a moment to sample these two ways of approaching and valuing the ventral state. What happens in our bodies when we put pressure on ourselves to activate the social engagement system? How is it different when we recall moments of being deeply received? Our muscles, belly and heart brains, breath, face, and eyes are often responsive to this change in focus. As we become familiar with these physiological shifts, they may come into consciousness more often to alert us to moments when we have adaptively shifted into left-centric attending. When we are able to receive these communications with compassion rather than judgment, with one part of our mind holding a safe space for the other to be heard, we are likely at the portal to ventral once again. If we are doing this process with a reading partner or friend, interpersonal deep listening and compassion may build another memory of how we touch and co-regulate each other's ANS.

Leading

One way we might think about a helpful approach to our work of providing safe space is to imagine a three-part process: *leading, following, responding.* Paradoxically, the kind of *leading* we want to offer is the opposite of taking control. Instead, it begins with accepting responsibility for getting support for our inner world and healing process to such an extent that the need for control recedes in favor of trust in the inherent healing capacity that is awakened when the necessary interpersonal sustenance arrives. When we have received deep listening and presence from another, we will have experienced their power to open our inner world to healing. Then, we can more easily let go of the need to take charge. As we have seen, relational neuroscience increasingly assures us that we are continually shaping one another's embodied brains, and that the safety provided by deep listening offers a unique support for engagement. However, it is one thing to believe it cognitively and quite another to grow into the practice of this belief.

The first two-thirds of this book have been dedicated to cultivating right-centric viewpoints and processes to such an extent that we experience not only a paradigm shift in our left-hemisphere emissary but a transformation and deepening of how we are able to be present with one another. There is no end to cultivating this inborn capacity. It often proceeds in a two-steps-forward, one-or-three-steps-back fashion, challenging us to let go of linearity in favor of fluidity. It asks us to be willing to be uncomfortable because of the tentative nature of what happens next when we stay in the moment. It requires the continual support of others on this particular path of development, both because we need each other just by how we are built and because our culture is an active force, implicitly and explicitly drawing us away from this interpersonally rich process. It is also likely one of the most meaningful and rewarding ways of living because of how it enriches every encounter we have in this world.

Following

When we are dedicated to such ongoing cultivation, the leadership we provide in our counseling rooms first becomes rooted in our way of seeing and being, not primarily in what we do. As McGilchrist (2009) suggests, how we attend changes us and changes the person we hold in this way. The deep trust in the process of healing that gradually emerges from our inner work then fosters our next way of being with our people: *following*. One gift of nonjudgmental, agendaless presence is that a wide road of acceptance opens, so that the inner world of our people gradually begins to sense, experience, and trust that every part is equally valued and equally welcome.

Ours is the work of invitation. In the movie *E. T.* (Kennedy, Spielberg, & Spielberg, 1982), the beloved alien's first encounter with Elliott involves an exchange of Reese's Pieces. E. T. eases Elliott's fear of him by dropping some of the peanut butter goodies in his lap, and Elliott then draws E. T. into his room with little piles of Reese's on the porch, the stairs, and at the doorway. Then they discover they can follow one another's gestures as a way of joining in safety. It doesn't matter if we see ourselves as E. T. or Elliott. They are inviting one another into relationship through a process of mutually following each other's delicious offerings. When our people arrive at our door for the first time, we are both invited into a similar process of mutual discovery. If I am able to be in a state of open receptivity (the ultimate Reese's Pieces for our neurobiology), this new person may be able to follow me toward the possibility of connection. At the same time, my system, without an agenda of its own, will begin to follow the underground communications of the multiple systems flowing in my patient. Much of this will be below the level of conscious awareness while some of it will be visible, even though we may not be able to attend to it with full awareness immediately.

In truth, we can't help but follow one another to some extent, given our capacity for resonance. However, if we have our own agenda for what needs to happen next, the process has a tendency to become more of a one-way street, with our patients often following us at the expense of their own sense of direction.* With an agenda, expectations, or judgments, we step out of relationship and onto the shaky ground of control. That can sound strange, since we usually think of control as providing stability and security. However, given our neurobiological preference and need for safety and connection, it has the opposite effect interpersonally.

Instead, our process of opening to receptivity establishes the rela-

---

* Because our systems are so dedicated to staying in connection with one another, many of us will abandon our own needs to remain attached without knowing we're doing it.

tional connection for us to be able to follow our patients. As we let go of agenda and expectations, we may find we become more quiet in both body and mind. The tensions that accompany the impulse to control subside, and the energies of our mental/emotional life are more other-directed and devoted to listening rather than speaking. If we pause for a moment here, we may be able to feel the quality of the onset of such a state in mind, heart, and body.

We may then be able to more easily attend to our people's communications that often remain below conscious awareness: subtle changes in breath, coloring, eye tension, prosody of voice; small movements toward or away; changes in the quality of eye contact. Receptivity means that we don't grasp and use what we notice for assessment. Instead, we are simply present to these implicit communications in the spirit of holding a tender space in which they can reveal themselves to whatever extent our patients' system feels safe to be vulnerable in the moment. Our left-hemisphere emissary may well understand that these emerging changes indicate increasing neuroception of safety or threat in our people, but that perspective will not dominate the right-centric relatedness that is holding the experience. It will instead become a supportive voice that has the potential to clarify and focus the compassion we are experiencing for our people.

Meanwhile, our resonance circuitry will also be following and recreating in our own bodies the sensations, feelings, and intentions of our patients. Because of our quiet attentiveness and ongoing neuroception of safety, we may be able to hold our own activations as well as theirs within a broad window of tolerance. Both of us contribute what we can to cultivating such a safe holding space by directing our joint attention to what is unfolding in this moment. When this happens, the mutuality of following becomes a beautiful circle of support surrounding the hurt and frightened parts of our people. We have been open to receiving them, and their systems, following our lead, are now also becoming more able to stay in touch with both the reassuring quality of our relatedness and the sensations, images, feelings, and thoughts that are emerging in their inner world. The image of a waterwheel of mutual care that draws on the flowing connection in the space between to provide energy for integrating embedded traumas comes to mind.

These moments of deep mutual discovery have their own unique rhythm and felt sense that I can only describe as sacred. They are so extraordinarily nourishing for both people. In addition, they are, of course, interspersed with ordinary times of daily conversation and deeply human moments of rupture and repair. If we are at ease with these missteps, we will more likely be able to move in and out of safety together, with us returning to our baseline ventral state if we have left it during the rupture. One woman said to me, "Your screw ups are really something. They don't seem to bother you at all." While that overstates my healing in the area of shame, it is certainly more true now than it was a few years ago. Occasionally, there is almost a sense of gratefulness in the midst of the latest mistake. Most importantly, if my missteps are welcome, so are theirs, and that is often a revolutionary and transformative experience all on its own.

Responding

Stepping back a bit to take in the overall process so far, we can see that the leading we offer comes from our cultivation of an emotional/relational safe space that has brought on the possibility of us welcoming and following our people. From there, the following becomes mutual and another word for that process is "responding." Initially, this responsiveness may primarily be our inner worlds coming into more synchrony with each other within our joined windows of tolerance (Beckes & Coan, 2011; Hasson et al., 2012; Porges, Badenoch, & Phillips, 2016). Soon, this joining may also become a call to responsive action on behalf of the frightened and hurt parts who carry our patients' embedded traumas and are now coming forward for help.

Again, we are at that familiar crossroads. Will we respond by stepping in to intervene based on what we believe is most likely to alleviate this suffering, or will we remain quiet and listening until we sense a response drawn out of us by our less-than-perfect resonance with our person? This is such a paradox for our system. The path of intervention can have a settling quality of certainty and conviction. It draws on our left hemisphere's storehouse of healing techniques, matching them to the symptoms we notice. The felt sense of the rightness of this goal-directed approach is supported implicitly and explicitly by our culture's norms for our profession and for our society at large. If we focus on the means to change this person's state in the direction of what we believe is greater health, we are also stepping out of empathic connection. This is a violation of our innate expectation, at every biological level, that we are meant to be embedded in a nest of warm relationships (Beckes & Coan, 2012; Cozolino, 2014).

On the other hand, the path of waiting and listening foregoes certainty and exposes us to a sense of tentative unknowing, which is often uncomfortable at best. This may only be tolerable when we have developed some degree of trust in the inherent healing capacity built into the human system and the power of interpersonal receptivity to animate this process. For most of us, this trust arrives because we have experienced it ourselves and can now embody it for others. As this deep learning proceeds in us, we may be able to rest more easily into the waiting because the unknowing is increasingly being held within our expanding window of tolerance. As we are able to work in this way, I believe our people get a felt sense of our profound and enduring respect for their inherent wisdom, something that is likely a unique and healing experience given their history of traumatic relationships. I don't believe I have found any offering that is more empowering than respect.

What does responding look like in our counseling rooms? When we begin with both a well-fed left-hemisphere emissary and a healthy respect for our fallibility, we listen for which of our left-centric supplies swims to the surface and then offer it as a possibility with no preference for how it will be received. Most importantly, we check in with our people to see how their inner world responds to the suggestion. Earlier in this chapter, we asked our young woman about placing her hand on her belly and then turned to her belly see how it had received that gesture. We followed the lead of her system, which seemed to know how much warmth was tolerable in the moment. Then we finished with some words that were a left-centric translation of a right-centric awareness to support trust in the wisdom of her system, particularly in regard to pacing and protection. It may be helpful to reread that exchange \ in light of this current discussion.

It sometimes surprises me that people don't find questions addressed to their bodies silly, especially early in therapy, but they rarely do. Perhaps getting into relationship with the sensations our bodies offer is natural for many of us once we are supported to be in a more right-centric state. Relationship is quite irresistible from that perspective. Often, those whose histories have precluded them from listening to their bodies feel sad or irritated that they can't, but it seems only a very small percentage actually find it an odd thing to do. In the asking, it is crucial that we don't have a preferred answer in mind, because that will be felt in the room, probably below the level of conscious awareness, as a subtle coercion. At that point, safety diminishes and the inner worlds of our people are less likely to make contact with us. Instead, when we offer receptive listening, with warm curiosity for the truth of the moment in our person's system, we can trust that its guidance will be far more helpful than anything we might independently imagine. Gentleness, humor, and abundant support are wonderful resources on this ever-unfolding, stubbornly nonlinear journey from control to receptivity.

In this chapter, there has been a good deal of repetition of the same processes from different perspectives, partly because it isn't always easy to get in touch with the subtle distinctions we are exploring. In addition, there is a circular or almost simultaneous quality to the way leading, following, and responding relate with one another. They overlap, intertwine, and transform into each other in a fluid way. The movement toward leading through settling into receptivity draws us into following, which becomes a kind of underground leading offered to the other person so she may follow herself—and us. If that sentence is hard to understand and easier to feel, we are likely on the right track. As our people keep to the inward path, they take the lead and we follow/respond, while staying steadfast in our return to ventral leadership after many ruptures, since this movement out of safety and back is the foundation for the dance. We could go on. Since it may be challenging for our left hemispheres to understand, there is less risk of this process trying to become a protocol. Instead, it is simply the unfolding of how we are intended to be with each other, a river into which we sometimes fall—together.

To keep our focus on the process itself, we began by focusing on two unique but fairly simple examples of leading, following, and responding, hoping to offer a felt sense of how the three are interwoven with each other and with our human limitations. As we move forward in these chapters, we will spend time with people experiencing challenges of greater complexity. For now, it may be enough to settle into the felt-sense differences between intervention and receptivity, carrying this awareness into our work with our patients and encounters with others to deepen our compassionate sensitivity to how safety enters and leaves the space between. In the next chapter, we will build on this by attending to the process of co-attaching in the context of leading, following, and responding.

19

Co-attaching

The Foundation of Relational Healing

There are wolves
everywhere and closer

Your parents are busy
flailing at the snarling snouts and dripping fangs

Busy wrapping their own, and each other's bloody wounds

While you curl up, cold and lonely in the bottom of the sled
thinking, I'll die if someone doesn't pick me up and hold
me soon

—A. NEIL MEILI (2013)

Over the years, many of my colleagues in the world of play therapy told me they were cautioned in their training not to allow their young patients to attach to them because it would disrupt their bonds with their parents. Perhaps even more challenging was the injunction to not become attached to their kiddos. We now know that both of these are neurobiological impossibilities—and that is quite a relief. In the *Handbook of Attachment* (2016), James Coan says, "In truth, because so many neural structures are involved in one way or another in attachment behavior, it is possible to think of the entire human brain as a neural attachment system" (p. 244). That is quite a profound statement and draws us back toward what we have been experiencing about our embodied brains.

Our infant muscles let go and mold to the shape of our mother's bodies when we are securely held. Our bellies learn the meaning of the sensations of hunger and thirst from the interpersonal sweetness of our need being seen, met, and satisfied by our mother as food is offered. We take in her attentiveness along with the nourishment, and this shapes our openness to all kinds of nurturance throughout our lives (Harshaw, 2008). Our hearts beat more slowly and our amygdalae calm when she is in a ventral state, her presence reassuring us of the possibility of safety in connection (Beckes & Coan, 2011; Porges, 2013). At that moment, our very hearts are also encoding a preference for warm connections, and the answer to our autonomic nervous system's (ANS's) question, "Are you with me?" is "Yes!" Our brainstems take in the rhythmic movements of her body and emotions as she attentively follows our bid for play, our drift toward sleep, our signal that it is time to be quietly together (Perry & Hambrick, 2008). In our midbrain, our SEEKING system finds the waiting eyes and arms of our mother's CARE system in times of PLAY or GRIEF, patterning the expectation that connections will be restored when they are momentarily lost (Panksepp & Biven, 2012), that ruptures will call forth repairs (Tronick, 2003).

When we are infants, all of this is gathered up into our limbic region, shaping our perceptual lens and forming the embodied anticipations that will guide us toward sustaining relationships as we move out into the broader world (Cozolino, 2014; Schore, 2012; Siegel, 2015b). Then, as we grow a little older, our thoughts about ourselves and the world will turn experience into narrative. Throughout all of this, we and those closest and dearest have become thoroughly interwoven at every neural level (Iacoboni, 2011). Paradoxically, at exactly the same time, when there has been such responsive care (with abundant rupture and repair), we also emerge with a strong sense of ourselves as individuals. The potential we brought into the world has been so consistently reflected and supported that our many inborn possibilities gain solid manifestation. *The interpersonal nourishes the personal into existence while we remain permanently part of each other.* We live within and beyond our own skin at the same time. Daniel Siegel's (2015a) term "mwe" seeks to capture the simultaneous existence of both of these processes.

While our embodied brains will never be as fully open, sensitive, and malleable as they are in utero and in early infancy when we are mainly a sea of potential, these mutually shaping processes and internalizations continue throughout our lives. Much of it unfolds below conscious awareness in the midst of our expanding community of relationships, similar to the rich network of roots and fungi doing their mostly unseen work to connect the apparently individual trees into an interdependent forest (Simard, 2016).

Many of us, about 40 percent according to a recent study, do not experience this kind of supportive care early in life and form insecure attachments (Moullin, Waldfogel, & Washbrook, 2014). Even more concerning is a study by Sara Konrath and her colleagues (Konrath, Chopik, Hsing, & O'Brien, 2014) showing that by the time students reach college, the percentage of security declines from 60 percent to about 41 percent. Somewhere between the first year of life and the eighteenth, 20 percent of our young people lose touch with their security. This latter statistic may even be skewed in a more positive direction than the reality in the general population because at-risk children who are not even able to graduate from high school have much higher rates of insecure attachment to begin with (Moullin et al., 2014). It might make us wonder if the pressures of adulthood diminish access to security even more.

Our purpose here is to be with the experience of reparative co-attaching in our counseling room, so we will not be delving deeply into statistics or listlike descriptions of attachment styles (see Badenoch, 2008, for a summary of the neurobiology of attachment). However, the contrast between these two studies does bring the challenge of this culture to our attention again. The implicit and explicit forces of left-shifted attending move us away from the rich interpersonal interactions that strengthen our relational pathways. We literally cannot attend to each other when we are in that state, and we do not even notice the loss because we can't feel our bodies' distress signals until the internal situation becomes catastrophic, often in the form of major depression (McGilchrist, 2009). It may be possible that when our SEEKING system is pulled into the service of only pursuing tasks, goals, solutions, and success, its primary purpose of maintaining connection is subverted to the point that it eventually gives up, and we fall into despair (Panksepp & Biven, 2012).

Because of the work we have been doing throughout this book to cultivate our capacity to lead, follow, and respond, we can offer our people a relationship that holds many of the qualities of secure parenting. (We will explore this in detail below.) Our right-centric way of attending will leave us less inclined to pigeonhole our clients into a particular attachment style. Once we see our people as being a specific way, we are less able to notice aspects of them that don't conform to the type. As McGilchrist reminds us, how we attend changes the other person as well us, and our patients may find that they, too, focus on this narrower version of themselves. Instead, because of our right hemisphere's both/and way of perceiving and its focus on what is emerging in the present moment, we may experience attachment as more of an ever-shifting continuum as different aspects of our people emerge in the room with us. We can more easily welcome the multiplicity of attachment* experiences we all have had and be open to how different ones may awaken in various relational contexts. If our left-hemisphere emissary is familiar with the characteristics of attachment styles, we might hear, "Ah, that's a more avoidant way of responding" rather than "This person is avoidantly attached."

Pause for Reflection

Attachment is first a unique visceral experience in our bodies rather than a set of characteristics with a name. The latter emerges when we think about the experiences we have already had. In any attachment encounter, there is both what we perceive being offered and our embodied response to it. If we call to mind, heart, and body three or four people with whom we've had particularly close relationships, how do our bodies respond to their offers of connection? We can begin by being with muscles, belly, heart, and breath. How does our body want to move? Does what they bring and how we respond vary from time to time? We may want to sample some childhood relationships and some that are more current. After spending some time with the experience, we may sense that our left-hemisphere emissary wishes to add some thoughts about the kinds of attachment patterns we found, or not.

---

* Sometimes the word "attachment" means only the experiences we have with our primary people early in life. Here, honoring the primacy of our system's ongoing capacity for attaching, it will apply to the many significant connections we have throughout our lives that shape and reshape our relational circuitry and experience.

Flowing with the shifting patterns of attachment our patients bring lets us be present to how their system has adapted to the many connections they have experienced. To stay in proximity and contact, we humans will twist ourselves into whatever shape the relationship requires, not only but especially when we are very young. We must stay connected at all costs, as the experience of the Romanian orphans has shown us. Their pervasive struggles with cognition, behavior, and relationships are a reflection of losses in brain development because there was no possibility of attachment with those caring for them (Chugani et al, 2001). Sometimes, as in families who have adapted by becoming avoidant, this need to attach leads to paradoxical experiences where staying connected means staying separate.

Each of our parents and others close to us offer their unique version of attachment, so while we have four categories to give us a general outline of what may occur, we will find that each person's expression of each style is as individual as a fingerprint. Some of these experiences are ingrained when we are very young and, because of familiarity, we may find we are drawn to replicate them with variations over our lifetimes. Some come later and may have less durability over time, although not always.

One young woman taught me more than anyone else about how multiple attachment styles come into play in daily life. Liza and I worked together for about four years. During that time, she had three significant personal relationships and felt forced into leaving a job she loved because of an interpersonal situation that was not of her making. She and I had a remarkably easy time attaching with warmth and openness from the beginning. Prior to meeting one another, she'd had a therapist with whom she had what she experienced as a good relationship in which she worked out some of her anger, so perhaps I was the beneficiary of that helpful pairing. Recently, her insecure attachment adaptations awakened in her daily life, drawing her back into therapy. They became the focus of our most powerful work. We will touch on the nature of these relationships first to get a picture of what she was experiencing outside the counseling room and then spend some time with what emerged from our work.

Her first boyfriend during our time together was a gregarious, unreliable young man who was rarely on time and didn't follow through with plans. Most challenging was his inability to understand how that could be irritating. They laughed a lot and she said she felt like a teenager with him, but she also had a lot of anxiety and a persistent need to cling because it always felt like he could go away at any moment. His response to her clinging was to become "even more flaky, like he was shaking off an irritating mosquito." Eventually, she left because the anxiety became unbearable, and she noticed she was also starting to feel an understandable and adaptive anger.

A few months later, she met a man who was a little older, stable to a fault, and had some pretty strong expectations of her. At first, she felt secure because he was so dependable and she enjoyed the challenge of being her most creative self, but then she noticed she began to shut down and grow distant from him. She was bewildered because she was sure this was what she wanted—a relationship that was safe, calm, contained, predictable. After a few months of wrestling with herself, she decided to leave because she felt emotionally dead all the time, but she also felt like a failure.

Right about then, her work as creative director for a company that owned preschools became unbearable because of the arrival of a hypercritical female boss. Her workplace was emotionally chaotic for all the creative staff, but she, more than the others, found she couldn't think or do even the simplest parts of her job. She was quite angry with herself for not being able to just get her act together and ignore her boss. After being very sick twice in one month, she realized that her immune system was being deeply challenged by the environment and reluctantly left without even getting another job, something that was completely at odds with her work ethic. She felt as though she was fleeing for her life.

Through all of this, Liza and I had been doing deep work with the implicit inheritance of her early family life: an angry alcoholic father who was controlling when he wasn't drunk, a mother who seemed to be more of a child than a parent, an older brother who turned his own misery into torturing her with his cruel teasing and occasional violence, an older sister who hid from the chaos inside her books, and a much older brother who had left home when she was four. Among these six, there were at least ten unique attachment patterns—five that Liza had internalized from them and five that had arisen from her own adaptive responses to the others. For most of us, there are multiple attachment experiences, and picturing these pairings of the connections offered by others and the adaptations made by us may illuminate the complexities of current relational experience.

During the time her relationship with her first boyfriend was deteriorating, Liza's feelings with him became the focus of our time together. As we were present with the sensations of anxiety she was experiencing, she began to get a felt-sense awareness that she was with him the way she was with her undependable mother, always trying to regulate her so she would be an adult who could protect her from her father (what our left hemisphere could call an ambivalent style). It made sense to her that she felt like a teenager with him, too, because that is when she was most involved in managing her mother. Being with her teenage self's loneliness and anxiety, listening in quietness, and providing a safe haven became the necessary disconfirmation that began to heal this embedded trauma. Making sense helped, too, alleviating her tendency to be critical of her responses to her boyfriend. Even though this man never left her in danger, his cheerful, heedless unpredictability and inability to understand her upset could not be the foundation for a secure relationship even as we were resolving the implicit roots of her response to him.

Time passed, the new man arrived, and we celebrated the relative calm. Then, as she began to shut down in her second relationship, we welcomed the deadening feelings coming up in her body, seeking to value them as meaningful rather than wrong. She was quite surprised to see her mother's father, who lived with them for substantial periods of time, coming persistently to mind. She saw him sitting calmly behind his newspaper while her father raged. She also caught glimpses of her sister reading and reading. Her body shared feelings of envy that they could stay away from the chaos and curiosity about how they did that. She began to sense that in her focus on these two people, she had internalized the way they protected themselves by disengaging. But why had they made an appearance in this current relationship? As she let go of judging herself, she began to sense that this man was not able to invest himself emotionally in her, so her shutdown was also a mirror for his own way of relating (multiple layers of an avoidant style). As we sat with the intensity of her focus on her grandfather and sister, she found her aliveness was returning on its own.

With the arrival of this new boss, we entered the most challenging work we did because of the massive disorganization that came with it. Liza's inner world quickly connected this response with memories of her brother's physical and emotional cruelty. No wonder the office chaos touched her differently than it did the others. As these inner spaces where she had embedded memories of terror with no resolution emerged, some from her father's rage and some from the helplessness she felt at the hands of her brother, they brought overwhelming anxiety, deep ache, and dissociation into the space between. She could feel that the primary root of her terror was that she was absolutely alone in it with both these men. Because the trust was strong in our relationship, her system allowed these threatening experiences into the room, where they could be met with the disconfirmation of accompaniment, safety, comfort, and kind awareness.

At no point in our work did we talk about which attachment style was in play, but instead we received all of these experiences as they came to us through focusing on her bodily sensations as each of these relationships was being lost. I trusted that we were making our way through the forest of painful attachment memories that had drawn in these romantic partners and made her boss unbearable, that we were headed toward new ways of relating. However, part of her struggle was that she felt she was so inconsistent in her response to the challenges that are inevitably part of relationships that she couldn't trust how she would be with her next person. I believed that the trust and care between us would gradually grow into an embodied anticipation of security on which her inner world could draw for guidance. Her next partner might feel more like the two of us. That isn't exactly what happened.

One day, as we were doing some work with sand and miniatures, a tray emerged that was different from any she had done before. It was more peaceful, organized, and beautiful, with curving inclusive lines instead of jagged confining spaces. This particular change in the way space was defined had such a strong resonance for her that we stayed with it for quite some time. For the first time in any tray, the people in it seemed to like one another, an unfamiliar feeling. Savoring the mystery, we held a space for something more to be known if her inner world felt the time was right. She began to feel a large hand holding her small one, and it seemed as though someone much taller was walking at her side. We stayed with her body's feelings as tears of gratitude came for the safety and gentle joy of this memory. She had no idea who the other person in the experience was.

In the process of looking for a new job, she met a man who evoked these very same feelings in her almost immediately. Understandably hesitant at first, slow to trust herself or him after so many painful relationships, she found her heart (the physical heart in her chest, she said) opening to him, all on its own. The next time I saw her, she asked to see the picture of the peaceful sand tray, and as we sat with it, she said, "I believe this is the feeling of my oldest brother. It came to me the other day, and I asked my sister. She said he came home on leave a few times when I was very small before the army sent him overseas for good. Apparently, he walked and talked with me for a long time whenever he was home. Sometimes I was at his side, and sometimes he carried me. She told me she felt jealous because she didn't have anybody to keep her safe except Nancy Drew and Black Beauty." As an adult, Liza saw her brother only occasionally, and while they were comfortable with each other, she didn't have the same feeling as when she was small. He had endured several tragedies in his life and seemed to carry them as a heavy weight on his heart.

With reflection, I realized that Liza and I had voyaged through ambivalent, avoidant, and disorganized attachments, experienced in the past and reawakened in the present. Some were her adaptations to the disruptions of family life, and some were internalized from others. We finally arrived on the shore of security and found it to be a little island in her childhood, inhabited by her and her brother, in the midst of all the chaos. It has seemed to me that we needed to be with the big embedded traumas before this delicate flower could find room to show itself, but perhaps it is something quite different than that. Whatever the reason, it was a blessed arrival.

Over the years of our working together, our relationship continued to be mostly secure. When we had a rupture, she was most likely to adapt by becoming anxious and working hard to bring us back together. Her mother's unpredictability and lack of protection had ingrained similar but not identical responses in Liza. If we think in terms of disconfirming experiences, coming from listening, following, and responding, I could be a much more steady, safe, predictable companion for her, and a person who was as eager to repair as she was. Over months and years of working through embedded traumas, this quiet daily offering provided the steady disconfirmation that was likely part of her brother's inner arrival, too, and certainly fostered her earned security. What a teacher she was for me! After my time with Liza, any urge to categorize people by attachment style left, and I see these patterns more as a wheel now.

At any given moment, we, too, are somewhere on this wheel, or maybe several places at once sometimes. When we consider our rich inner communities in Chapter 21, we will find it is quite possible that more than one pattern of attachment can arise at the same time, sometimes in support of the others and sometimes in conflict. However, as

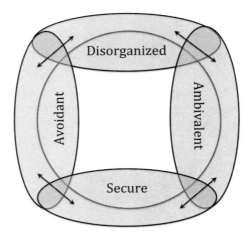

FIGURE 19.1 Wheel of attachment. It is impossible to capture the complexity of the flow between attachment styles, but perhaps this gives more of a sense of a continuum than of discrete categories. Many of us spend more time in our version of one style than another, although even in the course of a single day, we likely slip around some. Perhaps this can help us be a little more present with that fluidity in ourselves and others.

part of our preparation for the work we do with our people, along with seeking healing for our parts wounded through attachment, we can dedicate ourselves to staying connected to supportive people who will receive us without expectations or judgments. In that process, we will internalize them as they nurture our wounded ones. They then will join and foster those parts of ourselves who can be present with the ones who come to us in their suffering and recovery.

As we welcome our people in the state of receptivity available to us this particular day, we hope to lead with this self who has few expectations about what will come back to us relationally. We aren't expecting to be seen, acknowledged, nurtured, and received, at least consciously (although some or all of this nourishment may be offered by our people in the course of therapy, which is quite an unexpected gift). Through both the internalization of supportive others and cultivating a state with few expectations, we are likely partially protecting the parts of us who are carrying some of our unhealed attachment wounds, making it less likely that they will come to the surface and influence the flow of the therapy. Many of the practices in this book are intended to nurture this receptive self.

"Partially protecting" is an important phrase. All of us are vulnerable to the awakening of past attachment responses when we least expect them. Humility and willingness to repair are what we have to offer. I have found that many of my people have felt encouraged by the vulnerability that we share in common. If we counselors are able to be both accountable and compassionate toward ourselves in those times, some powerful disconfirmations may arise.

Of the numerous possible examples I could offer, let me share two. The first time I met Andrew, he strode in the door and offered me a strong handshake. "Hi, doc. Can you fix me?"

I laughed and found myself jovially saying, "I'm not in the fixing business. I'm in the listening business." I saw his face redden a bit and thought, "Wow. I believe I just caused a rupture before we got to know each other at all." I immediately recognized that this kind of banter was one of the few ways I could join with my father. It kept us connected but at a distance that was tolerable because he was so afraid of intimacy. It certainly lacked the warm receptivity I hoped to offer Andrew. As we sat down, my therapist self partially arrived and I added, "How was that for you?" I meant both me not doing any fixing and the way I had responded to him but didn't yet have my wits about me enough to be clear.

"Oh, I just meant it as a joke," he said, with his eyes down. The bravado was gone, and it seemed like a shamed child had come instead.

"That was a pretty flippant way for me to reply. I'm sorry." My voice was quieter, the pace slower.

"Oh, that's all right. You didn't do anything wrong. I shouldn't have said what I did."

I could feel my tendency, born of years of practiced compliance and pacification, to make everything all right for him, and began to sense that we were both being drawn toward trying to regulate one another by taking the blame on ourselves. Right after our rough initial move into relationship, we had both possibly next been touched in the place where ambivalent attachment lives, where we had given up our own reality and needs to quiet the inner world of another so he or she would stay with us. Being aware helped me let go of the impulse to continue to reassure him that it was my fault.

Instead, I felt my eyes and face soften and made a nonspecific comforting sound. He took a deeper breath and relaxed a bit. It seems the nonverbal holding may have been a more helpful repair than the apology this time. Then I said, "Would you tell me what brings you here today?" We began again.

Not all attachment awakenings in us are that easily recognized and held, and not all repairs happen so quickly. My single greatest ongoing vulnerability is around being treated as a cardboard cutout with no feelings, although every time I respond with an automatic and powerful withdrawal of empathy, it surprises me. As children, we were primarily the receptacle for our mothers' unhealed traumatic wounds. The only way she could attach was through abuse, which brought the only kind of proximity and contact she could imagine. She was so lost in her own pain that I don't believe she ever actually saw us as human beings. I have worked with this for decades with so much loving support and will continue to do so, but it is such a pervasive primary wound to my sense of existing that it may never fully heal.

Many of the people who have come to me over the years have experienced similar attachment failures, and for some, it has left them with a sense that they are so empty and nonexistent that what they say or do can't hurt others. They also feel like cardboard cutouts, and this sometimes leads to interactions that awaken my wound when they treat me as if I have no feelings. If it is short-lived and followed by some experience that recognizes our mutual humanity, my embodied brain has become resilient enough to stay in a ventral state and empathically available. However, when it is sustained, my ANS eventually protects me with a pronounced flight response that takes the form of a sensation like pulling the bathtub plug as the empathy drains out of me. No amount of conscious choosing or understanding can stop this automatic adaptive and protective response.

We had an unexpected death in our family that meant I needed to be out of town for a week or so. I was deeply sad and concerned for the well-being of those who had been tragically left behind. One of my people, who struggles so much with feelings of abrupt abandonment, called and left emails and texts repeatedly about when our next appointment would be, with no acknowledgment of my loss. By the second day of this, even in the midst of understanding his distress and how his ANS was protecting him by pursuing me, my system pulled the plug. As I helplessly felt the empathy drain away, I was concerned that it might never come back. The inner repair has always been difficult when this happens because my system seems mostly unwilling to be that vulnerable again with this person.

It didn't feel helpful to talk with him about what he had done or how it had affected me. Adding to the overwhelming shame that was always his close companion couldn't be part of repair. I am fortunate to have abundant support, so I began to share my experience, felt acknowledged in the wisdom of my body's response, and, once heard, found myself softening toward him somewhat, as though my cognitive understanding of his plight and the felt sense of my response were able to integrate and modify each other a bit. However, to this day, I stand closer to that fine line where empathy can be lost with him than I do with my other people. The repair isn't complete and perhaps never will be, and yet we go down the road together, human to human.

Over our years of practice and in our daily life, we will have many opportunities to become aware of our vulnerabilities. It isn't helpful to imagine that they will one day all be healed, although some will surely lessen as we receive the care we need. One or two trustworthy people with whom we can safely share even what feels most embarrassing to us, knowing that we will simply be received without judgment, are the indispensable companions for this walk.

Pause for Reflection

Reading these stories, some memories of similar attachment awakenings may have arisen. Receiving them with kindness, noticing if there is a sense of shame or blame—and receiving that as well—let's just be present with them for a moment. We may feel the flow from rupture to repair or the sense that no complete repair is possible, both within ourselves and with our people. If the latter is the case, sensing how our systems are offering protection can help us be gentle with ourselves, and this, in and of itself, is a kind of repair.

Who supports you in these times? We are often so eager to support others, while our culture and even the conditions of our practices make it difficult to imagine or seek support for ourselves. We aren't meant to carry suffering alone. If you don't have the people you need, perhaps you can be with that without judgment, too, because just the compassionate recognition can be the beginning of opening to companionship.

Now we are going to spend some time with the conditions that support attachment repair for our people. As we lead, follow, and respond, what qualities do we bring that foster security? Each of us likely has our own words for what we sense is needed to cultivate a relational space like this. My five, born of a long journey toward earned security, are *presence, contact, reflection, responsiveness*, and *delight*, experiences that unfold easily from one to the next. I believe we will find that what we have been practicing throughout this book and particularly in the last chapter bears a close resemblance to secure parenting.

Presence

To begin, when we open the door to welcome our people, our receptive *presence* is very similar to what we offer our babies: curiosity about who and how they are in this moment and the next, without agenda or judgments. If in that moment our inner world is settled enough for us to see more of them than of our own implicit coloring, they will feel safe and known. This is the foundation for all that follows.

Many of our people have been wounded in relationships in which the other person's pain made presence impossible some or most of the time. Asa, a young man who came from a mostly warm southern family, found it terrifying to go toward romantic relationships. His parents had a longstanding marriage that was okay and his younger brother was married with children, so the terror didn't make much sense to him. Then he shared his history with me. Asa's mother had been severely depressed during her pregnancy with him and for about two years after. Her depression lifted before his capacity for explicit memory developed, so he recalled her consciously only as the playful, concerned, and sometimes critical mom of his elementary school years and beyond.

As we worked together, slowly, slowly, the implicit memories from his earliest days began to come up in his body, bringing waves of terrifying disorganization that made it difficult to breathe, think, or move. He began to feel how his mother's depression robbed her of the ability to offer him the most rudimentary sense of true presence, leaving him to fend for himself with his infant needs for co-organization, safety, and closeness almost completely unmet. With his dad working many hours and no siblings at that point, he had literally been unseen most of his early days. Any movement toward the intimacy of a romantic relationship awakened these earliest implicit memories. It was also quite ter-rifying for him to experience me seeing him because it brought us so close to the neural nets that held his profound loss and accompanying disorganization. As a result, his system's wisdom guided us toward very slow pacing in our work.

For a long time, whenever we came together, Asa found that his body was tight and curled in at the beginning, and as we were present with this tension without expectation of change, his muscles would gradually soften so his body could literally unfold into the relaxation brought on by a growing neuroception of safety. I believe he would say now that for many months, all we practiced was being quietly present with what his body was sharing before we were invited by his healing inner world to make the contact of sustained gaze. Asa's need for such slow pace and patient support told me all I needed to know about the magnitude of his almost invisible injury.

Contact

With most of our people, once we are able to offer presence, *contact* seems to follow quite naturally. Just as a parent reaches out to his child with gentle hands and warm eyes, we may find ourselves drawn to offer contact of several kinds. Our ventral voice will send waves of reassur-ance to touch our people's ears, and the relaxation around our eyes, the flow of our breath, and the mobility of our faces will touch their ANS with a felt sense of safety (Porges, 2011). The availability of our open, receptive gaze offers an invitation to a particular kind of intimacy that is deeply connecting, sometimes fostering an infant sense of merging (Shepherd, 2010). As trust grows between us, our amygdalae will natu-rally calm as well (Beckes & Coan, 2011). At times, as connection deep-ens, our PLAY systems may awaken with sparkling eyes and laughter to animate our exchanges (Panksepp & Biven, 2012). All of these are a kind of contact.

Then we come to the question of physical touch. In Chapter 3, we talked about our skin's intimate relationship with our brain and how, once we feel connected, our most natural impulse is to reach out to touch one another (Liberators International, 2015). In infancy, abundant physical affection ameliorates the stress response in babies whose moth-ers, like Asa's, were depressed during pregnancy (Sharp et al., 2012).

Touch affects our neurochemicals directly: As levels of oxytocin and endogenous opioids increase with gentle contact, cortisol goes down (Panksepp & Biven, 2012). At every stage of life, our health and well-being improve with kind touch (Field, 2014; Linden, 2015). However, cultural variations in the acceptability of touch may add implicit coloring to how we feel about offering this nourishment. Dr. Ken Cooper studied how often people in several cities spontaneously touch one another in an hour of conversation: Puerto Rico, 180; Paris, 110; Florida, 2; London, 0 (Pease & Pease, 2004).

Our societal aversion to touch coupled with legitimate safety concerns, given our people's often troubled history with physical contact, may make us wary. Even if we become convinced of the value of touch in our work, if we feel concerned, the sympathetic activation that may bring on will be communicated to our people's ANS. Returning to the practices in Chapter 3, particularly if we do them often with a friend, may help clarify our relationship with touch. If we feel more at ease over time and couple that with the most profound respect for our people's history with this kind of contact, we may be ready to offer it in moments when it can provide a restorative disconfirming experience, especially for those who have endured painful or frightening contact or been deprived of much touch at all. In addition, there is something uniquely grounding about being in stabilizing connection with the body of another person in the midst of strong implicit arisings.

A young woman who came to us for help with violent impulses felt the need for touch as we went toward the frightening implicit memories embedded by her rageful, abusive upbringing. She sensed she would be better able to stay in connection with me (within our joined windows of tolerance) if she could hold on to me physically. As we asked more about how she pictured that happening, she sensed she also felt frightened at the prospect of me holding her hand (her original more left-centric thought), primarily because I would have to sit closer to her. As we continued to ask for guidance from her inner world about what kind of touch might be okay, she got an image of me holding her feet. With just a little rearranging, the coffee table became our meeting place. We experimented with various ways I might hold her, discovering that one hand on the bottom and one on the top of both feet felt most supportive. This gesture of envelopment, with both of us comfortable physically and emotionally, let us settle into the deeper work that was needed.

Reflection

In whatever way contact unfolds with ease and safety, it leads to the possibility of *reflection*. The more we are without judgment or agenda, the more our abundant resonance circuitry will help us see and reflect back what we are seeing to our people. It will also help us notice when what we offer doesn't echo what they are experiencing so that we have the opportunity to offer a repair. It is difficult to get into words the importance of such reflection. The poem at the beginning of this chapter is about the loss of presence, contact, and reflection. Neil (Meili, 2013) wrote a second one after sharing the first with someone who held and reflected his experience to him. Being received that way seems to have integrated the trauma and then extended his vision to the pain of his parents, where compassion for the whole family emerges.

Now you have seen me in the sleigh
it is more filled with warmth and light

See parents fighting wolves inside
each from a parent eaten young

And huddle grateful tight and tight
alive because they fight the fight

Reading the two poems together may help us recall times when our systems relaxed into safety and even contentment with just feeling certain we were heard because of the clarity of the reflection—with or without words, even when none of the troubling circumstances changed.

We can return to the African greeting "I see you" and the response "I am here" to sense the depth of meaning it has for us to be known in this way. How we are seen can literally call parts of us into existence and shape new selves in the image of the one seeing us. A little girl runs excitedly into the room and encounters a frown with the message that she is too rambunctious. A new shamed self begins to form. If this happens repeatedly, this part of her will grow strong and its presence often felt. On another day, she is quietly exploring the pictures in a new book, filled with the sense of discovery. This time, her book-loving father gazes at her with affection, and the part of her who loves to learn becomes a little more known as a real piece of who she is. His gaze isn't telegraphing approval, which often brings anxiety lest we not be able to repeat the desired behavior, but simply enjoying who she is in that moment.

As she becomes an adult, she is noticeably wounded when she sees a frowning face of disapproval and noticeably buoyed when someone enjoys her curiosity. These kinds of reflections stay implicitly with us and guide our responses to others in ways that we sometimes have trouble understanding. When they seem out of proportion, it is easy for us to fall into judgment of ourselves. If only we could see that child who felt the sting of shame when her wrongness was reflected, we might better be able to be tender with ourselves when she awakens again. When we can do that for ourselves, it is much more likely we will be able to offer that to our people as well.

Here is a poem by Neil Meili (2013) that illuminates the power of the reflection we receive.

> *My mother was afraid of everything*
> *She may have been afraid of me*
> *even before I was born*
>
> *I can almost remember*
> *pulling knees and elbows in*
> *so as not to cause her pain*
>
> *Afraid even in the womb to whisper*
> *anything she didn't want to hear*
> *That sort of thing stays with you*
>
> *Perhaps I should be thankful*
> *for the cliffs I didn't step off of*
> *too brave and blindly in the night*
>
> *but what about the doors*
> *the doors I didn't open*
> *into rooms filled with light*

Reflection shapes us, and lack of reflection also has its consequences. A young girl, born into outwardly very fortunate circumstances, remained largely unseen by her parents who were preoccupied with status on the outside and their childhood wounds on the inside. Her need for connection, her sadness, her fear, and even her interests received next to no confirming reflection. Because she was viewed through the lens of her family's wealth and status, it never occurred to others outside the family that this little one would lack for anything, so there was no help at school or with other families.

With no one to co-organize with her, she sank into a sea of agonizing disorganization and survived by developing a kind of "straight jacket, narrow feeling" in her body and mind that likely held her together. This state also made it profoundly challenging for her to think, learn, remember, or tap into any of her abundant creativity, and also left her feeling physically ill much of the time. When she reached adulthood, she had no idea who she was or what she wanted. Hovering on the edge of major depression most days, she was well into middle age before anyone listened to her closely enough to call her childhood experience by its right name, neglect. The combination of outward privilege and emotional invisibility is one of the most hurtful and confusing ways to live. Nothing appears to be wrong and yet every day is a torturous maze of unreflected chaotic emotional upheaval, ameliorated only by regular descents into dorsal numbness. Without a narrative or any way to make sense of this misery, people can usually only conclude that there is something profoundly wrong with them. Recovery began for this woman when her current state was accurately reflected by another.

In potentially traumatic circumstances, the presence or absence of reflection of our state can make the difference between whether the fear and pain embed or are able to integrate, even if the circumstances don't change (Bobrow, 2015; Hari, 2015a; Kohrt et al., 2010). As people come to us for help with traumas that did embed for lack of companionship, it is our reflection of their state in the moment that offers enough safety for them to become vulnerable to remembering. This is the core of our practice of following, to initially be available to take in and reflect back what our people bring, with no impulse to fix or change anything. This is so counter to what we are mostly taught in our training and what our culture tells us is the path to healing. Yet the wisdom of the relational neurobiology we have been studying and our felt-sense experience repeatedly point us in this direction.

When we are working together on specific traumatic memories, each time we offer reflection, we are also quietly repairing/disconfirming attachment wounds that always contain elements of our parents or others not being able to see us because of their own injuries. The recurring presence of attending, acceptance, clarity, and compassion gradually transforms those implicit neural nets that hold the embodied anticipation of absence, criticism, bewilderment, and coldness. Bit by bit, our people begin to embody the changed anticipation of being cared for and treated with kindness and respect. Part of what strengthens this new way of being comes from us having co-internalized one another. We will continue to be their reflective companion on the inside, and they will feel how we also continue to carry them with us in our inner world. It is quite beautiful to watch this healing unfold, often revealing itself as changes in body, feeling, behavior, and relational choices first, then later affirmed in more frequent words of tenderness toward themselves. Sometimes it happens the other way, too.

Responsiveness

In the last chapter, we saw how our practice of following leads to responding. In the same way, reflection brings on *responsiveness* in our attaching relationships. We can picture how a parent and baby attend to each other and then begin to move. One giggles and the other responds, which encourages a further response from the first one. The little one cries, her father's GRIEF system feels her distress, and he reflects his felt-sense understanding to her with the look on his mobile face and his sounds of concern. His resonance with her GRIEF also awakens his CARE system, and he tries on different responses until they are able to settle again together. As he follows attentively, his actions are drawn out of him to meet his little one right where she is, no matter how long it takes. He may have a lot of ideas of what it may be about, but ultimately she is the authority on what helps most. In this dance of co-regulation, repeated experiences of response, rupture, and repair build in the strong embodied anticipation of help arriving that is one foundation of security and resilience. At the same time, her father is gaining trust in his ability to be her parent. They are both growing through their interwoven responsiveness to one another.

For us therapists, our intention to continue following until our inner world offers a possible response may be one of the most challenging aspects of our work. Our left-hemisphere emissary has often built up a varied and useful storehouse of supplies in the form of ideas and techniques for healing trauma. Our culture tells us to set goals and make treatment plans. Because we are so dedicated to relieving suffering, we can feel catapulted into efforts to change what is hurting our people. We develop agendas that then often generate expectations of what should come next, leaving us vulnerable to disappointment in ourselves or our patients when the uniqueness of the situation brings a different outcome. The initiative becomes ours, and many, if not most, of our people will comply because their attachment with us is more important than staying in contact with what their inner world needs. Often, it's easier— even relieving—to go along with us, to see us as the authority, because it is so hard to trust that their inner world has anything helpful to offer. Without meaning to, we may replicate one of their core attachment wounds: being with parents who are unable to listen and reflect so that their child doesn't have support to practice hearing and trusting herself.

When we continue waiting for an inner response to come to us before tentatively suggesting a possible course of action as we did in the last chapter, we are offering our people a potential embodied disconfirmation and repair of implicit messages about the untrustworthiness of their inner experience that is often part of attachment wounding. They may begin to sense that it's okay to wait, to listen, to not know immediately, to know incompletely, and that we will wait with them.

Our learning to not trust ourselves early on is often profound, pervasive, woven into attachment, and not at all what our parents intended. When I was about six, one of my few friends moved away. I felt so sad and helpless that my RAGE system awakened for one of the few times in my childhood. My father was there and became the recipient of my outrage. "It's not *fair* they moved away!" I yelled. He replied in a disconnected way, "Of course it's fair. Her father's job changed and they had to go." He wasn't able to be present or reflect my experience, and a left-centric response was all he had to offer. What I remember most powerfully is the feeling of withdrawal in my belly and chest and a kind of spinning confusion in my head. A number of similar experiences, before and after, drove home the implicit knowing and explicit belief that my father knew and I didn't, cementing in a core piece of our attachment with each other.

Now, from my more mature left-centric understanding, I can sense how the requirements were clear: Abandon myself or lose him. I also know that his intention was to give me guidance about how to hurt less about this loss. However, as a little one, I didn't have the capacity to analyze or see his intention. Instead, a trauma embedded not only around the particular unacknowledged loss, but as a core part of our attachment in the form of shame, doubt, and abandonment because this beloved person was not able to be with me many days.

The beginning of our reparative responsiveness with our people is to model it through waiting for our inner world to guide us. Equally important is to then offer the suggestion that arose in a tentative way that comes from our humble conviction that it may or may not match what our person's inner world is needing in this moment. Our inner state is as important as our words. If we believe we're right while offering the suggestion, it will resonate differently than if we feel the respectful uncertainty. Probably the most frequent words my people hear are some version of "How is that for you?" Then we listen together for how their inner world responds to what is being offered.

At the beginning of practicing inner listening together, our people may feel nothing but confusion, no response at all, moments of clarity followed by doubt, relief and gratitude at our offer to truly listen, or something I can't even imagine right now. If we truly believe that whatever happens is just what we need to be with in this moment, our people may be able to continue feeling reassured that it isn't about doing it right or wrong, but simply being present. They may even be able to feel safe in the midst of what is sometimes a frustrating experience by left-hemisphere standards.

As we receptively attend together to whatever has arisen, we are moving from response back to receiving and reflecting without judgment or agenda. Most often, something new will come as we attend in this way, and then we wait again for our inner response. As halting and unfamiliar as this may feel to our adult minds and bodies, we are actually participating in a dance that is very similar to the spontaneous flow of reflection and response between parents and their babies, just with more content. In the next chapter, we will attend to how this process unfolds in healing particular embedded traumas; here, we may be able to sense that repeating this pattern over and over can support changes in the overall attachment pattern of how we are with one another.

Pause for Reflection

If "halting" and "unfamiliar" resonate with you at times, perhaps we can surround that experience with compassion. So many of us who choose this work come from backgrounds of pain and fear that have been instrumental in calling us to now co-suffer with others as they find the courage to approach their wounds. Sitting with the flow of presence, contact, reflection, and responsiveness, not as separate steps but as an unfolding process in which each part is interwoven with the others, what do our bodies tell us about our comfort with this process? We might ask our muscles, belly and heart brains, and autonomic nervous system as a beginning, listening without judgment, and drawing comforting arms around any moments of difficulty.

Inviting that pause in which we are both attentively present to the wisdom of our person's inner world is a gift to both of us really. I am not sure how we came to believe that we know more about what our people need than they do. A core, culturally supported assumption about their brokenness may have something to do with it, and so might our left-dominant culture and training that makes it more challenging to be present to anyone's implicit experience. Maybe it is equally about our inability to trust our own inner wisdom to guide us because no one helped us listen when we were young. Without that trust, we may get frightened for our people and about the process, and such feelings bring on the need to assert control. Under these circumstances, it is understandable that we might want to take refuge in left-centric protocols rather than be met by the uncertainty of the emerging moment. When we do shift left, our people's safety is unintentionally subverted and we may take on a needless ongoing burden of sole responsibility or find ourselves blaming our patients for not succeeding. As we experiment with the pause, remembering that rupture and repair are optimal, trust will grow as we and our patients stumble together into the tentative, fluid process of attunement with one another that supports the awakening of the inherent wisdom and health our people bring.

Delight

This brings us to *delight*, the sweetness that lets us know we are loved no matter our state. Perhaps it springs from the confluence of our CARE and PLAY systems where warmth and joy meet. At its best, it transcends being delighted with a particular happening and is instead the reflection to us, and often to one another, of an enduring bond that is bigger than any single occurrence between us. When we are small and see that look on our parents' faces, there is such an affirmation that we are good, lovable, welcome. These experiences go deep into us and become an implicit foundation for resilience in challenging times and the pattern for drawing in warm companions throughout our lives. We are never too old or too wounded to receive healing waves of the persistent delight of another.

How do we maintain delight when our people's words or behaviors are filled with pain, fear, and rage, sometimes at us, or when we are impaired with exhaustion, illness, or the stirring of implicit memory? We might begin with kindness by not expecting to have that expansive feeling all the time, by again accepting our human limitations and welcoming the optimal ruptures and repairs that happen. It seems helpful to build a storehouse of felt-sense moments when the delight did spontaneously emerge. For me, picturing the young ones that my people bring into the space between, often from our first time together, is a reliable way to return to delight. I often see these little ones not only in their wounded state but in the full flower of the inherent health I know is theirs as well. The more we become connected, the more we may catch sight of their joy, their curiosity, their loving natures. As we open ourselves to becoming aware of moments of delight, each of us will find our own doorways into this secret garden.

Pause for Reflection

This chapter has likely touched our own attachment experiences deeply, so it is perhaps fitting to end with recalling moments when we have been both the receiver and giver of delight. Perhaps breathing a little more deeply, dropping our request for those moments into our right hemispheres and waiting, we may be surprised by who arrives.

In the first two chapters of Part Two, we have explored an overall process of therapy—leading, following, and responding—and its application to repairing torn attachments. Now we are going to invite that same process to guide us in transforming the specific implicit memories that hold the embedded traumas that are often intermingled with our sea of attachment.

20

Opening to Implicit Memory

Come out into the dark
where I can see you.

—A. NEIL MEILI (2016)

The movement toward healing embedded traumas often takes us into the darkness so we can bear witness to what remains of these events. Here, we are going to begin differently to remind ourselves that implicit memories also form in the light. My good friend shared this story with me:

> I feel so warm and content whenever I'm pinching the ends off beans and snapping them into smaller pieces. Since I don't get this feeling with other kinds of cooking, it's made me wonder. Then one day, it came back to me: It's like being with my mother and grandmother, talking, laughing, or quiet, just the rhythm of the beans snapping, just together. What's so interesting is that my daughter loves to do this, too, and she doesn't even know the story. (M. Helene, October 2015, personal communication)

We so often think of implicit memory as a storehouse for painful and frightening memories. It is equally the home of legacies of goodness that stay with us. In our deeper mind, these memories support hope, belief in the possibility of care, the felt sense of connection with one another, and much more. They foster our ability to move through the most challenging times without falling into despair. Whether we are consciously linking these experiences to specific explicit memories or not, they are the unseen foundation that colors our perception in the direction of expecting life to be good.

We can hear some of the elements of implicit memory in her story: muscles relaxed, autonomic nervous system (ANS) in social engagement, brainstem enjoying the rhythm of connection and working together, an awakened CARE and maybe PLAY system, neurotransmitters of warm attachment flowing freely, and limbic circuits gathering up the experience and encoding it all for the future. These kinds of embodied memories integrate widely in our brains and come into awareness as waves of sensation and feeling, often easily linked to the explicit memory of the nourishing experiences that generated them. Like all implicit memories, when they are active, they have the quality of happening right now, a visitation from our eternally present past. Often, they are contagious in the most beautiful way as they are passed down through the generations as sacred rituals in the midst of ordinary life. They are visceral witnesses of what is best in our families and culture.

Everyone I have worked with has at least a small storehouse of these experiences, no matter how challenging childhood may have been. Sometimes it takes a while for them to make themselves known in therapy because there is so much pain and fear asking for our attention. If we keep making room in our minds and hearts for the possibility, they seem to eventually come. One day, as she watched track and field on TV, Jordie remembered the feeling of running freely through the woods whenever she could escape the violence in her house. A hiking trip brought Allan to the renewed experience of how he found and cataloged rocks, loving their textures and colors as well as the contrast between their beauty and the ugliness of his alcoholic and poverty-stricken home. A time in her spring garden helped Molly remember lying face down on the warm sidewalk to watch snails and caterpillars make their slow and beautiful way toward her, forgetting for the moment the abuse that unfolded almost every night in her family. Even if we cannot always remember the specifics of these memories, our bodies recall that goodness, peace, and beauty are possible. These implicit memories can be sanctuaries for our people and for us in the midst of the co-suffering and hard work of recovery.

Pause for Reflection

Our unique storehouse may have already opened its doors as we read about others' experiences. When we pause to listen, we may feel the echoes in our bodies and see pictures in our minds. Each time these memories fire anew, whether they bring explicit knowing with them or not, they become stronger and more reliable for us in times of need. Let's pause for a bit and sense which embodied memories might want to come in this moment. There may be two or three that have particular sweetness for us, inviting us to visit regularly.

Resting into the goodness of whatever came from this reflection, let's begin to talk about the embedded traumas that also linger in implicit memory. At my very first meeting with Maria, she made this wise statement: "I feel like I understand why my father screamed insults at me every day and even like I have forgiven him, but what upends my life are these terrifying sensations of his face close to mine, the look on his drunken face, how he was breathing, the smell of him. They come out of nowhere, sometimes several times a day, to make me feel so scared and small I can barely function." She was speaking to the relative importance of embodied implicit memory (we feel what happened and it isn't over) and explicit memory (we know what happened and that it is over) in terms of their effect on our lives. This points us toward the need for implicit resolution so we can experience a different quality of life.

In Chapter 15, we explored the way our wise brains manage overwhelming experiences and how these processes leave us in a good position to support the needed shift in the felt sense of implicit memories. In very brief review, chemical changes that activate when an experience is too strong for our current internal and external regulatory resources to manage tuck these pathways into our right-centric limbic circuitry and body (Jovasevic et al., 2015). In this way, our ongoing lives are protected from the constant incursion of the raw pain and fear, and the injured parts of ourselves are partially shielded from new injury. We might say that they have been *enwombed*, awaiting the arrival of support.

At the same time, the memories also remain malleable enough that they can be touched and awakened, which is essential for healing. However, we also remain vulnerable to them being brought into activity when support isn't available, precisely what Maria was describing. Someone standing overly close to her, a frowning face (man or woman), certain breathing patterns, and even sensory fragments (the color of a person's shirt or hair, the smell of alcohol on someone's breath) all had some probability of awakening the terror. The widely dispersed individual streams that make up these memories are all gathered into the neural net that formed at the time of the initial experience, and when our outer or inner world tugs on any strand, there is some probability that more of the neural net will open, bringing the rush of embodied feelings. Most often, the explicit memory does not arrive at the same time, so there is no context for the flood of sensations and emotions, which feel as if they are related to what is happening right now. Our system adaptively enters a sympathetic (or possibly dorsal) state that matches the perceived level of threat. What can look like an out-of-proportion response to what is happening in the moment is actually exactly in proportion to what is unfolding internally. If we sense this so deeply that this knowing is viscerally available when our patients are having strong emotional experiences, we will be able to offer them acknowledgment of the validity of their experience rather than needing to control or change it.

This brings us to the ways our left-hemisphere emissary might help us think about implicit memory to steady us as we support our people moving toward resolution through what are often very rough waters. When we view these arisings as negative and something to be gotten rid of, we may inadvertently set up an internal war for our people between the parts who are caught in the pain and fear and the parts who want to send them away. One of my people felt profound hatred and disdain for the small child within her who cowered in a corner. She wanted her destroyed. The weakness of this little one was understandably terrifying for her adult self because she felt so dangerously vulnerable if she got anywhere near this child's experience. As we sat with both parts of her, acknowledging the validity of the feelings from both viewpoints, my person began to have visceral sensations that her hatred inflicted a burning sensation on this child and that the disdain brought on further cowering. Without me suggesting that she feel differently, being able to physically sense what was happening for her child self gradually softened the energies she directed toward this younger part. This internal tenderness offered more safety for this little one so she could be available for the help we wanted to bring. Shifts toward such emotional safety may often begin with the broad acceptance and ventral space we offer our people. Through resonance and internalization of us as companions, our way of holding them may gradually become the way they are able to hold themselves.

If we can approach these implicit arisings as a gift rather than an attack, as an opening toward healing, we may be able to help our people get into relationship with their implicit world in a more compassionate and collaborative way. Perhaps we can begin with considering these memories, no matter how challenging, to be messengers of life-giving truth. Our explicit memories, to the extent that they formed at all in times of potential trauma, carry some small portion of the facts, although even these will be altered over time. Implicit memory speaks to the truth of what remains, in this moment, in our bodies, behaviors, beliefs, and relational expectations from the experience. The sensations and impulses to move reveal the remnants of the event as we responded to it. If we become convinced of that (usually through our own experience), then it gets so much easier to be openly receptive to—and perhaps even grateful for—whatever is arising in the moment. The impulse to try to change it eases. In its place, an open ventral space becomes more available for our people.

A young woman with a history of daily humiliation by both parents taught me so much about this. Our first couple of sessions were about history, and after that everything changed. Each time, very soon after she arrived and we had greeted one another, something would touch this implicit wound. Perhaps it was just being in the presence of someone who was paying attention to her, but we never knew for sure. Her hands would come up to cover her face, and tears would flow. There were no words and very few images, simply the anguished sensations and movements of a deeply shamed child. I could feel my left hemisphere yearning for more content, and yet something in the depth of her experience led me to only make sure that we were still connected. "Can you feel me here with you?" There would be a head nod and sometimes a hand reaching out to take mine. With this depth of emotional outpouring, I needed to know that we were still within our joined windows of tolerance, that she felt our connection. Otherwise, she would be reexperiencing the humiliation alone again and there would be no possibility of disconfirmation. Over the months, we moved through waves of anguish into moments of deep settling, then back to anguish and more settling. I was unsure of how all this was touching her daily life because she was rarely able to talk with me before the shame took over her body. Part of me felt trust in our process and part felt anxious because of the depth of her ongoing suffering and my very limited sense of anything outside of our process.

When such powerful implicit waves arrive, our wish for it to be different is understandable, since our caring hearts want so much to ease suffering. Our conviction that staying with "what is" will support these changes is not easy ground to hold. Being with both these parts of ourselves, the one who stands witness to anguish and the one who wishes for change, broadens the foundation that anchors us and ultimately may also help our people hold the ambiguity of their feelings toward implicit arisings.

Pause for Reflection

With as little judgment as we have this day, let's ask about how we are with the arising of our own painful implicit memories. Do we have at least a moment of wishing them to go away? If that is present, simply acknowledging the humanity of this is helpful. Then we can perhaps hold both the desire to separate from these bodily memories and the willingness to be with them in the broad embrace of welcome and compassion. I do believe this kind of acceptance is a lifetime's work that inevitably leads to failure at times. Our biology wants to protect us from what may harm us, and the arising of implicit memory can feel quite threatening. If we can soften toward our own tendency to want to move away and offer to begin again with gestures of inclusion, this is likely what is possible and optimal for us humans. Humility and grace are perhaps the gifts of this tension, gifts that we can then extend to our people in the form of honoring their struggle.

How we speak about the awakening of these memories may influence the ferocity with which they arrive, especially if we do it because we sense the changed language better reflects what happens rather than as a technique to control how these memories come to awareness. In Chapter 17, we suggested exchanging "touched and awakened" for the familiar "triggered." One therapist says this: "Even the gentlest sensory breeze can touch and awaken these old memories in our bodies. We are so tender and so available for healing" (K. Massoll, October 13, 2014, personal communication). It may sound strange to our left-hemisphere ears, but the shift in language seems to put us in a different relationship with the memories, and they begin to respond by arriving more gently. We might imagine that the prosody of our voice would be governed more by the ventral vagal parasympathetic, and that we would even listen differently because of this shift into a neuroception of safety in regard to the arising of implicit memories. All of this will resonate with our people, influencing their system's response. Perhaps it also better honors that the implicit is awakening in search of healing rather than to harm us. As always, it can be helpful to try it on with our own awakening memories for a while to see how our inner world responds to this offer.

One other shift in language seems to also soften how we tend to our inner world. "I just want this anxiety to go away! *It* makes my days miserable," any of us might say. It makes sense for us to want a symptom, an "it" to go away. If we begin to sense that we are made up of many selves (the subject of the next chapter), then we might instead say, "The anxious part of me is really suffering. I wonder how we might help *her*?" There is often a palpable softening as we gaze on a person inside who has value apart from the distressing symptom. We also may sense more clearly that this experience isn't all of us, but belongs to a part who has had encounters that give this anxiety context and meaning. The change of pronoun, granting personhood, may move us into a more right-centric way of perceiving, which also opens us to a more both/and perspective of broad acceptance, arouses our warm curiosity, and expands receptivity to the present moment. It can really be a very profound change.

Now for one last nourishing reminder for our left hemispheres before turning to the experience of implicit healing. In Chapter 15, drawing on the work of Bruce Ecker and his colleagues (Ecker, Ticic, & Hulley, 2012; Toomey & Ecker, 2007) we find this statement: "A client's seemingly irrational, out-of-control presenting symptom is actually a sensible, orderly, cogent expression of the person's existing construction of self and world, not a 'disorder' or pathology" (Toomey & Ecker, 2007, p. 210). All of us develop the protections our implicit memories need to keep what are perceived to be worse dangers from us. For many of us, the connection between symptom and implicit remains out of awareness for the most part, although certain of my people have come in making very clear statements. "If I stop drinking, I'm going to have to feel what it was like when my father left me." "When I stop cutting, I feel dead and want to kill myself." Our initial work isn't about making those connections, but about respectfully acknowledging that our people's system is acting wisely in this moment no matter what it looks like on the outside. Holding this firmly in our own body, heart, and mind is of inestimable benefit to those who come to us. They are often feeling crazy, bad, undisciplined, stupid, and all the rest, so to encounter someone who believes them to be wise and capable, even in this moment, is quite a disconfirmation to begin with.

These collaborative efforts between our right and left hemispheres, with the right opening to receptivity and the left backing us up by providing some clear principles and language, are the initial leadership that quietly accompanies us in the room. Then it becomes about the dance of following and responding, supported by the co-attaching that reliably (but with unpredictable specifics and pacing) unfolds in the presence of safety. At this point, our left hemispheres may long for a protocol to guide what comes next. While I can offer a few suggestions, the very idea of following our patients precludes that kind of protocol.

As we enter the tender territory of opening to implicit memory, we can begin by exploring one particular primary disconfirmation/restoration that our people need—relief from isolation. Traumas embed when our system is overwhelmed by pain and fear without having sufficient internal resources or companionship to help integrate the experience. As we begin working with our people, when we encounter parts inside who are carrying trauma, they almost always feel completely alone with the event. If there is an explicit memory as well, our people may see others being present, but as either unavailable for support or actively injurious, or the experience may have been so terrifying that even had someone tried to help, our patients might not have been able to receive it. In any of these cases, what remains now is a sense of isolation with the remaining anguish and terror. Over the years, I have found that as soon as a sense of accompaniment enters the memory, there is a new foundation for doing the work. Just as our people have internalized those who injured them, that same capacity can bring us inside to support processing the emotions and to resolve this primary wound of being alone. The sense of accompaniment increases safety, joins our windows of tolerance to support co-regulation, and opens the space where the work can unfold; GRIEF and FEAR are met with CARE so our systems can begin to settle; and gradually a rhythm of expecting painful arisings to be met by dependable and abundant comfort comes into their system as well.

This process of joining and accompaniment can start when our people first hear our voice or when we welcome them at the door for the first time. As we begin with receptivity, the offering of a nonjudgmental ventral space invites their social engagement system to come online as well. In this newly forming space between, resonance circuitry begins the co-internalization process. As they share what brought them here, we begin to follow not only their words but also their bodies. This is where all the practicing we've been doing attuning with our own sensations and movements becomes a gift to our people. With our increased sensitivity and awareness, we might notice small shifts in breathing or coloring, a little greater tension around the eyes. We might feel our muscles tense a bit or our stomach tighten, perhaps in tandem with theirs, perhaps not. As best we can, we just receive and hold without too much speculation about what it means, and also with awareness of our human limitations as our perceptions are colored by our own implicit memories. Our availability to deeply listen, even when we get it wrong, is likely also the beginning of a disconfirming/reparative experience.

For me, hearing a relational history at the beginning of our work helps me form pictures of some encounters that brought pain and others that offered empathic support. Early in life, who comforted this person? Who kept her safe? Who was distant? Who needed her to regulate them? Who felt dangerous? Who brought confusion or chaos? Who criticized and who was accepting? We might quickly discover that one person brought contradictory experiences—the confusing one also comforted, or the dangerous one at home was a primary support of safety in the outside world. All of this helps us begin to feel into the qualities of relatedness our person has taken in.

At this point, the process takes on its own unique shape. In general, as a Sherpa, I have a sense of the journey—make space for implicit memories to arise at their own pace, follow what comes, respond with what feels called forth in me by what my person is offering, and be open to awareness of ruptures so repair may happen as well. At the same time, I also have no idea how this person will approach that journey. What follows are two very different stories of how my person and I held this process in our welcoming hands. Neither of them is a script for what to do, but perhaps gives something of a felt sense that there is an underlying path that knows where it's going, and how much trust it takes to follow it. The two preceding chapters also have stories that may be worth rereading after spending time here to see other examples of implicit awakenings.

Sometimes the initial phone call starts the implicit process moving. Saralynn told me she had seen several other therapists over the years, had "talked her history to death," and was "madder than hell" because she still felt sick to her stomach every time she left the house for any reason. She assured me she wasn't agoraphobic and just gutsed it through. "I'm not scared of anything. It's just my damn body. Oh, and the doctors tell me I'm just fine!" Enjoying her abundant energy along with the hope and resilience she was demonstrating by trying therapy again, I felt moved to tell her that I believed her body was talking to us and, if we listened, might point us in the right direction to help. Having no sense of how that landed, I asked, "How's it for you that I say that?"

"Well, I actually wondered about that. This shit doesn't happen for no reason, right?"

"Right. We actually have a brain in our belly, a very sophisticated one, and it responds to everything that's happened in our lives, so it accumulates a lot of stories over time."

"Let's do it," she said with what sounded like enthusiasm and skepticism all rolled into one. I thought, "I'd be skeptical, too, if I had her history with trying to heal."

By the time we got together the following week, it felt to me like she was bringing her belly into the room, ready to see what it had to say. We might equally say that her belly was bringing her. A therapist interested in implicit memory can't ask for more than that. Since she had to leave the house to see me, her stomach was pretty active when she arrived. After acknowledging her belly, we did some history, beginning with listening to the trajectory of her intestinal distress. She couldn't remember a time when it wasn't either knotted up, unable to digest food well, or feeling sick at least part of the day. She repeated that going away from home was especially challenging, and added that she felt most at ease when she had hours of reading ahead of her for her work as an editor, with no threat or thought of leaving the house. Living alone really suited her.

As she shared some about her early life, we included her belly's sensations. Both her parents were loving, but she felt her mother was pretty worried and anxious. (This brought a tightening in her upper stomach.) Her father was quiet, studious, and shy. (No particular change.) Smiling, she said, "But I always thought that if someone tried to hurt me, he would leap off the couch like Superman and stop them!" (Her belly relaxed some for just a moment.) Saralynn was an only child and felt that had been good for her. She loved school and hated gym class. (The thought of being outside to play brought a wave of nausea.) Nothing else in her history seemed remarkable or relevant to her. I was quietly absorbing that there were no obvious traumas, while her belly was suggesting otherwise. Pictures of the relationship between her ANS and belly were floating through my mind.

We began to explore her relationship with her belly. "I don't like it. It's ruined my life in some ways. Other people enjoy food and I'm afraid of it. Other people can go hiking and feel good. I'm trapped in the house or else I go out and fight with my insides all day." She seemed more angry than sad, although as she talked and I listened, she softened some and I could almost feel some tears creeping in around the edges. Then she stiffened again. "Everyone is sick of me talking about it, too, so now it's just a sad fact of life."

I was touched by the pervasiveness of her misery and how she had become more isolated with these feelings over time. My strongest sense was of the adversarial relationship that had naturally developed. "I can easily understand why you would not like anything about this belly." I could feel a little tension in me about whether to go on and suggest that we see if we could start to meet and listen to her. I also noticed that in my mind, the pronoun for her stomach had started to shift from "it" to "her." Being aware of the tension, I paused, since that is usually the sign that I'm pushing ahead of where my person is. We were quiet for a moment, and then her hand found its way to her belly.

"Is that where there's the most pain right now?" I asked.

Her hand began to massage her belly a bit. "Yeah. When you said you could understand why I don't like my belly, I thought how strange that was. How does somebody get to hating a part of themselves? It's almost like I've separated myself from my own insides."

By now, my hand was on my belly in about the same place as hers. The room was very quiet with that familiar deepening that arrives when something is happening underneath, beyond the words. We paused until the energy in the room began to grow more active, and I found myself saying, "I wonder how it would be to invite her back in?" The tension had left my body, indicating to me that I was following her again, so the words came easily.

"I'm not sure. Why did you say 'her'?" Her hand hadn't left her stomach and was still moving in what looked like comforting circles.

"Two things come to me. I do believe your belly has her own voice, and can speak if we get into relationship with her. It's hard to relate to an 'it.'" Saralynn nodded. "And the other part is, from what you have shared, I am imagining there is a little girl inside, maybe even a baby, who first began to have a troubled tummy. These feelings may be her voice." A pause came naturally before I continued. "We may never know exactly when or how this began, but if we acknowledge this little one, she will somehow know that we are listening to her."

When I mentioned her little one, she took her hand off her belly, sat up straight, looked right at me in a kind of piercing way, and said, "That's enough for today."

Was this a rupture? I wasn't sure, but felt we had been heard by her inner world, had made some genuine contact. Feeling no resistance to what she sensed we needed to do, I said, "I trust you knowing when it's time to stop."

She spontaneously began talking about her work, how much she loved words, and how fortunate she felt that she could work at home and do what she enjoyed so much. While we shifted into conversation, it still felt to me like the underneath connection was alive in the room. We had certainly made a good beginning.

Over the following weeks, we developed a familiar rhythm in our work. Warm greeting, snarky comment or two, laughter, then settling toward her belly as it was in that moment. With all my people, that sense of a rhythm establishing itself, of moving more in tandem, is one of the ways my body feels reassured about our growing bond. We might chat a bit, but she was usually enthusiastic about connecting with her belly's sensations, an eager learner as she had been in school. She recognized that her biggest challenge was slowing down to truly listen. Her more natural pace was to ask questions and expect quick answers. She had been in sympathetic activation in this fight with her belly for two decades, so her urgency made sense. My contribution was to show up in a ventral state, listening to her sympathetic system, validating its activity on her behalf without having an agenda that it shift. The beautiful paradox is that by aligning with her ANS activation instead of trying to move her toward a ventral state, ventral could arrive on its own. And that's what happened.

First for moments and then for longer periods, we began practicing social engagement with her belly, a visceral disconfirming experience. This was also exercising the ventral branch of her ANS that had little support as a child growing up with an anxious mom. As Saralynn's capacity for deep listening grew, she was open to the myriad experiences that came. She saw some fleeting images from childhood, felt the relationship between her tight muscles and painful belly, and discovered that the deeper she listened, the more her belly relaxed. There were regular surges of tears and anger, which we were able to hold in our joined windows of tolerance. When the big emotions came, I was regularly checking to be sure she still felt our connection. Sometimes her body made pushing-away movements, sometimes her head turned away, and sometimes she felt a vast tiredness, all of which we followed. When she invited it, we fed her left hemisphere settling information about the relationship between sympathetic activation and difficulties with the belly brain. This integration between experience and knowing was deeply satisfying for her.

Over time, there was some gradual easing of her pain, moments of greater comfort when going outdoors, and an important shift in her expectations. Rather than waiting on pins and needles to see how her stomach would respond when she needed to go out, she got into conversation with her belly, listening to how "she" felt about the trip. Once they were in relationship, it seemed easier to get through the days when her belly was upset. Letting go of the left-hemisphere expectation that her stomach would be a little better each day, she began to flow with what was actually happening.

After we had been together for about six months, she came in with a remarkable experience to share. "I don't know why, but it seems like people are being warmer toward me these days. When I go into the local coffee shop, the barista wants to talk a little bit. Even people on the street seem friendlier. It's weird." We checked in and her belly seemed "cautiously optimistic." What came to my mind was that I wasn't sure if people were actually friendlier or if her being in a ventral state more often allowed her to feel their warmth. What did seem clear was that these deepening connections were gradually making it easier for her to look forward to going out without her belly sending a protective and painful warning that it was dangerous out there. Ready to try "flying without a net," as she said, we parted for a while. When her first child was born about six years later, her belly was doing well, but she felt a strong rise in anxiety and came back for another round of inner exploration.

During our first series of working together, Saralynn was never drawn to any explicit memories that seemed directly related to her digestive misery. Certain images would float by as we were attending to her belly's sensations, but they never seemed compelling to her. Instead, she was drawn to practicing a new way of being present with me and with herself. If I were to imagine what happened in her early life in the explicit sense, perhaps her loving mother's pervasive anxiety, likely present when she was feeding her infant daughter, became epigenetically entangled with the food (Harshaw, 2008), unintentionally pairing sympathetic activation with eating and with close relationships. Implicitly embedded at such an early age, it became a foundational way for her to experience the world. Her original belief that she wasn't agoraphobic was probably right because it seems it wasn't the open space outdoors but the anticipation of not connecting with people that upset her belly. I believe that the disconfirming/reparative experience was our joining in safety, allowing her ANS to move from sympathetic to ventral often enough that that became her baseline. Relationships could now be experienced as warm and safe when they truly were. That's the simple story my left hemisphere has crafted, and it may or may not be true.

My experience with Saralynn was most unusual, and once again taught me the wisdom of following what our people bring rather than leading with what I feel may be best. Had I suggested that she connect with the images that arose (which I sometimes felt tempted to do), I would have gone against her own inner wisdom, and I imagine we might have wound up in the ditch together, rehashing history as she had in previous therapy. Moving slowly, listening, noticing when my own intentions are trying to take over, and pausing in that moment have so often proved to be the most respectful and effective path of healing.

The second story is how implicit healing unfolds with greater frequency. It is never exactly like this, but the movement inward has a certain shape that is similar. Carlos came to therapy with only the spottiest explicit recall of his childhood. He grew up in a dangerous neighborhood and family, so there were virtually no places or people with whom he could take refuge. He described his experience as one dedicated to survival rather than connection. When he was five, his only little friend was shot and killed by accident in gang-related violence, so he had not even sought sanctuary with other young men. He considered it a blessing and a curse.

He chose me as his therapist because I was old enough to be the grandmother he never had. He had been a big reader as a child and had a particular affection for stories with grandmas who saved the day. We internalize not only living people, but characters who come alive in our reading and viewing. It felt lovely to me that in the midst of so much horror, he had these wise old women for allies, and that now I was to join their esteemed company. At least initially, he would attribute their characteristics to me, giving us both a foundation for joining and rich territory for ruptures and repairs, since I would likely never live up to these glorious beings.

Rather than talking about the specifics of his long history, it may be more helpful to focus on the first time we made a connection with the implicit world being protected by his symptoms. What brought Carlos to therapy was his concern about alternating flares of rage followed by severe withdrawal from all relationships. It was easy for me to see them as strong adaptive protectors of the anguish and terror embedded underneath rather than as standalone pathologies. He was most afraid he was going to seriously hurt someone before he could do anything to stop himself. That it hadn't happened yet was barely reassuring. Fear of himself was closest to the surface, so that is where we began.

"Carlos, can you sense where you feel the fear in your body?"

This is where all the work we have done with ourselves to sense the connection between our bodily sensations and implicit memories comes to help our person. Our conviction that this is a doorway to the deeper places provides a foundation, through resonance, for him to slow down and attend to his body. Carlos paused to take in this unfamiliar question and then got quiet. "My throat is so tight I can barely swallow."

"Does it feel like we can stay with that for a bit?" I found my hand going gently to my throat. This may sound odd to say, but when this happens it doesn't feel like a decision to move my hand so much as a behavioral impulse prompted by my CARE system wanting to meet his FEAR right there in his throat.

He nodded. We paused. After a little while, I said, "Let me know if there are any images or sounds or feelings that also come." Many of our people are so unused to being heard and reflected that they may need support to share what else may be arising.

"I see a little boy sitting on the floor while my father screams and beats my mother. Maybe four years old at most. It feels like a really dark place." He took a deeper breath and looked at me, shifting his gaze from inner to outer. I said, "I will go into the dark with you," returning his gaze while feeling so much sadness for this little one, and also feeling grateful for the connection he was able to make in our eye contact. It was as though this little boy and the whole scene were held in the space between us. At the same time, he had intuitively sensed he needed to move a bit away from the intensity by shifting his attention from quite so much direct contact. This felt like such a delicate and beautiful dance of co-regulation in the service of his inner wisdom. We were beginning to find our way, guided by all the skills he had developed to manage the intolerable pain and fear of childhood.

After a significant pause, I said, "Does it feel like we could be with him some more? We can do that, and I also trust that you will be able to sense if now is the right time."

"I'm not sure. He's kind of faded away. Should we go after him?"

"Let's trust how your inner world is guiding us. You've been chased and hurt so much in your life that it might be frightening for him if we're forceful at all. If your system believes it's time to go deeper with him, he'll come back."

"I want to wait a minute and see if he returns." The image swam back into view. I had been most touched by the complete isolation of this child in the midst of the violence, so that provided guidance for our first movement, hoping to establish a foundational sense of "we" in the memory. "Does it seem like you and I could move toward him?" He nodded. "Let me know what happens as we get closer."

"I'm seeing his eyes. He's terrified."

"Yes. Does he feel us coming to be with him?"

"Maybe a little."

"Let's just take it very slowly. He's not used to someone coming." It was quiet again for a moment.

"He sees us, but he's afraid to move."

"Could we come close to him, sit by him?"

"Yes."

"Could you take his hand, and just let your boundaries down a little so you can begin to feel what he's feeling?" This is the moment when two neural nets may meet and begin to join. Carlos's adult self was still more in the present-day world, and this little one was in a long-buried neural net that was just now opening to receive the disconfirmation that he was not alone, that help had come. As Carlos touched him, some of this boy's visceral sensations came into Carlos's body, and he immediately felt such compassion for what this boy had endured—not the intellectual compassion he always felt, but the sense of whole-bodied, whole-hearted empathy with his small self that moved him to tears.

As the feelings deepened, it was as though Carlos's adult was absorbed into his little boy, and I was now the adult with him. He carried me with him through the emotions and bodily sensations of the memory, sharing the depth of the implicit experience. I checked with him to be sure he still felt me here. He had reached out for my hand, and that helped anchor the two worlds together, perhaps part of the bridge to bring the disconfirmation into the implicit neural net. We were in no rush to leave this memory, because if we went too soon without the child feeling felt and understood, the resolution was apt to be incomplete. He needed what occurred to be witnessed. At some point, the intensity lessened, and I said, "We're just here together now, safe and quiet." We rested in this for a moment, and gradually his adult self began to emerge. As the little one receded, he took with him the experience of accompaniment and safety, and as the neural net reconsolidated over the next few hours, these experiences were permanently seeded as part of his history. In addition to changing the felt sense of this particular implicit memory, some healing of the sea of attachment was also beginning. As we continued in the weeks ahead, our steady presence with one another and with his inner world amplified the sense of security.

We may ask how important it is for us to enter the memory with our people. For some counselors, this feels potentially invasive or simply arrogant. I believe it is a way of consciously honoring and enhancing the internalization process that is underway anyway. It also provides our people with a resource that we hope comes to every child—the accompaniment of caring others whom they can consciously carry with them internally for the rest of their lives. Perhaps most important in the moment is the sense of additional comfort and regulation that comes from us being together in this way. One of my people said this: "When I'm at home and these memories come, I draw you in with me to comfort him. It makes all the difference."

In keeping with the theme of self-reliance in our left-centric culture, we may sometimes ask our people to care for this child themselves, concerned about them becoming dependent on us. However, when there has been little nurturance in early life, they may not have the inner resources to do that. Their adult self may need our care as much as the young ones. The addition of our presence provides that care and, perhaps more importantly, brings in a person from the outside who is safe and responsive. As this is deeply internalized, it builds trust in the possibility of having safe relationships in the world. In a broad way, it also embeds the implicit experience of not having to do it alone. For us to provide this kind of accompaniment, we need to become comfortable with offering ourselves in this way. If we feel anxious in doing this, that becomes part of the internalized experience, too. With kindness toward ourselves and with support of another, we may be able to find our way toward more comfort with the process of inviting our people into the process of internalization. That will be the right time to begin doing this with our patients.

Every story we might share will be different in its specifics, and every session with the same person will be different as well. With Carlos this time, the image might not have returned, his child may not have trusted us to come close, at any point the memory could have suddenly evaporated, or the unfolding sensations and arousal might have pulled Carlos out of our joined windows of tolerance. Each of these call on us to follow. Trusting the inherent wisdom of our people's system, we can support the image not coming back, a child who wants us to keep his distance, or a memory simply evaporating. When sympathetic or dorsal activation overwhelms the connection, we can respond by helping the process slow down, usually with the resources we have discovered together, and offering co-regulation to come back into our joined window of tolerance. In each case, what we offer next is a response that flows from what our person's system has brought, unless it is a rupture, and even then we can offer repair.

Each time we move through one of these sequences with our people, it is changing our embodied brains as well. In resonance, we experience the implicit arising, the sustained activation, and the resolution. Over time, the embedding of this complete process ingrains in us an embodied implicit anticipation that healing is possible; we recognize that the process follows a recognizable course; and as we stay in following and responding, our combined wisdom is trustworthy. We carry this hope and conviction in our bodies and our people rely on it.

I want to finish this chapter by saying how much respect I have for each person's system knowing what will support healing. Not everyone responds to the process of going directly into the body toward the root of implicit memory. For some, being consistently in the presence of a caring other provides disconfirmation for attachment losses. For others, sand tray or art may be the resonant support, or EMDR or Somatic Experiencing. So many modalities have emerged in recent years, primarily in response to our expanded understanding of the neuroscience of wounding and healing. Each way of working has value and may become even more supportive of our people if it rests on the practice of leading, following, and responding. In this way, we are able to cultivate a safe space for the fluid emergence of any specific protocol. Let's close with two very different possible approaches that offer implicit disconfirmation of embedded trauma in an unusual way. The first may help us ameliorate the traumatic stress of daily life.

In Japan (and now other places as well), shinrin-yoku or forest bathing is fostering healing through relationship with nature (Park, Tsunetsugu, Kasetani, Kagawa, & Miyazaki, 2010). Cortisol lowers, heart rate variability increases, and ventral activation calms the sympathetic ANS as we stroll for half an hour or so under the canopy of trees. If we are city dwellers, regular immersion in the beauty and stillness of the forest can become a visceral disconfirming/restorative experience for the cultural trauma that accrues for so many of us in daily life. With all devices left behind, our senses have the opportunity to come alive, nurturing a right-centric way of attending and of establishing a different rhythm than the one dictated by the anticipation of incoming email and texts (N. Carr, 2011; Richtel, 2010). It is possible that the network of roots and fungi beneath our feet offer some kind of tangible nurturance for the parallel systems in our bodies.

We are so immersed in and acclimated to the experience of our fast-paced, digital lives that it is challenging to gain a sense of the traumas subtly embedding each day. Our dependence on devices is influencing attention, memory, relationships, learning, neurotransmitters, and more (N. Carr, 2011) and changing our brains in ways that are diametrically opposed to the heart of our neurobiology—the need for sustained warm relationships. We are increasingly lost to each other. Nicholas Carr (2011), student of the web's influence on our wiring, sums up the cognitive challenge this way.

> The influx of competing messages that we receive whenever we go online not only overloads our working memory; it makes it much harder for our frontal lobes to concentrate our attention on any one thing. The process of memory consolidation can't even get started. And, thanks once again to the plasticity of our neuronal pathways, the more we use the Web, the more we train our brain to be distracted— to process information very quickly and very efficiently but without sustained attention. That helps explain why many of us find it hard to concentrate even when we're away from our computers. (p. 194)

As an antidote, imagine even longer periods of being untethered from devices. In 2010, a group of brain scientists spent several days on the river together, discovering the gradual letting go of the need to constantly check in, even the need to know what time it is (Richtel, 2010). In those circumstances, it seems our brains begin to find their way back to the inherent health waiting under the stress adaptations of our society. Even in so short a period of implicit disconfirmation through nature's tender influence, thoughts, feelings, behaviors, and relationships change. Not permanently, however. Once back in the culture, the implicit swirl and the embedded familiarity can consume us again. May we each find a forest-bathing path that can be a daily balm in this taxing world.

At the other end of the spectrum from those of us experiencing almost invisible daily wounding are those men and women, our first responders and military, who adapted to the intolerable with complex posttraumatic stress adjustments and cannot seem to find resolution with any of the traditional means of healing. Instead, they can come to psychologist Lorin Lindner's aviaries, perfectly named Serenity Park, at the Veteran's Center in Los Angeles to engage with the wounded parrots there (Siebert, 2016).

Parrots and their cousins are so socially attuned and cognitively sophisticated that when they are first stripped away from their flock to become pets and then afterward lose their human companion, they suffer a double trauma and begin to exhibit the signs of posttraumatic stress—pacing, screaming, nightmares, self-mutilation. When these wounded human veterans come to them, there is profound recognition across species in a most unexpected way and everyone begins to heal. As they pair up, they seem to find one another around particular injuries. The vet who developed epilepsy because of a traumatic brain injury was chosen by the only bird with seizures. A parrot with a severely wounded wing chose the helicopter pilot with a crippled arm. One of the veterans who has become a permanent part of Serenity Park shared his touching experience:

I had learned that yellow-headed Amazons are not that friendly, so when Joey made an effort to befriend me, that meant even more. We were different species, but we got each other. I was shy, burned by humans, isolated, angry. Joey had what seemed to me the same attitude. So we bonded. He let me touch him. Only me. (quoted in Siebert, para. 44)

The author of the article says that in his time at Serenity Park, he "came to think in terms of the expansive anatomy of empathy" (para. 48). The humans and birds find one another, co-suffer together, and care for each other in a deeply touching process of co-healing.

Lindner says this about what she witnesses from her psychologist's viewpoint:

> There's definitely something different going on at this place. We know that what's preserved across species, all vertebrates truthfully, is the ability to feel compassion. As for birds and humans, we both have sympathetic nervous responses. We react the same way to trauma on the physiological level and in terms of the reparative nature of compassion and empathy. That's what is doing the healing. That's what is bringing the broken halves together. We don't know what the actual healing factor is, but I believe that it has to do with mental mirroring. That the parrots get what the veterans are going through and, of course, the veterans get them, too, because, hey, they are all pretty much traumatized birds around here. (para. 37)

One of the veterans says it very simply: "They look at you, and they don't judge. The parrots look at you and it's all face value. It's pure" (para. 34).

This is where our journey has taken us, too—*recognizing the injury in all of us and cultivating our capacity for nonjudgmental presence, an ever-evolving process.* In these three chapters, we have established the foundation of leading, following, and responding to open a safe space for the work to unfold; co-attaching as the interpersonal ground for implicit change; and the process of disconfirmation/restoration in the embrace of the relationship to transform the felt sense, behavioral impulses, and perceptions of embedded traumas. As we have come to expect, these three processes are interwoven and mutually supportive, and we will add a final stream now as we deepen the healing process from the viewpoint of inner community.

21

Radical Inclusiveness
"Everyone Is Welcome Here"

I was noticing again the other day
watching a movie, strangely enough
called "Remains of the day"
that even though you died
you haven't gone away

—A. NEIL MEILI (2003A)

When Carlos began to see his four-year-old self in the midst of the violence between his parents, he also saw his mother and father. His experience was shaped by their presence then, and they have been internalized as part of his inner world now. As the trauma embedded, time stopped for his parents and his child self, with their embodied experience sequestered in his subcortical circuits and body for later healing. When the time is right in therapy, Carlos can step into each person's shoes to touch their emotions, bodily sensations, behavioral impulses, and intention, and together his adult self and I will be able to offer each of these inner ones disconfirmation of the pain and fear that has overwhelmed this family. It is quite a gift that our inner world includes the others in the memory so there can be inner resolution, especially when no outer reconciliation is possible. This is the essence of inner community* work.

---

* The idea of multiple selves has deep and varied roots in the work of the object relations theorists (Scharff, 2012), Eric Berne (1966), Fritz Perls (Perls, Hefferline, &

In Chapter 16, we spoke about the process of co-internalization, building on the work of Marco Iacoboni (2009, 2011). It is worth hearing what he says again.

> We empathize effortlessly and automatically with each other because evolution has selected neural systems that blend self and other's actions, intentions, and emotions. The more we learn about the neural mechanisms of mirroring, the more we realize that the distinction between self and other may be almost fictitious in many cases. We have created the self-other distinction in our explicit discourse, along with many other constructs that divide us. Our neurobiology, in contrast, puts us "within each other." (Iacoboni, 2011, p. 57)

To touch back in with what we talked about in that earlier chapter, we are each endowed with a rich array of resonance circuitry that enables us to take in and encode one another's bodily sensations, emotions, behavioral impulses, and intentions—basically, the aspects of implicit memory. As Carlos connects with his father inside, he might feel the surge of sympathetic activation, the feeling of rage, the impulse to lash out, and the intention to protect himself from the implicit pain of his own abandonment rising in him. If he turns to his mother, he might feel her dorsal withdrawal, terror, bodily cringing, and her intention to survive this violence. He might experience his little boy caught between sympathetic and dorsal responses to his helplessness, terror, and anguish, frozenness in his body, and the intention to make it stop without being able to do anything. He would encounter three different perceptual universes in that single memory. At the level of our senses, we are also encoding how the person looks and sounds, the quality of their touch, perhaps how they smell and taste. This is the minimum of what we take in. Mirror neurons are being found throughout our brains now (Iacoboni, 2011), and it will be quite some time before we understand all of what we are exchanging with one another, just how deeply interwoven and influential we are.

To have a further sense of the power and pervasiveness of this

---

Goodman, 1951), Roberto Assagioli (1971), John Watkins (Watkins & Watkins, 1997), and Richard Schwartz's (1995) Internal Family Systems model. One contribution of inner community work is its emphasis on the process of internalization and how that guides the course of resolution.

process, we can consider when this encoding begins. In utero, our system develops in parallel with our mother's at many levels, a kind of pervasive pre-internalization experience of near-oneness. As we are born into this vast outside world, our parents awaken our resonance circuitry as they make faces, delighting in us as we return their gestures. With our systems fully directed toward attaching, we eagerly attend and deeply draw in these beloved others. Our bodies remember the father who was present, the one whose attention was elsewhere, the unsure parent who was anxious, or the mother whose eyes were filled with hatred. Even with implicit-only memory in those early months, bits of sensory experience encode that remind us how much remains of those who are with us: a fragrance, a rough beard, warm hands on our belly, and especially eyes. The sustained, loving gaze of our mother can draw us almost all the way back to the womb, then and now.

These experiences stay with us and with our people. Looking at a photograph of her mother holding her when she was an infant, Jalene says, "I see it, but my body doesn't know anything about being held." As we look at the picture together, we can see her mother's vacant eyes, so it is no wonder that her body remembers that touch more as absence than presence. Stepping into her mother's experience for a moment, Jalene feels her chest open into a black hole, making it hard to breathe. David shows me a photograph of his father tossing him up in the air when he is just a few months old and feels ripples of joy running so powerfully through his body that he feels like he could fly. Changing to dad's perspective, a tear wells up: "He loves me."

Pause for Reflection

Inviting a warm memory from early in life to arrive, let's see if we can sense the experience from our own perspective, then from that of the other person. If you can, spend a little time going back and forth between the two. How does your body—muscles, belly, heart, breath—speak to you about this experience from each perspective? There tends to be less difference between the two when there is mutual joy and caring, although David's delight is somewhat different than the love he felt in his father. If you are doing this with a reading partner or friend, you might each want to invite a painful or frightening experience, and, if one arrives, gently touch the felt sense of each person in the memory. Returning to the warm experience together is a helpful way to conclude.

In the last chapter, we talked about being with our native parts, mostly the younger ones, and here we are expanding to include the people we have taken in through internalization our whole life long. We might call these our imported parts. Over the years, it has seemed to me that working with the children inside is only half the process. These imported others continue to add their pain, fear, and associated capacity for wounding other people to the stream of implicit memory that can be touched and awakened. They are equal members of our inner community. *This internalization process may be a primary way that wounds get passed from generation to generation.* My father's harshly critical voice can be touched and awakened in me, then directed at my own child. At the same time, the ongoing wounds these internalized ones carry can mean that our protective parts need to keep vigilant so that the remaining distress doesn't overwhelm our outside world all the time and to ensure that the still-wounded ones aren't further hurt. This continuing sense of danger requires us to devote resources that otherwise might flow toward warm relationships and creativity to containing the injury. Additionally, the bodily experience we have taken in from them will affect our muscles, belly and heart brains, ANS, eyes, ears, and vocal cords when they are active in us. While carrying this much of others can feel like an overwhelming burden, it is also the open door to healing, since their aliveness inside us means they can be touched with the disconfirming care others might offer us.

The process ahead will ask us, in our role as counselor, to cultivate increased understanding and compassion to enliven the *radical inclusiveness* that can make a safe space for these internalized ones. Some of these people inside have caused grave injury, and some of the protectors wreak havoc in our daily lives while intending only to do good. To truly welcome them without judgment or requirement to change is the greatest gift and asks so much of us.

We can begin with some nourishment for our left hemispheres to deepen our understanding, which often provides a more stable foundation in the midst of challenge. Each of our inner communities is completely unique, and yet there are certain pathways of development we share. From early in life, we will have relationships that nurture us and ones that bring pain and fear. Usually, the same person brings both. Our tender, comforting mother also requires standards of behavior that are beyond our developmental capacity, for example. As we discovered in speaking about implicit memory in the last chapter, the dyads (or larger groups) that sustain us also integrate broadly in our brains, so we have easy access to their implicit (and sometimes explicit) support. Those that hold embedded traumas will be sequestered in subcortical circuits and our bodies. Part of the shelter for these wounded ones involves the emergence of what we are calling *protectors*, aspects of ourselves that actively engage our inner and outer worlds to keep more hurt from coming to those already injured. They also support the seawall that keeps the pain, fear, rage, sorrow, and other inner experiences from continually welling up to threaten daily functioning. We can imagine them facing inward and outward at the same time to gauge how much protection is needed, given the magnitude of the wounding and current unfolding events. In general, the greater the wounding, the more numerous and powerful our protectors need to be.

In various paradigms of practice, we have called these protectors "defenses" or "resistances," as though they were objects that needed to be moved out of the way. This is understandable, because we see that these parts of ourselves sometimes cause injury if we view them only from the outer perspective without opening to the ways they are sheltering our inner world. The Reader of Books in Figure 21.1 lets us safely inhabit other worlds while also keeping us isolated and afraid in our aloneness. The Hungry One fills the empty places with something she can control, and also may injure health and keep us from taking in other kinds of human nurturance. Both may seem to stop us from moving forward in therapy by keeping vulnerability at bay. Only if we are able to widen the lens to take in the bigger picture that includes both the outer challenges and the inner distress do we begin to sense that the protectors are in proportion to what is in need of shelter. It is our system's sense that moving the safeguard aside and allowing the implicit to emerge would be more harmful than whatever the protector is doing in this moment.

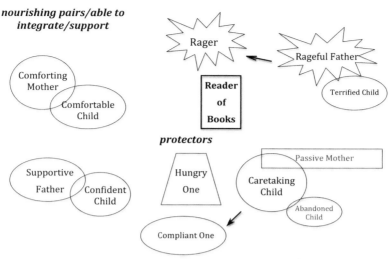

nourishing pairs/able to integrate/support

protectors

unresolved groups/sequestered/time stops/vulnerable

FIGURE 21.1 Each of us could draw a partial map of our inner world that would be different than this one. What we do hold in common are the layers themselves. On the left are the internalized ones who can support hope and resilience, and on the right, the holders of embedded traumatic experience. Standing between are aspects of ourselves who are actively protective. Some of them are modeled on what we have learned from native and imported selves, while some seem to spring more from inherent capacities and preferences. In this example, the Reader of Books and the one who finds soothing in food seem more related to who this person is, while the Rager and Compliant One transfer parts from the wounded layer to become protectors. They are actually simultaneously protectors and parts of injured groups, something that is challenging to picture. As we encounter our people's inner worlds and our own, we will find our parts to be more fluid than static or boxed up, even though we have to draw them that way here.

Pause for Reflection

In order for us to offer this kind of acceptance to our people, it is helpful to again sense how it is for us. As we begin to talk about protectors, which of yours come easily to mind? In the first moment of their appearance, how do you feel about them? If the first impulse is to push them away, can we, with as little judgment as possible, include this response as well as the protector him/herself in a gesture of welcome? Doing this repeatedly is like exercising a muscle. It builds a neural pathway that can hold both our judgments and our compassionate receptivity at the same time. As our people resonate with this developing capacity in us, they, too, may get into relationship with their protectors a little differently than ever before.

Acknowledging, valuing, and respecting these protectors, not as a technique but because we truly see them as indispensable to our people's functioning, deepens the safety in the room. Let's look at how this might happen between our people and us. After every disappointment with her husband, mainly around his inability to listen to anything that had to do with her needs or achievements, Sylvia found herself depressed and in bed for hours or days. "I hate this about myself," she said. "Why do I let him have this much power over me?"

That crossroads between attempting to shift a symptom and being with what is present came alive in me again. I could understand her frustration at the regularity with which this happened and also feel something important in the depth of the collapse his abandonment brought forward. These two protectors—depression and frustration—were clearly in conflict with each other. At this point, I might align with the frustrated one and offer suggestions for staying out of bed, or sit with the possibility that both the part of her who felt frustrated and the part who collapsed needed attention. "Your frustration is certainly understandable. It is hard to feel like you're losing this time when you want to move forward. I wonder what the part of you who gets so depressed is needing."

That brought on a little rupture. "She needs to get up!" Sylvia's frustration had shifted to me. Sometimes in the effort to align with their protectors, our people may feel we are going to leave them in the grip of a part who is hurting them. In this case, it was easy to sense how the frustrated part was protective. She was the prod who wasn't going to let Sylvia be overpowered by husband or depression, and I had become the enemy by not supporting her prodding with my own. In an attempt at repair, I said, "You need me to want you to get up, too."

"Otherwise, what are you good for?"

"Maybe I'm good for believing that everything you are doing is meaningful and important, even collapsing in bed. Maybe together we can discover how this part is trying to protect you."

"Maybe. But I still don't like it."

"This I completely understand. I do believe that if we can hear what this part is telling us, she can lead the way to whoever needs our attention deeper inside so she doesn't need to go to bed." With that agreed on, we started down the familiar road to implicit disconfirmation, beginning with the sensations in her body just before and during the collapse. As we gently moved toward this embodied experience, the protector stepped aside to allow us access to a very young child who was systematically ignored when her baby brother was born. Going to bed when she felt abandoned now had been the only thing standing between her and revisiting this intolerable anguish alone. The restorative experience arose with ease, as my CARE system was immediately responsive to her GRIEF. From there, with a gentle question about whether she was ready to shift her focus, we were able to move toward the parents who had stepped away from her. Just as we had with her little one, we touched their inner experience, beginning with the bodily traces of their presence inside her.

In this kind of work, we are making the commitment to attend to deeper implicit healing rather than focusing on symptom change. One may not be better than the other, but they are different. Quicker relief of some particular symptoms may happen if we emphasize cognitive or behavioral change. Moving more deeply into the territory of embedded traumas often increases the need for protection for a while as the pain comes to the surface. However, in my experience, if the symptom-generating pain locked in implicit memory is not healed, the need for protection will stay the same, and another kind of symptom will likely be needed to continue shielding the intense emotions, behavioral impulses, and beliefs that remain. One client said she played a game with herself called "Pick Your Poison." She could shop, eat, or gamble to quiet the deep distress of her mother's abuse; at the same time, she recognized that each brought a significant downside along with the protection offered. Simply being conscious of her options didn't quiet the protectors or lessen her fear of what she was implicitly holding. When we are able to provide disconfirmation/repair at this deeper level, the protections are needed less and have a tendency to transform or fade away.

We might picture it this way. Prior to implicit healing, our protectors are responding to the magnitude of pain they need to sequester. It is as though they are facing mainly inward to keep track of the suffering there while devoting just enough resources to the outside world to modulate the degree of protection needed according to the emerging moment. That is why our responses can sometimes look wildly out of proportion to those only seeing our outer circumstances. As we heal, there is less need for protection from implicit wounds, so more of our protective resources can be devoted to the needs of the current moment. A compliant protector who has indiscriminately given herself away in an attempt to keep everyone calm now becomes able to offer kindness and care while also taking her own needs into account. A raging protector who has lashed out in proportion to the inner danger is able to keep his anger available only for times when defense is warranted by current circumstances. This transformation often comes slowly while it reliably reflects the state of our inner world.

Some protectors do eventually dissolve in their current manifestation. Cutting or purging stops. Addiction to alcohol or drugs abates. Suicide plans become ideation and finally depart, although none of this happens as linearly as I have stated it. Often, they are first replaced by less harmful protectors, and then those may be able to transform, bringing helpful gifts. Most important for us with our people is to welcome these parts, listen to them, and let them become our guides. Many of us have experience doing this with our people's child parts, so it is simply a matter of offering the same receptivity and following to these protective ones. They will have a better sense of pacing than we can because they are so connected to the wounded ones inside. As the ones in distress have less hold on thoughts, feelings, behaviors, and relationships, we can know that less vigilance over the inner world is needed.

As we make the journey inward with our people, we will come to the next challenge to our compassion: those inner community members who have actively brought harm to the young ones inside. *This is such tender territory, a place where we need to acknowledge the suffering our people have sustained without demonizing and alienating the ones who brought it, for they are now part of the ones in our care as well.* This can be radical inclusiveness at its most healing, widening our joined windows of tolerance to truly accept every part. Along the way, our own inner community wounds will be touched, our system's natural protections will cause us to pull back at times, judgments will come unbidden. If we can open into receptivity enough to hold all those experiences, both the ones of rejection and acceptance, this will resonate deeply with our people. As our embodied brains become increasingly interwoven over time, our expanding compassion becomes theirs as well.

It can help us keep our balance to distinguish between the living people who were hurtful and the internalized ones who are now part of our neurobiology. Those who harmed us may never change, but once they become part of us, they seem to partake of our impulse toward healing. I don't know that neuroscience can yet help us understand quite how this happens, but I would like to share a story, one that is emblematic of many I have been privileged to witness.

Joshua came from a chaotic home ravaged by a mentally ill father and a mother who had withdrawn into addiction for safety. Even though he had two brothers, the three of them remained isolated from each other. He always felt like an only child to me. By the time he came to therapy in his mid-thirties, he had almost died twice in car crashes that may have been of his own making, married and divorced twice, fathered three children, and torn through a series of jobs as a graphic artist because of his unpredictable behavior. Most of these painful experiences seemed to be driven by relentless anxiety and a diverse group of protectors who were barely able to hold the system together. "It's as though I'm being chased by demons day and night."

I could easily imagine that as he shared his history, allowing me to begin to picture the dyads and triads inside. We worked slowly over several months, following his protectors inward, being drawn to little ones in need of accompaniment and disconfirmation. Perhaps as hardworking and resilient a person as I had ever encountered, Joshua seemed to flourish with the combination of his deepening understanding of the effects of the continual trauma he had sustained and our strong connection. The depth of relational goodness we experienced created a substantial window of tolerance for the intensity of the emotions and bodily sensations that came to us. He moved rather quickly from self-hatred to taking in the reflection of his worth in my eyes and became more gentle with himself. As he inhaled relational neuroscience from books and our conversations, his left hemisphere became a most supportive emissary, aiding him in moving toward respect and appreciation for his highly activated protectors. With acknowledgment of them and the work we were then able to do with his little ones, mostly in regard to his mother's nonprotection, life was getting a little more predictable in his outside world.

Then we hit a major turning point. Without warning, he plunged into depression for the first time in his life. Taking in what Jaak Panksepp (Panksepp & Biven, 2012) offers, depression always brings to mind the possibility that the person's SEEKING system may have turned off. SEEKING had clearly been Joshua's driver since childhood, particularly seeking safety. To see him without it was stunning. His sleep was troubled by the presence of his father, who had been haunted by paranoid delusions, and Joshua began to talk about being pursued by demons again. Our mutual trust in his system's wisdom kept us from being swept away by the despair he felt. We began to ask, "What is this depression, this one who is so still, wanting to tell us?" Then we waited.

We stayed with the one who felt dead inside, acknowledging his protective value even though we had no cognitive awareness of who and what he was sheltering. Joshua, who had become very skilled at listening inside, began to feel a rapid heartbeat "in the distance." It wasn't quite fully in his body, but he could feel it approaching. This feeling of danger coming, coupled with the inability to move, continued for several sessions. He could tolerate it for about ten minutes; then it would evaporate, and we would talk about other matters for the rest of our time. Joshua is one of the people who taught me about respecting pace, particularly when it is very slow. I do believe we all heal as quickly as we can given the co-integrating nature of our embodied brains, so when the process unfolds very slowly, it often speaks to us of the perceived magnitude of what is coming.*

Joshua had never been drawn to working with sand and miniatures but now found his eyes pulled to the shelves in search of a particular image. When this one chose him, he felt something release inside. He spent quite a bit of time holding it in both his right and left hands, finding that it only felt comfortable in his left. Since implicit arisings are right-centric experiences, this made sense to both of us. This figure became our regulating companion for the next opening, perhaps holding and reflecting a bit of the upset that was coming so slowly toward us.

---

* Sometimes slow pace may also be speaking to diminished safety in the relationship, which is to say that it is wise to only move as fast as interpersonal conditions can support and hold what is arising. Struggles between our people and us over the pace of therapy can dysregulate the process into a frenzy or stall it. Returning to following and responding may ease this.

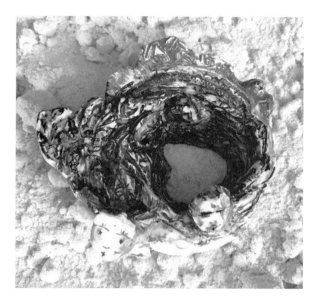

FIGURE 21.2 The whirling, fragmented sensation of this image felt like the space between Joshua and his father. One face is darkened, the other trying to escape. "Both of us are helpless in the swirl. It could pull us under or throw us into outer space on a whim." (Image by Georgia Mann, http://georgiamann.com)

Joshua's nightmares about his father had been increasing and were now to the point that he was able to bring the embodied experience of them fully into the room. He saw his father holding him, faces close together—a little boy frozen in terror, a father distraught in the grip of his illness. Being familiar with engaging an inner parent from our work with his mother, he sensed that being with his father first would help the little boy most. Just as we would with any other part, we let his father know that we just wanted to be with him, that we wouldn't ask him to be any different. This reassurance that we only want to witness and acknowledge what is happening may be the essential stance that deepens safety. When we have no intention of being an active agent of change, the feeling of possible coercion seems to leave the relationship.

I asked Joshua, "Do you sense he knows we're here?"

"Maybe a little bit. I can feel his terror in my arms and forehead. He's holding on so tight to keep from losing it completely." He paused before continuing in a hushed voice. "And it seems he loves me." This was the first time Joshua had any sense that his father cared about him. It was an astounding and deeply moving moment. It stopped Joshua's breath.

"It's okay to breathe," I said. He inhaled deeply, and as he exhaled, powerful sobs broke loose, perhaps from both father and son. That held breath was a moment's protection from the anguished yearning to be with each other these two had. After the sobs subsided, we four rested quietly together—Joshua's adult, his little boy, his father, and me. He felt an impulse to touch his father's cheek and, doing this inside, could feel him soften a bit, become just a little more organized. As we were getting ready to stop for the day, Joshua paused a moment and said, "I believe I feel more peaceful than I ever have before. No demons for the moment. I believe that's what my father felt, too, like demons were always chasing him." I agreed, also feeling grateful for the depression that had moderated our pace enough for us to be able to hold this most significant arrival when he came. Each time I experience the unseen wisdom of a person's system, it deepens my trust in the inner process unfolding and my awe at the way we are organized to be protected until the possibility of healing arrives.

We spent several months with his father, and as so often happens, he was able to carry us back to his own childhood. There is no science to support this yet, but my consistent experience has been that when we internalize someone, it is as though we take in the part that is active in that moment. If people have harmed us, that part is usually a protector whose need to cause injury comes from desperate attempts to not feel destroyed by the pain and fear they are carrying. Generally, they are not conscious of this process, but it likely mirrors what has been passed down through the generations in the family. As we offer ourselves to this protector without judgment or agenda, the one the protector is sheltering often begins to appear, and that is usually the child within the one who hurt us. These are often moments of deep transformation as our people begin to have a felt sense of the pain and fear that drove their beloved parent (or other person) to hurt them. There may have been what we could call intellectual compassion before, an understanding of how family history has simply flowed downstream. This new arising is different because now, as our people embody the experience of the one who caused them harm, a whole-hearted, whole-bodied compassion arrives that brings a different quality of forgiveness.

Pause for Reflection

This shift from intellectual to embodied compassion is at the heart of deep forgiveness, or what we could call compassionate release that gives us the gift of not needing to fend off the ones who hurt us anymore. It is a letting go at a different depth. Let's take a moment here to invite any experiences we may have had of this kind of shift in our embodied relationship with someone who has harmed us. Even developing intellectual compassion requires wisdom and integrity, a willingness to let go of blame. We can honor that process when it has occurred. It is usually the indispensable beginning. Wherever we are in this process of compassionate release, perhaps we can hold that with gentle nonjudgment, opening a space in which our inner world may prepare to take the next steps.

As we continued to welcome Joshua's internal father, he began to carry us back to his household where his own father's violence left all the children alternating between active terror and stunned dissociation. We stayed close to him in the closet where he was locked for hours at a time, stood with him as he saw his younger brother beaten into unconsciousness, and felt his terror rise as his mother was forced out of the house into the snow in her nightie.* With each experience, Joshua wept for his father's child, and his internal father gradually calmed. What had been called delusions turned out to be a child's mind inhabited by the active images of terrifying abuse. If, after this work, Joshua had still felt the visceral sense of upset coming from his father, we might have traveled back an additional generation to be present with his grandfather's inner world. The depth at which we take in the preceding generations astonishes me. There is likely an epigenetic component to this as well as transmission through the internalizations that get passed down through the generations. Whole cultures are carried forward that way, so it makes sense that family legacies might be transmitted that way as well.

As we follow and respond, our people have the opportunity to teach

---

* We don't yet know how specific memories are transmitted internally when the younger generation has no knowledge of the story. Danah Zohar's *Quantum Self* (1991) suggests that when we join through powerful emotions, a wave state containing the relational history is created that continues on eternally, so could be passed on through the generations. Another possibility is that the mirror neurons that have been discovered in the hippocampus and other regions of the brain may play a role (Iacoboni, 2011). We might also wonder what role epigenetics might play. We have so much more to learn!

us about the intricacies of our multigenerational inner world and the processes that can heal at such a deep level. The last story I want to share is about a sand tray process involving an inner parent who inserted her presence—her cry for help—in the middle of some trays about something else entirely. Caroline and I had worked together for a number of years in the past, and now she was returning to do a kind of vision quest in the sand. As she grew older, spiritual concerns had been calling her. One day, perhaps five trays into our process, mystery came into our work.

FIGURE 21.3 From the center of the tray down to the lower right corner, it felt to Caroline that this was continuing with the spiritual thread we had been following. The lower left corner has a cradled baby with Robin Hood watching over her in his tree. A ring of white stones separates this from the rest of the tray. The upper left corner contained the mystery.

As she shared her tray with me, she kept coming back to a sense of blankness about how the figure of rage and the empty bench belonged. It had never occurred to me before, but I found myself asking if those two pieces wanted to do a sand tray of their own next time. She paused to take in the question and offer it to these tray inhabitants. She felt a very strong confirmation in her body that this would be the way to proceed. Years of doing this process together had given both of us a deep sense of trust.

Sand tray can be an embodied conversation between our inner world and outer awareness, held and witnessed by another. Because of the tactile experience of the sand and miniatures and the symbolic nature of the figures, we have the opportunity to make contact with implicit memories that have no words. We follow our body's guidance in arranging the sand and in allowing the miniatures to choose us. It is a right-centric process that allows us to let go of meaning-making in favor of following our felt sense and behavioral impulse. Meaning may arrive later, but we at least begin, as best we can, without expectation to give our inner world the most freedom we can.*

FIGURE 21.4 Rage and an empty bench. (Image by Georgia Mann, http://georgia mann.com)

Caroline returned and placed the two figures in the same corner after checking with them to be sure this was the place they wanted to begin. By following them, we were offering her inner world the freedom to guide us.

The process of working with the sand, selecting the pieces, and making the tray felt foreign to Caroline, although she also had the sense she was following something important. The tray was mostly built in silence; then we quietly held it for a while to see if words wanted to emerge. She started by saying, "I felt angry making those boulders, but strong too. The foil feels cold and disruptive. The only thing that feels good is the drum, which can echo throughout the tray." Then her focus was drawn to the upper left corner.

Here, there were more questions than answers. "Who is that pleading figure? What are they saying to one another? Who is that bench for?" We can hear this as her left hemisphere asking for some kind of story to relieve the uncertainty and, at the same time, her right hemisphere

---

* For details about the process of sand tray with the brain in mind, there is a chapter in *Being a Brain-Wise Therapist* (Badenoch, 2008).

FIGURE 21.5 This is moldable sand, so Caroline made boulders and then scattered wadded-up foil. The cement faces throughout the tray are anguished, angry, rageful. The lower right corner holds a spiritual space and the upper right, a person who is oblivious with her back turned and covered up. The upper left was where we began and now has an additional pleading figure and the whirling chaos figure that held Joshua's father. (Cement faces by Andrew Lonnquist, https://www.olanderearthworks.com)

FIGURE 21.6 Closer view of the rager, pleading figure, and chaos holder.

simply tossing questions into the abyss of the tray to see what might arrive. By midweek, she was preoccupied day and night by the two figures facing one another, so she asked me to take a picture of them and email it so she could see them more clearly.

FIGURE 21.7 Rage is swirling orange and red. The pleading figure, who is modeled after Oedipus when he gouges his eyes out after realizing he has murdered his father and slept with his mother, is black with blood running from his eyes.

As she sat with them, she suddenly knew, with that kind of certainty we feel throughout our bodies, that her mother had come into the tray to be heard and healed, originally as the raging one and now as both of these figures mirroring two aspects of what was left in them by abuse that began in infancy and had been passed on to Caroline in infancy as well. She wrote this to me: "There is this unfathomable conversation between Rage and Odysseus—guilt, horror, wanting to make amends, wanting to be seen like this with his eyes ripped out. It gives me chills to remember that my mother was blind when she died. At the same time, I feel as though I am standing entirely in her shoes, and yet it isn't my story at all."

When she returned, she felt sad, a little frightened, but mostly grateful for what had originally felt like an intrusion into her spiritual process. As soon as she touched the molding sand, powerful energy moved into her whole body and shoved the sand strongly to one side. The two familiar figures came again with only a very few other images this time.

FIGURE 21.8 A rage face overlooking the sea, a baby in the womb tossed on the sand in the middle, the two figures trapped inside a fence, and a snake making its way between the fence posts.

FIGURE 21.9 Rage and Odysseus mirroring each other, snake just coming through the fence into their enclosure.

As Caroline quickly completed the tray, she became very quiet. We beheld it together. Then she said with absolute clarity, "I am the snake that bit my mother, that started the abuse all over again. It was torture for her. She thought she wanted a baby and what she got instead was a reawakening of everything that happened to her." Caroline was completely immersed in her mother's viewpoint. In our earlier work, she had felt this same experience from the child's perspective of being the bad one who ruined everything. What was happening now was an entirely different perception that was giving her the felt sense of her mother's crushing disappointment and horror when this baby arrived. She was the one providing care for her mother as I had for her little one in the earlier memory. I was transfixed by the way her internal mother had simply arrived and begun to tell her story in the sand.

Eventually, the face embedded in the cliff drew her strongly.

FIGURE 21.10 Wrath (Cement face by Andrew Lonnquist, https://olanderearth works.com)

Tears welled up as she said, "He is screaming out over the ocean—a mixture of rage and anguish, and no one to hear, no one. There seems to be a direct conduit between the two in the corner and this face. He needs desperately to be heard and there is no help ever. That's what did in my mother, no help ever."

I believe her mother must have felt heard then, because Caroline's next tray moved on to more clearly point to the source of the anguish, both carrying us back to her mother's childhood experience and revealing it as the source of her own violence toward her children.

FIGURE 21.11 Rage stands in the middle on a buried knife, while six snakes go beneath the ground to attack her silently from underneath. At the top of the tray stands a distorted black figure whose energies seem to consume the tray.

When Caroline arrived, it was clear that her inner world had been preparing for the next steps, since she tentatively asked if she could use my biggest butcher knife in her tray. Since there was no safety concern, she chose from what I had to offer and buried it in the center of the tray.

Caroline spent a long time building a ring of sand around the exposed knife, being sure that the sand remained loose. Then she placed Rage on the exposed knife. As she tunneled the snakes into the hill, she started to feel sick with horror. "I believe this is how it must have been for my mother, this sense of unknown horrors coming toward her, but she couldn't see what they were. I kept tunneling the creatures further in and feeling sick when the sand would move. The figure at the top is

FIGURE 21.12 Rage stands directly on the knife blade, and even though it is difficult to see in this picture, he is in quite a deep hole that gives the snakes full access to him. The arrival of the pronoun "he" seemed significant.

like God, only a spirit of Malevolence instead, that touches everything, governs everything. The question that comes to me is what happens for her if she doesn't stand on the foundation of violence? What if she doesn't hurt us?" The questions were just a wondering, not in search of an immediate answer. We were holding this together, and our joined windows of tolerance seemed able to contain the physical and emotional intensity. Witnessing and empathizing at the same time, it seemed we were able to bring some ventral presence to this world.

We stayed in touch for the next couple of days as Caroline's inner world and body continued to process and integrate the experience. She was having waves of horror that were alternately causing severe nausea and a sense of dropping into deadness as her ANS cycled from sympathetic to dorsal and back again. At one level, this was happening to her; at another, she clearly felt these sensations belonged to her mother. Sometime on the second day, she also became aware that the rage was equally her grandfather's presence in the tray, and likely brought the shift in pronoun to "he." The addition in her awareness of a third generation seemed to change something. On the third day, she felt her breathing shift, more down in her belly than ever before, as though an invisible weight she didn't know was there had been lifted from her chest, making room for more air. Some of our embodied wounds are so familiar that we believe them to be part of who we are until something happens and a new aspect of our inherent health becomes experientially real.

As she moved through the week, she felt that maybe this last tray had completed something with her mother, so she approached the sand and miniatures anticipating something new would begin. She was drawn to a particular Native American piece, one that had fallen numerous times, been broken, glued, broken again, and reglued. There are several pieces on my shelf that are missing limbs or have obvious cracks, and these seem to be used more than most.

FIGURE 21.13 The corn maiden is buried in the middle, her face turned to the right, a dragon on her feet and a cage of spikes on her head. The face of tragedy is in the upper left corner and a small chameleon tries to make her way toward her mother. Pieces of glass surround her so no one can come near. The bell is by her head, marking the spot of most importance in the tray. Caroline's inner world frequently chooses big and small bells for this purpose.

Caroline could stay with this tray for only a little while. She looked, walked away, looked, asked me to take the pictures instead of her, then held my hand as we looked together. After a long silence, she said, "This is about the broken mothers who want to sing and love, but are already ruined—this piece is broken and mended, but still broken. Her mouth is full of sand, a raging dragon guards her feet, shards of glass surround

FIGURE 21.14 This is where we are asked to attend.

FIGURE 21.15 The cracks aren't obvious in the photo but are all up around her arms and neck. There are some small missing pieces as well. She is a singing corn maiden, the one who feeds the children in times of famine and carries the story of the tribe. Caroline would not necessarily have known this story and told me later she was simply drawn to the brokenness of the image.

her, and a crown of thorns hurts anyone who tries to come near her. This mother hurts everyone without ever wanting to. The grief is too deep for tears. The child on the walkway has already told us her story of no access to this broken mother. My mother was blocked off from her sadness, which might have healed her—already too wounded to grieve by the time I came. I feel my mother wanted to love me and care for me, but this was all she had to offer. I just know that mother and I both wanted to sing. Instead, there was crucifixion with no resurrection for her." I was so touched by the depth of her experience and her eloquence as she sought to give it words. At that moment, we couldn't know how deep the resolution would go. Time was needed for that.

There were no more trays from her mother, and we seemed to be guided back to her spiritual concerns. One day she was talking with a friend who said something about seeing our parents on the other side after death. Caroline said that everything paused inside her when she heard that. She realized that prior to now, when she heard that belief voiced, she had always thought, "I understand this was the best my mother could do, but I really really don't want to see her when I die." This moment, everything was different. She told me, "If I saw her here or on the other side, I would feel nothing but love for her. I would embrace her. And I don't even know if there is another side." As we checked inside, it seemed that her mother had come to rest as well.

Over the years, I have come to realize that we just can't know how or when resolution will come. Joshua's depression brought his father to us, and Caroline's mother simply came unbidden when the time was right. At other times, our people may be more intentional in opening to inner parents. As a dedicated follower, I have been privileged to witness and support the wisdom that emerges from all of these. I expect to be surprised by what the next people will teach me as they pursue their unique path toward resolution and open to inhabiting their inherent health.

We might ask what role relational neuroscience plays in these kinds of experiences. For me, it begins with the body. Cultivating an understanding—and most importantly, a felt sense—of these neural pathways helps us attune body to body with our people as they enter these deeper, more challenging realms. Through resonance, our capacity to attend to our bodies while remaining in a ventral state gradually becomes theirs. An indispensable support comes from our left hemisphere's deepening understanding of the particulars of the healing process. The stability this provides helps our right stay as engaged as possible in the relationship with all its emerging uncertainty. When Joshua became suddenly depressed, Jaak Panksepp came to mind, so I could remain curious rather than scared. When Caroline entered increasingly intense states with her mother, Stephen Porges helped me remain mindful of our joined windows of tolerance and the necessity of staying in connection for co-regulation and disconfirmation to occur. The whole process of leading, following, and responding rests on his statement, "Safety IS the treatment." In the broadest way, Dan Siegel's voice fosters deep acquaintance with the principles of interpersonal neurobiology, which supports hope for healing, confidence in our inherent health, and appreciation for our co-organizing brains. Each of these strands of knowledge potentially increases our trust in the process. You may sense yourself adding those that have been most helpful for you to this list.

The way I see my people and myself, my gradually growing ability to attend from the right, the language that comes most naturally, the certainty that implicit healing is the foundation for long-term change, the awareness of our body's importance in guiding recovery, and my growing sensitivity to what is unfolding in these bodies—mine and theirs—can be laid at the feet of the discoveries of relational neuroscience. Compassion and humility grow when we go deep with both understanding and experience. For example, as one who will continue to practice radical inclusiveness as I fail again and again, I can say it is quite a relief to embrace the limitations of being human. On that note, we are going to spend a little time with a reflection that may bring both comfort and discomfort.

When Therapy Fails

This is such difficult language, and we may hear it spoken quite often. There are surely times when we don't find a good fit with someone who comes to us, and we send that person on to another counselor who may be more helpful. A few times, I have experienced a painful implicit entanglement very early in the relationship, likely at the intersection of our mutual wounds, so we weren't able to establish the initial bond that could carry us across ruptures later in the relationship. Sometimes people begin, discover how much pain and fear they are holding, and adaptively decide to take what gains they have made and stop. Occasionally, we reach the limits of our competence or capacity and must help one of our people find someone or a nest of people who can hold their wounds when we can't. We could each likely add other situations in which we have parted with someone early in the relationship or at a time that seemed premature. All of this is part of human limitation in both of us.

In my long years of being with these courageous ones who come for healing, there have been a few times when all of our listening and following have not helped this dear person's inner world and body settle in an ongoing way. For all of these people, I was a last-ditch effort after many unfulfilling experiences in therapy. We found we could co-regulate when we were together, but the new state continued to fall apart very soon after our time ended. All of these experiences have one common thread: No one seems to have been present for this person at the time of the abuse or any stage of life—no teacher, neighbor, auntie, friend, or sense of the presence of the Divine. It is as though their embodied anticipation of "no help" is so strong that moments of disconfirmation through deep connection aren't able to take hold. It is heartbreaking for both of us to experience this cycle over and over. How do we hold on to hope? I don't have an answer for that except to say that hope without expectation of healing, often supported by the love we feel for our people, may have a value all of its own for both of us.

Pause for Reflection

As we settle here together for the last time, let's make room for these experiences when our best efforts together don't seem to take hold. If you have someone with whom you've been doing these reflections, this would be a good time to tenderly hold one another's experience. Since there are no answers to be found, there is nothing asked of us except to be present in the midst of tragedy. We may find this is enough.

For all of us, there are likely also times when therapy simply doesn't seem to move forward as we had imagined it would. At this crossroads, we often either question ourselves or blame our patients. Between what our culture requires and what we have experienced in childhood, we might go either direction. We have a particular challenge to feeling competent right now. Our left-centric society has done its best to codify the healing process, leaving us with a set of procedures and expected outcomes that don't welcome the individuality of our people or the fluidity of each person's unpredictable and unique process of recovery. This is doubly difficult, because when we follow the course culture provides, safety is already undermined to a greater or lesser extent. I believe it wounds us when we feel we aren't helping a person because we set out with such good hearts to relieve suffering. A well-practiced protector may try to guard our hearts by blaming our people's resistance. When a wounded part of us is afraid we are inadequate, this often generates a critical protective voice trying to urge us toward a better performance. In both instances, our ability to be present for our people gets lost in the need to protect. How can we hold these experiences kindly, recognizing that they are part of the human experience? Right now, we might be able to open the arms of inclusion to these parts of us.

Warm curiosity about what is happening is a different kind of experience than judgment. It can help us open to the bigger picture beyond this moment of what feels like failure. We may consider our person's history and our own. We might bring in our left-hemisphere emissary to see how we could understand where we are in the process. In this quieter internal place, sometimes an intuitive sense of trust will come even when we can't figure it out. At moments of deep uncertainty, I find that I sometimes jump the tracks into taking control, and in those moments, if I can move back toward following, the process often finds its own feet again. All of this has gradually led me to believe that letting go of expectations about the outcome of therapy as much as possible gives the process the most room to show itself. *The balance between this letting go and the wisdom of our developing Sherpa who has been on many journeys may make room for the emergence of some surprising experiences.* In the last chapter, I have the privilege of sharing a story with you about the person who is teaching me the most about letting go of expectations.

22

A Sacred Space Opens

Opening the door, I saw a small, bright, birdlike woman in her sixties. She seemed a bit hesitant, and then found the place she would most like to sit, in the middle of the long couch. I settled into the loveseat. When Pearl had called for an appointment a few days earlier, I had said yes even though I wasn't taking new people right then. Something in the quality of her voice touched a deeper place and I felt drawn to her.

She began to tell me a bit about her birth family: A mother who seemed to hate her and have no room for her at all, but who had an insatiable need to be adored by everyone else. A father whose role in his birth family was to be a failure, filled with shame at his ongoing incapacity. An angry adopted older brother and eventually a much younger brother, both of whom appeared to be beloved by her mother, although their emotional struggles as older adults would belie that. What I felt most was the severe attachment loss she had suffered because, as best I could tell, her mother needed Pearl to carry all the parts from her own childhood that she had to disown in order to stay connected to the cold demanding father who was her only parent. However, at that point, I had no real sense of the depth of Pearl's injury.

As we reached a lull in the conversation that first day, she suddenly and quietly got up, came toward me, and sat on the floor, leaning against the loveseat and my leg, gently putting her head on my knee. For some reason, it seemed not at all out of place, and I found my hand resting on her head. We sat quietly for a long while. Then we made another appointment for the following week.

Only much later did I learn what Pearl was thinking even before she came in. She eventually told me that she had "failed" therapy many, many times. She spoke of other therapists who would see her for a while and then send her away, often in what seemed to me to be most demeaning or dishonest ways. She said that when her mother learned she was in therapy, she sometimes sought out these therapists, becoming friends with them, and that often signaled the end of any care for Pearl. As I listened, I imagined these counselors becoming entangled not only with her mother and her need to deprive her daughter of nurturance, but also with the depth of Pearl's pain and couldn't tolerate it, so wound up replicating it. This can happen to any of us at any time. Now, as she came to me, she desired to learn how to hate herself well enough for things to settle inside her once and for all. She wanted me to teach her the best way to hate. When she came over to me that first day, it was for a moment of comfort because she knew that she would likely not see me again, especially since she had followed her impulse to sit by me on the floor. On reflection now, it seems to me she was already telling me what she needed most—a place to settle in proximity, safety, warmth, and quiet because she had none of that as a child.

Within a few sessions, her core patterns of relatedness began to reveal themselves. Her mother's primary implicit and mostly unspoken instruction to Pearl had been that any apparent outward offer of connection by mother meant for her daughter to go away. We might begin to get an embodied sense of the confusion and disorganization that would arise in a baby, child, and adolescent, hungry for connection and reflection, who received those messages every day. How does anyone adapt to that? I began to hear that her attachment system's foundational and ongoing encoding were wired backwards, that instead of her need for connection leading to joining, the only way to remain in contact with her mother was to go away. This experience violates the core assumptions and needs of our inherent neurobiology, leaving profound disorganization, indescribable anguish, and unbearable ache in its wake. Pearl's system had to find a way to adapt to this attachment catastrophe that both followed the family rules while protecting her from the constantly upwelling disorganization. She developed an unbreakable law that said the more a relationship mattered, the more important is was go away.

In relationship with me, this manifested as her feeling the insistent twin pulls of the healthy urge to be together inextricably coupled with the profoundly encoded message that this meant she must go away, particularly when I was responding to her need with offers of connection. This wasn't a cognitive idea, but an embodied anticipation and certainty about how things work that required her body to behave in a particular way. The more bonded she and I became, the greater her struggle between these two pulls. She would linger on the threshold of the office at almost every visit, painfully frozen at the crossroads of these two incompatible implicit and nervous system commands. In the early days of our time together, I was filled with optimism that this old way would be infused with this new care and gradually the passage into our time together would become less conflictual for her. This is not what happened, and, in fact, to this day, the struggle remains in place.

As our relationship developed, it gradually became clear that she paid an enormous price for allowing for the possibility that we could really be together, especially if it was good for both of us. As she would open enough to just begin to feel the care, she would immediately come into contact with the profound disorganization that had been her dominant experience from the beginning of life. In that state it was almost impossible to think, talk, or breathe while panic that threatened to dissolve her swept through her system. Even just at the edge of the disorganization, a nearly intolerable ache would take over her body. Sometimes she would feel as though she were drifting away in pieces, disappearing, or dying. Immediately, her adaptive protectors would rush in to reorganize her, with the primary guardian being intense self-hatred. Well learned from her mother's loathing of her, this profound experience of self-rejection was able to reassemble her and return her to her primary identity of being a loathsome inhuman creature—a dangerous "it" who had to be on guard every second so that ugliness wouldn't spill out, who knew that her role was to move away to protect others from her venom. Especially as she became able to speak more about these inner convictions, I believe I retained hope, almost certainty, that our deepening care for each other would gradually provide enough disconfirmation to dissolve the self-hatred. As we will see, that isn't the way it went for us either.

She shared these small pieces of her life with me, bit by tiny bit.

By five, she was suicidal on a daily basis.

Going to the fair as a little girl, she longed to be the goldfish in the small plastic bag she saw people taking home because she knew it would be briefly wanted and then die.

After she graduated as valedictorian of her high school (while fully experiencing herself as stupid) and was accepted at Stanford, her mother talked with the admissions people to tell them why they should not accept her because she would fail. A guidance counselor from her high school was able to intervene.

Her mother also told a boyfriend and several girlfriends that they could do better than her daughter. No one spoke up there and those relationships were lost.

The few times Pearl asked her mother if there was anything she liked about her daughter, her mother would change the subject and talk about the glories of a cousin.

In her adult life, she wouldn't use the air-conditioning in her car even if it was 100 degrees because she didn't feel it was right for her to use up any resources or have any comfort. Instead, she would pray that others' pains come to her so she might be useful in some way.

Pearl often said to me that it was more important that she be allowed to like me than that I like her. This was one of her most painful wounds—that her mother, who insatiably needed adoration, didn't want this daughter to like her. I am still struck silent by those words. Her question, "It's still okay to like? Even after today?" is part of our ritual with one another. I always say, "Yes, every day, without exception." I don't know if there are enough tomorrows for either of us, now in our seventies, for her to ever rest in complete assurance of my ongoing welcome, yet she finds enough support and comfort in these repeated words to sometimes sign her emails "edwe" (abbreviating "every day without exception").

If we multiply these experiences with her mother by many thousands, we can have some sense of Pearl's implicit sea of rejection and humiliation, more thorough and intense than any words can capture. The only person she could identify with was her father, who very occasionally acknowledged her existence until her mother made it clear that was not to happen. Pearl's attempt at being with him by empathic identification meant that in addition to being her mother's hated one, she helped her father carry his failure by becoming one herself. While she may never be able to acknowledge what I am about to say without encountering disorganization, being a failure was no easy task because she is, in my experience, highly intelligent and curious, has a kind and tender heart toward the suffering of others, is resourceful and resilient, has supported so many wounded and recovering children as a physical therapist, and consistently goes out of her way to help people and animals in need.

To counteract this obvious goodness and success in order to maintain her sense of badness and failure, her wise and creative inner world then developed a pattern in which any time she does or says anything positive, it must almost immediately be taken away by doing or saying something that negates the positive. This is a profound behavioral impulse rooted at the deepest implicit level. She is helpless in its grip. It has the feeling of being a reflex that can't be denied. I experience this pattern as a pair of scales that must always lean toward the side of "failure" and "bad person" for her to stay out of the disorganization.

Two of the more pervasive protections that keep her intact are having her house in a constant state of chaos and dramatic sleep deprivation almost every day of her life that make it very challenging for her to think or speak or organize her thoughts. Many might see this as self-sabotage, but Pearl taught me this is wisdom of a high order. Keeping herself mired in shame, disorder, inability to make decisions, and exhaustion means she gets to keep being a force for good in the world—while knowing next to nothing about it because there is all this proof of badness. Each day she tallies the evidence to be sure that she is right in her assessment of her evilness.

At this juncture, we may begin to sense the daily sea of paradoxes that define her world. It seems as though her earliest implicit learning that the only way to be attached to mother was to go away initiated a pattern that permeates so much of her perceptual and behavioral world. To be an honest and acceptable person, she must continually prove she is a bad human being. To be successful at staying connected with and protecting her father, she must remain a failure. One of the most binding paradoxes is revealed when she says almost every time we are together, "I want to be what I'm not." What she wishes not to be is this "cockroach" of a dangerous person, and yet, she already is not that by such a wide margin of kindness and concern for others. Yet to see herself in this way exposes her to the danger of disintegration and threatens her place in her family-of-origin. So here we are, with her deepest wish to be a good person also the most profound threat to her survival, with the additional painful irony that what she wishes for is already here, but she may not touch the hot stove of perceiving herself as the lovely human she is.

How do we be with the paradoxes our people bring? We can align with one side of the conundrum and dismiss the other in an effort to relieve the unsettling experience that the logically unresolvable contradiction brings to us and our people. However, if we do this, we are stepping away from our person's experience because he or she is living inside the paradox and can't move away. Staying present asks us to hold the full paradox within our own minds and bodies, to enter the suffering that entails. If we are able to do this and remain in a ventral state, it seems that something happens and we may be able to enter a state in which the paradox begins to reveal its value a little differently than ever before. With Pearl, what helped most was to recognize the necessity of the paradox so that I could hold my perception of her without needing her perception to change. As we settled into this broader acceptance together, I believe we made room for the possibility of the arrival of a resolving third thing in its own time.

It took me quite a long while to let go of the quiet hope that Pearl's suffering in these areas would be relieved in ways that my logical mind might imagine. It is so natural for us to hold a vision of what health might look like—self-compassion in the place of self-hatred, ease of social interaction, a good feeling in opening to being cared for, and recognition of her goodness. How do we be with the process and our response to it when what actually happens is very different? It isn't that I gave up on her healing, but, as she continued to struggle to get in the door and actively needed her self-hatred to stay functional, I began to realize more deeply that her patterns had meaning and that it wasn't useful for me to predetermine what recovery might look like for her.

What helped me get to that point was that something else unexpected had started to happen. I'm not sure how, but we somehow began to sit in silence with one another for some substantial portion of our time together. Although it didn't occur to me at the time, she had already showed me that she needed this as she quietly settled on the floor by my side at our very first meeting. As we entered this space of silence, one day her very quiet, awestruck voice said, "Everything changes." In place of the hatred, failure, and conviction of badness welled up some combination of infant well-being and mystical experience of God's love. It seems to me this was the unexpected arising of the third thing, the unforeseeable resolution of the paradox where her personal goodness was no longer the issue because it had been replaced by the sweetness of relationship. It took her over completely, body, mind, heart, and soul. Her being overflowed with gratefulness and she settled into sweet rest in the arms of the Divine, perhaps the first she had consistently known. She began to be hungry for certain Rūmī poems and the words of the

Franciscan mystic, Father Richard Rohr, asking me to read to her so she also had my voice. We particularly began to invite all parts of her into Rūmī's *Guest House* (1270/2004), where "the dark thought, the shame, the malice" (p. 109) are all especially welcome. This is very challenging for her because it begins to touch the place where she might be a loved human being, an "I" instead of an "it." Yet, somehow, this place of deep settling has opened a door where she can tolerate this possibility just a little bit differently than ever before.

At the same time, the self-hatred ebbs for a little while, then flows strongly again, the house is relentlessly messy (leading to more harsh judgment), and her sleep is becoming even more disturbed (although naps seem more possible sometimes). I wonder if this is because she has to be more on guard as the protections around the disorganization are softening. Perhaps she has to work harder to maintain the balance in favor of failure and badness. Sometimes the struggle between coming toward me and pulling away dominates her for a few miserable days. Frequently, she is in even more pain and anger when she feels abandoned, perhaps because it is harder to blame it all on herself. At moments when we are together and I am letting her know that I enjoyed our time, the anguish of the disorganization breaks through for a moment until her familiar patterns can reestablish her old identity and organization. I believe it is becoming more and more challenging for her to perceive herself only according to how she was shaped by her mother. Ten years is a substantial amount of warm contact and deepening care, certain to be noticed by her inner community who are now left with their own terrible paradox—how to keep her safe from the disorganization and let her be loved at the same time.

So here we are together now, in the midst of a spiritual awakening and some of the most profound suffering I have witnessed. Sometimes Pearl calls my voice mail and whispers into the phone, "Today was a little better than expected" or "It's okay to like." Just lately, she has begun experiencing small spikes of the deep rest and felt sense of being loved coming into daily life, at the dentist, in the midst of a physical therapy session, while driving her car, during acupuncture. Like little sprouts of light, they blossom in the midst of the devastated field of her earliest experiences. None of this is what I expected, and I am so profoundly grateful to Pearl for helping me release my expectations and follow her inner wisdom.

There is a little more to our story. About three years into our time

together, she told me this. One day, long before we met, she had been
in the waiting room of a place where I taught a class. She heard a voice
that touched something in her, and the next week, when she traveled to
New Jersey, she went to the arboretum. She saw a gardening shirt that
said, "I like playing in the dirt," and knew that it somehow belonged to
that voice—even though she was also convinced that she was crazy. So
she bought a much larger size than she wears, even though she hadn't
seen me, and took it home. A while later, she asked a friend for a refer-
ral for therapy, somehow finding the resilience to try again, even if it
was only to learn how to hate more efficiently. That friend gave her my
name, and she recognized the voice she had heard in the other room on
my answering machine. Three years after we met, she gave me the shirt,
which fits me perfectly as I spend countless hours in my beloved garden.

Her remarkable intuition and capacity for caring beyond what seems
possible in her circumstances also revealed themselves when her only
child was born, long before we met. As this little one was placed in
her arms, she fell in love with him, breaking the cycle of hatred in this
family once and for all. The roots of her inherent health came forth to
meet this precious child against all odds.

I have other stories just as mysterious, just as beautiful, just as sacred,
but it seems good to stop here and wonder if it is possible for us to begin
to let go of our expectations about the shape in which healing may
arrive, to trust the treatment plan lying dormant and waiting within
our people, to cultivate a gradually gathering stillness so that, in the
safety of the space between, healing pathways have the possibility of
revealing themselves.

References

Alexander, B. K. (1987). The disease and adaptive models of addiction: A framework evaluation. *Journal of Drug Issues, 17,* 47–66.

Alexander, B. K. (2010a). Addiction: The view from Rat Park. Retrieved from http://www.brucekalexander.com/articles-speeches/rat-park/148-addiction -the-view-from-rat-park

Alexander, B. K. (2010b). *The globalization of addiction: A study in poverty of the spirit.* London, UK: Oxford University Press.

Alexander, B. K., Beyerstein, B. L., Hadaway, P. F., & Coambs, R. B. (1981). Effect of early and later colony housing on oral ingestion of morphine in rats. *Pharmacology, Biochemistry and Behavior, 15*(4), 571–576.

Amaral, D., & Lavenex, P. (2006). Hippocampal neuroanatomy. In P. Andersen, R. Morris, D. Amaral, T. Bliss, & J. O'Keefe (Eds.), *The hippocampus book.* London, UK: Oxford University.

American Autoimmune Related Diseases Association, Inc. (2015). Autoimmune statistics. Retrieved from http://www.aarda.org/autoimmune-information/autoimmune-statistics/

American Psychiatric Association. (2013). *Diagnostic and statistical manual of mental disorders* (5th ed.). Washington, DC: Author.

Anderson, C. H., Van Essen, D. C., & Olshausen, B. A. (2005). Directed visual attention and the dynamic control of information flow. Retrieved from http://redwood.berkeley. edu/bruno/papers/attention-chapter.pdf

Armour, J. A. (1976). Instant-to-instant reflex cardiac regulation. *Cardiology, 61,* 309–328.

Armour, J. A. (2003). *Neurocardiology: Anatomical and functional principles.* Boulder Creek, CO: Institute of HeartMath.

Armour, J. A. (2008). Potential clinical relevance of the "little brain" on the heart. *Experimental Physiology, 93*(2), 165–176.

Armour, J. A., & Ardell, J. L. (Eds.). (1994). *Neurocardiology.* London, UK: Oxford University Press.

Assagioli, R. (1971). *Psychosynthesis: A manual of principles and techniques.* New York, NY: Viking Compass.

Avey, H., Matheny, K. B., Robbins, A., & Jacobson, T. A. (2003). Health care providers' training, perceptions, and practices regarding stress and health outcomes. *Journal of the National Medical Association, 95*(9), 833, 836–845.

Badenoch, B. (2008). *Being a brain-wise therapist: A practical guide to interpersonal neurobiology.* New York, NY: Norton.

Badenoch, B. (2011). *The brain-savvy therapist's workbook.* New York, NY: Norton.

Bader, M. (2016, January 29). Healing our wounded warriors. Retrieved from http://www. huffingtonpost.com/michael-bader-dmh/healing-our-wounded-warri_b_9095104.html

Banich, M. T. (2003). Interaction between the hemispheres and its implications for the processing capacity of the brain. In R. J. Davidson & K. Hugdahl (Eds.), The asymmetrical brain (pp. 261–302). Cambridge, MA: MIT Press.

Barbas, H. (2007). Flow of information for emotions through temporal and orbitofrontal pathways. *Journal of Anatomy. 211,* 237–249. doi: 10.1111/j.1469-7580.2007.00777.x

Bauer, P. J. (1996). What do infants recall of their lives? Memory for specific events by one- to two-year-olds. *American Psychologist, 51,* 29–41.

Baumeister, R. F., Finkenauer, C., & Vohs, K. D. (2001). Bad is stronger than good. *Review of General Psychology, 5*(4), 323–370. doi:10.1037/1089-2680.5.4.323

Beckes, L., & Coan, J. A. (2011). Social baseline theory: The role of social proximity in emotion and economy of action. *Social and Personality Psychology Compass, 5*(12), 976–988. doi: 10.1080/10926771.2013.813882

Beebe, B., & Lachmann, F. M. (1994). Representations and internalization in infancy: Three principles of salience. *Psychoanalytic Psychology, 11,* 127–165.

Benarroch, E. E. (2009). The locus coeruleus norepinephrine system: Functional organization and potential clinical significance. *Neurology, 73*(20), 1699–1704.

Berne, E. (1966). *Games people play: The psychology of human relationships.* New York, NY: Grove Press.

Bishop, O. (2014). Sawubona. Retrieved from https://www.globalonenessproject.org/library/interviews/sawubona

Bobrow, J. (2015). *Waking up from war: A better way home for veterans and nations.* Chicago, IL: Pitchstone.

Bornstein, D. (2014, March 19). Teaching children to calm themselves. *New York Times.* Retrieved from http://opinionator.blogs.nytimes.com/2014/03/19/first-learn-how-to-calm-down/?_r=0

Bosemans, W., Martens, M. A., Weltens, N., Hao, M. M., Tack, J., Cirillo, C., & Vanden Berghe, F. (2013). Imaging neuron-glia interactions in the enteric nervous system. *Frontiers in Cellular Neuroscience.* Retrieved from http://journal.frontiersin.org/article/10.3389/fncel.2013.00183/full

Boyce, W. T., & Ellis, B. J. (2005). Biological sensitivity to context: An evolutionary-developmental theory of the origins and functions of stress reactivity. *Development and Psychopathology, 17,* 271–301.

Bracha, H. S., Garcia-Rill, E., Mrak, R. E., & Skinner, R. (2005). Postmortem locus coeruleus neuron count in three American veterans with probable or possible war-related PTSD. *Journal of Neuropsychiatry and Clinical Neurosciences, 17*(4), 503–509.

The brain from top to bottom. (n.d.). Retrieved from http://thebrain.mcgill.ca/flash/a/a_11/a_11_cr/a_11_cr_cyc/a_11_cr_cyc.html

Breedlove, S. M., Watson, N. V., & Rosenzweig, M. R. (2010). *Biological psychology: An introduction to behavioral, cognitive, and clinical neuroscience* (6th ed.). Sunderland, MA: Sinauer Associates.

Burns, A. J., Roberts, R. R., Bornstein, J. C., & Young, H. M. (2009). Development of the enteric nervous system and its role in intestinal motility during fetal and early postnatal stages. *Seminars in Pediatric Surgery, 18*(4), 196–205. doi: 10.1053/j.sempedsurg.2009.07.001

Bush, G., Luu, P., & Posner, M. I. (2000). Cognitive and emotional influences in anterior cingulate cortex. *Trends in Cognitive Science, 4*(6), 215–222. doi: 10.1016/S1364-6613(00)01483-2

Cahill, L., & McGaugh, J. L. (1995). A novel demonstration of enhanced memory associated with emotional arousal. *Consciousness and Cognition, 4*(4), 410–421. doi: 10.1006/ccog.1995.1048

Campbell, V. (2010, May 12). Glial cells: Interview with R. Douglas Fields [Transcript]. Brain Science Podcast. Retrieved from http://brainsciencepodcast.com/episodes-page

Campbell, V. (2014, February 17). The cognitive-emotional brain: Interview with Dr. Luiz Pessoa [Transcript]. Brain Science Podcast. Retrieved from http://brainsciencepodcast.com/episodes-page

Cantin, M., & Genest, J. (1986). The heart as an endocrine gland. *Clinical and Investigative Medicine, 9*(4), 319–327.

Carr, L., Iacoboni, M., Dubeau, M., Mazzlotta, J., & Lenzi, G. (2003). Neural mechanisms of empathy in humans: A relay from neural systems for imitation to limbic areas. *Proceedings of the National Academy of Sciences of the United States of America, 100,* 5497–5502.

Carr, N. (2011). *The shallows: What the Internet is doing to our brains.* New York, NY: Norton.

Chakravarthy, V. S., Joseph, D., & Bapi, R. S. (2010). What do the basal ganglia do? A modeling perspective. *Biological Cybernetics, 103*(3), 237–253. doi: 10.1007/s00422-010-0401

Chugani, H. T., Behen, M. E., Muzik, O., Juhász, C., Nagy, F., & Chugani, D. C. (2001). Local brain functional activity following early deprivation: A study of postinstitutionalized Romanian orphans. *NeuroImage, 14,* 1290–1301. doi:10.1006/nimg.2001.091

Clem, R. L., & Huganir, R. L. (2010). Calcium-permeable AMPA receptor dynamics mediate fear memory erasure. *Science, 330,* 1108–1112. doi: 10.1126/ science.1195298

Coan, J. A. (2016). Toward a neuroscience of attachment. In J. Cassidy & P. R. Shaver (Eds.), *Handbook of attachment: Theory, research, and clinical applications* (3rd ed., pp. 242–269). New York, NY: Guilford.

Coan, J. A., & Sbarra, D. A. (2015). Social baseline theory: The social regulation of risk and effort. *Current Opinion in Psychology, 1,* 87-91. doi: 10.1016/j.copsyc.2014.12.021

Cohen, H., Kotler, M., Matar, M. A., Kaplan, Z., Loewenthal, U., Miodownik, H., & Cassuto, Y. (1998). Analysis of heart rate variability in posttraumatic stress disorder patients in response to trauma-related reminder. *Biological Psychiatry, 44,* 1054–1059. doi: 10.1016/S0006-3223(97)00475-7

Collins, F. (2012). *The symphony inside your brain.* Retrieved from http://directorsblog.nih.gov/2012/11/05/the-symphony-inside-your-brain/

Conradt, E., Measelle, J., & Ablow, J. C. (2013). Poverty, problem behavior, and promise: Differential susceptibility among infants reared in poverty. *Psychological Science, 24*(3), 235–242. doi: 10.1177/0956797612457381

Corrigan, F., & Grand, D. (2013). Brainspotting: Recruiting the midbrain for accessing and healing sensorimotor memories of traumatic activation. *Medical Hypotheses, 80*(6), 759–766. doi: org/10.1016/u.mehy.2013.03.005

Corrigan, F., Grand, D., & Raju, R. (2015). Brainspotting: Sustained attention, spinothalamic tracts, thalamocortical processing, and the healing of adaptive orientation truncated by traumatic experience. *Medical Hypotheses, 84*(4), 384–394. doi: 10.1016/j.mehy.2015.01.028

Costa, M., Brookes, S. J. H., & Hennig, G. W. (2000). Anatomy and physiology of the enteric nervous system. *Gut, 47*(4). Retrieved from ut.bmj.com/content/47/suppl_4/iv15.full

Cozolino, L. (2014). *The neuroscience of human relationships: Attachment and the developing social brain* (2nd ed.). New York, NY: Norton.

Cryan, J. F., & O'Mahony, S. M. (2011). The microbiome-gut-brain axis: From bowel to behavior. *Neurogastroenterology and Motility, 23*(3), 187–192. doi: 10.1111/j.1365-2982.2010.01664.x

Dafny, N. (1997). Anatomy of the spinal cord. Retrieved from http://neuroscience.uth.tmc.edu/s2/chapter03.html

Damasio, A. (2000). *The feeling of what happens: Body and emotion in the making of consciousness.* New York, NY: Mariner.

Dartington TV. (2011, May 23). Iain McGilchrist@Schumacher College: Things are not what they seem [Video file]. Retrieved from https://www.youtube.com/watch?v=oXiHStLfjP0

Debiec, J., Díaz-Mataix, L., Bush, D. E. A., Doyère, V., & LeDoux, J. E. (2010). The amygdala encodes specific sensory features of an aversive reinforcer. *Nature Neuroscience, 13,* 536–537. doi: 10.1038/ nn.2520

de Jager, P. (2006). From mere greetings, to great meetings. Retrieved from http://www.technobility.com/docs/article092.htm

de Jong, T. R., Chauke, M., Harris, B. N., & Saltzman, W. (2009). From here to paternity: Neural correlates of the onset of paternal behavior in California mice (Peromyscus californicus). *Hormones and Behavior, 56,* 220–231.

de Jonge, W. J. (2013). The gut's little brain in control of intestinal immunity. *ISRN Gastroenterology.* Retrieved from http://dx.doi.org/10.1155/2013/630159

De Pittà, M., Volman, V., Berry, H., & Ben-Jacob, E. (2011). A tale of two stories: Astrocyte regulation of synaptic depression and facilitation. *PLoS Computational Biology, 7*(12), e1002293. doi: 10.1371/journal.pcbi.1002293

Devinsky, O., & Laff, R. (2004). Callosal lesions and behavior: History and modern concepts. *Epilepsy and Behavior, 4*(6), 607–617. doi: 10.1016/j.yebeh .2003.08.029

Dias, B. G., & Ressler, K. J. (2014). Parental olfactory experience influences behavior and neural structure in subsequent generations. *Nature Neuroscience, 17,* 89–96. doi: 10.1038/nn.3594

Díaz-Mataix, L., Debiec, J., LeDoux, J. E., & Doyère, V. (2011). Sensory specific associations stored in the lateral amygdala allow for selective alteration of fear memories. *Journal of Neuroscience, 31,* 9538–9543. doi: 10.1523/jneurosci.5808-10.2011

Drake, R. L., Vogl, A. W., & Mitchell, A. W. M. (2014). *Gray's anatomy for students.* Philadelphia, PA: Churchill Livingstone.

Dunbar, R. (2004). *The human story: A new history of mankind's evolution.* London, UK: Faber.

Duvarci, S., & Nader, K. (2004). Characterization of fear memory reconsolidation. *Journal of Neuroscience, 24,* 9269–9275. doi: 10.1523/jneurosci.2971-04.2004

Ecker, B. (2015). Memory reconsolidation understood and misunderstood. *International Journal of Neuropsychotherapy, 3*(1), 2–46. doi: 10.12744/ijnpt.2015 .0002-0046

Ecker, B., & Hulley, L. (2000). Depth oriented brief therapy: Accelerated accessing of the coherent unconscious. In J. Carlson & L. Sperry (Eds.), *Brief therapy with individuals and couples* (pp. 161–190). Phoenix, AZ: Zeig, Tucker & Theisen.

Ecker, B., Ticic, R., & Hulley, L. (2012). *Unlocking the emotional brain: Eliminating symptoms at their root using memory reconsolidation.* New York, NY: Routledge.

Eisenberger, N. I., & Lieberman, M. D. (2004). Why rejection hurts: A common neural alarm system for physical and social pain. *Trends in Cognitive Sciences, 8*(7), 294–300. doi: 10.1016/j.tics.2004.05.010

Eklund, A., Nichols, T. E., & Knutsson, H. (2016). Cluster failure: Why fMRI inferences for spatial extent have inflated false-positive rates. *Proceedings of the National Academy of the United States of America, 113*(28), 7900–7905. doi: 10.1073/pnas.1602413113

Ellis, B. J., & Boyce, W. T. (2008). Biological sensitivity to context. *Current Directions in Psychological Science, 17*(3), 183–187.

Elzinga, B. M., & Roelofs, K. (2005). Cortisol-induced impairments of working memory require acute sympathetic activation. *Behavioral Neurology, 119*(1), 98–103. doi: 10.1037/0735-7044.119.1.98

Engel, G. (2007). Evidence for wavelike energy transfer through quantum coherence in photosynthetic systems. *Nature, 446*(7137), 782–786. doi: 10.1038/nature05678

Farroni, T., Menon, E., & Rigato, S. (2007). The perception of facial expressions in newborns. *European Journal of Developmental Psychology, 4*(1), 2–13. doi: 10.1080/17405620601046832

Fehmi, L., & Robbins, J. (2007). *The open-focus brain.* Boston, MA: Trumpeter.

Ferber, R. (2006). *Solve your child's sleep problems: New, revised, and expanded edition.* New York, NY: Touchstone.

Field, T. (2014). *Touch* (2nd ed.). Cambridge, MA: MIT Press.

Field, T., Diego, M., & Hernandez-Reif, M. (2006). Prenatal depression effects on the fetus and newborn: A review. *Infant Behavior and Development, 29*(3), 445–455.

Fields, R. D. (2011). *The other brain: The scientific and medical breakthroughs that will heal our brains and revolutionize our health.* New York, NY: Simon & Shuster.

Fields, R. D., & Stevens-Graham, B. (2002). New insights into neuron–glia communication. *Science, 298*(5593), 556–562.

Fisher, R. P., & Craik, F. I. (1977). Interaction between encoding and retrieval operations in cued recall. *Journal of Experimental Psychology: Human Learning and Memory, 3*(6), 701–711.

Fivush, R., & Hudson, J. A. (Eds.). (1990). *Knowing and remembering in young children.* New York, NY: Cambridge University Press.

Flaxman, G., & Flook, L. (2012). *Brief summary of mindfulness research.* Retrieved from http://marc.ucla.edu/workfiles/pdfs/marc-mindfulness-research-summary.pdf

Fox, E. A., & Murphy, M. C. (2008). Factors regulating vagal sensory development: Potential role in obesities of developmental origin. *Physiology & Behavior, 94,* 90–104. doi:10.1016/j.physbeh.2007.11.024

Fox, G. R., Kaplan, J., Damasio, H., & Damasio, A. (2015). Neural correlates of gratitude. *Frontiers in Psychology.* Retrieved from http://journal.frontiersin.org/article/10.3389/fpsyg.2015.01491/full

Fredrickson, B. L., Grewen, K. M., Coffey, K. A., Algoe, S. B., Firestine, A. M., Arevalo, J. M. G. . . . Cole, S. W. (2013). A functional genomic perspective on human well-being. *Proceedings of the National Academy of Sciences of the United States of America, 110*(33), 13684–13689. doi: 10.1073/pnas.1305419110

Furness, J. B. (2006). *The enteric nervous system.* Hoboken, NJ: Wiley-Blackwell.

Furness, J. B., Clerc, N., & Kunze, W. A. A. (2000). Memory in the enteric nervous system. *Gut, 47*(4). Retrieved from http://gut.bmj.com/content/47/suppl_4/iv60.full

Gage, F., & Temple, S. (2013). Neural stem cells: Generating and regenerating the brain. *Neuron, 80*(3), 588–601. doi: 10.1016/j.neuron.2013.10.037

Gallese, V., Fadiga, L., Fogassi, L., & Rizzolatti, G. (1996). Action recognition in the premotor cortex. *Brain, 119,* 593–609.

Geddes, L. (2015, February 25). *Why your brain needs touch to make you human.* Retrieved from https://www.newscientist.com/article/mg22530100-500-why-your-brain-needs-touch-to-make-you-human/

Gendlin, E. T. (1982). *Focusing.* New York, NY: Bantam.

Gershon, M. (1999). *The second brain: A groundbreaking new understanding of nervous disorders of the stomach and intestine.* New York, NY: Harper.

Gomez, J., Barnett, M. A., Natu, V., Mezer, A., Palomero-Gallagher, N., Weiner, K. S. . . . Grill-Spector, K. (2017). Microstructural proliferation in human cortex is coupled with the development of face processing. *Science, 355*(6320), 68–71. doi: 10.1126/science.aag0311

Gordon, I., Voos, A. C., Bennet, R. H., Bolling, D. Z., Pelphrey, K. A., & Kaiser, M. D. (2013). Brain mechanisms for processing affective touch. *Human Brain Mapping, 34*(4), 914–922. doi: 10.1002/hbm.21480

Grand, D. (2013). *Brainspotting: The revolutionary new therapy for rapid and effective change.* Boulder, CO: Sounds True.

Hardee, J. E., Thompson, J. C., & Puce, A. (2008). The left amygdala knows fear: Laterality in the amygdala response to fearful eyes. *Social Cognitive and Affective Neuroscience,* 3(1), 47–54. doi: 10.1093/scan/nsn001

Hari, J. (2015a). *Chasing the scream: The first and last days of the war on drugs.* New York, NY: Bloomsbury.

Hari, J. (2015b, June). Everything you think you know about addiction is wrong [Video file]. Retrieved from http://www.ted.com/talks/johann_hari_everything_you_think_you_know_about_addiction_is_wrong

Harshaw, C. (2008). Alimentary epigenetics: A developmental psychobiological systems view of the perception of hunger, thirst and satiety. *Developmental Review,* 28(4), 541–569. doi: 10.1016/j.dr.2008.08.001

Hasson, U. (2010, December). I can make your brain look like mine. *Harvard Business Review.* Retrieved from https://hbr.org/2010/12/defend-your-research-i-can-make-your-brain-look-like-mine

Hasson, U., Ghazanfar, A. A., Galantucci, B., Garrod, S., & Keysers, C. (2012). Brain-to-brain coupling: A mechanism for creating and sharing a social world. *Trends in Cognitive Sciences,* 16(2), 114–121. doi:10.1016/j.tics.2011.12.007

Hawkins, J., & Blakeslee, S. (2004). *On intelligence: How a new understanding of the brain will lead to the creation of truly intelligent machines.* New York, NY: Times Books.

Hebb, D. O. (1949). *The organization of behavior: A neuropsychological theory.* New York, NY: Wiley.

Hilbert, M., & Lopez, P. (2011). The world's technological capacity to store, communicate, and compute information. *Science,* 332(6025), 60–65. doi: 10.1126/science.1200970

Hill-Soderlund, A. L., Mills-Koonce, W. R., Propper, C., Calkins, S. D., Granger, D. A., Moore, G. A. . . . Cox, M. J. (2008). Parasympathetic and sympathetic responses to the Strange Situation in infants and mothers from avoidant and securely attached dyads. *Developmental Psychobiology,* 50(4), 361–376. doi: 10.1002/dev.20302

Hoban, A. E., Stilling, R. M., Ryan, F. J., Shanahan, F., Dinan, T. G., Claesson, M. J. . . . Cryan, J. F. (2016). Regulation of prefrontal cortex myelination by the microbiota. *Translational Psychiatry, 6,* e774. doi: 101038/tp.2016.42.

Hurley, D. (2013, June 25). Grandma's experiences leave a mark on your genes. *Discover Magazine.* Retrieved from http://discovermagazine.com/2013/may/13-grandmas-experiences-leave-epigenetic-mark-on-your-genes

Iacoboni, M. (2008). *Mirroring people: The science of empathy and how we connect with others.* London, UK: Picador.

Iacoboni, M. (2009). Imitation, empathy, and mirror neurons. *Annual Review of Psychology, 60,* 653–670. doi: 10.1146/annurev.psych.60.110707.163604

Iacoboni, M. (2011). Within each other: Neural mechanisms for empathy in the primate brain. In A. Coplan & P. Goldie (Eds.), *Empathy: Philosophical and psychological perspectives* (pp. 45–57). New York, NY: Oxford University Press.

Iacoboni, M., Woods, R. P., Brass, M., Bekkering, H., Mazziotta, J. C., & Rizzolatti, G. (1999). Cortical mechanisms of human imitation. *Science,* 286(5449), 2526–2528.

Jarome, T. J., Kwapis, J. L., Werner, C. T., Parsons, R. G., Gafford, G. M., & Helmstetter, F. J. (2012). The timing of multiple retrieval events can alter GluR1 phosphorylation and the requirement for protein synthesis in fear memory reconsolidation. *Learning and Memory, 19,* 300–306. doi: 10.1101/ lm.024901.111

Johns Hopkins Medicine. (2015). Positron emission tomography (PET). Retrieved from http://www.hopkinsmedicine.org/healthlibrary/test_procedures/neurological/positron_emission_tomography_pet_scan_92,p07654/

Jovasevic, V., Corcoran, K. A., Leaderbrand, K., Yamawaki, N., Guedea, A. L., Chen,

H. J. . . . Radulovic, J. (2015). GABAergic mechanisms regulated by miR-33 encode state-dependent fear. *Nature Neuroscience, 18,* 1265–1271. doi: 10.1038/nn.4084

Kanouse, D. E, & Hanson, L. (1972). Negativity in evaluations. In E. E. Jones, D. E. Kanouse, S. Valins, H. H. Kelley, R. E. Nisbitt, & E. Weiner (Eds.), *Attribution: Perceiving the causes of behavior.* Morristown, NJ: General Learning Press.

Kelso, B. S., & Engstrøm, D. (2006). *The complementary nature.* Cambridge, MA: MIT Press.

Kennedy, K., & Spielberg, S. (Producers), & Spielberg, S. (Director). (1982). *E. T. the extra-terrestrial* [Motion picture]. United States: Amblin Entertainment.

Kestly, T. (2014). *The interpersonal neurobiology of play: Brain-building interventions for emotional well-being.* New York, NY: Norton.

Kini, P., Wong, J., McInnis, S., Gabana, N., & Brown, J. W. (2015). The effects of gratitude expression on neural activity. *Neuroimage, 128,* 1–10. doi: 10.1016/j.neuroimage.2015.12.040

Kinomura, S., Larsson, J., Gulyás, B., & Roland, P. E. (1996). Activation by attention of the human reticular formation and thalamic intralaminar nuclei. *Science, 271*(5248), 512–515. doi: 10.1126/science.271.5248.512

Kohrt, B. A., Jordans, M. J. D., Tol, W. A., Perera, E., Karki, R., Koirala, S., & Upadhaya, N. (2010). Social ecology of child soldiers: Child, family, and community determinants of mental health, psychosocial well-being, and reintegration in Nepal. *Transcultural Psychiatry, 45*(5), 727–753. doi: 10.1177/1363461510381290

Kolb, B., & Tees, C. (Eds.). (1990). *The cerebral cortex of the rat.* Cambridge, MA: MIT Press.

Kolb, B., & Whishaw, I. Q. (2003). *Fundamentals of human neuropsychology* (5th ed.). New York, NY: Worth.

Konnikovajan, M. (2014, January 12). Goodnight. Sleep clean. *New York Times.* Retrieved from http://www.nytimes.com/2014/01/12/opinion/sunday/goodnight-sleep-clean.html?emc=edit_tnt_20140111&tntemail0=y

Konrath, S. H., Chopik, W. J., Hsing, C. K., & O'Brien, E. (2014). Changes in adult attachment style in American college students over time: A meta-analysis. *Personality and Social Psychology Review, 18*(4), 326–348. doi: 10.1177/1088868314530516

Konrath, S. H., O'Brien, E. H., & Hsing, C. (2011). Changes in dispositional empathy in American college students over time: A meta-analysis. *Personality and Social Psychology Review, 15*(2), 180–198. doi: 10.1177/1088868310377395

Koob, A. (2009). *The root of thought: Unlocking glia—the brain cell that will help us sharpen our wits, heal injury, and treat brain disease.* Upper Saddle River, NJ: Pearson FT Press.

Korb, A. (2015). *The upward spiral: Using neuroscience to reverse the course of depression, one small change at a time.* Oakland, CA: New Harbinger.

Kramer, G. (2007). *Insight dialogue: The interpersonal path to freedom.* Boulder, CO: Shambhala.

LeDoux, J. E., Romanski, L., & Xagoraris, A. (1989). Indelibility of subcortical emotional memories. *Journal of Cognitive Neuroscience, 1,* 238–243. doi: 10.1162/jocn.1989.1.3.238

Levine, P. (2010). *In an unspoken voice: How the body releases trauma and restores goodness.* Berkeley, CA: North Atlantic Books.

Levine, P., & van der Kolk, B. (2015). *Trauma and memory: Brain and body in a search for the living past: A practical guide for understanding and working with traumatic memory.* Berkeley, CA: North Atlantic Books.

Levitin, D. (2014, August 9). Hit the reset button in your brain. Retrieved from http://www.nytimes.com/2014/08/10/opinion/sunday/hit-the-reset-button-in-your-brain.html?module=Search&mabReward=relbias%3Ar%2C{%221%22%3A%22R1%3A6%22}&_r=0

Li, Y., & Owyang, C. (2003). Musings on the wanderer: What's new in our understanding of vago-vagal reflexes? *American Journal of Physiology, Gastrointestinal and Liver Physiology, 285*(3), G461–9. doi: 10.1152/ajpgi.00119.2003

Liberators International. (2015, September 10). Berliner eye contact with strangers [Video file]. (2015). Retrieved from https://www.youtube.com/watch?v=CGQGgOOWXWE

Lieberman, P. (2006). *Toward an evolutionary biology of language.* Cambridge, MA: Harvard University Press.

Linden, D. J. (2015). *Touch: The science of hand, heart, and mind.* New York, NY: Viking.

Lipton, B. (2008). *The biology of belief: Unleashing the power of consciousness, matter, and miracles.* Carlsbad, CA: Hay House.

Livingstone, M., & Hubel, D. (1988). Segregation of form, color, movement, and depth: Anatomy, physiology, and perception. *Science, 240*(4853), 740–749. doi:10.1126/science.3283936

Llinas, R. R. (1990). Intrinsic electrical properties of mammalian neurons and CNS function. *Fidia Research Foundation Neuroscience Award Lectures, 4,* 175–194.

Llinas, R. R. (2008). Of self and self-awareness: The basic neuronal circuit in human consciousness and the generation of the self. *Journal of Consciousness Studies, 15*(9), 64–74.

Lyte, M., & Cryan, J. F. (Eds.) (2014). *Microbial endocrinology: The microbiota-gut-brain axis in health and disease.* New York, NY: Springer.

Main, M. (1996). Introduction to the special section on attachment and psychopathology: 2. Overview of the field of attachment. *Journal of Consulting and Clinical Psychology, 64,* 237–243.

Marci, C. D., Ham, J., Moran, E. K., & Orr, S. P. (2007). Physiologic concordance, empathy, and social-emotional processing during psychotherapy. *Journal of Nervous and Mental Disease, 195,* 103–111.

Marci, C. D., & Reiss, H. (2005). The clinical relevance of psychophysiology: Support for the psychobiology of empathy and psychodynamic process. *American Journal of Psychotherapy, 259,* 213–226.

Markowitsch, H. J. (1998). Differential contribution of right and left amygdala to affective information processing. *Behavioral Neurology, 11*(4), 233–244.

Marzi, C., Perani, D., Tassinari, G., Colleluori, A., Maravita, A., Miniussi, C. . . . Fazio, F. (1999). Pathways of interhemispheric transfer in normals and in a split-brain subject: A positron emission tomography study. *Experimental Brain Research, 126*(4), 451–458. doi: 10.1007/s002210050752

Maté, G. (2010). *In the realm of hungry ghosts: Close encounters with addiction.* Berkeley, CA: North Atlantic Books.

McCraty, R. (2015). *The science of the heart: Exploring the role of the heart in human performance* (Vol. 2). Boulder Creek, CO: Institute of HeartMath.

McGilchrist, I. (2009). *The master and his emissary: The divided brain and the making of the Western world.* New Haven, CT: Yale University Press.

Meaney M. J. (2001). Maternal care, gene expression, and the transmission of individual differences in stress reactivity across generations. *Annual Review of Neuroscience, 24,* 1161–1192. doi: 10.1146/annurev.neuro.24.1.1161

Meewisse, M.-L., Reitsma, J. B., de Vries, G-J., Gersons, B. P. R., & Olff, M. (2007). Cortisol and post-traumatic stress in adults: Systematic review and meta-analysis. *British Journal of Psychiatry, 191*(5), 387–392. doi: 10.1192/bjp.bp.106.024877

Meili, A. N. (1994). *Prairie boy's springtime.* Austin, TX: New Texas Press.

Meili, A. N. (2003a). *Shrinking heads: Expanding hearts.* Austin, TX: New Texas Press.

Meili, A. N. (2003b). *The sound of one cowherd clapping.* Austin, TX: New Texas Press.

Meili, A. N. (2012). *Wood River windings.* Austin, TX: New Texas Press.

Meili, A. N. (2013). *The silence of sleighs.* Austin, TX: New Texas Press.

Meili, A. N. (2016). *Putting aside the mask for the moment.* Austin, TX: New Texas Press.

Merriam-Webster. (2014). Retrieved from http://www.merriam-webster.com/

Mesulam, M. M. (1990). Large-scale neurocognitive networks and distributed processing for attention, language, and memory. *Annals of Neurology, 28,* 597–613. doi: 10.1002/ana.410280502

Michelangelo. (n.d.). Collection of quotations. Retrieved from http://www.brainyquote.com/quotes/authors/m/michelangelo.htm

MIT News. (2015, August 31). Parts of the brain can switch functions. Retrieved from http://news.mit.edu/2011/brain-language-0301

Montagu, A. (1986). *Touching: The human significance of the skin* (3rd ed.). New York, NY: Harper.

Morley, C. A., & Kohrt, B. A. (2013). Impact of peer support on PTSD, hope, and functional impairment: A mixed-methods study of child soldiers in Nepal. *Journal of Aggression, Maltreatment and Trauma, 22,* 714–734. doi: 10.1080/10926771.2013.813882

Moullin, S., Waldfogel, J., & Washbrook, E. (2014). *Baby bonds: Parenting, attachment and a secure base for children.* London, UK: Sutton Trust. Retrieved from http://www.suttontrust.com/wp-content/uploads/2014/03/baby-bonds-final.pdf

Mumme, D. L., Fernald, A., & Herrera, C. (1996). Infants' responses to facial and vocal emotional signals in a social referencing paradigm. *Child Development, 67,* 3219–3237.

Murphy, D. A., Thompson, G. W., Ardell, J. L., McCraty, R., Stevenson, R. S., Sangalang, V. E. . . . Armour, J. A. (2000). The heart reinnervates after transplantation. *Thoracic Surgery, 69*(6), 1769–1781.

Murray, M. A. (n.d.). *Our sense of hearing.* Retrieved from https://faculty.washington.edu/chudler/hearing.html

Nader, K., Schafe, G. E., & LeDoux, J. E. (2000). Fear memories require protein synthesis in the amygdala for reconsolidation after retrieval. *Nature, 406,* 722–726.

Narvaez, D. (2011). The dangers of "crying it out." Retrieved from http://www.psychologytoday.com/blog/moral-landscapes/201112/dangers-crying-it-out

Narvaez, D., Panksepp, J., Schore, A. N., & Gleason, T. R. (2012). *Evolution, experience and human development: From research to practice and policy.* Oxford, UK: Oxford University Press.

Newman-Norlund, R, D., van Schie, H. T., van Zuijlen, A. M., & Bekkering, H. (2007). The mirror neuron system is more active during complementary compared with imitative action. *Nature Neuroscience, 10*(7), 817–818. doi: 10:1038/nn1911

Ng, M. Y., & Wong, W. S. (2013). The differential effects of gratitude and sleep on psychological distress in patients with chronic pain. *Journal of Health Psychology, 18*(2), 263–271. doi: 10.1177/1359105312439733

Ogden, P., & Fisher, J. (2015). *Sensorimotor psychotherapy: Interventions for trauma and attachment.* New York, NY: Norton.

Ogden, P., & Minton, K. (2006). *Trauma and the body: A sensorimotor approach to psychotherapy.* New York, NY: Norton.

Olausson, H., Cole, J., Rylander, K., McGlone, F., Lamarre, Y., Wallin, B. J. . . . Vallbo, Å. (2008). Functional role of unmyelinated tactile afferents in human hairy skin: Sympathetic response and perceptual localization. *Experimental Brain Research, 184*(1), 135–140. Retrieved from http://www.ncbi.nlm.nih.gov/pubmed/17962926

Olausson, H., Lamarre, Y., Backlund, H., Morin, C., Wallin, B. G., Starck, G. . . . Bushnell, M. C. (2002). Unmyelinated tactile afferents signal touch and project to the insular cortex. *Nature Neuroscience, 5,* 900–904. doi: 10.1038/nn896

O'Neill, J. O., Boccara, C. N., Stella, F., Schoenenberger, P., & Csicsvari, J. (2017). Superficial layers of the medial entorhinal cortex replay independently of the hippocampus. *Science, 355*(6321), 184–188. doi: 10.1126/science.aag2787

Online etymology dictionary. (2014). Retrieved from http://www.etymonline.com

Oostenbroek, J., Suddendorf, T., Nielsen, M., Redshaw, J., Kennedy-Costantini, S., Davis, J. . . . Slaughter, V. (2016). Comprehensive longitudinal study challenges the existence of neonatal imitation in humans. *Current Biology, 26*(10), 1334–1338. doi: http://dx.doi.org/10.1016/j.cub.2016.03.047

Ort, V., & Howard, D. (2015). Development of the eye. Retrieved from http://education.med.nyu.edu/courses/macrostructure/lectures/lec_images/eye.html

Panksepp, J. (1998). *Affective neuroscience: The foundations of human and animal emotions.* New York, NY: Oxford University Press.

Panksepp, J., & Biven, L. (2012). *The archaeology of mind: Neuroevolutionary origins of human emotions.* New York, NY: Norton.

Panksepp, J., Normansell, L. A., Cox, J. F., & Siviy, S. (1994). Effects of neonatal decortication on the social play of juvenile rats. *Physiology and Behavior, 56,* 429–443.

Park, B. J., Tsunetsugu, Y., Kasetani, T., Kagawa, T., & Miyazaki, Y. (2010). The physiological effects of Shrinrin-yoku (taking in the forest atmosphere or forest bathing): Evidence from field experiments in 24 forests across Japan. *Environmental Health and Preventive Medicine, 15*(1), 18–26. doi: 10.1007/s12199-009-0086-9

Pasricha, P. J. (2011). Stanford's Hospital's Pankaj Pasricha discusses the enteric nervous system, or brain in your gut [Video file]. Retrieved from https://www.youtube.com/watch?v=UXx4WTVU34Y

Patel, U. (2011, December 5). Hasson brings real life into the lab to exam cognitive processing. Retrieved from http://www.princeton.edu/main/news/archive/S32/27/76E76/index.xml?section=science

Pearce, N. (2009, July/August). Connecting with the person inside Alzheimer's. *Social Work Today, 9*(4), 26.

Pease, A., & Pease, B. (2004). *The definitive book of body language.* Buderim, Australia: Pease International.

Pedreira, M. E., & Maldonado, H. (2003). Protein synthesis subserves reconsolidation or extinction depending on reminder duration. *Neuron, 38,* 863–869. doi: 10.1016/S0896- 6273(03)00352-0

Pedreira, M. E., Pérez-Cuesta, L.M., & Maldonado, H. (2004). Mismatch between what is expected and what actually occurs triggers memory reconsolidation and extinction. *Learning and Memory, 11,* 579–585. doi: 10.1101/lm.76904

Perkel, J. M. (2013). This is your brain: Mapping the connectome. Retrieved from http://www.sciencemag.org/site/products/lst_20130118.xhtml

Perls, F., Hefferline, R. F., & Goodman, P. (1951). *Gestalt therapy: Excitement and growth in the human personality.* New York, NY: Delta.

Perreau-Link, E., Beauregard, M., Gravel, P., Paquette, V., Soucy, J. P., Diksic, M., & Benkelfat, C. (2007). In vivo measurements of brain trapping of C-labelle alpha-methyl-L-tryptophan during acute changes in mood state. *Journal of Psychiatry and Neuroscience, 32*(6), 430–434. Retrieved from http://www.ncbi.nlm.nih.gov/pubmed/18043767

Perry, B. D. (2014). Rhythm regulates the brain. Retrieved from http://attachmentdisorderhealing.com/developmental-trauma-3

Perry, B. D., & Hambrick, E. P. (2008). The neurosequential model of therapeutics. Retrieved from https://childtrauma.org/wp-content/uploads/2013/08/NMT_Article_08.pdf

Pessoa, L. (2013). *The cognitive-emotional brain: From interactions to integration* [Kindle for iPad version]. Retrieved from http://www.amazon.com

Petrovich, G. D., Canteras, N. S., & Swanson, L. W. (2001). Combinatorial amygdalar inputs to hippocampal domains and hypothalamic behavior systems. *Brain Research Reviews, 38*(1–2), 247–289.

Pine, A., Mendelsohn, A., & Dudai, Y. (2014). Unconscious learning of likes and dislikes is persistent, resilient, and reconsolidates. *Frontiers in Psychology, 5*(1051), 1–13. doi: 10.3389/ fpsyg.2014.01051

Porges, S. W. (1995). Orienting in a defensive world: Mammalian modifications of our evolutionary heritage: A Polyvagal Theory. *Psychophysiology, 32,* 301–318. doi: 10.1111/ j.1469-8986.1995.tb01213.x

Porges, S. W. (2007). The Polyvagal perspective. *Biological Psychology, 74,* 116–143. doi: 10.1016/j.biopsycho.2006.06.009

Porges, S. W. (2009a). Reciprocal influences between body and brain in the perception and expression of affect: A Polyvagal perspective. In D. Fosha, D. J. Siegel, & M. F. Solomon (Eds.), *The healing power of emotion: Affective neuroscience, development, clinical practice* (pp. 27–54). New York, NY: Norton.

Porges, S. W. (2009b). The Polyvagal Theory: New insights into adaptive reactions of the autonomic nervous system. *Cleveland Clinic Journal of Medicine, 76*(2), S86–90. doi: 10.3949/ccjm.67.s2.17

Porges, S. W. (2010). Music therapy & trauma: Insights from the Polyvagal Theory. In K. Stewart (Ed.), *Music therapy & trauma: Bridging theory and clinical practice.* New York, NY: Satchnote Press.

Porges, S. W. (2011). *The Polyvagal Theory: Neurophysiological foundations of emotions, attachment, communication, and self-regulation.* New York, NY: Norton.

Porges, S. W. (2013, September). A neural love code. In M. Kern (Chair), *Breath of Life Conference 2013.* Symposium conducted at a meeting of the Craniosacral Therapy Educational Trust, London, UK.

Porges, S. W. (2015). A moderated discussion of Stephen Porges's work, including a discussion of the clinical application of Polyvagal Theory [transcript]. Online symposium, Psychotherapy 2.0, Sounds True. Retrieved from http://www.soundstrue.com/store/psy20/

Porges, S. W., Badenoch, B., & Phillips, M. (2016). Feeling and expressing compassion [Webinar]. Retrieved from http://bestpracticesintherapy.com/silver-month-long-july/

Porges, S. W., Doussard-Roosevelt, J. A., & Maili, A. K. (1994). Vagal tone and the physiological regulation of emotion. *Monographs of the Society for Research in Child Development, 240/59*(2–3), 167–186.

Porges, S. W., & Phillips, M. (2016). Connectedness: A biological imperative [Webinar]. Retrieved from http://bestpracticesintherapy.com/silver-month-long-july/

Post, R. M., Weiss, S. R. B., Li, H., Smith, M. A., Zhang, L. X., Xing, G. . . . McCann, U. D. (1998). Neural plasticity and emotional memory. *Development and Psychopathology, 10,* 829–856.

Przybyslawski, J., & Sara, S. J. (1997). Reconsolidation of memory after its reactivation. *Behavior and Brain Research, 84,* 241–246. doi: 10.1016/S0166-4328(96)00153-2

Purves, D., Augustine, G. J., Fitzpatrick, D., Katz, L. C., LaMantia, A. S., McNamara, J. O., & Williams, S. M. (Eds.). (2001). *Neuroscience* (2nd ed.). Sunderland, MA: Sinauer Associates. Retrieved from https://www.ncbi.nlm.nih.gov/books/NBK10893/

Qiu, A., Anh, T. T., Li, Y., Chen, H., Rifkin-Graboi, A., Broekman, B. F. P. . . . Meaney, J. (2015). Prenatal maternal depression alters amygdala functional connectivity in 6-month-old infants. *Translational Psychiatry, 5*(2). doi: 10.1038/tp.2015.3

Raichle, M. E. (2010). Two views of brain function. *Trends in Cognitive Science, 14*(4), 180–190. doi: 10.1016/j.tics.2010.01.008

Ramos, B. P., & Arnsten, A. F. (2007). Adrenergic pharmacology and cognition: Focus on the prefrontal cortex. *Pharmacology and Therapeutics, 113,* 523–536. doi: 10.1016/j.pharmthera.2006.11.006

Remen, R. N. (1996). *Kitchen table wisdom: Stories that heal.* New York, NY: Riverhead Books.

Richtel, M. (2010, January 15). Outdoors and out of reach, studying the brain. *New York Times.* Retrieved from http://www.nytimes.com/2010/08/16/technology/16brain.html?pagewanted=all

Riener, A. (2011). Information injection below conscious awareness: Potential of sensory channels. Retrieved from https://www.pervasive.jku.at/Research/Publications/_Documents/Automotive%20UI%202011%20-%20Information%20injection%20below%20conscious%20awareness%20CR%20v2.pdf

Rohr, R. (2014, February 22). The true self: The gaze of grace. Retrieved from http://cac.org

Rombouts, S. A. R. B., Barkhof, F., & Sheltens, P. (2007). *Clinical applications of functional brain MRI.* New York, NY: Oxford University Press.

Rūmī, J. a.-D. (2004). *The essential Rumi: New extended edition.* (C. Barks, Trans.). New York, NY: HarperCollins. (Original work published 1270)

Sasselli, V., Pachnis, V., & Burns, A. J. (2012). The enteric nervous system. *Developmental Biology, 366*(1), 64–73. doi: 10.1016/j.ydbio.2012.01.012

Scharff, D. E. (2012). *Object relations theory and practice: An introduction.* Lanham, MD: Jason Aronson.

Schmahmann, J. D., & Caplan, D. (2006). Cognition, emotion and the cerebellum. *Brain, 129*(2), 290–292.

Schore, A. N. (1994). *Affect regulation and the origin of the self: The neurobiology of emotional development.* Mahwah, NJ: Erlbaum.

Schore, A. N. (2012). *The science of the art of psychotherapy.* New York, NY: Norton.

Schwartz, G. M., Izard, C. E., & Ansul, S. E. (1985). The 5-month-old's ability to discriminate facial expression of emotion. *Infant Behavior and Development, 8*(1), 65–77.

Schwartz, R. C. (1995). *Internal family systems therapy.* New York, NY: Guilford.

Sekiguchi, T., Yamada, A., & Suzuki, H. (1997). Reactivation-dependent changes in memory states in the terrestrial slug *Limax flavus. Learning and Memory, 4,* 356–364. doi: 10.1101/ lm.4.4.356

Sender, R., Fuchs, S., & Milo, R. (2016). Revised estimates for the number of human and bacteria cells in the body. Retrieved from http://biorxiv.org/content/early/2016/01/06/036103. doi:http://dx.doi.org/10.1101/036103

Seung, S. (2013). *Connectome: How the brain's wiring makes us who we are.* New York, NY: Mariner.

Shaffer, F., McCraty, R., & Zerr, C. L. (2014). A healthy heart is not a metronome: An integrative review of the heart's anatomy and heart rate variability. *Frontiers in Psychology, 5,* 1040. doi: org/10.3389/fpsyg.2014.01040

Sharp, H., Pickles, A., Meaney, M., Marshall, K., Tibu, F., & Hill, J. (2012). Frequency of infant stroking reported by mothers moderates the effect of prenatal depression on infant behavioural and physiological outcomes. *PLoS ONE, 7*(10), e45446.

Shepherd, P. (2010). *New self, new world: Recovering our senses in the twenty-first century.* Berkeley, CA: North Atlantic Books.

Sherrington, C. S. (1907). On the proprioceptive system, especially its reflex aspect. *Brain, 29*(4), 467–485. doi: 10.1093/brain/29.4.467

Shewmon, D. A., Holmes, G. L., & Byrne, P. A. (1999). Consciousness in congenitally decorticate children: Developmental vegetative state as self-fulfilling prophecy. *Developmental Medicine and Child Neurology, 41,* 364– 374.

Shubin, N. (2009). *Your inner fish: A journey into the 3.5-billion-year history of the human body.* New York, NY: Vintage.

Siebert, C. (2016, January 28). What does a parrot know about PTSD? *New York Times.* Retrieved from https://www.nytimes.com/2016/01/31/magazine/what-does-a-parrot-know-about-ptsd.html?rref=collection%2Fsectioncollection%2Fscience&_r=2

Siegel, D. J. (2015a). *Brainstorm: The power and purpose of the teenage brain.* New York, NY: TarcherPerigee.

Siegel, D. J. (2015b). *The developing mind: How relationships and the brain interact to shape who we are* (2nd ed.). New York, NY: Guilford.

Sills, F. (2010). Craniosacral biodynamics. Retrieved from http://www.craniosacral -biodynamics.org/the-inherent-treatment-plan.html

Simard, S. (2016, June). How trees talk to each other [Video file]. Retrieved from https://www.ted.com/talks/suzanne_simard_how_trees_talk_to_each_other ?language=e

Slater, L. (2004, March 21). Monkey love: Harry Harlow's classic primate experiments suggest that to understand the human heart you have to be willing to break it. Retrieved from http://www.boston.com/news/globe/ideas/articles/2004/03/21/monkey_love/

Smith, P. A. (2015, June 23). Can the bacteria in your gut explain your mood? Retrieved from http://www.nytimes.com/2015/06/28/magazine/can-the-bacteria -in-your-gut-explain-your-mood.html?_r=0

Squire, L. R., Knowlton, B., & Musen, G. (1993). The structure and organization of memory. *Annual Review of Psychology, 44,* 453–495.

Steiner-Adair, C., & Barker, T. H. (2014). *The big disconnect: Protecting childhood and family relationships in the digital age.* New York, NY: Harper.

Stephens, G., Silbert, L., & Hasson, U. (2010). Speaker–listener neural coupling underlies successful communication. *Proceedings of the National Academy of Sciences of the United States of America, 107,* 14425–14430.

Swain, J. E, Lorberbaum, J. P, Korse, S., & Strathearn, L. (2007). Brain basis of early parent–infant interactions: Psychology, physiology, and in vivo function neuroimaging studies. *Journal of Child and Adolescent Psychiatry, 48,* 262–287.

Thompson, C. L., Wang, B., & Holmes, A. J. (2008). The immediate environment during postnatal development has long-term impact on gut community structure in pigs. *ISME Journal, 2,* 739–748.

Ticic, R., & Kushner, E. (2015, January). Deep release for body and soul. *The Neuropsychotherapist, 10,* 24–28. Retrieved from http://www.coherencetherapy .org/files/TNPTissue10.pdf

Toomey, B., & Ecker, B. (2007). Of neurons and knowings: Constructivism, coherence psychology, and their neurodynamic substrates. *Journal of Constructivist Psychology, 20*(3), 201–245. doi: 10.1080/10720530701347860

Törk, I. (1990). Anatomy of the serotonergic system. *Annals of the New York Academy of Sciences, 600,* 12. doi: 10.1111/j.1749-6632.tb16870.x

Tronick, E. Z. (1989). Emotions and emotional communication in infants. *American Psychologist, 44,* 112–119.

Tronick, E. Z. (2003). Of course all relationships are unique: How co-creative processes generate unique mother–infant and patient–therapist relationships and change other relationships. In *New developments in attachment theory: Application to clinical practice*, proceedings of conference at UCLA, Los Angeles, CA.

Tyszka, J. M., Kennedy, D. P., Adolphs, R., & Paul, L. K. (2011). Intact bilateral resting-state networks in the absence of the corpus callosum. *Journal of Neuroscience, 31*(42), 15154–15162. doi: 10.1523/JNEUROSCI.1453-11.2011

Twenge, J. M., & Campbell, W. K. (2009). *The narcissism epidemic: Living in the age of entitlement.* New York, NY: Free Press.

Twenge, J. M., & Foster, J. D. (2010). Birth cohort increases in narcissistic personality traits among American college students, 1982–2009. *Social Psychological and Personality Science, 1*(1), 99–106. doi: 10.1177/1948550609355719

Twenge, J. M., Konrath, S., Foster, J. D., Campbell, W. K., & Bushman, B. J. (2008).

Egos inflating over time: A cross-temporal meta-analysis of the Narcissistic Personality Inventory. *Journal of Personality, 76*(4), 875–902. doi: 10.1111/j.1467-6494.2008.00507

Van Essen, D. C., Smith, S. M., Barch, D. M., Behrens, T. E. J., Yacoub, E., & Ugurbil, K. (2013). *The WU-Minn Human Connectome Project: An overview.* Retrieved from http://dx.doi.org/10.1016/j.neuroimage.2013.05.041

Veebiakadeemia. (2013, January 10). Jaak Panksepp—in the lab of happy rats [Video file]. Retrieved from https://www.youtube.com/watch?v=WLfubEzV23M

Vilares, I., Howard, J. D., Fernandes, H. L., Gottfried, J. A., & Kording, K. P. (2012). Differential representations of prior and likelihood uncertainty in the human brain. *Current Biology, 22*(18), 1641–1648. doi: 10.1016/j.cub.2012.07.010

Wager, T. (2002). Functional neuroanatomy of emotion: A meta-analysis of emotional activation studies in PET and fMRI. *NeuroImage, 16*(2), 331–348. doi: 10.1006/nimg.2002.1087

Walker, M. P., Brakefield, T., Hobson, J. A., & Stickgold, R. (2003). Dissociable stages of human memory consolidation and reconsolidation. *Nature, 425,* 616–620. doi: 10.1038/nature01930

Watkins, H. H., & Watkins, J. G. (1997). *Ego states: Theory and therapy.* New York, NY: Norton.

Weinstein, A. D. (2016). *Prenatal development and parents' lived experiences: How early events shape our psychophysiology and relationships.* New York, NY: Norton.

Weisberg, D. S., Keil, F. C., Goodstein, J., Rawson, E., & Gray, J. R. (2008). The seductive allure of neuroscience explanations. *Journal of Cognitive Neuroscience, 20*(3), 470–477. doi: 10.1162/jocn.2008.20040

Wipfler, P., & Schore, T. (2016). *Listen: Five simple tools to meet your everyday parenting challenges.* Palo Alto, CA: Hand in Hand Parenting.

Wittgenstein, L. (1998). *Tractatus logico-philosophicus* (471st ed.). Mineola, NY: Dover. (Original work 1922)

Yehuda, R., Cai, G., Golier, J. A., Sarapas, C., Galea, S., Ising, M. . . . Buxbaum, J. D. (2009). Gene expression patterns associated with posttraumatic stress disorder following exposure to the World Trade Center attacks. *Biological Psychiatry, 66*(7), 708–711. doi: 10.1016/j.biopsych.2009.02.03

Yehuda, R., Teicher, M. H., Seckl, J. R., Grossman, R. A., Morris, A., & Bierer, L. M. (2007). Parental posttraumatic stress disorder as a vulnerability factor for low cortisol trait in offspring of Holocaust survivors. *Archives of General Psychiatry, 64*(9), 1040–1048. doi: 10.1001/archpsyc.64.9.1040

Yoonessi, A., & Yoonessi, A. (2011). Functional assessment of magno, parvo, and koniocellular pathways: Current state and future clinical applications. *Journal of Ophthalmic and Vision Research, 6*(2), 119–126.

Zahn, R., Moll, J., Paiva, M., Garrido, G., Krueger, F., Huey, E. D., & Grafman, J. (2009). The neural basis of human social values: Evidence from functional MRI. *Cerebral Cortex, 19*(2), 276–283. doi: 10.1093/cercor/bhn080

Zohar, D. (1991). *The quantum self: Human nature and consciousness defined by the new physics.* New York, NY: William Morrow.

Index

In this index, *f* denotes figure.